Strange Tales from Edo

Rewriting Chinese Fiction in Early Modern Japan

Harvard East Asian Monograph Series 465

Strange Tales from Edo

Rewriting Chinese Fiction in Early Modern Japan

William D. Fleming

Published by the Harvard University Asia Center
Distributed by Harvard University Press
Cambridge (Massachusetts) and London 2023

Printed in the United States of America

The Harvard University Asia Center publishes a monograph series and, in coordination with the Fairbank Center for Chinese Studies, the Korea Institute, the Reischauer Institute of Japanese Studies, and other facilities and institutes, administers research projects designed to further scholarly understanding of China, Japan, Korea, Vietnam, and other Asian countries. The Center also sponsors projects addressing multidisciplinary, transnational, and regional issues in Asia.

Cataloging-in-Publication Data is on file at the Library of Congress

ISBN 9780674293809 (hardcover)

Index by Mary Mortensen

♾ Printed on acid-free paper

Last figure below indicates year of this printing
32 31 30 29 28 27 26 25 24 23

For Kathy

Contents

Figures and Tables

Figures

Tables

Acknowledgments

The kernel of this project took shape while I was a graduate student in the Department of East Asian Languages and Civilizations at Harvard University. Under the mentorship of Adam Kern, I began in earnest to explore the world of Edo literature and popular culture, learning to decipher hastily scrawled calligraphy, thorny theoretical texts, and many things in between. Edwin Cranston and Shigehisa Kuriyama inspired me with their generosity and profound insights across a dizzying range of subjects. Hal Bolitho gave valuable guidance early in my studies, and I cherish the memory of my sadly few conversations about Edo fiction with Howard Hibbett. I am also thankful for the camaraderie and support of many others I first crossed paths with during my years in Cambridge, particularly Fumiko Cranston, Matthew Fraleigh, Will Hedberg, Kuniko McVey, Jay Rubin, Glynne Walley, Kristin Williams, Mark Woolsey, and Jian Zhang.

In the years since, I have taught in the Department of East Asian Languages and Cultural Studies at UC Santa Barbara and, before that, in the Department of East Asian Languages and Literature and the Theater Studies program at Yale. I am grateful to numerous people at both institutions for their contributions to this project and for their collegiality and friendship. At UCSB, these include Sabine Frühstück, Xiaorong Li, Kate McDonald, John Nathan, Fabio Rambelli, Luke Roberts, Kate Saltzman-Li, Naoki Yamamoto, Xiaowei Zheng, and the HASC staff. At Yale, I would especially like to thank Dani Botsman, Kang-i Chang, Fabian Drixler, Adam Haliburton, Seth Jacobowitz, Ed Kamens, Dominika Laster, Kathi Matsuura, Drisana Misra, Haruko Nakamura,

Joe Roach, John Treat, Mimi Yiengpruksawan, and the staff in EALL, Theater Studies, and the Council on East Asian Studies.

Many others have supported the completion of this book in one way or another. Erin Brightwell, Michael Emmerich, Josh Fogel, Yulia Frumer, David Gundry, Keller Kimbrough, Peter Kornicki, Satoko Shimazaki, Kai Xie, and Eve Zimmerman have offered valuable suggestions, words of encouragement, or opportunities to present work in progress. My research in Japan would not have been possible without the generosity of Robert Campbell, Loren Fykes, Ichinohe Wataru, Kawasaki Noriko, Kim Shiduck, Ōtaka Yōji, Suzuki Jun, and Ivan Vartanian, not to mention the numerous librarians and archivists at the scattered collections visited in the course of completing this project.

Several institutions have supported my research with generous grants and fellowships, including the Japan Foundation, the Reischauer Institute for Japanese Studies at Harvard, the National Institute of Japanese Literature, and funding agencies at UCSB, Yale, and Waseda University. I am also grateful to Bob Graham at the Harvard University Asia Center; to the anonymous readers of my manuscript submission for their thoughtful, serious engagement with my work; to Kristen Bettcher and Michelle Asakawa for their editorial acumen; to Jacob La Fleur and Jason Tranchida for their graphic design work; and to Mary Mortensen for preparing the index.

A few sections of this book appeared in earlier form in two publications: "Strange Tales from Edo: *Liaozhai zhiyi* in Early Modern Japan," published initially in the journal *Sino-Japanese Studies* (2013) and later reprinted in revised form in Joshua Fogel and Matthew Fraleigh, eds., *Sino-Japanese Reflections: Literary and Cultural Interactions between China and Japan in Early Modernity* (De Gruyter, 2022); and "Plotting War during the Great Peace: The Uses of Warfare in Historical Fiction of the Late Edo Period," in Elizabeth Oyler and Katherine Saltzman-Li, eds., *Cultural Imprints: War and Memory in the Samurai Age* (Cornell University Press, 2022). I am grateful to both publishers for allowing the inclusion of this material in the present volume.

Last, I would like to express my gratitude to my family. My parents and siblings have supported me in all my endeavors, and my wife, Kathy, never fails to amaze me with her emotional, intellectual, and editorial astuteness. Thank you.

Abbreviations

The following abbreviations are used in the text.

LZ	*Liaozhai zhiyi: huijiao huizhu huiping ben* 聊齋誌異 : 會校會注會評本
MCS	*Morishima Chūryō shū* 森島中良集
NKBT	*Nihon koten bungaku taikei* 日本古典文学大系
NZT	*Nihon zuihitsu taisei* 日本随筆大成
SNKBT	*Shin Nihon koten bungaku taikei* 新日本古典文学大系
SNKBZ	*Shinpen Nihon koten bungaku zenshū* 新編日本古典文学全集
ZNZT	*Zoku Nihon zuihitsu taisei* 続日本随筆大成

INTRODUCTION

Eighteenth-century China had its share of self-styled eccentrics, but few could rival Scholar Yan of Xunyang. The scion of a prosperous merchant family, Yan is reported, according to the only known account of his life, to have used his abundant wealth to indulge a taste for all things Japanese. Eschewing kunqu and Chinese verse in favor of shamisen ballads and waka, he lined the walls of his home with an impressive Japanese library that ranged from *The Tale of Genji* (*Genji monogatari*) and major poetic anthologies to contemporary pulp fiction and kabuki criticism. He even owned the very latest Japanese comic books, all carefully preserved in their original packaging. Yan could be spotted around town wearing a chic Japanese jacket and matching black cowl (to shield himself from prying eyes), and he accented his dress with fashionable accessories seen more commonly in Edo than in Hangzhou, including a long Japanese pipe that often dangled from his lips. He was even known to wash down morsels of fresh sashimi with imported Yamaya sake.

The story of Scholar Yan is, of course, pure fiction, the plot of a madcap comic book, or *kibyōshi*, dreamed up by the Japanese writer and Sinologist Ōta Nanpo (1749–1823). First published in 1783 as *The Salt Merchant's Felicitous Wedding* (*Kotobuki shioya no konrei*), the piece was reissued the following year and more widely read under the catchier title *Japan for This Guy!* (*Koitsu wa Nippon*).[1] Many of the scenes are conceived

1. The piece is included in Kimura Yaeko, Uda Toshihiko, and Koike Masatane, eds., *Kusazōshi shū*, in *SNKBT* 83 (Iwanami shoten, 1997), 211–26.

for maximum comic effect. As spring arrives, Yan organizes an ikebana exhibition at Yueyang Tower on the shores of Lake Dongting, where he displays a series of increasingly idiosyncratic flower arrangements. Later, following the pattern of the rake's progress prevalent in the *kibyōshi* genre, Yan finds himself disowned by his father and spends a period in exile on the island of Hirado, in Japan's far west, before finally returning to China, begging his father's forgiveness, and happily marrying his courtesan lover.

However preposterous the storyline, a figure like Scholar Yan was not *completely* inconceivable. One real-life Chinese Japanophile was a merchant by the name of Lu Mingzhai.[2] During a series of voyages to Nagasaki beginning in the early 1770s, Lu learned the basics of jōruri chanting, cavorted with Japanese courtesans, and developed a taste for the local cuisine. At home in the port of Zhapu in Zhejiang Province, he erected a two-story Japanese-style house complete with tatami flooring where he treated guests to Japanese delicacies served in imported dishware. He was even known to perform a line or two from *Chūshingura* (A Treasury of Loyal Retainers, premiered 1748), the perennial favorite of the Japanese stage. Some of Lu's countrymen were able to take in *Chūshingura* without ever leaving the continent. In the early nineteenth century, a handful of Japanese scholars translated excerpts of this and other Japanese texts into vernacular Chinese. Although it is not known if these translations ever left Japan, it has recently come to light that a version of the play had been performed in front of the Qianlong emperor in Beijing decades earlier, around 1782.[3]

By and large, however, cultural influence flowed overwhelmingly the other direction. Where Chinese Japanophiles like Lu were rare oddities,

2. Lu's story was not widely known until the inclusion of a short biography and an illustration (which depicts him seated before a jōruri libretto in the company of a Japanese courtesan) in the early nineteenth-century gazetteer *Nagasaki meishō zue*, and was unlikely to have been known to Nanpo when he wrote his piece. *Nagasaki meishō zue*, in Ikeda Yasaburō et al., eds., *Nihon meisho fūzoku zue* 15 (Kadokawa shoten, 1983), 120–21.

3. On translations of *Chūshingura* into vernacular Chinese, see William C. Hedberg, "The Chinese Afterlives of Coxinga and the Forty-Seven Rōnin of Akō: Japanese Puppet Theatre and Cultural Encounter in Edo-Period Nagasaki," *Sino-Japanese Studies* 20 (2013): 34–65. On the Beijing performance of *Chūshingura* and how word of it reached Japan, see Luke S. Roberts, "Shipwrecks and Flotsam: The Foreign World in Edo-Period Tosa," *Monumenta Nipponica* 70, no. 1 (2015): 107–8.

early modern Japan—which is to say, Japan of the Edo period (1600–1868)—overflowed with his mirror images. Ogyū Sorai and his followers applied themselves to the excavation of new meanings from ancient, foundational Chinese texts. Scholars of vernacular Chinese churned out dictionaries and other reference works, as well as the occasional translation from Japanese, while students and curiosity-seekers thronged to Nagasaki to learn the language firsthand and imbibe the city's unique continental atmosphere. Readers devoured a steady stream of imported Chinese narratives in both the original and Japanese editions, and authors found inspiration in the unfamiliar characters, storylines, and stylistic elements they contained.

A more obvious reading of *Japan for This Guy!*, then, is as a parodic inversion of the actual state of affairs in early modern Japan. The absurdity of Scholar Yan's naïve, over-the-top enthusiasm for all things Japanese shines a satirical light on the excesses of a land overrun with Sinophiles and Sinologists obsessively poring over continental models and searching for profound truths in even the most trivial Chinese texts. At the same time, Nanpo celebrates the riches and dynamism of "native" cultural life, especially art forms associated with the city of Edo, as Yan is shown delighting in the pleasures of *ukiyoe* prints, Japanese ceramics, flower-arrangement, popular ballads, and much more.[4] This celebration may also involve a degree of wishful thinking manifesting the insecurities, subconscious or otherwise, of an intellectual who was himself deeply immersed in the Japanese Sinological tradition. After all, the implausibility of Nanpo's premise only underscores the fundamental imbalance wherein goods, ideas, and practices had since ancient times flowed from the continent into Japan while relatively little made the reverse journey. Not unlike those who translated Japanese texts for an imagined Chinese readership, Nanpo imagines a world where the balance of cultural power is tilted the other direction.

In the Edo period, the flow of ideas from the continent was embodied in a steady stream of imported books. If in Nanpo's imagined world

4. Several scholars have interpreted the piece along these or similar lines. See Uda Toshihiko, in Kimura Yaeko et al., *Kusazōshi shū*, 212; Wada Hiromichi, ed., *Shokusanjin kibyōshi shū* (Koten bunko, 1984), 133–34; and Hamada Giichirō, *Ōta Nanpo*, in *Jinbutsu sōsho* 102 (Yoshikawa kōbunkan, 1963), 96–97.

Japanese publications hot off the block flowed through Ningbo into the hands of an eager Chinese reader, in the real world thousands upon thousands of books, including the latest fiction, flowed through Ningbo and other Chinese ports en route to the Japanese port of Nagasaki. (One hiccup in Nanpo's parodic inversion concerns Yan's journey to his spiritual homeland: from the 1630s, Japanese were forbidden from traveling abroad. It follows that imported books were all transported from the continent by the Chinese themselves.) This study follows these books from their publication in China through their importation to Nagasaki and afterlives in the Japanese literary milieu, with the aim of reconsidering the status of Chinese fiction in early modern Japan and the processes through which, as well as the purposes *for* which, it was rewritten.

We begin with the very large picture, setting our sights on nothing less than the entire literary output of late imperial China and the substantial subset that was imported to Japan. Through a set of interconnected large-scale analyses, the first part of this study provides answers to fundamental questions that have usually been approached anecdotally if not ignored altogether: What portion of China's literary output, particularly fiction, reached Japan in the Edo period, and how quickly? How did the speed and scale of importation change over time? How accessible and how expensive were imported books? What percentage of titles were reprinted for the Japanese market in cheaper, more readily available domestic editions? How do these figures break down by genre, and how do they change over time? What types of texts, and what types of fiction, were most likely to be imported and reprinted? How might we estimate the incompleteness of the documentary record and account for gaps, not to mention those titles that are no longer extant?

Even a glance through the surviving Nagasaki import records reveals that fiction made up a relatively small portion of imported texts, vastly outweighed by materials such as local gazetteers, medical texts, Buddhist sutras, histories, and commentaries on the classics. In absolute terms, however, a great many titles of Ming-Qing fiction reached Japanese shores over the course of the Edo period. In fact, the macro-analysis in this book paints a detailed picture of the nearly wholesale and often virtually contemporaneous transport of an entire literary culture—the collective literary imagination of late imperial China—to early modern Japan. This included the *majority* of Chinese fiction. The permeation of these texts into Japanese literary consciousness is often taken for granted, evidenced by the popularity and wide reach of narratives such as *The Water Margin* (*Shuihu zhuan*), *Romance of the Three Kingdoms* (*Sanguo yanyi*), and *Journey to the West* (*Xiyou ji*), all of which were rewritten in countless forms and became familiar cultural touchstones. Other commonly cited examples include Qu You's *New Tales by Lamplight* (*Jiandeng xinhua*, lit. "New Tales for Trimming the Lamp-Wick"), which inspired many adaptations over an extended period of time—"The Peony Lantern" ("Mudan deng ji"), in particular, proved popular in any number of genres and media, including oral storytelling—and Feng Menglong's vernacular *Sanyan* collections, selections of which were reprinted, translated, and adapted into new genres.

At the same time, each of these examples illustrates the difficulties of assimilation. Qu You's tales circulated narrowly in manuscript form among Gozan monks for more than a century after their arrival in Japan. It was not until the appearance of a 1648 reprint edition with annotation and Japanese reading marks, and the reissue of this edition twice subsequently, that the text began to find more widespread familiarity. Even then, the language presented extraordinary challenges to Japanese readers of all abilities. The situation was more pronounced for texts in the vernacular register. *The Water Margin* was very gradually rendered accessible through successive annotations, commentaries, (partial) reprints, translations, and adaptations over the course of the eighteenth century, while Feng Menglong's stories became widely familiar only with the reprint of selections in a series of carefully annotated editions prepared by the Sinologists Oka Hakku and Sawada Issai in the mid-eighteenth century.

The vast majority of imported texts were never reprinted in domestic editions. Given that most titles were brought to Japan in vanishingly small numbers—often only one or two copies—the mere fact of importation is by itself of questionable significance. In the absence of a reprint edition, such books would seem bound to enjoy limited readership or to disappear altogether. In the rare case that a copy could be found at all on the open market, it was assured to be prohibitively expensive for all but the wealthiest collectors. As will be seen, even the most ordinary imported titles regularly sold for tens of times more than deluxe editions of domestic literature—thousands of dollars in today's money—while rare titles could fetch mind-boggling sums orders of magnitude higher still. What does it mean for a work to have been imported if it simply vanished into a void of inaccessibility?

As the monograph progresses, attention is increasingly focused on one text in particular: Pu Songling's (1640–1715) celebrated collection of strange tales *Liaozhai zhiyi* (Strange Tales from Liaozhai Studio; hereafter abbreviated as simply *Liaozhai*). The choice of text takes us away from the well-trod paths of reception history and opens up new perspectives on the ways Chinese fiction was circulated, read, and ultimately rewritten in the Japanese context. Unlike the examples mentioned above, *Liaozhai* is a title that seldom surfaces in discussions of Edo literary culture. Only a handful of copies were imported, and the collection was never reprinted in a domestic edition. Yet far from disappearing into obscurity, the tales reemerge in surprising, far-flung places. This points to a reception that unfolded beneath the surface, through practices largely hidden from sight. The excavation of these subterranean layers demonstrates the continued importance of manuscript culture and associated practices—the literal rewriting of texts through hand-copying—in an era thought of as dominated by print. At the far end of these processes, the trail resurfaces into the world of print, where we find adaptations of Pu's tales across diverse genres that resituated them in a complex intertextual web, molded them to new generic expectations, and grappled with the political realities of life under the rule of the Tokugawa shogunate.

Pu Songling in China and Japan

Readers on the continent were immediately drawn to *Liaozhai* for its strange conceits and alluring style, as well as the sheer scale and diversity of the collection, with nearly five hundred tales ranging from no more than a line or two to many pages in length. Selections began to circulate in manuscript form in the late seventeenth century, even as Pu remained at work on the collection, and the tales continued to spread among family, friends, and other enthusiasts in the decades that followed. The publication of the first print edition in 1766, half a century after the author's death, brought still greater visibility. The text began to accrue commentaries and annotations, and there arose a growing body of imitators.[5] In one often-cited passage, the Qing critic Yu Hongjian identifies several of the most familiar of these and positions them in a distinct hierarchy: "*Liaozhai* is widely enjoyed, but I myself take particular pleasure in *Yuewei caotang biji* (Notes from the Cottage of Close Scrutiny). . . . As for *Xieduo* (The Bell of Humor), *Yetan suilu* (Informal Record of Nighttime Stories), and the like, they all retread *Liaozhai*'s footsteps but are at least good enough to pass the time between meals. At the bottom is Yuan Mei's *Zi bu yu* (That of Which the Master Did Not Speak). It should just be tossed into the fire."[6] Yu's personal favorite, *Yuewei caotang biji*, was the work of the prominent scholar Ji Yun, one of *Liaozhai*'s most vociferous critics. Ji disparaged *Liaozhai* for blending and bending genres, and for its resistance to categorization—the same qualities that for many readers, then as now, were part of the collection's appeal. Still, *Liaozhai* served as the reference point by which Ji distinguished his own strange tales, a privileged status underscored in the hierarchy laid out by his admirer Yu.

Liaozhai would eventually assume a secure place in the literary canon in Japan as well, but this process did not get underway until well into the Meiji period (1868–1912). In 1883, Kikuchi Sankei, a Confucian scholar who had formerly served as personal tutor to the penultimate Tokugawa shogun, published his own collection of curious, if for the most part ostensibly true, tales from contemporary Tokyo. In choosing a title, Sankei settled on *Japanese New Tales of Yu Chu* (*Honchō Gu Sho shinshi*), presenting the collection as an updated domestic counterpart to Zhang Chao's *New Tales of Yu Chu* (*Yu Chu xinzhi*, preface dated 1700). Nevertheless, the style and literary sensibility of the work were also deeply informed by Sankei's reading of Pu Songling, as he himself proclaims in the explanatory notes that precede the body text. The stylistic similarity extends to the commentaries by Sankei and several members of his

5. For a thematic overview of responses to *Liaozhai* in China, see "The Discourse on the Strange," in Judith T. Zeitlin, *Historian of the Strange: Pu Songling and the Chinese Classical Tale* (Stanford, CA: Stanford University Press, 1993), 15–42; for a concise overview of the Chinese reception history in the Qing, see Luo Hui, "The Ghost of *Liaozhai*: Pu Songling's Ghostlore and Its History of Reception" (PhD diss., University of Toronto, 2009), 153–56.

6. Zhu Yixuan, ed., *Liaozhai zhiyi ziliao huibian* (Zhengzhou: Zhongzhou guji chubanshe, 1986), 503–4.

literary cohort appended to many of the tales; in fact, in the original manuscript Sankei attributed his own remarks to the "Historian of the Strange," assuming the same self-appellation used by Pu Songling.[7]

Sankei was hardly the only Meiji literary luminary to feel a deep connection with Pu Songling. Mori Ōgai (1862–1922), who recalled eagerly reading Sankei's tales as a young man in his semi-autobiographical *Vita Sexualis* (1909), also spent many hours poring over *Liaozhai*; his well-worn personal copy, featuring extensive annotations in his own hand, survives today in his collection at the University of Tokyo. Ōgai was also one of the earliest to document Japanese rewritings of *Liaozhai* tales. In a piece that appeared in the *Yomiuri shinbun* newspaper in 1890, he noted that a smattering of "translations" had appeared to date and identified Yoda Gakkai's short story "Ono no Takamura," published a few weeks earlier in the literary serial *Shincho hyakushu*, as a close rewriting of Pu's "Princess Lotus" ("Lianhua gongzhu"). While praising Gakkai for his elegant style, Ōgai questioned the appropriateness of including such a piece in a publication with the words "new works" (*shincho*) in its very title.[8]

One month earlier, Ōgai's younger sister, Koganei Kimiko (1871–1956), still in her teens at the time, had published her own version of what is today one of Pu's best-known stories: "The Painted Skin" ("Hua pi"). Titled "A Single Layer of Skin" ("Kawa hitoe," 1890), the piece is presented in a self-consciously classical style and adds a clear seasonal setting—it begins with the words "In the dim light before daybreak one autumn morning"—where there was originally none. Befitting this "Japanification" of the narrative, the text is stripped of proper nouns that might betray a sense of place, the sole exception being the protagonist, Wang. (Even so, he is first named several paragraphs in, not at the outset, as in Pu's version.) Like Gakkai, Kimiko does not identify the source text, but she does acknowledge the existence of one, signing the piece "translated by Koganei Kimiko" (*Koganei Kimiko yaku*).[9]

7. Ikezawa Ichirō, "*Honchō Gu Sho shinshi* to kōdan," in Ikezawa Ichirō et al., eds., *Kanbun shōsetsu shū*, in *SNKBT Meiji hen* 3 (Iwanami shoten, 2005), 521.

8. Yang Shuang, "Yoda Gakkai to *Ryōsai shii* [*Liaozhai zhiyi*]: 'Ono no Takamura' to 'Lianhua gongzhu' to no hikaku kenkyū o chūshin ni," *Nihon kanbungaku kenkyū* 12 (2017): 121.

9. For a transcription of Kimiko's story, along with the text of "The Painted Skin" in parallel, see Odagiri Hiroko, "Hon'yaku bungaku no keifu: Kimiko yaku 'Kawa

Others of the same generation who formed a close relationship with *Liaozhai* include Kōda Rohan (1867–1947), Ozaki Kōyō (1868–1903), and Kunikida Doppo (1871–1908). Doppo, who earlier in his career had tried his hand at translating several of the tales, wrote in his final work, the posthumously published *Notes from My Sickbed* (*Byōshōroku*, 1908), of his boundless enthusiasm for ghost stories and—reflecting the continuation of a custom that had become popular in the Edo period—for passing the night reading and listening to them. Arguing for the superiority of Chinese strange tales, he described *Liaozhai* as "one of my favorite books."[10] This enthusiasm carried on unabated among prominent members of the next generation of writers, notably Akutagawa Ryūnosuke (1892–1927) and Dazai Osamu (1909–48), whose adaptations, reflecting broader literary trends, evince a particular interest in the collection's grotesque and satirical qualities.

Substantial Japanese translations did not come until relatively late. Western readers were able to access 164 stories in translation as early as 1880, the year of Herbert Giles's two-volume English translation *Strange Stories from a Chinese Studio*.[11] The translation was republished multiple times in subsequent decades. By contrast, the earliest modern anthology of Chinese strange tales in Japanese translation was a three-volume series from 1906 titled *An Anthology of Chinese Strange Tales* (*Shina kidan shū*), which presented a selection from multiple collections from ancient times through the Qing, of which about one-third of the total, or fifty-four tales, were from *Liaozhai*.[12] In 1921 the writer Tanaka Kōtarō (1880–1941) translated a smattering of ghostly love stories from several Chinese

---

hitoe,'" *Fukuoka jogakuin tanki daigaku kiyō* 24 (February 1988): 1–19. *Liaozhai* was also a favorite of Kimiko's grandson, the science-fiction short-story writer Hoshi Shin'ichi (1926–97). Saishō Hazuki, *Hoshi Shin'ichi: sen'ichiwa o tsukutta hito* (Shinchōsha, 2007), 42.

10. Doppo, *Byōshōroku*, in Kunikida Doppo zenshū hensan iinkai, ed., *Teihon Kunikida Doppo zenshū*, 2nd ed. (Gakushū kenkyūsha, 1978), 9:68.

11. Herbert Giles, trans., *Strange Stories from a Chinese Studio* (London: Thomas de la Rue, 1880).

12. Ōga Junji, ed., *Shina kidan shū: dai ippen, dai nihen, sanjūkyūnen gogatsu* [*dai sanpen*] (Kinji gahōsha, 1906). See Fujita Yūken, "Kunikida Doppo to Chūgoku kaii bungaku," in *geppō* accompanying *Kunikida Doppo zenshū* 4 (June 1966): 323.

collections, including *Liaozhai*. He and others produced more extensive translations later that decade.[13]

In 1933 the journalist Shibata Tenma embarked on a full translation, having serially published selected tales in a Japanese-language newspaper in Manchuria two decades earlier. However, the project was censored by the Japanese authorities after the publication of the first volume, and additional financial difficulties delayed the project's completion until the early 1950s.[14] Still, by the time Shibata conceived this project, *Liaozhai* was already firmly ensconced in the Japanese canon. A collection of Tanaka Kōtarō's original strange tales, titled *A Collection of Shadows* (*Kokuei shū*, 1921), was marketed to readers for being "not a rehash of [E.T.A.] Hoffmann or [Edgar Allan] Poe, but . . . comparable only to Pu Songling's *Liaozhai zhiyi* or Ueda Akinari's *Tales of Moonlight and Rain*," attesting to both collections' status as familiar cultural touchstones or "modern classics" by the Taishō period (1912–26).[15] A 1933 selection of nearly two dozen *Liaozhai* stories was published under the title *A Chinese Decameron* (*Tōyō Dekameron*), equating Pu Songling with Boccaccio in stature and structure if not style and subject matter.[16]

In contrast to the preceding, the evidence for engagement with *Liaozhai* in the Edo period initially appears very thin. Although it is possible that some of the tales arrived during the years they circulated in manuscript on the continent, the earliest attested copy appears in the import records in 1768, two years after the publication of the first printed edition. On the one hand, this exemplifies the considerable speed with which newly published Chinese books could reach Japan. It was, however, just one copy, and only a handful of additional copies are known to have been imported over the remainder of the Edo period. Given that the text was never reprinted in a domestic edition, it is un-

13. Tanaka Kōtarō, trans., *Ren'ai kigo* (Ten'yūsha, 1921), and *Ryōsai shii* [*Liaozhai zhiyi*], in *Shina bungaku taikan* 12 (Shina bungaku taikan kankōkai, 1926).

14. Yamada Hiromitsu, "*Ryōsai shii* to Nihon kindai bungaku," in Tezukayama gakuin daigaku sōritsu nijūgo shūnen kinen ronshū henshū iinkai, ed., *Sekai to Nihon* (Ōsakasayama-shi: Tezukayama gakuin daigaku, 1992), 53–54.

15. See advertisement in *Tosho geppō* 19, no. 7 (July 1921), reprinted in *Shoshi shomoku shirīzu* 19: *Kōkoku hen* (Yumani shobō, 1986), 171.

16. Seki Senshū, trans., *Tōyō Dekameron* (Mikasa shobō, 1933).

surprising that *Liaozhai* was long thought to have been virtually unknown in early modern Japan.[17]

Yet beneath this surface of apparent neglect lies a rich underground reception history. *Liaozhai* may not have attained the level of widespread familiarity enjoyed by *The Water Margin*, *New Tales by Lamplight*, or the other texts mentioned previously—a situation that owes in part to the collection's relative newness, as the diffusion and familiarization of texts was a process that unfolded over decades and centuries. Nevertheless, people *were* engaging with the text, and in remarkably diverse ways. The title appears in letters, literary prefaces, and marginalia. Stories depicting legal cases and the administration of justice were excerpted as case studies for instruction at a domainal academy. Teachers assigned the text to their students as required reading. More than a dozen tales were even translated into vernacular Japanese (albeit by way of a later Chinese anthology) in a collection published in the 1820s, long before the efforts of Koganei Kimiko and Yoda Gakkai, let alone Tanaka Kōtarō and Shibata Tenma.

Liaozhai was imported into a Japan awash in curiosity and a desire for the strange. The sense of wonder fueled by the European "Age of Discovery" had parallels in early modern Japan, where rising wealth and material comfort—enabled by what Hayami Akira has characterized as the period's "industrious revolution"—joined forces with Japan's own age of discovery, which unfolded through its encounter with the unceasing stream of goods from the outside world unloaded in Nagasaki.[18] This encounter fed itself, fueling desire for further wonders, curiosities, and strange experiences—all subsumed under the increasingly prevalent heading of *ki* 奇. Edo writers, steeped in this broader cultural context, found in Pu Songling a kindred spirit who shared their peculiar obsessions.

17. See, for instance, Masuda Wataru et al., trans., *Ryōsai shii*, in *Chūgoku koten bungaku zenshū* 21 (Heibonsha, 1958), 434.

18. On the European experience of wonder in the Age of Discovery, as well as its sinister appropriations, see Stephen Greenblatt, *Marvelous Possessions: The Wonder of the New World* (Chicago: University of Chicago Press, 1991). Hayami Akira originated the term "industrious revolution" in 1976 and developed the concept in numerous subsequent publications. Akira Hayami, *Japan's Industrious Revolution: Economic and Social Transformations in the Early Modern Period* (New York: Springer, 2015), 96.

These include some whose names have been mostly lost to history, such as Hattori Shukushin (1773?–1805) and Terasaki Reishū (1761–1822), a pair of literati-scholars from the small castle town of Takaoka on the Japan Sea coast who bonded over an enthusiasm for Pu's tales that few could rival. Shukushin found himself so immersed in Pu's fictional worlds that he would plunge into depression after finishing a story; according to Reishū, he was visited by Pu's spirit in a dream shortly before his untimely death at the age of thirty-three.[19] At the other extreme of celebrity sits Kyokutei Bakin (1767–1848), one of the giants of late Edo fiction. Among Bakin's nearly one hundred *kibyōshi* comic books, mostly published early in his literary career, is one from 1797 that depicts the life of a young man who naïvely turns to books for the answers to life's questions and challenges. Presented as a series of gently satirical episodes, the piece constitutes a rewriting of Pu Songling's "The Bookworm" ("Shu chi"). Given the pervasiveness of adaptation and allusion in the deeply intertextual Japanese literary tradition, Edo writers generally did not identify source texts, at least not overtly. In this instance, however, Bakin openly identified *Liaozhai zhiyi* by name in his preface, recounting the feeling of "immediate contentment" he experienced after immersing himself in Pu's tales.[20]

It is remarkable that a text should become so widely known—not just in Edo, but in Nagoya, Takaoka, and beyond—in spite of the existence of only a few printed copies in the entirety of Japan. That it did points to the continued importance of manuscript culture and related practices in a period usually characterized as dominated by print. To be sure, the Edo period *was* a golden age of print: already by the 1660s, readers in the major cities could purchase classical literature, vernacular fiction, poetry handbooks, Confucian classics, medical treatises, calendars, dictionaries, and more in woodblock editions. Nevertheless, manuscript culture remained vibrant long after the rise of print. It did so in many contexts, and for diverse reasons. Cultural conservatives espoused views that evoke Adorno's notion of the "aura" of the original, arguing for a perceived authenticity that was lost in mass reproduction. Copying texts by hand

19. Terayama Reishū, *Reishū yoshu* (1819), in Isobe Yūko and Moriga Kazue, *Toyama bungaku no reimei*, vol. 2 (Toyama: Katsura shobō, 2017), 4–5.

20. Kyokutei Bakin, *Oshiedori ahō no kōmyō* (1797), in Seida Keiko, "Honkoku Kyokutei Bakin no kibyōshi (3)," *Komazawa tanki daigaku kenkyū kiyō* 5 (March 1977): 71.

was also promoted as a valuable form of discipline and self-cultivation. Economic considerations played a further role. Many texts could not sustain the considerable outlay of capital necessary to produce a print edition. Even those that could yielded copies that were not so inexpensive as to completely disincentivize copying by hand, which required only ink and paper—for which sheets recycled from elsewhere often sufficed. The calculus shifts back somewhat in print's favor if we factor in the expenditure of time, but only somewhat. Early modern copiers were endowed with speed and stamina scarcely fathomable in our digital age.

Above all, there is the simple fact that what was available in print was far exceeded by that which was not. Here we come up against the logical extreme of economic considerations and the law of supply and demand. Rare texts, if they could be obtained at all, were prohibitively expensive for all but the wealthiest collectors; items that could not be tracked down on the market were, quite literally, priceless. It was only through borrowing and copying that such texts could be acquired, and many scholars spent their days eagerly borrowing, reading, and copying obscure, difficult-to-find titles. Through such labor, the contents of private and institutional collections were freed into the wider world. These collections included, for example, that of the Shōheikō, the bakufu academy, which, in spite of its Neo-Confucian underpinnings, held a selection of Chinese fiction several times larger than that which was cumulatively reprinted in Japanese editions over the entire duration of the Edo period.

Liaozhai was one of many texts that circulated widely through such "hidden" practices. Nevertheless, here and there the trail surfaces into the world of print, the visible evidence of a reception sustained largely by manuscript. The present study traces a total of around two dozen published adaptations, spin-offs, and translations of individual tales in literary genres ranging from historical fiction to the *kibyōshi* comic book. In addition, several tales were eventually reprinted in their entirety, and a few more were excerpted in part. The first of these traces in print appeared only a few years after the arrival of the first copy in Japan; after gaining steam in the 1790s, the decade that saw the publication of Bakin's comic-book adaptation of "The Bookworm," they continued unabated into the nineteenth century.

The most substantial of these engagements with Pu Songling is a virtually unknown collection of haunting supernatural tales by the writer Morishima Chūryō (1756–1810) titled *Tales from the Withering Wind* (*Kogarashi zōshi*, 1792). In the canon of Japanese supernatural fiction, pride of place is reserved for Ueda Akinari's (1734–1809) *Tales of Moonlight and Rain* (*Ugetsu monogatari*, 1776), a work whose familiarity outside Japan was greatly magnified by Mizoguchi Kenji's 1953 film adaptation *Ugetsu*. But Akinari's collection was joined by those of Chūryō and others as part of a much larger corpus of Edo-period strange tales. On one level, these narratives seem to exist in a world apart, their otherworldly subject matter and historical settings conveying detachment from the mundane concerns of the present. They direct their gaze inward to the world of the text and literary tradition, borrowing and adapting storylines, imparting meaning through allusion to classical texts, and engaging in a dialogue with other writers. Yet this very detachment from the present also represents, paradoxically, a concession to its realities, a necessary strategy by authors very much aware of the looming presence of shogunal power. Distancing the strange was a performance of submission to the Tokugawa order. Chūryō's tales exemplify this contradiction. They are exquisitely strange, richly intertextual, and at times deeply poetic—perhaps not quite the match of those of Akinari, but not deserving to be completely eclipsed by them either. At the same time, they were produced during a particularly repressive moment in Tokugawa rule, and as he rewrote Pu Songling's tales he remained keenly aware of the concerns of the present.

Situating the Present Study

This monograph navigates among several interrelated approaches and bodies of scholarship. It begins by considering texts as material objects, drawing on approaches and frameworks from book history as well as, in treating these objects en masse, methods that would now conventionally be described as the territory of "digital humanities." As the scope shifts from the text as object to the text as abstract entity, we enter the domain of literary studies, with forays into manuscript studies, adaptation and translation theory, and what is often termed "reception theory," although this study prefers the more encompassing term "rewriting."

More narrowly, this project participates in a renewed wave of scholarly interest in the status of Chinese texts in Japan in the premodern and early modern eras.

The broad outlines of the importation of Chinese texts to Japan have been traced by historians of the book including Peter Kornicki, who presents a chronological overview of this transmission history in his study of the book in Japan.[21] In the early modern period, the book trade left a rich, if fragmented, body of extant ship inventories, inspection lists, pricing documents, and auction records, particularly from the late seventeenth century onward, as inspection procedures were codified. Reproductions of these archival materials have been published by the Japanese historian Ōba Osamu, who has also written extensively on Sino-Japanese trade and cultural contact in the early modern era, and whose foundational work in the 1960s and 1970s did much to illuminate the sheer scale of the importation of Chinese texts. A selection of Ōba's ground-breaking work has also been made available in English translation through the efforts of Joshua Fogel, whose own work has contributed greatly to our understanding of Sino-Japanese history.[22]

The documents painstakingly collected and edited by Ōba offer an invaluable window into the titles and quantity of imported books. In his study of sentimental fiction during what he characterizes as Japan's "long nineteenth century," Jonathan Zwicker, taking an approach informed but not limited by Franco Moretti's proposal for "distant reading," observes the sheer number of imported titles attested in these records. Cognizant of the dangers of ascribing too much meaning to importation alone, Zwicker writes that "it is one thing to show that such and such a

21. Peter Kornicki, *The Book in Japan: A Cultural History from the Beginnings to the Nineteenth Century* (Honolulu: University of Hawai'i Press, 2001), especially 277–300 and 320–31.

22. Ōba Osamu, *Edo jidai ni okeru Chūgoku bunka juyō no kenkyū* (Kyōto: Dōhōsha, 1984), and *Edo jidai no Nit-Chū hiwa* (Tōhō shoten, 1980). Joshua Fogel translated the latter serially in volumes 8 through 13 of the journal *Sino-Japanese Studies*, then published a revised translation of the full work as *Books and Boats: Sino-Japanese Relations in the Seventeenth and Eighteenth Centuries* (Portland, ME: Merwin Asia, 2012). The import records themselves are reproduced primarily in Ōba, *Edo jidai ni okeru Tōsen mochiwatarisho no kenkyū* (Suita-shi: Kansai daigaku shuppanbu, 1967), 238–739, and *Hakusai shomoku*, 2 vols. (Suita-shi: Kansai daigaku shuppanbu, 1972).

book was imported at such and such a time; it is quite another to map out the course of that book's social life once it has cleared customs and the censor's eye and when the paper trail is likely to have ended."[23] Still, in examining a selection of several dozen works of Ming-Qing fiction, he takes the appearance of a majority of these titles in the import record as evidence that "virtually the entire literary imagination of late imperial China . . . was available to the Japanese reading public by the nineteenth century."[24]

Although I am sympathetic to the spirit of this assertion, at the very least it warrants further examination on several fronts. To begin with, can we take a small set of relatively prominent texts as representative of the whole? We must also remember that the appearance of a title in the archive tells nothing about quantity. Only one copy of *Liaozhai* is known for certain to have been imported before the year 1800; for many other texts, the first copy was also the last. Can books such as these really be said to be "available" to the reading public without our endeavoring to reconstruct something of their "social lives," to borrow Zwicker's term—that is to say, their physical and literary afterlives, as they continued onward to buyers, collections, and—possibly—readers across Japan? This study reopens the question of the availability of Chinese fiction in the Edo period by expanding the scope of inquiry to much larger bodies of texts and, in an effort to move beyond a focus on titles alone, by considering the role of domestic reprint editions. Charting the afterlives of texts is a far more daunting prospect, and it is here that the focus necessarily narrows, with the case of *Liaozhai* used to illustrate broader phenomena and practices through which Chinese texts were rewritten at the hands of Japanese authors.

The large-scale analysis in this monograph wrings greater nuance from Ōba's materials by considering them not in isolation but in conversation with other bibliographic scholarship and bodies of data. Bringing bodies of scholarly work together allows us to refine our image of the "big picture." Looking back to the continent, we are able to draw on the re-

23. Jonathan Zwicker, *Practices of the Sentimental Imagination: Melodrama, the Novel, and the Social Imaginary in Nineteenth-Century Japan* (Cambridge, MA: Harvard University Asia Center, 2006), 128.

24. Zwicker, *Practices of the Sentimental Imagination*, 135.

search of Chinese bibliographers including Yuan Xingpei, Hou Zhongyi, and Ning Jiayu, whose work includes extensive annotated catalogs of Chinese "fiction" (*xiaoshuo*) from the Ming and Qing dynasties.[25] Turning the other direction, we may rely upon the efforts of Nagasawa Kikuya, who has catalogued a large number of the domestic Japanese reprints of Chinese texts known as *wakokubon*.[26] These resources were all converted into digital forms to facilitate the present analysis. In some cases, this presented particularly acute challenges. Nagasawa's catalog, for example, is not only handwritten but intermingles modern woodblock and facsimile editions with those published in the Edo period. The one major "born-digital" resource used in this study, the Zenkoku kanseki dētabēsu (Japan-Wide Database of Chinese Texts) maintained by the Institute for Research in Humanities at Kyoto University, was an invaluable supplement to Nagasawa but presents challenges of its own: the back-end data is not available, and the entries need to be approached with caution, as they include not only *wakokubon* but also imported books and modern reprints, all without any standardized formatting.[27]

The use of existing and newly created data sets, text-mining, scripts, and other digital techniques in the first part of this study necessitates mention of the "digital humanities." As the term has been increasingly adopted in Chinese and Japanese studies over the past decade or two, it has been used ever more casually and over-broadly, often merely to denote the use of digital tools in service of humanistic inquiry. The problem is not unique to this field, and some of the factors behind such "mission creep"—the spread of access to digital tools, increasingly accessible interfaces, and increased technological literacy—are innocuous if not to be lauded. Yet there are also more insidious factors, many of which are interrelated. These include recourse to digital methods to overcome malaise (both personal and in the field at large), to impart perceived relevance,

25. Yuan Xingpei and Hou Zhongyi, eds., *Zhongguo wenyan xiaoshuo shumu* (Beijing: Beijing daxue chubanshe, 1981); and Ning Jiayu, *Zhongguo wenyan xiaoshuo zongmu tiyao* (Jinan: Qilu shushe, 1996).

26. Nagasawa Kikuya, ed., *Wakokubon kanseki bunrui mokuroku*, rev. ed. (Kyūko shoin, 2006).

27. Zenkoku kanseki dētabēsu (Japan-Wide Database of Chinese Texts): http://kanji.zinbun.kyoto-u.ac.jp/kanseki.

or as the logical conclusion of neoliberal profit-motives and attendant hopes of appealing to funding sources.[28]

While I am skeptical of many projects that self-identify as "digital humanities," at the same time I do not wish to malign the minority pursuing genuinely innovative work under its banner. My preference not to identify my own work as such is born not of disdain for the field—at least not as practiced by those who approach it with sufficient self-awareness and critical reflection—but out of a perhaps futile desire to prevent the term from being used so broadly as to obscure its legitimate meanings. It is in danger, if that point has not already been reached, of becoming an empty label. As the editors of one recent survey of the field succinctly put it, "the mere use of digital tools for the purpose of humanistic research and communication does not qualify as Digital Humanities."[29] I wish to hang onto this and recognize the distinction in work such as my own. While I use digital tools to expand the scope of my analysis to entire corpuses, they are merely that: *tools*. I also eschew the "digital humanities" label because my interest is fundamentally at the level of close reading. Although the opening chapters of my study do not neglect the text itself as an object of analysis, particularly from the third chapter on the focus shifts to individual copies of books, individual narratives, and the individual writers who wrote and rewrote them.

Recognition of the reality that ideas, texts, and books—and even people—flowed across "national" boundaries in the early modern era has been a recurring theme in historical scholarship of the past decades, part of a broader rejection of the once-prevalent *sakoku* (or "closed country") paradigm of Edo Japan. Ronald Toby's observation that the view of islands "shut off" from the outside world is rooted in a tendency to view Tokugawa foreign relations solely in terms of its policy regarding Europe has a counterpart in Ōba, who notes that the Chinese presence in Nagasaki was long overlooked in favor of the Dutch because whereas the for-

28. For a thoughtful and provocative consideration of some of these issues as they pertain to the field of modern Japanese literary studies, see John Whittier Treat, "Japan Is Interesting: Modern Japanese Literary Studies Today," *Japan Forum* 30, no. 3 (2018): 11–19.

29. Anne Burdick, Johanna Drucker, Peter Lunenfeld, Todd Presner, and Jeffrey Schnapp, *Digital Humanities* (Cambridge, MA: MIT Press, 2012), 122.

mer was everyday, the latter was rarer and thus deemed worthy of note.[30] Nor was Japan itself, prior to modern notions of nation and sovereignty, neatly defined at the periphery; spaces like Tsushima and the Ryūkyūs existed at once within and without Japan.[31] The move to consider early modern Japan within its East Asian and global contexts is now well established and has spread from history to other fields. As it has done so, the notion that Japanese studies of the West played a marginal role in the larger culture has also been questioned, for example by Timon Screech, who has shown how new technologies conveyed through the Dutch, particularly optical devices such as the microscope, took on new meanings in the Japanese popular imagination and gave rise to new ways of thinking about the world, often providing new metaphors and conceptual frameworks.[32]

In literary studies, the tendency to view Japan's foreign relations solely in terms of Western relations lies behind characterizations of Edo literature in earlier English-language scholarship as, to borrow Donald Keene's famous metaphor, a "world within walls."[33] From this vantage point, it is only in the Meiji period that Japanese literature emerged from its cocoon, "opening up" to Western literary movements as reformers such as Tsubouchi Shōyō advocated for what they saw as an evolutionary march toward literary modernity through the embrace of the novel, naturalism and realism, and—at least in Shōyō's case—Shakespeare. However, Japanese scholars of Edo literature have long recognized the flow of texts across boundaries within East Asia. In the *kokubungaku* ("national literature") tradition of literary scholarship, this has often taken the form of what we would term "reception history." Studies of the Japanese reception of

30. Ronald Toby, "Reopening the Question of *Sakoku*: Diplomacy in the Legitimation of the Tokugawa Bakufu," *Journal of Japanese Studies* 3, no. 2 (Summer 1977): 323–63, and *State and Diplomacy in Early Modern Japan: Asia in the Development of the Tokugawa Bakufu* (Princeton, NJ: Princeton University Press, 1984); Ōba Osamu, *Kanseki yunyū no bunkashi: Shōtoku taishi kara Yoshimune e* (Kenbun shuppan, 1997), 8 (quoted in Zwicker, *Practices of the Sentimental Imagination*, 129).

31. For Toby's more recent perspectives, see Ronald Toby, *Engaging the Other: "Japan" and Its Alter-Egos, 1550–1850* (Leiden: Brill, 2019).

32. Timon Screech, *The Lens within the Heart: The Western Scientific Gaze and Popular Imagery in Later Edo Japan*, 2nd ed. (Honolulu: University of Hawai'i Press, 2002).

33. Donald Keene, *World within Walls: Japanese Literature of the Pre-Modern Era, 1600–1867* (New York: Holt, Rinehart & Winston, 1976).

Chinese fiction began in earnest with the detailed mid-twentieth-century textual studies of scholars such as Ishizaki Matazō and Asō Isoji. Both conceived of this reception in terms of "literary influence" (*bungaku no eikyō*), the study of which in practice often consisted of the identification of Edo adaptations of Chinese narratives and the tracing of individual source texts.[34] In more recent years their legacy, which did much to illuminate the extent of the Japanese reception of Chinese fiction, has been carried on by Tokuda Takeshi and others with increasing detail and sophistication.[35]

Asō devoted particular energy to what he termed the "supernatural tale" (*kaii shōsetsu*), a body of literature in which he included the collections of Ueda Akinari, his predecessors Tsuga Teishō (1718–ca. 1794) and Asai Ryōi (d. 1691), and many others. Japanese scholarship on the strange tales and supernatural fiction of the Edo period has accelerated in recent years. Much of this work emerges from and carries on Asō's bibliographic and reception-based analyses, but there have also been efforts at new approaches, notably the proposals of Iikura Yōichi and others to consider alternative taxonomies and generic frameworks for these texts.[36] There has also been considerable expansion of the corpus through the anthologizing of previously neglected texts. Of particular note in this regard are two five-volume series, one edited by Takada Mamoru and the other by Kigoshi Osamu, that include not only numerous less-familiar printed collections but also examples from the distinct tradition of manuscript strange tales that circulated regionally.[37] With regard to the latter, the work of Sugimoto Yoshinobu merits particular mention; in addition to co-editing a volume in Takada's series, he has published a separate volume devoted to more fully exploring the picture-book and picture-scroll variants of one of the works in that volume, a narrative titled *An Account of Inō Heitarō's*

34. Ishizaki Matazō, *Kinsei Nihon ni okeru Shina zokugo bungakushi* (Kōbundō, 1940); and Asō Isoji, *Edo bungaku to Shina bungaku: kinsei bungaku no Shina-teki genkyo to yomihon no kenkyū* (Sanseidō, 1946).

35. See, for instance, Tokuda Takeshi, *Nihon kinsei shōsetsu to Chūgoku shōsetsu*, in *Nihon shoshigaku taikei*, vol. 51 (Musashimurayama-shi: Seishōdō shoten, 1987).

36. See, for instance, Iikura Yōichi, "'Kidan' no ba," *Gobun* 78 (May 2002): 22.

37. Takada Mamoru, ed., *Edo kaii kisō bungei taikei*, 5 vols. (Kokusho kankōkai, 2000–2003); and Kigoshi Osamu, ed., *Edo kaidan bungei meisakusen*, 5 vols. (Kokusho kankōkai, 2016–19).

Spirit Encounters (*Inō mononoke roku*) that originated in the Hiroshima region and circulated from the late eighteenth century onward.[38]

Western scholarship on Edo tales of the strange has been comparatively stagnant, leaving ample room for expanding the scope of inquiry. Stimulating work has appeared recently devoted to the adjacent field of *yōkai*—the menagerie of weird creatures of Japanese folklore—notably by Michael Dylan Foster, whose monograph, while mostly concerned with modernity and the imposition of order on this unruly tradition, reaches back as far as the late seventeenth century in tracing the Edo-period natural-historical discourses that lie beneath later interest from Meiji onward.[39] With regard to fictional tales specifically, however, there has been little aside from Noriko Reider's historical overviews and typologies of the Edo ghost story and the occasional translation, the main one of note being Anthony Chambers's now definitive translation of Akinari's *Tales of Moonlight and Rain*, which includes an introduction that is a valuable contribution in its own right.[40] While Japanese scholarship has moved on, the Western understanding of supernatural tales in Japan before the twentieth century remains largely limited to Akinari and Lafcadio Hearn (through whom Asai Ryōi's "The Peony Lantern" has also become widely familiar outside Japan).

Illustrative of this tendency is a recent anthology of Japanese strange tales that, in spite of having "Edo" in its very title, presents only one story that is actually from the Edo period, and one that is already well known to readers in English at that: Akinari's "The Chrysanthemum Vow" ("Kikuka no chigiri"), from *Tales of Moonlight and Rain* (1776).[41] In fact, the

38. Tsutsumi Kunihiko and Sugimoto Yoshinobu, eds., *Kinsei minkan ibun kaidan shūsei* (2003), vol. 5 of Takada, ed., *Edo kaii kisō bungei taikei*; and Sugimoto Yoshinobu, ed., *Inō mononokeroku emaki shūsei* (Kokusho kankōkai, 2004).

39. Michael Dylan Foster, *Pandemonium and Parade: Japanese Monsters and the Culture of Yōkai* (Berkeley: University of California Press, 2009).

40. Noriko T. Reider, "The Appeal of *Kaidan* Tales of the Strange," *Asian Folklore Studies* 59, no. 2 (2000): 265–83, and "The Emergence of *Kaidan-shū*: The Collection of Tales of the Strange and Mysterious in the Edo Period," *Asian Folklore Studies* 60, no. 1 (2001): 79–99; Anthony H. Chambers, trans., *Tales of Moonlight and Rain* (New York: Columbia University Press, 2007).

41. Masao Higashi, ed., *Kaiki: Uncanny Tales from Japan, Volume 1: Tales of Old Edo* (Fukuoka: Kurodahan Press, 2009). The title of Akinari's tale is translated in the collection as "The Chrysanthemum Pledge."

collection expressly limits its purview to pieces written within the arbitrary window of the "last hundred years," with the only other exception granted for Hearn's "In a Cup of Tea" (1902), another story that is readily available elsewhere. This in spite of the fact that the collection otherwise devotes itself, admirably, to previously untranslated work, including stories by writers such as Kōda Rohan and Tanaka Kōtarō whose tales were shaped by their readings of Edo strange tales and their Chinese counterparts. The failure to delve more deeply into the Edo tradition, or at least to stray from the well-worn path, represents a missed opportunity to expand the vision of the Japanese strange tale.

The recent stream of Japanese anthologies featuring previously untranscribed works, most of which were originally published as woodblock editions, gives an indication of the sheer scale at which these tales were published in the early modern period, and by extension the scale of the publishing industry as a whole. The decades after the onset of the Tokugawa peace witnessed a publishing revolution, and by the late seventeenth century Japan had entered what is often characterized as a sustained golden age of print. Print culture is an important component of what was "modern" about early modern Japan, which is to say what set the period apart from what came before. Mary Elizabeth Berry has argued that print created a sense of national space, both literally and in the abstract; cartographic materials constructed a shared sense of a territorial space that was Japan, while an ever-growing, regularly updated library of informational texts chronicling all observable aspects of culture and society fostered awareness among readers that they belonged to a shared community. This "library of public information," as Berry terms it, included maps, didactic texts, encyclopedias, directories of officials and professionals, manuals of various sorts, fiction, and more.[42] Insofar as this ventures into the territory of print media and imagined communities, we might note similarities with Benedict Anderson, although Berry's collective identity emerges more out of geographic consciousness, not to mention a distinct political and historical context. In her emphasis on the ability of print to compress spatial and temporal distance, we might

42. Mary Elizabeth Berry, *Japan in Print: Information and Nation in the Early Modern Period* (Berkeley: University of California Press, 2006).

also observe the reach of this function beyond the territory of Japan, as the inflow of printed material from Qing publishing houses enabled a high degree of synchronicity with the continent's cultural production.

Yet even in this world apparently dominated by print, manuscript was never far away. Most immediately, it is worth noting the obvious point that in contrast to books printed using typeface, woodblock print reproduced handwriting, as the process involved transferring a handwritten "clean copy" (*kiyogaki*) to the woodblock. (Even the so-called Saga-bon movable-type editions from the early Edo period sought to replicate the calligraphic style, extending to the use of ligatures.) That woodblock editions resulted in the mass-replication of handwriting, as opposed to typeface, has led Linda Chance and Julie Davis to propose a reconsideration of the print-manuscript dichotomy in premodern and early modern Japan, their view being that much of Edo printed matter might properly be considered manuscript for having propagated handwriting—that is, we should think in terms of "mode" instead of "medium"—and that manuscript did not have the same weight as an "epistemological category" in early modern Japan as it did in the European context.[43] This last point may be true in relative terms, yet it glosses over the fact that writers of the Edo period routinely distinguished between print and manuscript as essential categories, whether they were busy denouncing the pervasive reach of print, describing the format of individual books, or cataloging the contents of their libraries. More fundamentally, where the present study is concerned, the meaningful distinction lies in the technology of reproduction, not the surface appearance of the finished product. If we wish to emphasize manuscript as mode, we would do better to speak of the manuscript *style* or *aesthetic* of most Edo printed materials—or, to avoid confusion altogether, the *calligraphic* or *handwritten* style. Regardless of the pattern of ink on the page, a woodblock-printed book is no more manuscript than is a photographic facsimile edition of a handwritten text such as (to take one familiar, widely reproduced example) the signed copy of the United States Declaration of Independence.

43. L. H. Chance and J. N. Davis, "The Handwritten and the Printed: Issues of Format and Medium in Japanese Premodern Books," *Manuscript Studies* 1, no. 1 (2016): 90–114.

Besides, handwritten texts retained not only prestige but uses that extended far beyond their replication in the world of print. Peter Kornicki has outlined several categories of text for which scribal culture played a dominant role in their circulation, notably "news" and matters of local interest, as well as semi-fictionalized accounts of real-life rebellions and other politically sensitive content that risked censorship.[44] These categories are united by a common factor: they are all texts that could not sustain commercial publication, whether for political reasons or because of limited demand. Viewed in these terms, Kornicki's categories expand into other areas. Matters of local interest might include texts that circulated in other limited or restricted contexts. For our purposes, this would include the great majority of imported Chinese books, but also specialized or proprietary texts of other sorts, such as theatrical playscripts. Likewise, strange tales and anomaly accounts that circulated regionally in manuscript form can be considered both from the perspective of limited, local interest and, for their suggestion of disorder on the margins of Tokugawa rule, as politically sensitive content; printed strange tales had to tread much more delicately, actively distancing their material from contemporary realities.

In her study of Tao Yuanming's poems and manuscript culture, Xiaofei Tian emphasizes the instability, fluidity, variation, and slippage—often accidental, occasionally intentional—that occur in the manuscript circulation of texts.[45] Modern scholarship tends to fetishize the print edition for its authoritativeness even though, or perhaps precisely because, it glosses over this chaotic, unstable world that lies underneath, in which authoritativeness was contested by numerous individual readers and copiers. Some early modern Japanese commentators were similarly enthused by the promise of print to allow the fixing of variants (or at least their preservation for comparison), the resolution of ambiguity, and the wide dissemination of "definitive" versions. Others worried about what was being lost as print proliferated: the aesthetic qualities of handwritten texts, their perceived authenticity, and the value of manual reproduction as a

44. P. F. Kornicki, "Manuscript, Not Print: Scribal Culture in the Edo Period," *Journal of Japanese Studies* 32, no. 1 (2006): 23–52.

45. Xiaofei Tian, *Tao Yuanming and Manuscript Culture: The Record of a Dusty Table* (Seattle: University of Washington Press, 2005).

form of self-discipline or for the active engagement with the text it demanded. Yet manuscript thrived and proliferated all around them. Just as Tian paints a sweeping picture of the scale and commonness of copying by hand in the premodern Chinese context—a state of affairs that continued unabated as print ascended in the Northern Song—manuscript practices similarly persisted in early modern Japan long after the onset of the Edo publishing revolution. Copying by hand was an everyday activity, and early modern scribes churned out page after page with astonishing speed and stamina.

The divide between print and manuscript is often seen as one of public versus private. The proliferation of imported Chinese texts through manuscript practices occurred through the collective action of numerous individuals, a private realm shielded from view between these texts' publication on the continent and their republication as Japanese editions, translations, and adaptations. Indeed, behind virtually any early modern woodblock-printed book lies a larger body of manuscript texts, including draft manuscripts, clean copies, and correspondence between author and publisher. People's private lives were similarly filled with letters, journals, and many other handwritten documents. We might therefore see manuscript to constitute a vastly larger "library of private information."

At the same time, the public-private division is complicated in many ways. Commercial publishers may have offered their products for sale to the public and been motivated by market forces, but they were ultimately privately owned and controlled. Nor were all printed materials designed to be available to the public, as in the cases of deluxe *surimono* prints and similarly commissioned picture books, the private editions known as *shihan*, or certain domainal and bakufu editions. On the manuscript side, handwritten texts could be bought and sold, borrowed for a fee from lending libraries, or commissioned from scribes for hire. More importantly, handwritten texts became public through the very act of circulation. Indeed, Kornicki distinguishes a separate category of "public manuscripts" that were "produced with an eye to some form of circulation."[46] The distinction is not always straightforward. While Kornicki classifies some illicit materials that circulated in manuscript as private because copyists were putting themselves in danger, other content that courted

46. Kornicki, "Manuscript, Not Print," 33.

similar risks, such as *jitsuroku*, is assigned to the public category. These ambiguities can be resolved, at least in part, if we look not at the problematic question of intent but at the end result. Anything that escaped narrow control and was reproduced and circulated beyond its immediate source was, de facto, a public manuscript. Viewed in this light, the individual private interactions through which Chinese texts were borrowed and replicated collectively dissolve into the public at scale; it is the difference between sharing among friends and circulating at large.

Returning to the question of literary "reception," another possibility for compelling intervention is laid out by Michael Emmerich, whose study of *The Tale of Genji* and its canonization both in Japan and as world literature offers a thoughtful critique and alternative path forward.[47] Emmerich eschews the word "reception" for several reasons, among them its perceived connotations of passivity, that it looks backward instead of tracing a trajectory forward, and the way it overstates the material and textual stability of that which is transmitted. He argues that canonization is instead a process of "replacement" in which texts are substituted with other versions of themselves, including translations, adaptations, and parodies. We might view many of the major works of Chinese fiction that gained wide familiarity in the Edo period as having entered the Japanese canon through such a process of "replacement," often in the absence of a stable original. William Hedberg's recent study of the Japanese encounter with *The Water Margin* (*Shuihu zhuan*) offers a compelling illustration of precisely this process.[48]

However, familiarity through replacement pertains only to a select few texts. After all, Emmerich's and Hedberg's monographs both self-identify, in their very subtitles, as canonization studies. (In fact, Emmerich limits his call to replace reception to the field of canonization studies.) The present study is concerned with many adjacent issues, but not canonization itself. For texts of less prominence, different realities obtain. Here we find encounters both with the "original" and with replacements that do not

47. Michael Emmerich, *The Tale of Genji: Translation, Canonization, and World Literature* (New York: Columbia University Press, 2013).

48. William C. Hedberg, *The Japanese Discovery of Chinese Fiction: The Water Margin and the Making of a National Canon* (New York: Columbia University Press, 2019).

truly replace, as they were not read *as* replacements or substitutes but, by and large, on their own terms. Learned readers may have been aware, for example, that *Tales from the Withering Wind* included several rewritings of *Liaozhai* stories, but the average reader was not. While Emmerich posits that ordinary readers may not have *read* Ryūtei Tanehiko's *A Fraudulent Murasaki's Rustic Genji* (*Nise Murasaki Inaka Genji*, 1829–42) as a replacement of *The Tale of Genji*, they were at least *aware* of its status as replacement from their encounter with the title itself. If we can claim for *Liaozhai* to have achieved comparable status, it is only well into the twentieth century with its extensive translations and replacements—perhaps by 1921, when Tanaka Kōtarō's collection of supernatural tales could be marketed to the reading public as a modern-day *Liaozhai*.

Given the unsuitability of the word "replacement" where the present study is concerned, perhaps we would be advised not to throw out "reception" just yet. Linda Hutcheon's theorization of adaptation has sought to rehabilitate a similarly maligned term, seeing adaptation not as a derivative, secondary mode, or as an act of mere preservation, but as an act of engagement, interpretation, and creation—arguably the dominant or *only* form of creation.[49] We might likewise reclaim reception, recognizing that the critiques of its perceived passivity do not always persuade. Reception is not unthinking or uncritical; it involves judgment, choice, action, and agency. It is an act of consumption but also production. Just as receivers are vital components of radios and (American) football teams alike, literary reception encompasses all manner of dynamic processes: importation, circulation, reproduction, reading, editing, anthologizing, translation, adaptation, and assimilation. Agency is to be found even where it initially seems most absent, in the act of importing Chinese books. While the physical transport of texts lay outside Japanese hands, agency was exercised on the receiving end through the submission of requests, through regimes of censorship, and, most powerfully, through market forces. After all, what ultimately drove the book trade was its profitability, which depended on satisfying the desires of would-be Japanese buyers.

Nevertheless, it is difficult to shake off the baggage the term "reception" has accrued, and its close association with the older models of

49. Linda Hutcheon, *A Theory of Adaptation*, 2nd ed. (New York: Routledge, 2013).

scholarship exemplified by Ishizaki, Asō, and their inheritors. Accordingly, while the term is used as appropriate in the present study, I have instead foregrounded the alternative framework of "rewriting"—a word that appears in the very title of the monograph—as a way of resolving the problems of reception and replacement. Rewriting encompasses a larger body of practices. To rewrite is to transform through translation and adaptation. It is also to rewrite in the literal sense of copying and transmitting a text—the defining practice of manuscript culture. Rewriting encompasses both consumption and production, giving weight to tradition and intertextuality but also to creation and agency. It is a term that looks backward—as all "re-" words do—while also emphasizing what comes after.

Underlying many recent interventions in Sino-Japanese studies—indeed, implicit in the name of the field—is the desire to challenge received notions of China and Japan as discrete realms of cultural and literary production with clearly defined linguistic boundaries. Joshua Fogel, whose own scholarship is deeply informed by this approach, has occasionally reflected on the institutional progress made in academia in this regard over the past several decades. In the introduction to one of his edited volumes, he relates an anecdote about a proposal for a China-Japan panel at the annual Association for Asian Studies conference that was passed back and forth among members of the program committee until the deadline had passed.[50] It is hard to imagine such an occurrence in today's age of abundant "inter-area" and "border-crossing" panels.

Atsuko Sakaki has observed that the established Sino-Japanese "polarity" encompasses a number of further, attendant binaries, including masculine-feminine, traditional-modern, and abstract-concrete.[51] Renegotiating these structures in terms that escape modern national divisions often involves the reconsideration of what it means for a text to be "Chinese." Matthew Fraleigh, in his study of the neglected writer Narushima

50. Joshua Fogel, "Texts, Contexts, and Intellectual Contacts," in Fogel, ed., *Crossing the Yellow Sea: Sino-Japanese Cultural Contacts, 1600–1950* (Norwalk, CT: EastBridge, 2007), 5.

51. Atsuko Sakaki, *Obsessions with the Sino-Japanese Polarity in Japanese Literature* (Honolulu: University of Hawai'i Press, 2005).

Ryūhoku (1837–84), has argued for restoring Sinitic literature to the mainstream of Meiji literary history, while William Hedberg has, more radically, suggested a similar possibility for *The Water Margin*, that of reading it "as Japanese literature."[52] At the other end of the historical spectrum, David Lurie has observed the fundamentally "interlingual" nature of ***kundoku*** (lit. "reading by gloss"), the procedural reading of texts written using Chinese vocabulary and syntax into a hybrid form of vernacular Japanese. Given that even texts originating in China could be read in the local vernacular, early Japanese did not see themselves as reading (or writing) in a foreign language.[53]

One manifestation of the effort to avoid the retroactive imputation of national divisions on premodern and early modern texts is the increasing use in English-language scholarship of the term "literary Sinitic" in place of what has conventionally been referred to as "literary Chinese" or "classical Chinese," which is to say the shared language of scholarship and traditional literary endeavor that spread throughout the Sinosphere. First proposed by Victor Mair, this neologism has found adoption in recent scholarship by Peter Kornicki, Matthew Fraleigh, Brian Steininger, Si Nae Park, and others.[54] Fraleigh offers one of the clearest articulations of the rationale behind its use. Much as the Japanese term ***kanshibun*** (lit. "poems and prose of Han") is a modern invention that separates Japan's literary heritage into Chinese and Japanese components, "literary Sinitic" is an attempt in English to elide such national divisions, one that "affirms the ultimate linguistic origins of such writing but at the same time also inserts a slight distance between the form and the modern nation-state . . . accommodating the fact that such writing spread far

52. Matthew Fraleigh, *Plucking Chrysanthemums: Narushima Ryūhoku and Sinitic Literary Traditions in Modern Japan* (Cambridge, MA: Harvard University Asia Center, 2016).

53. David Lurie, *Realms of Literacy: Early Japan and the History of Writing* (Cambridge, MA: Harvard University Asia Center, 2011), 180.

54. Victor Mair, "Buddhism and the Rise of the Written Vernacular in East Asia: The Making of National Languages," *Journal of Asian Studies* 53, no. 3 (1994): 707–51; Peter F. Kornicki, *Languages, Scripts, and Chinese Texts in East Asia* (Oxford University Press, 2018); Brian Steininger, *Chinese Literary Forms in Heian Japan: Poetics and Practice* (Cambridge, MA: Harvard University Asia Center, 2017); Si Nae Park, *The Korean Vernacular Story: Telling Tales of Contemporary Chosŏn in Sinographic Writing* (New York: Columbia University Press, 2020).

beyond the borders of 'China.'"[55] It is not by chance that most of the scholars who have adopted the term work primarily on texts written in Japan or Korea, as there is not the same compelling need to separate language and nation in the case of texts that are both linguistically and geographically "Chinese."

At the same time, it can be argued that the term "literary Sinitic" does not so much *free* premodern and early modern texts from modern national divisions as *obscure* those divisions. After all, as others have noted, "Sinitic" is simply a Latinate word for "Chinese."[56] Moreover, while "Sinitic" may serve the additional function of distinguishing the written and spoken forms of the language, the modifiers "literary" or "classical" are, at least to those outside the field of linguistics, generally sufficient to denote that we are in the domain of written sources. All of this is to say that it is not out of ignorance of recent trends that the present study largely retains the term "classical Chinese." I have done so both for the sake of euphony and because most of the texts to which the term is applied are in fact of continental origin. In other words, not only do language and place align, but the terminology serves as a useful reminder of the geographic origins of these texts. An exception is made for Terasaki Reishū's collection, the only Japanese text discussed at length that was not written in the local vernacular. In this case, to underscore the work's Japanese authorship and its participation in the larger East Asian linguistic sphere, the term "literary Sinitic" is used instead.

Two of the most stimulating recent monographs to deal with Chinese texts in the Edo period specifically have been concerned not with classical texts or literary Sinitic but with the status of vernacular Chinese fiction. These, too, in their own ways, have challenged received binaries. William Hedberg notes that while among early modern Japanese commentators on *The Water Margin* there was certainly recognition of its distinct geographic and linguistic origins, they did not read the text in search of what might later be termed a "national essence." Rather, their primary concern lay in narrative and thematic elements, or in what was universal, not what was different and essentially "Chinese." This leads

55. Fraleigh, *Plucking Chrysanthemums*, 369n5.

56. See, for instance, Zev Handel, review of Kornicki, *Languages, Scripts, and Chinese Texts in East Asia*, H-Asia, H-Net Reviews (August 2019), 3.

Hedberg to propose reading *The Water Margin* not as "a source of inspiration *for* Japanese literature," but "*as* Japanese literature" (emphases in original). By this he means not to reprise the agenda of nationalist commentators in the era of Japanese imperialism, who positioned Chinese literature as "a second national literature of Japan," but as a way of thinking about how vernacular fiction, which defied traditional, normative categories, came to be defined and legitimated as literary expression, and how Japanese writers came to codify and define the concept of literature itself.[57] There is of course an unavoidable tension in this approach, reflected most conspicuously in the conscious decision to read the title of the central text as "*Shuihu zhuan*" throughout—as opposed to using the English translation *The Water Margin* or the Japanese reading *Suikoden*. This choice underscores the reality that even as the narrative worked its way into the canon and arguably became readable as Japanese literature, it nevertheless retained its aura of exotic apartness.

In his earlier study of the Japanese encounter with vernacular Chinese fiction, Emanuel Pastreich traces how awareness of China as a living, breathing thing transformed not only Japanese notions of China but broader discourses surrounding language and literature.[58] Ogyū Sorai was inspired to critique *kundoku*, arguing that the Chinese language, whether classical or vernacular, was best apprehended directly or through vernacular Japanese translation, not by reading through gloss. (Among later commentators, the inadequacies of *kundoku* were often compared to "scratching an itch through one's shoe.") Pastreich also charts how Chinese narratives, with their accounts of mundane experiences and casts of unfamiliar characters, not only spawned diverse adaptations and literary experiments but precipitated broader intellectual and epistemological debates. As writers reflected on the nature of narrative and fiction, they developed novel interpretive frameworks that allowed new and disparate texts to be subsumed under the heading of literature.

Even as both Hedberg and Pastreich demonstrate easy familiarity with orthodox reception study, their main concerns lie elsewhere. After

57. Hedberg, *The Japanese Discovery of Chinese Fiction*, 8–9.

58. Emanuel Pastreich, *The Observable Mundane: Vernacular Chinese and the Emergence of a Literary Discourse on Popular Narrative in Edo Japan* (Seoul: Seoul National University Press, 2011).

all, their focus on vernacular texts inherently problematizes notions of "reception," as the attendant linguistic and interpretive barriers fundamentally complicated any straightforward transposition of texts and ideas. The classical tales that are the touchstone of the present study represent a very different world. In many ways they were more readily accessible. While *The Water Margin* and *Romance of the Three Kingdoms* are sprawling epics, *Liaozhai* is a collection of strange gems in miniature. Although the language could still pose challenges even to the most erudite readers, it did not present the same fundamental obstacles as the vernacular register. Classical texts could be glossed and "read" through ***kundoku***, and it was possible to "translate" by simply "writing out" (***kakikudashi***) sentences according to these same procedures. Indeed, with some modification, this is more or less the approach that was taken to the handful of *Liaozhai* tales that were translated in the 1820s.

At the same time, the Chinese strange tale is by its very nature filled with characters and situations far removed from the "observable mundane" of much vernacular fiction. As a realm of anomalies and marvels, it appealed to the Edo desire for "***ki***"—the same insatiable sense of curiosity that undergirded and fueled the early modern Japanese age of discovery. But the Chinese strange tale could not simply be absorbed directly or "Japanified." The exploration of the rewritings through adaptation in the final chapters of this book also traces its lineage to the "impact-response" scholarship of Asō, Ishizaki, and Tokuda, but it seeks to trace not parallels but *difference*, and the meanings that emerge from these gaps. Japanese writers exercised great creativity as they wrote their strange tales, but they were also limited by all manner of constraints. Turning away from the linguistic and cultural factors on which much ink has already been spent, my concern lies primarily with the role of genre and literary convention, as well as the political context of Tokugawa Japan—constraints that, under authoritarian rule, were often interrelated, with the concerns of the state exerting a constant pull on those of literature.

This study is structured so as to progress from the very broad through the increasingly narrow, beginning by taking entire bodies of texts as its object of inquiry and concluding at the level of individual narratives. Chapter 1, "Importing Chinese Fiction in the Edo Period," offers a panoramic view of the Chinese book trade in early modern Japan, following boatloads of books, even entire genres, on their journey from the continent to Nagasaki, then onward to readers and collections across the archipelago. The bureaucratic procedures instituted to control the inflow of foreign texts left behind a rich, if fragmentary, body of documentary evidence that is brought into conversation with other primary and secondary sources—bibliographies, catalogs, auction records, journals, letters, and essays—to enable a set of interconnected large-scale analyses that collectively detail a story of temporal and spatial compression. Between the seventeenth and nineteenth centuries, China and Japan and their literary cultures came to be bound together ever more closely, with the onset of mass importation and near simultaneity by the late eighteenth century. At the same time, the breadth of importation was not matched by depth. Economics and market forces dictated that while a remarkable portion of texts reached Japanese shores—including a comfortable majority of published Chinese fiction—the scarcity of individual copies led to bidding wars, astronomical prices, and would-be collectors wasting years in the fruitless pursuit of specific titles or editions. Even the most unassuming works of fiction, when they could be found at all, sold for vastly more than luxury editions of comparable domestic fare. Items of greater interest routinely fetched the equivalent of tens of thousands of dollars or more. The amassing of a collection of imported books was primarily a pastime for wealthy institutions, elite daimyō, and the upper echelons of the urban merchant class.

Chapter 2, "*Wakokubon*: Chinese Books Printed in Japan," considers one avenue by which otherwise inaccessible imported texts became available to ordinary readers: through domestic reprint editions known as *wakokubon kanseki* ("Chinese books carved in Japan"), or simply *wakokubon*. Texts of continental origin were targeted from the very dawn of printing in Japan, with the earliest documented printed text, produced at the request of Empress Shōtoku in the 760s, consisting of excerpts of a Buddhist sutra transliterated in Chinese script that were enclosed in miniature wooden pagodas and distributed to temples across Japan. Reprints of secular texts first appeared in temple-sponsored editions in the fourteenth century and grew rapidly in number with the rise of commercial publishing in the 1600s. Commercial *wakokubon* brought a wide selection of Chinese cultural production within easy, relatively affordable reach. By the late seventeenth century, Confucian classics, histories, medical treatises, poetry, fiction, and more were piled high on bookstore shelves across Japan, and the selection grew rapidly through the nineteenth century. A number of titles that were lost on the continent survive thanks to these Japanese editions. Nevertheless, the fact remains that the great majority of imported Chinese books were never reprinted. Building on the analyses developed in chapter 1, this chapter traces the outlines of a two-tiered reception. On the surface sits a highly visible but relatively small corpus of texts whose reach was exponentially magnified through print. Beneath this lies a vastly larger body of texts, comprising nearly the entire literary imagination of late imperial China, that made the journey through Nagasaki only to be secreted away in scattered institutional and private collections. For these to slip their bonds and escape into the wider world, they would have to rely on other means—not the visible, public technology of print but the private practices of groups of individuals borrowing, sharing, and copying by hand.

To provide evidence for this hypothesis, and to illuminate broader trends in the circulation and reading of Chinese fiction, chapter 3, "Hidden Practices: Collectors, Borrowers, and Manuscript Culture in the Age of Woodblock Print," reconstructs the journeys taken by *Liaozhai* (with reference to many other texts along the way) as it percolated into the Japanese literary milieu. Although Pu Songling's collection falls within that great majority of texts that were never reprinted domestically—granting a minor exception, it is seen, for a half-dozen or so tales that were reproduced incidentally in sources not primarily concerned with the collection *as fiction*—the perception that his tales remained largely unknown until the modern period proves entirely unfounded. Quite the contrary, readers across Japan were not only familiar with the text but at times harbored an enthusiasm verging on obsession, and other eighteenth- and nineteenth-century collections of strange tales, similarly unavailable in domestic editions, enjoyed wide readership of their own. As *Liaozhai* passed through new hands, dozens of adaptations and translations of individual tales emerged in its wake, offering further evidence of its ever-expanding reach. Enabling such widespread circulation was a vibrant manuscript tradition that churned away steadily beneath the glossy surface of print culture. Scholars shared rare books for reasons noble and otherwise: out of a sense of moral obligation to the advancement of knowledge, but also in the self-interested hope of reciprocity. And as books circulated, they reproduced themselves. Copying texts by hand—literally rewriting them—remained widespread as a practice of self-cultivation, as a form of close reading that demanded careful engagement with the text, and above all as a technology of preservation through which readers augmented their own collections and ensured the survival and propagation of even the scarcest texts.

In the final chapters, the focus shifts from books as material objects to the texts they contained. As Chinese strange tales passed through various forms and stages of rewriting—copying, annotating, editing, reprinting, translating, adapting—they reemerged in altered form into the markedly different literary and political landscape of early modern Japan. Chapter 4, "*Kidan*: Strange Tales from Japan," maps the terrain of Chinese *zhiguai* anomaly accounts and *chuanqi* strange tales and examines the spectrum of translation and adaptation practices to which they and other Chinese fiction were subjected. Among the most significant sites for adaption was a genre known as the *kidan*. Collections of *kidan* tales, which originated with those of Teishō in the middle of the eighteenth century and were carried forward by Akinari, Chūryō, and many others, have traditionally been categorized under the catch-all heading of *yomihon* (lit. "books for reading"). In place of this undescriptive, overly broad, and anachronistic label, chapter 4 advances *kidan* as a more productive category not only for its relative precision and descriptive value (it means, literally, "strange tale") but as the label most commonly used by early modern authors themselves. Identifying several key differences in form and convention between the Chinese strange tale and the *kidan*, the chapter homes in on one in particular: the pervasiveness of warfare in the Japanese narratives. Through close readings of Chūryō's *Liaozhai* adaptations in *Tales from the Withering Wind*, supported by digressions into the tales of Akinari as well as other lesser-known *kidan* authors, this recontextualization is seen to serve a valuable narrative function. Rewriting tales against a backdrop of unrest provides an anomalous context that magnifies their anomalous content, enhancing the mood of uncertainty and strangeness in plots that often hinge on separation and individual anxiety. The effect is further strengthened by a reliance on complex intertextual associations that borrow meanings and significance from other texts both in and beyond the *kidan* genre.

Other conventions have the effect not of enhancing uncertainty but of collapsing it. Chapter 5, "Taming the Strange: Anomalies and the

Tokugawa Order," examines the many ways the *kidan* exerts control over the strange, rendering it palatable to authority. Resolving the temporal indeterminacy and sense of recency that prevails in many of its Chinese source texts, the Japanese strange tale is nearly always resituated in specific historical moments in the pre-Tokugawa past. Anomalies are also cast outward into Japan's geographic periphery, away from the urban centers that were the visible seats of Tokugawa power and control. This act of doubly distancing the strange—both temporally and spatially—points to an inherent conservatism in the genre, a cautious display of deference to the established political order. The *kidan* also seeks to account for the strange and explain it away, further neutralizing its unpredictability. The Chinese strange tale certainly gestures in this direction: anomalous events are routinely linked to immoderate behavior, and those in the grips of obsession often experience a particular subjectivity of vision that leaves them blind to the strange and uniquely susceptible to its harms. Japanese rewritings bring such didacticism to the surface, at times spelling out their lessons in terms that closely resonated with contemporary political concerns. The chapter's most extended analysis is reserved for the longest story in *Tales from the Withering Wind*, a rewriting of Pu Songling's "The Painted Skin" that serves in many ways as the collection's thematic center of gravity. At the same time that he preserves his source's cautionary depiction of the dangers of unrestrained sexual desire, Chūryō layers on new lessons that speak directly to a series of reforms being implemented by the bakufu at the moment of writing. And yet, in spite of a prevailing conservatism that at times verged on complicity, the *kidan* was not monolithic and unwavering in its submission to authority. As explored in the epilogue, even in this cautious literary space there are glimmers of the same subversive strain and resistance to the status quo seen elsewhere in the popular fiction of early modern Japan.

CHAPTER I

Importing Chinese Fiction in the Edo Period

Setting the Scene: Nagasaki and the China Trade

As the sun dropped low in the sky one evening in 1818, the scholar Rai San'yō (1781–1832) gazed out the window of his boat, which lay anchored for the night in the Sea of Amakusa off the west coast of Kyushu. Glimpsing a barely perceptible sliver on the horizon, he allowed himself a moment of elegant confusion. "Is it a cloud? A mountain? Wu or Yue?"[1] Was it just a thread of cloud, or was it some distant island—maybe even the coast of China itself? Only a few miles away, others stood with their gazes similarly fixed on the horizon. Day and night, maritime watchmen stood guard atop the mountain ridges of the Nagasaki Peninsula. Japanese boats plied these waters in great numbers: ferries and cargo ships sped up and down the coast, fishing skiffs dotted countless coves and inlets, and pleasure boats cruised the calmer waters of Nagasaki Harbor itself. But the watchmen were on the lookout for ships from foreign shores. Dutch vessels were relatively infrequent—only one or two in an ordinary year by the late eighteenth century—but Chinese ships regularly appeared on the horizon, bearing crates full of cargo fresh from the continent: silks and

1. Rai San'yō, "Anchoring in the Sea of Amakusa" ("Amakusa nada ni haku-su"), in Mizuta Norihisa, Rai Tsutomu, and Naoi Fumiko, eds., *Kan Chazan, Rai San'yō shishū*, in *SNKBT* 66 (Iwanami shoten, 1996), 195.

satins, sugar, ginseng and other medicines, minerals, animal products, and of course books. China was almost as close as San'yō imagined.

This nearness ebbed and flowed over the Edo period. From the end of the sixteenth century through the Qing conquest in 1644, Ming authorities officially forbade Chinese ships from sailing for Japan. Nevertheless, in a typical year several dozen vessels made the crossing in defiance of the ban, while others sailed from ports in southeast Asia outside Ming control. With the implementation of Japan's own restrictive maritime policies in the 1630s, these numbers rose further as Chinese merchants sought to capitalize on their advantageous position. Japan's isolationist policies came in response to the perceived threat of the spread of Christianity, and under them the shogunate exerted tight control over trade and foreign relations. After first requiring, in 1633, that Japanese vessels obtain an official license before sailing overseas, only two years later the shogunate issued far more sweeping restrictions: Japanese were forbidden from traveling overseas under penalty of death, and incoming Chinese vessels were limited to the single port city of Nagasaki. The Dutch followed shortly thereafter, relocated in 1641 from the comparative freedom of Hirado to the tiny man-made island of Deshima in Nagasaki Harbor. Where foreign ships had once dotted harbors across the southwest, Nagasaki was to be Tokugawa Japan's main window onto the outside world for two centuries to come.[2]

The number of Chinese vessels calling at Nagasaki fluctuated in response to political pressures in both countries. After the implementation of Japan's maritime controls, the already high numbers rose to nearly one hundred in some years as Chinese merchants sought to capitalize on their new monopoly. Following the Qing conquest, the yearly average dropped to around fifty. This figure soon fell further. As part of the ongoing Qing campaign against Ming loyalists and the allied maritime forces of Zheng Zhilong and his son Zheng Chenggong (better known as Coxinga), the Kangxi emperor evacuated residents along the southeastern coast to in-

2. Although Nagasaki was the official site for the conducting of foreign relations, relations with certain proximate regions were outsourced to nearby domains: relations with Ryūkyū were managed by Satsuma, those with Korea by Tsushima, and those with the Ainu by Matsumae.

land areas shortly after his ascent to the throne in 1661. This program, known as the *qianjie*, or "moving of the frontier" order, succeeded in severing the Zhengs' trade links with the mainland, and the number of ships sailing for Japan dropped for the duration to around twenty per year. With the defeat of Coxinga's son Zheng Keshuang and his surrender of Taiwan in 1683, the evacuation policy was reversed and the Qing promoted an active maritime regime of their own under the *zhanhai*, or "expansion to the sea" policy.[3] The number of ships sailing for Nagasaki swiftly rebounded and rose to unprecedented levels, approaching two hundred in 1688.[4] However, a peak in Japanese copper production in the late seventeenth century, coupled with increased domestic demand—copper, used in coinage, was one of Japan's main exports along with silver and various maritime goods—prompted the bakufu to introduce limits on the volume of trade.[5] In 1715 the number of ships was limited to thirty annually. This was gradually reduced further, first to twenty per year, then to ten or so by the end of the eighteenth century, although these later ships were larger than their predecessors and could carry more sizable cargoes.[6]

Even the smaller ships of earlier years could easily carry crews of several dozen, in some instances approaching as many as one hundred. Western observers including Engelbert Kaempfer and Carl Peter Thunberg marveled at the numbers they carried in relation to their size.[7]

3. For overviews of the *qianjie* and *zhanhai* policies, see Yamamoto Noritsuna, *Nagasaki Tōjin yashiki* (Kenkōsha, 1983), 76–82; and Ōba, trans. Fogel, *Books and Boats*, 22–24.

4. Yamamoto, *Nagasaki Tōjin yashiki*, 91, 96, 100–102, presents various tabulations (drawing on earlier work by Iwao Seiichi) of the number of ships calling between 1611 and 1852. See also Iwao Seiichi, "Kinsei Nis-Shi bōeki ni kansuru sūryōteki kōsatsu," *Shigaku zasshi* 62, no. 11 (November 1953): 1–40.

5. Ryuto Shimada, *The Intra-Asian Trade in Japanese Copper by the Dutch East India Company during the Eighteenth Century* (Boston: Brill, 2006), 15.

6. Ōba Osamu, "Chinese Travelers to Nagasaki," in Joshua A. Fogel, ed., *Sagacious Monks and Bloodthirsty Warriors: Chinese Views of Japan in the Ming-Qing Period* (Norwalk, CT: EastBridge, 2002), 114–15.

7. Engelbert Kaempfer, trans. J. G. Scheuchzer, *The History of Japan, Together with a Description of the Kingdom of Siam, 1690–92* (New York: Macmillan, 1906), 2:250; and Carl Peter Thunberg, *Travels in Europe, Africa, and Asia, Performed between the Years 1770 and 1779*, 3rd ed. (London: F. and C. Rivington, 1796), 3:21.

With so many merchants and sailors pouring into Nagasaki, by the late seventeenth century the city was home to a community of several thousand Chinese residents. The city magistrate responded to the influx and an accompanying rise in unauthorized trade by setting aside a seven-acre property, formerly the site of a medicinal herb garden, for construction of the "Chinese Residence" (Tōjin yashiki), a compound of twenty two-story buildings surrounded by a formidable wall that stood as high as twelve feet in places. With the completion of the compound in 1689, the Chinese community that had previously intermingled with the Japanese in the city proper was isolated and found their movements significantly restricted, although not to the same extent as the Dutch on the fan-shaped island factory of Deshima a short distance away.[8]

In spite of their remove to this enclosed space, it continued to be the Chinese in Nagasaki who gave the city much of its unique foreign flavor, far more than the smaller, less visible Dutch presence. Nagasaki drew tourists and scholars from throughout Japan, some eager merely to revel in its exotic atmosphere, others desirous of studying the Chinese language or otherwise acquiring knowledge of the continent and its culture. Often the line between tourist and scholar was blurred, as in the case of the physician and geographer Furukawa Koshōken (1726–1807), who visited the city in 1783 and wrote excitedly of his experiences in and around the Chinese compound. Throughout his account, Koshōken's tone remains one of unflagging delight, whether he is describing the great throngs and bustling atmosphere (there were no fewer than twelve ships anchored in the harbor during his visit), the refined manners and dress of the Chinese, the playful antics of the low-level officials who greeted him at the entrance to the compound, or the peculiar, unfamiliar sounds of the spoken language. Koshōken was even thrilled to find himself the victim of petty crime. As he lingered by the waterfront gazing at a team of Chinese carpenters busily at work on a ship, he cooled himself with a folding fan personally inscribed by Rai San'yō's father, the Confucian scholar Rai Shunsui. A moment later, one of the younger workers darted over and plucked the fan right out of his hands. To judge by his written account,

8. However, whereas the Dutch made regular visits to Edo to pay their respects to the shogun, the Chinese were generally forbidden from leaving Nagasaki.

nothing could have brought Koshōken greater joy than having this authentic tourist experience.[9]

Koshōken's visit, which took place the very same year Ōta Nanpo published *Japan for This Guy!*, further illustrates the way in which the comic book inverts reality: just as the fictional Scholar Yan eagerly immerses himself in all things Japanese, real-life Japanese scholars sought Chinese experiences in any form they could. Two decades later, Nanpo himself would take in the sights of Nagasaki during a year-long official deployment. The city enjoyed the distinction of being governed directly by the bakufu through rotating magistrates and other bureaucrats from Edo, and Nanpo, who had distinguished himself three years earlier at the Osaka copper exchange (*dōza*), was assigned to Nagasaki in 1804 to oversee various financial matters and to work as an inspector at the Nagasaki Customs Hall (Nagasaki kaisho), where bakufu officials reporting to the city's resident governor managed trade with both the Dutch and the Chinese. Setting off from Edo late in the seventh month, he reached his destination a month and a half later and began his official duties the next month, after recovering from an illness that had afflicted him en route. He served in his new post for almost exactly one year.

In addition to writing numerous letters to friends and family back home in Edo, Nanpo filled seven volumes with a detailed record of his daily activities, encounters, and interesting news and gossip.[10] Each day brought new and stimulating experiences in a city whose bustle he deemed to surpass even that of Osaka, whose memory was still fresh in his mind. The year 1804 was an especially exciting time to be sent to Nagasaki. Not only were there various colorful incidents involving the Dutch, but Nanpo arrived just at the right moment to watch as the Russians were thrown into the city's cosmopolitan mix. That November, the envoy Nikolai Rezanov sailed into Nagasaki Harbor to request formal trading rights on behalf of the czar. Although he was eventually refused after waiting half

9. *Saiyū zakki*, in Miyamoto Tsuneichi, Haraguchi Torao, and Higa Shunchō, eds., *Nihon shomin seikatsu shiryō shūsei* (San'ichi shobō, 1969), 2:381. A summary of Koshōken's journal, interspersed with translated excerpts, is included in Herbert Plutschow, *A Reader in Edo Period Travel* (Folkestone, Kent: Global Oriental, 2006), 89–101.

10. *Mozu no kusaguki* (A Shrike in the Grass, 1804, 2 vols.), *Keiho zattetsu* (Jottings from Nagasaki, 1805, 3 vols.), and *Keiho yūtetsu* (Further Jottings from Nagasaki, 1809, 2 vols.). In Hamada Giichirō, ed., *Ōta Nanpo zenshū* (Iwanami shoten, 1985–90), 8:431–677.

a year for a decision, in the interim Nanpo secured the privilege of visiting him aboard his ship and, in a moment of particular note, shaking his hand—possibly the earliest documented handshake in Japanese history.

These European encounters notwithstanding, it remained the Chinese who occupied the largest share of Nanpo's attention, mirroring their presence in the city itself. Nanpo spent much of his time in and around the Chinese compound, composing verse with Chinese ship captains, studying unfamiliar continental customs and social conventions, and observing the diversity and mutual incomprehensibility of the various regional dialects. He took in performances of unfamiliar continental forms of theater—battle reenactments, brothel pieces, plays about bandits, domestic dramas, and spectacles involving jugglers and acrobats—and gorged himself at banquets with elaborate spreads of strange food and drink, partaking of pork, fish, pickles, winter melon, cakes, jujubes with sesame, longan fruit, plum wine, and more. And like Koshōken, he observed the arrival of many Chinese ships and marveled at the array of goods that was unloaded onto the docks.

Importing the Library of Late Imperial China

One of the main attractions of Nagasaki for Nanpo and like-minded scholars was the opportunity to acquire the latest books from the continent. Chinese books did occasionally reach Japan by other routes. The library of the Sō clan, which governed the island of Tsushima and exercised control over Japan's relations with Korea throughout the early modern period, included a considerable number of books from China and Korea, some of which were sent to Edo for the bakufu's own collections. The Shimazu clan in Satsuma exercised a similar monopoly over relations with Ryūkyū, and Chinese texts came this way, too. However, only one title, the moral textbook *Liuyu yanyi* (J. *Rikuyu engi*), is known to have entered Japan solely by this southern route; for the most part, Chinese texts flowed the other direction, from Japan to Ryūkyū.[11]

11. On *Liuyu yanyi*, see Kornicki, *Languages, Scripts, and Chinese Texts in East Asia*, 142. Gregory Smits notes that Chinese visitors to Ryūkyū observed many of the local

Leaving aside these exceptional pathways, access to which was restricted to narrow circles, the trade in Chinese books went through Nagasaki. Ship captains filled crate after crate with a steady stream of foundational texts that were in perennial demand, including lexicons such as the Kangxi Dictionary (*Kangxi zidian*) and the *Peiwen Treasury of Rhymes* (*Peiwen yunfu*), Li Shizhen's *Compendium of Materia Medica* (*Bencao gangmu*), annotated editions of the Confucian classics, and the dynastic histories. Along with these came many less-familiar titles, published in some cases just weeks earlier.[12] It is common to characterize this importation, like the more abstract concept of reception itself, as "largely passive."[13] In some sense this is a fair assessment, as it was the Chinese merchants who ultimately decided which titles to import. Yet specific titles—known from mention in other works or imported catalogs—were brought by requests both from the bakufu and, through bookseller liaisons, individual buyers. More fundamentally, the characterization of importation as passive underestimates the agency of market forces. Given the potential for sizable profits (a topic explored at length later in this chapter), importers had strong incentives to cater to Japanese desires whether by fulfilling specific demands or by anticipating items of interest. Aside from reliable standbys, the latest titles hot off the blocks were likely to attract attention. If importers tested the water and interest failed to materialize, at the very least the bakufu could be counted on to acquire books that had not been previously imported. If, on the other hand, demand was strong, then more copies could be imported at a later date.

Nanpo, who encountered a steady stream of imported titles in his day job at the Customs Hall, kept a keen eye on the latest arrivals. Many pages of his Nagasaki journals are given over to long lists of titles (sometimes

Chinese texts to be editions published in Japan. Smits, *Visions of Ryukyu: Identity and Ideology in Early-Modern Thought and Politics* (Honolulu: University of Hawai'i Press, 1999), 79–80.

12. The explorer Adam Johann von Krusenstern estimated that Western ships could cover the corridor from Ningbo to Nagasaki (a common route for Chinese merchants) in four days. Chinese ships were somewhat slower but could still make the journey in one to two weeks. Krusenstern, trans. Richard Belgrave Hoppner, *Voyage Round the World in the Years 1803, 1804, 1805, & 1806 [. . .]* (London: John Murray, 1813), 1:278.

13. Kornicki, *The Book in Japan*, 299.

including also the number of volumes and copies, prices, and overviews of the contents) that arrived aboard vessels between 1801 and 1805. Nanpo was an active collector, and Chinese books made up a sizable portion of his voluminous personal library.[14] Although the catalog of his collection contains almost no information concerning edition or format aside from noting which items were in manuscript form, many of the titles were not available in domestically printed editions and must have been imported copies. It is telling that while officials stationed in Nagasaki often returned to Edo laden with the exotic gifts that were one of the perquisites of the position, Nanpo kept only a single European wool jacket, having liquidated the other items to fund book purchases.[15]

Books were only a small portion of the goods brought to Nagasaki aboard Chinese ships, and most boats did not carry any as part of their cargo. Between 1709 and 1713, a window for which the extant record is relatively robust, only slightly more than one in ten boats carried books, and often only a crate or two at that.[16] Nevertheless, ships occasionally would arrive with much larger quantities. During the same interval, five ships arrived with sizable cargoes of books, ranging from forty to ninety-three crates.[17] As time passed, the volume increased. By Nanpo's day, fewer ships were making the crossing each year, but those that did were larger. Coupled with shifting origins—most ships now came from Ningbo or Nanjing, close to centers of publishing—and unflagging Japanese demand, the majority of vessels arrived with books on board. Of eleven ships that called on Nagasaki in 1804, ten brought books. This trend continued through midcentury, when ships regularly arrived with dozens or hundreds of individual items typically consisting of multiple volumes each. Although the record is fragmentary at best, it is evident that cumulatively Chinese ships transported many tens of thousands of books, comprising hundreds of thousands of volumes, if not more.

14. For a facsimile reproduction of the catalog to his collection, see *Shokusanjin zōsho mokuroku* [*Nanpo bunko zōshomoku*], in Shoshi kenkyūkai, ed., *Shoshi shomoku shirīzu* 13 (Yumani shobō, 1984).

15. Nabeshima Naotomo, "Shokusanjin no Nagasaki taizai: sakuhin *Mozu no kusaguki* sono ta ni miru," *Nagasaki daigaku kyōyōbu kiyō: jinbun kagaku* 7 (1967): 4–5.

16. Crates varied in size and fullness, with inventories revealing that some contained fewer than thirty volumes while others were packed with hundreds of volumes.

17. Ōba, *Books and Boats*, 85–86.

The procedures for inspecting, pricing, and auctioning these books to authorized buyers were codified in the late seventeenth century, roughly concurrent with the construction of the Chinese compound on the city waterfront.[18] As a result of this systemization, there survives an extensive, if fragmentary, documentary record, much of which was made available as reproductions and transcriptions in a series of publications prepared several decades ago through the hard legwork of the Japanese historian Ōba Osamu.[19] Before following imported books onward on their journeys to collections and collectors across Japan, let us pause to consider these procedures and the different forms of documentary evidence that survive. These materials allow us to identify imported titles and their date of importation, and they are an important part of the large-scale analyses in this chapter and in chapter 2.

After ships arrived in the harbor, initial onboard inspections were conducted, and captains submitted inventories of their cargo, which were known as *sairai shomoku* or *tairai shomoku* in the case of books.[20] The morning after arrival, cargo was unloaded into onshore warehouses and carefully compared with the written inventories. In 1630 the bakufu established a censorship office tasked with monitoring imported books for forbidden content, especially material related to Christianity. The head of this office later came to be known as the Inspector of Books (Shomotsu aratameyaku), a position that was held by successive generations of the Mukai family. From 1693 on, the censorship office prepared book summaries known as *taiisho* that were forwarded to the bakufu in Edo for approval before items could be released for sale.[21] These summaries served a dual function, also alerting the bakufu to items of potential interest for which they had the right of first refusal. Although book orders could be placed by individual officials of sufficiently high status, the largest purchasers were the two major institutional collections: the bakufu library, or

18. The procedures are outlined at various levels of detail in many sources. See, for example, Yamawaki Teijirō, *Nagasaki no Tōjin bōeki*, in Nihon rekishi gakkai, ed., *Nihon rekishi sōsho* 6 (Yoshikawa kōbunkan, 1964), 197–209; and Ōba, *Books and Boats*, 36–38.

19. For a convenient overview, see Ōba Osamu and Wang Yong, *Tenseki*, in *Nit-Chū bunka kōryūshi sōsho* 9 (Taishūkan shoten, 1996), 99–114.

20. Extant *sairai shomoku* are reproduced in Ōba, *Tōsen mochiwatarisho*, 241–63.

21. Extant *taiisho* are reproduced in Ōba, *Tōsen mochiwatarisho*, 267–450.

Momijiyama Bunko, and the library of the bakufu academy, or Shōheikō. *Taiisho* were prepared for all imported titles through 1756, after which only books imported for the first time were subjected to this level of scrutiny.

After inspections were completed and the summaries had been prepared, books were transferred to the Nagasaki Customs Hall, where negotiations took place to determine the prices Chinese ship captains would receive for their goods. The results of these negotiations were recorded in a ledger called the *negumichō*.[22] In the rare event that a price could not be agreed upon, the items in question were returned to China. (Book prices and the factors behind their determination are discussed later in this chapter.) Otherwise, a list of titles and the negotiated price (hereafter referred to as the "fixed price") were recorded in a second ledger known as the *shojaku motochō*, and a date was set for an auction at which items would be bid on by authorized merchants from the five cities of Edo, Kyoto, Osaka, Sakai, and Nagasaki.[23] Prospective bidders were allowed to view items in advance and recorded their observations and planned bids in notebooks called *kenchō*, which they referred to during the auctions themselves. After each auction, the top three bids were recorded in an official ledger of bids, the *rakusatsuchō*, and the winning bids were sometimes added to the *shojaku motochō* as well.[24]

Many of the primary documents produced during the importation process were prepared in multiple. Nevertheless, the extant record covers only a limited number of years and ships. The mid-nineteenth century is well represented, with nearly all surviving *shojaku motochō* falling between 1840 and 1855, the sole exception being those for a few ships in 1803 and 1804. The extant *rakusatsuchō* cover 1843 to 1845 and 1858 to 1862. *Negumichō* and *kenchō* are exceedingly rare, with the only known instances dating from 1829 to 1830 and 1843 to 1844, respectively. The *sairai shomoku* and *taiisho* extend coverage back into the eighteenth and late seventeenth centuries, but they are few and far between. *Sairai shomoku* survive for scattered groups of ships between 1714 and 1801, along with those for two ships that arrived in 1805 that are transcribed in Nanpo's

22. Extant *negumichō* are reproduced in Ōba, *Tōsen mochiwatarisho*, 583–87.

23. Extant *shojaku motochō* are reproduced in Ōba, *Tōsen mochiwatarisho*, 453–583.

24. Extant *kenchō* and *rakusatsuchō* are reproduced in Ōba, *Tōsen mochiwatarisho*, 588–600 and 600–656.

journals. *Taiisho* survive for individual ships or groups of ships once every decade or so between 1694 and 1812, along with a fragment from 1860.

The main window onto the eighteenth century and earlier is provided by secondary records compiled after the fact. These include *Shōhaku sairai shomoku*, an 1804 compilation by Mukai Genchū, the fifth Inspector of Books, based on family documents.[25] Although it is not a complete record of the censorship office's activities through that year, it does include entries for nearly five thousand titles inspected between 1693—the year the *taiisho* were first prepared—and 1803, among them some later editions of titles predating 1693. The entries are listed not by year of importation but by the year in which the inspection was completed. The two are often the same, but there could be a lag of up to a few years, as was the case with *Gujin tushu jicheng* (Complete Collection of Illustrations and Writings Old and New), which arrived in 1750 (as known from the *taiisho*) but had not been fully inspected until 1753.[26] The work of the censorship office could take time, especially for books of such monumental scale.

Complementing *Shōhaku sairai shomoku* is a further body of compilations based on Mukai family documents, the most extensive of which is titled *Hakusai shomoku*.[27] The compiler is not known for certain, but the most likely candidate is Nakagawa Tadateru (1753–1830), who served as Nagasaki magistrate from 1795 to 1797, during which time he interviewed numerous local Chinese informants in the course of preparing his most famous work, a study of Chinese manners and customs titled *Shinzoku kibun* (1799).[28] *Hakusai shomoku* records books imported to Nagasaki

25. A transcription appears in Ōba, *Tōsen mochiwatarisho*, 659–739.

26. Ōba, *Tōsen mochiwatarisho*, 103; and Ōba and Wang, *Tenseki*, 106–7.

27. For a complete facsimile of the former with introduction and index, see Ōba, ed., *Hakusai shomoku*. Related titles include *Hakurai shomoku*, which survives only in incomplete later copies; a substantial catalog titled *Hakusai shomoku tsūran*, no longer extant; and a shorter manuscript derived from it titled *Bunrui hakusai shomoku tsūran*, which is reproduced in Ōba, *Hakusai shomoku*, vol. 2. Ōba and Wang, *Tenseki*, 107–9. For a straightforward bibliographic overview, see Yamanaka Hiroyuki, "Shinshutsu Ozaki Masayoshi hen *Hakurai shomoku* genpon ni tsuite," *Higashi Ajia bunka kōshō kenkyū* 8 (March 2015): 2–3.

28. The attribution was first proposed by Nagasawa Kikuya and later reiterated by Ōba on the basis of similarity with Tadateru's *Hakusai shomoku tsūran*, an uncategorized catalog of nearly the same length that is no longer extant. Yamanaka does not come down definitively on the attribution, but he does provide a detailed weighing of

between 1694 and 1754, albeit with significant gaps. Moreover, it does not contain many of the titles found in *Shōhaku sairai shomoku*. Nevertheless, because it does not limit its coverage to books that were being imported for the first time, *Hakusai shomoku* has more entries. There is also often more detail, which generally includes the number of volumes each title comprises, the transporting vessel, and sometimes tables of contents and prefaces—offering glimpses inside several titles that are otherwise lost.

Related to *Hakusai shomoku* is the similarly titled *Hakurai shomoku*, compiled by the Osaka scholar Ozaki Masayoshi (1755–1827).[29] Although generally less thorough in its coverage of the censorship office's early years, *Hakurai shomoku* extends its reach into the 1790s and early 1800s and supplements its content with material from two printed catalogs that had been published many decades earlier. These are Isshiki Tokimune's *Niyūdō* (1699) and Yamada Saburobē's *Tōhon ruisho kō* (1751), copies of both of which survive in many collections today. *Niyūdō* was prepared as a reference work for students at the author's private academy and surveys the contents of Tokimune's sizable personal library, which comprised hundreds of titles in diverse fields. Yamada conceived *Tōhon ruisho kō* as a successor to *Niyūdō* that would remedy some of its lacunae and challenge what he perceived as a monopoly on information by self-anointed and unreliable experts.[30] Among later printed reference materials, of particular note is Shūsuien Shujin's *Shōsetsu jii* (1791), a dictionary of vocabulary from Chinese fiction. The front matter features a list of 160 works that provided the basis for the entries, allowing the dictionary to double as a catalog of the titles available to the author at the time.[31] Although these and similar printed materials do not allow us to pinpoint when titles were imported, they nevertheless provide valuable upper bounds, showing what was available domestically at the time of publication.

In addition to all of the preceding, there are numerous other resources that supplement our understanding to a lesser degree. These include

---

the evidence and comparison of *Hakusai shomoku* and *Hakusai shomoku tsūran*. See Yamanaka, "*Hakurai shomoku* genpon," 1–21.

29. On *Hakurai shomoku*, see Ōba and Wang, *Tenseki*, 108–9.

30. For discussions of these works, see Ōba, *Tōsen mochiwatarisho*, 100–102, and *Tenseki*, 103–4.

31. *Shōsetsu jii*, in Nagasawa Kikuya, ed., *Tōwa jisho ruishū* (Kyūko shoin, 1959–76), 15:3–5.

smaller or fragmentary primary materials devoted to relatively narrow time periods.[32] There are also lists of books scattered in journals and diaries, such as those Nanpo kept during his year in Nagasaki. Some Edo collections survive in one form or another today, while many more can be glimpsed through the surviving catalogs of individual collectors or institutional collections such as those of the Momijiyama Library, the Shōheikō Academy, or the many domainal academies. Booksellers' catalogs are another valuable resource, with one from 1688 offering one of the earliest records of imported books.[33] Finally, we are also able to glean information from modern catalogs such as that of Nagasawa, which includes titles that were reprinted in early modern Japanese editions and are thus known to have been imported in or before the Edo period. We will return to this last resource in chapter 2, where these reprint editions become our primary focus.

Chinese Fiction by the Numbers

Fiction was a relative trickle amid the stream of Chinese books that poured into early modern Japan. Nevertheless, Edo readers became intimately familiar with many of the best-known titles, at least through their replacements and rewritings, from *The Water Margin*, *Romance of the Three Kingdoms*, and *Journey to the West* to *Jin Ping Mei*, Qu You's *New Tales by Lamplight*, and the vernacular collections of Feng Menglong.[34] As explored in chapter 2, some works of fiction were lost in China and not

32. Two examples, covering windows from 1722–26 and 1835–44, respectively, are reproduced in Ōba Osamu, "Seidō bunko no *Fueki fukenshi mokuroku*," *Kansai daigaku tōzai gakujutsu kenkyūjo kiyō* 3 (March 1970): 91–97; and Ōba Osamu, "Naikaku bunko no *Kōrai shoseki mokuroku* (honkoku)," *Kansai daigaku tōzai gakujutsu kenkyūjo kiyō* 1 (March 1968): 33–84.

33. Ōba Osamu, "Genroku gannen no Tōhon mokuroku," *Shisen* 35–36 (December 1967): 151–67.

34. In addition to the work of Ishizaki Matazō, Asō Isoji, and Tokuda Takeshi discussed in the introduction, for a brief overview of Edo adaptations of some of the less familiar Ming-Qing "masterpieces," see Nagasawa Kikuya, "Sono ta no Min Shin no kessaku to sono yunyū," in Nagasawa Kikuya sensei kiju kinenkai, ed., *Nagasawa Kikuya chosakushū* (Kyūko shoin, 1982–87), 5:292–95.

only survived in Japan but enjoyed active afterlives. Indeed, even limited forays into the import records reveal that many lesser titles likewise made their way through Nagasaki, often to resurface in surprising places downstream. The initial picture seems to support Jonathan Zwicker's assertion that "virtually the entire literary imagination of late imperial China" was available to the late-Edo reading public.

In arriving at this claim, Zwicker gestures toward the possibility of a large-scale quantitative analysis by examining a selection of seventy-two titles, including twenty categorized as "masterpieces" or "bestsellers," of which the majority appear in the records compiled by Ōba.[35] Bringing the complete body of texts attested in Ōba in conversation with other bibliographic resources offers the promise of a more careful quantification of the importation of Chinese fiction, one that allows us to assess not only the full extent to which the Chinese literary imagination was imported to Japan but other large, unanswered questions about the speed of this importation—and, more significantly, what it really meant for an imported text to be "available." Of course, the extant Nagasaki records are far from complete, and even titles that *do* appear do not necessarily accurately reflect the year a work first reached Japan. Zhang Chao's *New Tales of Yu Chu* was adapted and reprinted in a Japanese edition long before it is attested in the surviving import records. Feng Menglong's *Sanyan* collections appear in rapid succession in 1727, 1731, and 1743, but a half-century earlier, in 1683, the Confucian scholar Itō Jinsai (1627–1705) was already borrowing a copy of *Constant Words to Awaken the World* (*Xingshi hengyan*, 1627), the last of the three, from a seller of Chinese books.[36] Of course, such gaps mean only that we are at risk of *under*stating the importation of Chinese fiction, and in any event there are, as will be seen, independent data sets that allow us to estimate the degree of incompleteness and correct for it.

The first step as we proceed into the analysis is to identify the body of texts we wish to follow on its journey to Japan. Anticipating the examination of reprint editions and their significance in the next chapter, as well as the subsequent focus on the case of *Liaozhai*, this section will be limited to

35. Zwicker, *Practices of the Sentimental Imagination*, 128–35.

36. See entries in Ōba, *Tōsen mochiwatarisho*, 735, 717, and 700, respectively. On Jinsai's borrowing, see "Kogidō no shōsetsuka-tachi," in Nakamura Yukihiko, *Kinsei sakka kenkyū* (San'ichi shobō, 1961), 132. Quoted in Ogata Tsutomu, "Kaisetsu," in Ogata, ed., *Shōsetsu sangen* (Yumani shobō, 1976), 867.

printed editions of classical Chinese fiction, which were more amenable to straightforward reprinting than their vernacular counterparts. The main resource is Yuan Xingpei and Hou Zhongyi's *Zhongguo wenyan xiaoshuo shumu*, an extensive bibliography of works in the classical style categorized under the heading of *xiaoshuo*.[37] This is a label that includes categories of texts such as *zhiguai* strange tales and *biji* miscellanies that, to varying degrees, cannot be unproblematically equated with fiction. Writers of *zhiguai* often described their work as "transmitting" but not "creating" (after Confucius), which is to say that they presented themselves as merely reporting ostensibly true events. Ji Yun fervently subscribed to this view and felt that narratives must demonstrate their "plausibility."[38] Still, many writers used such arguments as mere rhetoric and freely fictionalized their tales. Moreover, *zhiguai* and *biji* collections were rewritten unambiguously as fiction in the Japanese context, as we will see in the final chapters, where I address questions of genre and literary convention. For the purposes of analysis, then, we consider the entries in Yuan and Hou's catalog to provide a corpus of Chinese classical fiction that lends itself to analysis. It would, in any event, be an impossible endeavor to assess the "fictionality" of each individual title on a case-by-case basis.

Yuan and Hou's bibliography includes 696 Ming titles and 555 from the Qing. Among these are 265 for which we can confirm the existence of a print edition dating to 1850 or earlier. This subset was taken as the corpus for analysis. (Titles with tentative or otherwise questionable years of publication were generally omitted from analysis, but a few cases were resolved through reference to Ning Jiayu's *Zhongguo wenyan xiaoshuo zongmu tiyao*.[39]) Ming editions were included regardless of whether a specific date could be established, as these necessarily predate 1645, while only Qing editions that could be confidently dated to early 1850 or before (predating the reign of the Xianfeng emperor) were included. As discussed momentarily, the figure of 265 inevitably underestimates the actual number of titles of classical fiction in print editions, not just because of the limitations of modern bibliographic study but for other reasons as well.

37. Yuan Xingpei and Hou Zhongyi, eds., *Zhongguo wenyan xiaoshuo shumu* (Beijing: Beijing daxue chubanshe, 1981).

38. Leo Tak-hung Chan, *The Discourse on Foxes and Ghosts: Ji Yun and Eighteenth-Century Literati Storytelling* (Honolulu: University of Hawai'i Press, 1998), 165.

39. Ning Jiayu, *Zhongguo wenyan xiaoshuo zongmu tiyao* (Jinan: Qilu shushe, 1996).

However, just as we are able to correct for incompleteness in the import record, we are also able to estimate and correct for this.

Following these 265 printed editions of Ming-Qing fiction after their publication, 69 (26 percent) appear in the extant import records.[40] This is a substantial figure, but it is one that obviously understates the amount of Chinese fiction that arrived in Japan, given the fragmentary nature of the historical record. Correcting for this requires a set of titles known to have been imported but independent from (orthogonal to) the import records, which would allow us to estimate their completeness. Fortunately, Japanese *wakokubon* editions offer precisely such a data set. Here we may draw in advance on the analysis developed in chapter 2, where it is found that seven of the above 69 classical titles attested in the import records were later reprinted in Japanese editions, and that there are a further eight titles among the 265 print editions in Yuan and Hou that, while absent in the import records, were also reprinted in Japanese editions. These appear in table 2.1 as titles known to have been reprinted (as detailed in the last column) but not attested in the import records (the second-to-last column). All fifteen of these titles must have been imported, yet only seven appear in the Nagasaki records. Although the sample size is small, it is statistically significant. The data suggests that not only are the import records incomplete, they are *very* incomplete, with eight out of fifteen titles unattested. In other words, while the extant records document the importation of 69 out of 265 titles, a better estimate is that 148 (that is, $69 \cdot \frac{15}{7}$) were imported, or around 56 percent. Suddenly it seems plausible that more than half of published Ming-Qing classical fiction made it to Japanese shores.

One final complication lies in the existence of known *wakokubon* editions of titles that could not be verified as print editions relying on Yuan and Hou's bibliographic data (a distinction noted in the middle column of table 2.1). These are thirteen in number. If we assume, for the sake of establishing a lower bound on the rate of importation, that the Japanese reprint editions all reproduce Chinese print editions—which was the case for the later editions that could be examined but is not necessarily the case for movable-type editions or woodblock-printed editions based on them—then we can estimate the incompleteness of Yuan and Hou's data on print

40. The analysis in this section uses all of the documents reproduced in Ōba, *Tōsen mochiwatarisho* and *Hakusai shomoku*.

editions the same way we estimated the incompleteness of the import record. In this case, we revise the figure of 265 titles of classical fiction published on the continent up to 495 such titles ($265 \cdot \frac{15+13}{15}$).

Only 4 of the additional 13 titles appear in the import records. In other words, the record is even less complete for these titles, and accounting for them revises the estimate of importation rates further upward. Scaling the 69 titles from Yuan and Hou attested in the records in proportion to our revised estimate of the number of print titles yields 129 ($69 \cdot \frac{495}{265}$). Refining the preceding analysis, we now have 328 ($129 \cdot \frac{15+13}{7+4}$) titles imported out of 495 that were published—that is, we have scaled by the total number of titles in table 2.1 divided by the number of titles in table 2.1 that appear in the import records. This final revised figure points to the importation of around 66 percent—nearly two-thirds—of the entire corpus of classical fiction published in late imperial China.

Temporal Compression: Toward Simultaneity

Within imported Chinese fiction, some genres were more likely to be imported than others. Jonathan Zwicker's analysis of twenty bestsellers—including the vernacular "masterworks" *The Water Margin*, *Journey to the West*, *Romance of the Three Kingdoms*, *Jin Ping Mei*, and *Dream of the Red Chamber* (*Hongloumeng*)—finds that eighteen, or 90 percent, are known to have been imported.[41] These are works that arrived in such quantities, and over such extended swaths of time, that the incompleteness of the import records has much less of an impact on the estimates. More interestingly, Zwicker considers an additional fifty-two titles across three fictional subgenres drawn from Robert Hegel's study of illustrated fiction in late imperial China: late Ming historical novels, Qing military romance novels, and Qing scholar-beauty romance novels. The rates of importation of these titles range from 40 percent to 70 percent, with the earliest titles showing the lowest rates of importation.[42]

41. Zwicker, *Practices of the Sentimental Imagination*, 133.

42. Zwicker, *Practices of the Sentimental Imagination*, 134–35; and Robert E. Hegel, *Reading Illustrated Fiction in Late Imperial China* (Stanford, CA: Stanford University Press, 1998), 45, 49–50, 65.

Of course, these figures are not the actual rates of importation but the rates at which such titles are attested in the extant records. Given that the documentation is more extensive for later periods, the relatively low rate for late Ming historical novels is at least in part a reflection of the available evidence. At the same time, the story of Edo engagement with the continent is one of increasing awareness of the proximity of China, of its existence as a living, breathing thing, not merely a repository of the past. Unsurprisingly, there is no dearth of anecdotal evidence to suggest temporal compression in the flow of texts from China. Even in the seventeenth century, where the import records run thin, we find examples such as Tokugawa Ieyasu's son Yoshinao, daimyō of the Owari Domain for much of the first half of the seventeenth century, who is known to have acquired a number of titles just two years after their publication on the continent.[43] In the eighteenth and especially nineteenth centuries, examples become only more common. Ōba Osamu lists twenty-three titles accessioned by the bakufu at either the Momijiyama Library or the Shōheikō Academy between 1807 and 1852, of which all but five reached Japan within a decade of publication. One of these was imported the same year, several others just one year later. Inspection and other bureaucratic procedures could add months or even a few years to the process, but two-thirds of the titles were available for reading within a decade of publication.[44]

Examples of rapid importation are also frequent among fiction. A copy of *Liaozhai* was unloaded in Nagasaki in 1768, just two years after the publication of the first print edition in Hangzhou. A sizable shipment of twenty-one copies of Yuan Mei's *Zi bu yu* (That of Which the Master Did Not Speak), one of *Liaozhai*'s most popular successors, arrived aboard a ship from Nanjing in 1794, six years after the collection's publication. The same vessel carried many other important works of fiction, including the first recorded copies of *Dream of the Red Chamber*, which had been published just three years earlier.[45]

Bringing together the different data sets introduced thus far allows us to widen our gaze beyond these individual cases. This bigger picture emerges in figures 1.1 through 1.3, which visualize the time between publication and importation for fifty-two titles of classical fiction in fifty-six

43. Ōba, "Chinese Travelers to Nagasaki," 112.
44. Ōba, *Tōsen mochiwatarisho*, 238.
45. Ōba, *Tōsen mochiwatarisho*, 252.

different editions. Most are drawn from Yuan and Hou, the requirements being (1) that their publication is datable to a precise year between 1600 and 1850, and (2) that they are attested in the Japanese import records. There are forty-eight works that fit these criteria. To these have been added four titles from Leo Tak-hung Chan's study of Qing classical fiction that fulfill the same criteria but are absent in Yuan and Hou.[46] Some minor dating errors and irregularities have also been corrected.[47]

Given that information about edition is rarely recorded in Edo import documents, it is assumed that imported copies reflect the most recent available edition at the time. Thus, four titles that were imported in more than one year—with new editions published in the interim—are represented twice in the data. By way of example, *Liaozhai zhiyi* was imported not only in 1768 but also in 1800 and 1854. The 1800 copies are excluded from analysis, as the most recent edition at that time remained the Qingketing edition of 1766, and our concern is with when editions were *first* imported. However, the 1854 copies *are* reflected in the data, because (although there is no way to know for sure) they were presumably a more recent edition, the latest of which had been printed in Shanghai a decade earlier.

Figure 1.1 presents the data in relatively simple form as a histogram of the number of titles that reached Japan after a given number of years. It is immediately evident that there is a handful of works that are not known to have arrived until many decades after their publication. For some the gap is a century or more. At the same time, the evidence as a whole supports the anecdotal case that the temporal lag between publication and importation was generally low. The majority of titles can be documented to have reached Nagasaki within two decades (the median is nineteen years), and more than one-third arrived within a decade of publication. Dividing the titles into four groups by year of publication adds

46. Chan, *Discourse on Foxes and Ghosts*, 15. Three of the titles are component texts of *Yuewei caotang biji*, which does not appear itself in Ōba: *Luanyang xiaoxia lu* (1789), *Rushi wowen* (1791), and *Huaixi zazhi* (1792). The fourth text is *Qiuping xinyu* (1792).

47. Yuan and Hou give 1765 for *Yetan suilu*; I have followed instead Chan's date of 1791. One of the titles added from Chan, *Huaixi zazhi*, in spite of generally being dated to 1792, appears in the import records in 1791. A similar issue occurs with *Zhiwen lu*, the earliest printed edition of which is given as 1843, but which appears in 1841. For the purposes of analysis, I have considered both titles to have been published the same year they were imported.

greater nuance. Those published before 1690 account for most of the slowest titles, while those published between 1696 and 1710 arrived somewhat more quickly, but still with a lag of a half-century or more. Excluding the earlier titles group by group steadily lowers the median crossing time, first to fifteen years (for titles from 1680 and after), then ten years, and finally seven years for titles published after 1750. Although this suggests a process of temporal compression, the evidence is not unambiguous. Particularly for books published prior to the codification of record-keeping in the 1690s, we cannot exclude the possibility of importation at an earlier date.

If this form of visualization offers a glimpse of historical change and the possibility of a progression toward simultaneity, figure 1.2 brings these things into clearer focus by presenting the data instead as a scatter plot from 1680 to 1860, roughly the period of the extant import record. The data points sweep downward from the upper left to the lower right, suggesting that fiction did indeed flow into Nagasaki more quickly as time passed. However, it is not a steady progression. Allowing for some slight regression in the early nineteenth century, around the time Nanpo arrived in the city, the mid-eighteenth century emerges with greater clarity as a sort of demarcation line. Texts published before this (the last of which dates to 1710) took many decades to reach Japan; those published afterward arrived with relative quickness. The story is still one of temporal compression, but compression that arrives suddenly, not gradually.

Figure 1.3 offers further nuance to our interpretation of the same data. Here the horizontal axis is provided by year of importation instead of year of publication. It is again apparent that the small number of texts that arrived before around 1750 were already many decades old, whereas those that came afterward were, by and large, much more recent. That said, we discern more clearly the verticality of discrete waves of importation. These vertical lines correspond to multiple titles that arrived in the same year, usually on a single ship—like the boat that arrived from Nanjing in 1794 bearing the first copies of *Zi bu yu*, *Dream of the Red Chamber*, and several other works of fiction. Additional lines corresponding to three or more works arriving simultaneously appear in 1754, 1782, 1791, 1803, 1829, and 1840.

Shifting the horizontal axis to the year of earliest known importation also brings back into view several titles published before 1680 that lie outside the range of figure 1.2. These are distinguished with X-shaped markers. All are confined to the upper reaches of the plot, with several

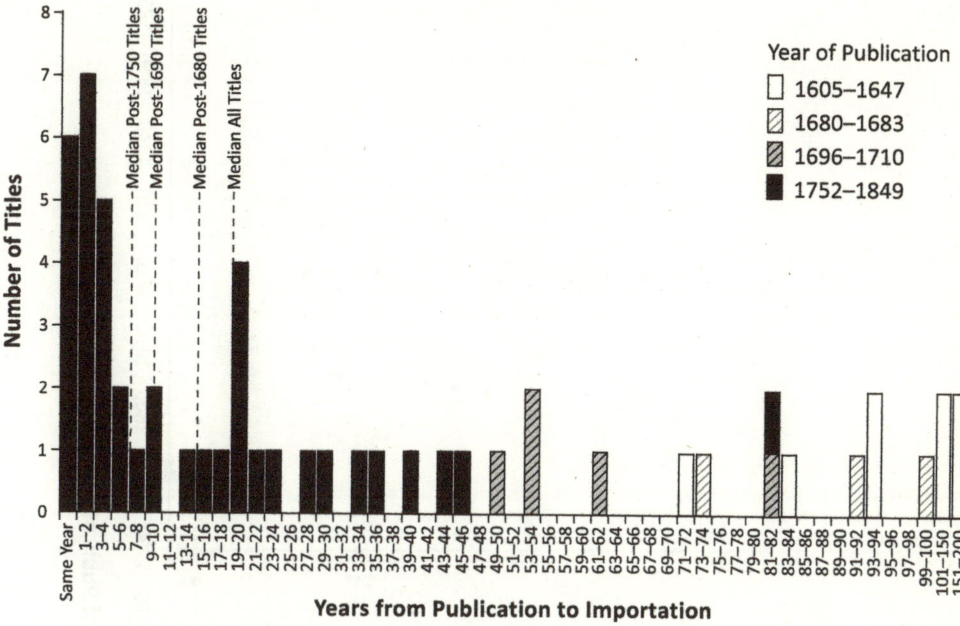

FIGURE 1.1 How quickly did Chinese fiction reach Japan?

lying in the top margin, indicating that their first recorded arrival occurred more than a century after publication. As stated previously, it is possible, even likely, that some of these reached Japan at an earlier date—after all, there is little record of importation prior to 1690—and without the early titles the median importation time is several years faster. Yet even this likely overstates the actual time it took for titles to arrive, as the import record remains fragmentary and incomplete through the end of the Edo period. The first documented importation of a given title provides only an upper bound.

If we treat the X-shaped data points in figure 1.3 with a measure of skepticism—recognizing that these pre-1680 titles are relatively likely to have been imported earlier than shown—what emerges most clearly from the distribution is, again, not gradual temporal compression but the sudden onset of large-scale importation around the middle of the eighteenth century. Older works also came along with this wave, as attested by the appearance of the pre-1680 titles in the upper margin around the same

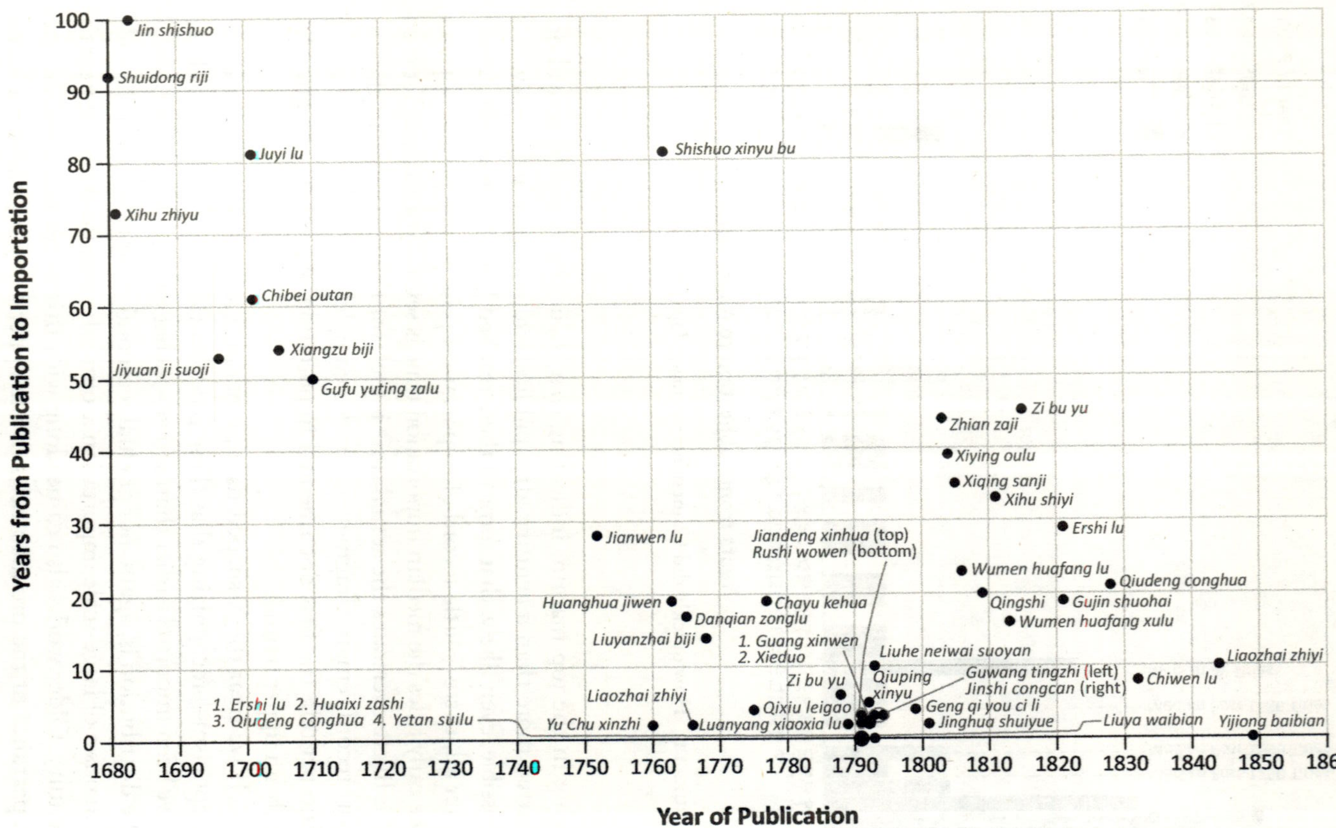

FIGURE I.2 Speed of importation of Chinese fiction by year of publication

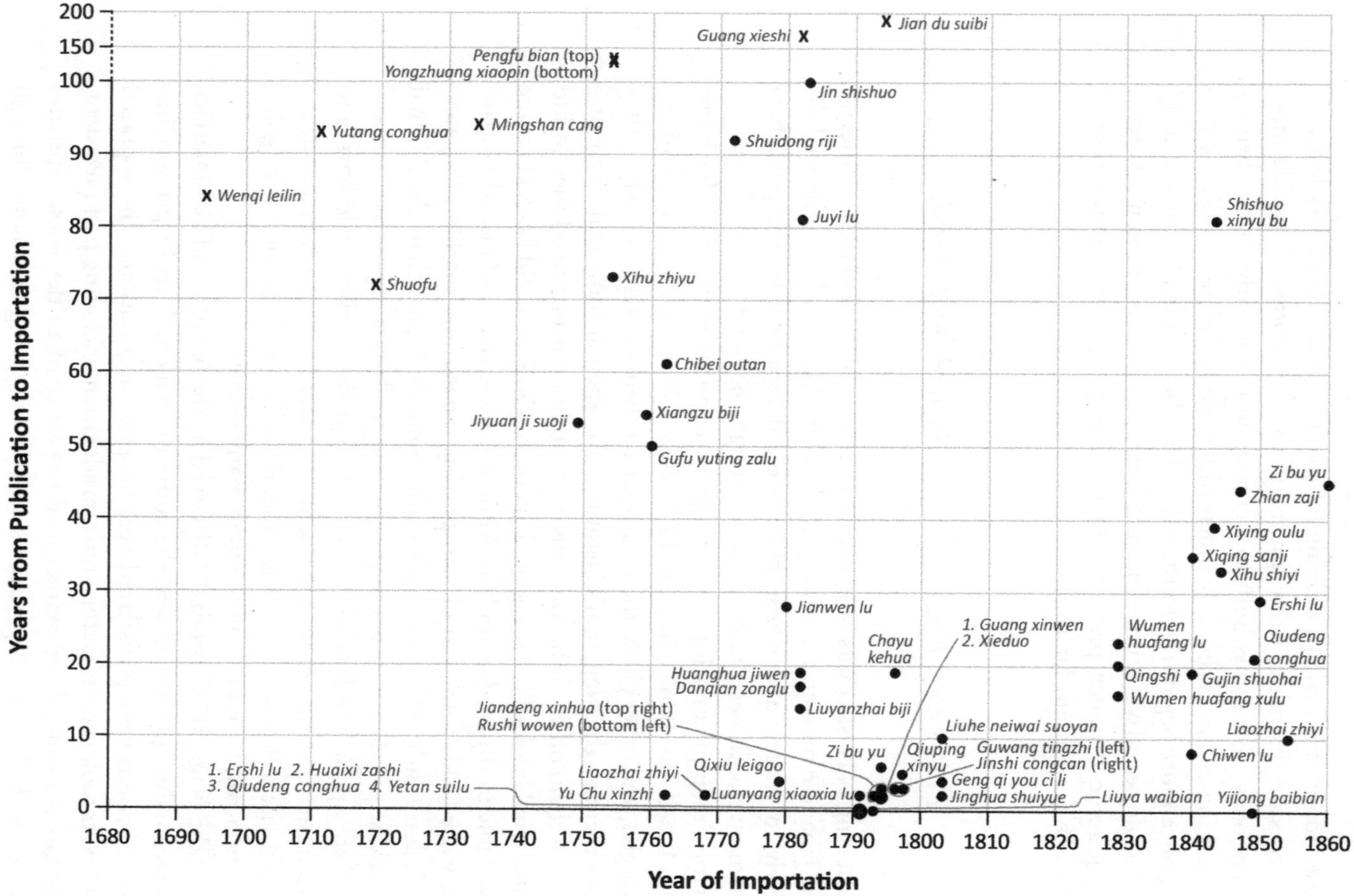

FIGURE I.3 Speed of importation of Chinese fiction by year of importation

time. Some were perhaps arriving for the first time. At the very least, we can be sure that older titles continued to be imported alongside more recent ones. This influx built to a crescendo in the early 1790s, then retreated somewhat in the early nineteenth century before steadily increasing once more beginning in the 1830s. In other words, the final century of the Edo period was a time of both mass importation *and* near-simultaneity. Geographic distance presented little hindrance to the permeation of Chinese fiction into Japan.

Prices and Profits in the Chinese Book Trade

Reaching Nagasaki was only one step in an imported book's journey to the Japanese market. In contrast to domestic books, which were sold directly to readers and whose prices were determined by the publishers themselves, Chinese books passed through the hands of many intermediaries, their prices rising with each transaction along the way. Merchants purchased the books from publishers based in Hangzhou, Nanjing, Ningbo, and other cities, then transported them to Nagasaki, where they sold them to the Nagasaki Customs Hall. The Customs Hall then auctioned them off to authorized buyers, who in turn auctioned them off to individual booksellers at regional auctions. Only then did books become available to the reading public. Although these steps did not add intrinsic value (aside from that of transporting the items to market), they nevertheless resulted in prices orders of magnitude higher than the original purchase prices. This is not to suggest that the laws of supply and demand did not apply. The final cost reflected what the market could bear, and given their scarcity many items sold for prices out of reach of all but the wealthiest collectors. However, rather than the enormous profits all going to one actor, they were split among many parties.

The Nagasaki Customs Hall served as the bakufu's official interface between foreign markets and the domestic market. After inspection, imported goods were transferred here for price negotiations. The appraisal of books took various factors into consideration, including past precedent, the current state of the market, and the rarity of a title. These estimates served as the basis for negotiations with the importing merchants, through which adjustments were made and the final price mutually agreed upon.[48] In the event that no agreement could be reached, books were returned to China unsold. Ōba describes a Song edition of the Five Classics that the bakufu requested in 1803 based on the inspection summary. By the time the request reached Nagasaki, the book had been returned to China owing to a disagreement over a suitable price.[49]

Within a day or two of the price negotiations, those titles not whisked away by the bakufu were auctioned off to authorized booksellers from the five major cities of Edo, Kyoto, Osaka, Sakai, and Nagasaki.[50] A portion of the profits went into the shogunate's coffers, while the remainder went to Customs Hall officials as salary and to annual payments made to the residents of Nagasaki. Secondary auctions further distributed titles among booksellers who specialized in Chinese books or who sold imported titles alongside domestically published materials. Extant notes from several such auctions held in Osaka and Kyoto in 1831 and 1832 record the participation of dozens of individual booksellers.[51] Finally, following these auctions, the books at last became available for purchase to the reading public at individual shops across Japan.

Before we delve into the prices of imported books and interpret their significance, we must first reckon with a number of fundamental challenges. Transformations in the monetary system within the Tokugawa period make comparisons across time difficult, while incommensurabilities with our own economic system preclude the straightforward conversion of historical figures into present-day terms. More immediately, the Tokugawa monetary system presents a complicated amalgam of currencies and varying exchange rates. Book prices, where they are found, are recorded using diverse units of currency, often in combination with each other. Common units include *mon* (coppers), *hiki* (10 coppers), *kan* and *monme* of silver (approximately 3.74 kilograms and 3.74 grams, respectively), and *ryō* (the value of one gold piece, or *koban*). One *ryō* typically

48. For a concise summary, see "Tōhon no yunyū," in Yayoshi Mitsunaga, *Mikan shiryō ni yoru Nihon shuppan bunka* (Yumani shobō, 1988–93), 2:124–25.

49. Ōba, *Books and Boats*, 79.

50. For a short overview of the bidding process, see Ōba, *Books and Boats*, 79–81.

51. *Shinto Tōhon-ichi hikaechō*, in Yayoshi, *Mikan shiryō ni yoru Nihon shuppan bunka*, 2:343–406. A brief description of the document is included in Yayoshi, *Mikan shiryō ni yoru*, 8:480. This auction was conducted not only through the submission of paper bids, as at the primary Nagasaki auctions, but also through oral bidding. See Hashiguchi Kōnosuke, "Edo no furuhon'ya," *Nihon kosho tsūshin* 942 (January 2008): 30–31.

equaled between 50 and 60 *monme*, while one *monme* fluctuated around 66⅔ *mon* from the 1690s (when the rate was set at 60 *monme* = 4,000 *mon*) through around 1770, then rose rapidly to around 100 to 110 *mon* before dropping off slightly in the last decades of the Edo period. Two additional units, based on divisions by four, are the *bu* and the *shu*, where one *bu* equals a quarter of a *ryō*, and one *shu* a quarter of a *bu*.

These complicated constellations of currencies, along with floating exchange rates among the different metals and the fundamental differences between the Tokugawa economy and that of our own day, have led some, including Kornicki, to declare efforts at interpreting book prices doomed from the outset.[52] But if we are to make any sense of the available data, and to compare figures across time, we cannot give up so easily. Recognizing the caveats and challenges involved in diachronic comparison, my approach is to borrow, with modification, one of the conventional bases for price comparison: the cost of a bowl of soba noodles.[53] The choice fulfills several important criteria. It was a staple item regularly consumed from the seventeenth century onward; it experienced steady inflation but few erratic fluctuations, and price data is available across time.[54] It is also an item that maps onto our own lived experience: for the purposes of analysis, we can value it at the price of an inexpensive lunch, or five dollars. The precise number is arbitrary, but assigning a modern-day value is necessary to allow us to convert prices to an approximate dollar equivalent that accounts for inflation within the Edo era. For example, a book that cost ten coppers in the 1760s, when soba cost about twelve coppers, would be the equivalent of $4.17 today; the same price a century later, by which time the price of soba had risen to 16 coppers, is equivalent to $3.13.

For all the differences between our economic systems, the price of a basic meal is commensurate with the present day in surprising ways. A typical Edo laborer's wages circa 1820—5.4 *monme* a day, or roughly 1,500 *monme* per year—would, by this metric, correspond to an annual salary

52. Kornicki, *The Book in Japan*, 185–86.

53. For examples of the cost of soba being used as a basis for comparison, see Utano Hiroshi, "Edo jidai no hon no nedan kō," *Nihon kosho tsūshin* 772 (November 1993): 12–13; and Tanahashi Masahiro, *Edo gesaku sōshi* (Shōgakukan, 2000), 12.

54. Price data is taken from Uehara Rorō, *Soba jiten* (Tōkyōdō shuppan, 1972), 40. In the year 1664: 8 coppers; 1684–88: 6 coppers; 1690: 7 coppers; 1723: 7–8 coppers; ca. 1764–72: 12 coppers; 1791: 14 coppers; 1804: ~15 coppers; 1818–30: 16 coppers; 1830–44: 16 coppers; 1860: 16 coppers. Prices for other years are interpolated based on these figures.

of $52,400.[55] The mean annual salary in the United States in 2019 across all occupations was $53,490.[56] Whatever advantages and previously unimaginable luxuries workers may enjoy today, not much has changed in terms of how many meals their salary can buy. While not perfect, at the very least the soba metric provides a rudimentary basis for interpreting the significance of prices across time.

Let us begin, then, to look at the prices of Chinese books, using the soba metric to derive price equivalents for all figures, accounting as best as possible for the changing price of soba and shifting conversion rates between different metals, given that books were usually priced in silver *kan* and *monme*, not copper *mon*.[57] The records from the Nagasaki Customs Hall present a natural starting point. In his brief discussion of book prices, Ōba selects eight titles from the fixed-price ledger (*shojaku motochō*) for 1845, the prices of which he compares with those of imported luxury items.[58] Observing that the books are less expensive, often much so, than items such as Dutch pocket watches, telescopes, or music boxes, Ōba concludes that Chinese books were not particularly expensive. But what if we put these figures in perspective not by comparing them to some of the most expensive luxury items available at the time, but by assigning our dollar equivalents, as in table 1.1?

Suddenly the prices paid for these titles no longer appear particularly low. In fact, these fixed prices point to considerable profit margins for Chinese merchants. There is a paucity of reliable data on market prices for books in China, fiction included, equal to or greater than the already considerable limitations of the Japanese record.[59] However, an anecdote from the Ming that offers some valuable perspective concerns an outlay of around 100 ounces of silver—roughly 760 *monme*—for the carving of woodblocks for the Thirteen Classics with commentaries.[60] An edition

55. Daily wages are based on Ono Takeo, *Edo bukka jiten* (Tenbōsha, 1979).

56. United States Bureau of Labor Statistics, https://www.bls.gov/oes/2019/may/oes_nat.htm.

57. Exchange rates are based on Shinbo Hiroshi, *Kinsei no bukka to keizai hatten: zen-kōgyōka shakai e no sūryōteki sekkin* (Tōyō keizai shinpōsha, 1978), 171–73.

58. Ōba, *Books and Boats*, 81–82.

59. On book prices in the Ming, see Shen Jin [Chum Shum], "Ming dai fangke tushu zhi liutong yu jiage," *Guojia tushuguan guankan* 1 (June 1996): 101–18.

60. Joseph McDermott, "The Ascendance of the Imprint in China," in Cynthia J. Brokaw and Kai-wing Chow, eds., *Printing and Book Culture in Late Imperial China* (Berkeley: University of California Press, 2005), 102n133.

Table 1.1 Fixed Prices and Winning Bids for Selected Imported Titles, 1845

Title	Fixed price		Winning bid		Increase
Peiwen yunfu 佩文韻府	1 *kan*	($31,250)	1.71 *kan*	($53,400)	71%
Siku quanshu tiyao 四庫全書提要	40 *monme*	($1,250)	520.3 *monme*	($16,300)	1,201%
Wubian tongjian 五編通鑑	400 *monme*	($12,500)	1.234 *kan*	($38,600)	209%
Zhibuzuzhai congshu 知不足齋叢書	300 *monme*	($9,380)	367 *monme* (corrected from 345 in Ōba)	($11,500)	22.3%
Shisanjing zhushu 十三經注疏	250 *monme*	($7,810)	465 *monme*	($14,500)	86%
Qinding sijing 欽定四經	180 *monme*	($5,630)	411.5 *monme*	($12,900)	129%
Huangchao jingshi wenbian 皇朝經世文編	150 *monme*	($4,690)	310 *monme*	($9,690)	107%
Ming shi gao 明史稿	150 *monme*	($4,690)	352.1 *monme*	($11,000)	135%

of the Thirteen Classics with commentaries (*Shisanjing zhushu*) appears in the table, where the fixed price for a single copy is already some 250 *monme*. One would need to sell just three copies at this price to recoup almost the entire investment of capital for the blocks themselves; clearly this represents an enormous markup from the market price in China.

One item in table 1.1, the *Siku quanshu tiyao* (Overview of the Complete Library of the Four Treasuries), stands out for having been bought from the Chinese at a relatively low fixed price. In the course of bidding at Nagasaki, however, the price increased more than twelvefold. Indeed, auction incorporated substantial markups into the price of all but one of the titles; typically the price roughly doubled. Moreover, these figures represent only the first steps of the books' journey to the domestic market. As explored later in this chapter, additional costs downstream continued to add substantially to the final retail price. In other words, Chinese books could easily end up costing considerably *more* than imported telescopes and watches—items that were already extraordinarily expensive in their own right.

To expand the chronological range of our examination of prices, table 1.2 presents the prices of a handful of titles imported in 1784, several decades before the earliest extant price ledgers. These figures, recorded by Ōta Nanpo in his miscellany *Ichiwa ichigen*, reflect the amounts paid

Table 1.2 Prices of Chinese Books Purchased by Nagasaki Magistrate's Office in 1784

Title	Price	
Taiping yulan 太平御覧	~175 *monme*	($6,790)
Peiwen yunfu 佩文韻府	227.63 *monme*	($8,830)
Yuanjian leihan 淵鑑類函	350.2 *monme*	($13,600)
Pinzi jian 品字箋	105.6 *monme*	($4,100)
Tong ya 通雅	280.16 *monme*	($10,900)
Zhengzi tong 正字通	29.767 *monme*	($1,150)
Qianque leishu 潛確類書	~54 *monme*	($2,090)
Zheng shuofu 正説郛	~90 *monme*	($3,490)
Xu shuofu 續説郛	~54 *monme*	($2,090)
Yiwen leiju 藝文類聚	~36 *monme*	($1,400)
Kangxi zidian 康熙字典	113.815 *monme*	($4,410)

for items that were purchased directly by the Nagasaki magistrate's office. As such, they likely reflect a surcharge on the fixed price less than the price increase that would have come through bidding had they first gone through auction.[61]

Neither table 1.1 nor table 1.2 suggests that books were particularly cheap. At the same time, neither constitutes a random or representative sample of titles. Nanpo's list consists of items significant enough to be of official interest, while Ōba limits his selection to titles that fetched 150 *monme* ($4,690) or more, making his assertion of their affordability all the more puzzling. They are, after all, among the most expensive items imported that year. They are also mostly well-known, foundational texts. This last point has competing implications where price is concerned. On the one hand, demand for such works was relatively high, and many came in sizable multivolume sets. On the other hand, they were not exceedingly rare titles likely to incite frenzied bidding or speculation. In any event, the question remains just how representative these selections were of prices more generally.

We can begin to answer this question by expanding our analysis to the extant price records as a whole. Table 1.3 presents total and average figures by ship and by auction, as well as in the aggregate, over the sixty-year

61. Ōba, *Tōsen mochiwatarisho*, 232–33.

Table 1.3 Total and Average Fixed Prices and Winning Bids for Imported Chinese Books, 1803–62

Year and ship number	Auction year and number or date	Number of titles	Number of items	Number of subunits	Total fixed price, *monme* (dollars)
1803.7		22	157	185	1,892.5 ($67,800)
1803.8		11	64	535	3,275 ($117,000)
1803.9		19	282	425	3,514 ($126,000)
1803.10		4	4	31	210 ($7,530)
1804.2		22	200	420	3,096 ($112,000)
1804.3		9	25	288	4,625 ($168,000)
1804.x1		1	2	40	560 ($20,300)
1804.x2		3	3	8	203 ($7,370)
1804.4		4	47	94	587 ($21,300)
1804.5		3	3	30	290 ($10,500)
1804.6		26	45	204	3,507.5 ($127,000)
1804.8		17	260	706	3,295 ($120,000)
1829.5		92	1,291	—	1,206 ($40,900)
1829.7		18	307	—	1,230.9 ($41,800)
1829.8		3	3	—	36 ($1,220)
1830.1		1	12	—	40 ($1,330)
1839.5		4	4	9	64 ($2,260)
1839.6		15	15	19	109 ($3,840)
1839.7		3	3	6	38 ($1,340)
1839.8		2	2	2	11 ($388)
1840.1		182	410	1,197	10,705 ($368,000)
1840.2		97	200	846	6,953.5 ($239,000)
1840.3		100	394	786	4,935 ($170,000)
1841.1		35	92	282	4,493 ($154,000)
1841.2		132	236	632	5,981 ($205,000)
1841.4		11	33	86	855 ($29,300)
1841.6		1	1	2	16 ($549)
1842.1		6	6	13	275 ($9,190)
1842.2		93	176	321	4,325 ($145,000)
	1843.10.8 (w/ fixed price)	9	10	30	220.8 ($6,900)
	1843.10.8 (only bids)	102	424	857	—
	1844 #2	79	149	806	—
	1844 #6	196	729	1,613	—
1844.5–7 (w/ bids)		216	488	1,414	17,996.9 ($562,000)
1844.5–7 (w/o bids)		39	79	121	1,313 ($41,000)
1845.3–5		186	830	1,388	13,520.2 ($423,000)
	1845 #2	205	512	870	—
	1845 #6	75	364	546	—
1846.1		64	117	374	3,319.5 ($104,000)
1846.2		118	378	541	3,255 ($102,000)
1846.3		42	46	122	1,644 ($51,400)
1846.4		88	474	839	8,118.6 ($254,000)

Average fixed price, *monme* (dollars)		Total winning bids, *monme* (dollars)	Average winning bid, *monme* (dollars)	
per item	per subunit		per item	per subunit
12.1 ($432)	10.2 ($367)	—	—	—
51.2 ($1,830)	6.12 ($219)	—	—	—
12.5 ($447)	8.27 ($296)	—	—	—
52.5 ($1,880)	6.77 ($243)	—	—	—
15.5 ($562)	7.37 ($268)	—	—	—
185 ($6,720)	16.1 ($583)	—	—	—
280 ($10,200)	14 ($508)	—	—	—
67.7 ($2,460)	25.4 ($921)	—	—	—
12.5 ($454)	6.24 ($227)	—	—	—
96.7 ($3,510)	9.67 ($351)	—	—	—
77.9 ($2,830)	17.2 ($624)	—	—	—
12.7 ($460)	4.67 ($169)	—	—	—
0.934 ($31.70)	—	—	—	—
4.01 ($136)	—	—	—	—
12 ($407)	—	—	—	—
3.33 ($111)	—	—	—	—
16 ($564)	7.11 ($251)	—	—	—
7.27 ($256)	5.74 ($202)	—	—	—
12.7 ($446)	6.33 ($223)	—	—	—
5.5 ($194)	5.5 ($194)	—	—	—
26.1 ($899)	8.94 ($308)	—	—	—
34.8 ($1,200)	8.22 ($283)	—	—	—
12.5 ($431)	6.28 ($216)	—	—	—
48.8 ($1,680)	15.9 ($547)	—	—	—
25.3 ($869)	9.46 ($325)	—	—	—
25.9 ($889)	9.94 ($341)	—	—	—
16 ($549)	8 ($274)	—	—	—
45.8 ($1,530)	21.2 ($707)	—	—	—
24.6 ($821)	13.5 ($450)	—	—	—
22.1 ($690)	7.36 ($230)	583.3 ($18,200)	58.4 ($1,820)	19.5 ($608)
—	—	27,652.6 ($864,000)	65.2 ($2,040)	32.3 ($1,010)
—	—	26,966.5 ($843,000)	181 ($5,660)	33.5 ($1,050)
—	—	43,441.52 ($1,360,000)	59.6 ($1,860)	26.9 ($842)
36.9 ($1,150)	12.7 ($398)	30,400 ($950,000)	62.3 ($1,950)	21.5 ($672)
16.6 ($519)	10.9 ($339)	—	—	—
16.3 ($509)	9.74 ($304)	—	—	—
—	—	31,341.01 ($979,000)	61.2 ($1,910)	36.0 ($1,130)
—	—	9,614.41 ($300,000)	26.4 ($825)	17.6 ($550)
28.4 ($887)	8.88 ($277)	—	—	—
8.61 ($269)	6.02 ($188)	—	—	—
35.7 ($1,120)	13.5 ($421)	—	—	—
17.1 ($535)	9.68 ($302)	—	—	—

(*continued*)

Table 1.3 (*continued*)

Year and ship number	Auction year and number or date	Number of titles	Number of items	Number of subunits	Total fixed price, *monme* (dollars)
1846.5		29	155	292	2,278 ($71,200)
1846.6		26	83	284	2,701.5 ($84,400)
1846.7		38	161	307	2,148 ($67,100)
1846.4–7, 1847.1 (new titles)		27	96	116	440.5 ($17,200)
1847.2		56	168	480	5,739 ($179,000)
1847.3		13	25	26	67 ($2,090)
1847.4		69	148	226	2,765 ($86,400)
1848.2		67	331	666	6,153 ($192,000)
1848.3		71	137	229	3,434.5 ($107,000)
1848.4		127	269	377	3,404.5 ($106,000)
1849.1		31	49	63	585.8 ($18,300)
1849.2		13	19	27	694 ($21,700)
1849.3		173	234	748	14,858 ($464,000)
1849.4		75	225	482	7,947 ($248,000)
1849.5		173	422	793	8,591.7 ($268,000)
1849.6		30	78	274	2,935 ($91,700)
1849.7		13	22	32	426.5 ($13,300)
1849 shipwreck 1		103	133	245	2,661.4 ($83,200)
1849 shipwreck 2		30	30	102	359.6 ($11,200)
1850.1		62	76	145	1,733.2 ($59,200)
1850.4		72	87	244	3,531 ($121,000)
1851.1		16	16	21	409 ($13,400)
1851.2		23	29	117	6,660.5 ($218,000)
1851.4		55	473	537	3,517.7 ($115,000)
1852.2		89	107	416	13,172.9 ($425,000)
1852.3		6	6	15	160 ($5,170)
1852.5		6	8	12	391 ($12,600)
1854.1		45	82	237	4,075.6 ($128,000)
	1858.10.15	12	30	86	—
	1859.6.25–26	44	73	382	—
	1859.6.25–26 w/o subunits	99	146	—	—
	1860 #1 (i3.29)	37	46	315	—
	1860 #1 (i3.29) w/o subunits	3	3	—	—
	1862 #2	16	16	—	—
Total (with subunits)		**4,104 (3,872)**	**12,860 (11,082)**	**24,984**	—
Total with fixed price (and subunits)		**3,236 (3,122)**	**10,368 (8,755)**	**19,509**	**217,557.3 ($7,090,000) (215,044.4) ($7,010,000)**
	Total with bids (and subunits)	**1,093 (975)**	**2,990 (2,825)**	**6,919**	—

Average fixed price, *monme* (dollars)		Total winning bids, *monme* (dollars)	Average winning bid, *monme* (dollars)	
per item	per subunit		per item	per subunit
14.7 ($459)	7.80 ($244)	—	—	—
32.5 ($1,020)	9.51 ($297)	—	—	—
13.3 ($417)	7.00 ($219)	—	—	—
4.59 ($179)	3.80 ($148)	—	—	—
34.2 ($1,070)	12.0 ($374)	—	—	—
2.68 ($84)	2.58 ($81)	—	—	—
18.7 ($584)	12.2 ($382)	—	—	—
18.6 ($581)	9.24 ($289)	—	—	—
25.1 ($783)	15.0 ($469)	—	—	—
12.7 ($396)	9.03 ($282)	—	—	—
12.0 ($374)	9.30 ($291)	—	—	—
36.5 ($1,140)	25.7 ($803)	—	—	—
63.5 ($1,980)	19.9 ($621)	—	—	—
35.3 ($1,100)	16.5 ($515)	—	—	—
20.4 ($636)	10.8 ($339)	—	—	—
37.6 ($1,180)	10.7 ($335)	—	—	—
19.4 ($606)	13.3 ($417)	—	—	—
20.0 ($625)	10.9 ($339)	—	—	—
12.0 ($375)	3.53 ($110)	—	—	—
22.8 ($779)	12.0 ($408)	—	—	—
40.6 ($1,390)	14.5 ($494)	—	—	—
25.6 ($836)	19.5 ($637)	—	—	—
230 ($7,520)	56.9 ($1,860)	—	—	—
7.44 ($243)	6.55 ($214)	—	—	—
123 ($3,970)	31.7 ($1,020)	—	—	—
26.7 ($861)	10.7 ($344)	—	—	—
48.9 ($1,580)	32.6 ($1,050)	—	—	—
49.7 ($1,560)	17.2 ($538)	—	—	—
—	—	2,220.96 ($64,800)	74.0 ($2,160)	25.8 ($754)
—	—	11,722.9 ($344,000)	161 ($4,710)	30.7 ($900)
—	—	17,179.45 ($504,000)	118 ($3,450)	—
—	—	2,992.2 ($83,000)	65.0 ($1,800)	9.50 ($263)
—	—	337.9 ($9,370)	113 ($3,120)	—
—	—	1,418.06 ($36,800)	88.6 ($2,300)	—
—	—	—	—	—
21.0 ($684)	**11.0 ($359)**	—	—	—
—	—	**205,870.81 ($6,360,000)** **(186,935.4) ($5,810,000)**	**68.9 ($2,130)**	**27.0 ($840)**

period from 1803 to 1862. The numbers are based on the surviving *negumichō* (price-negotiation ledgers), *shojaku motochō* (fixed-price ledgers), *kenchō* (inspection notebooks), and *rakusatsuchō* (bid ledgers).[62] Only bound volumes have been included for analysis. Other types of printed and manuscript materials, including single-sheet prints, ephemera, and albums of various sorts, are excluded. These other materials were imported in bulk, sometimes by the hundreds, and appear alongside books in the *shojaku motochō*. Single ships regularly arrived with hundreds of copies of items including the *Thousand-Character Classic* (*Qianzi wen*), *The Hundred Surnames* (*Bai jia xing*), or reproductions of stone inscriptions in small albums or single-sheet impressions. Not only do these materials follow different pricing conventions—they are often very inexpensive, given their slight format—but they are also not books, and my analysis is concerned only with imported books.

To account for variation in size, which ranges from single fascicles to monumental compendia in hundreds of volumes, the table gives averages not just per item but also per subunit, typically a folding case (*tō* 套) or satchel (*hō* 包). (Larger works were usually divided into multiple cases containing several bound volumes each, and the number of cases is generally recorded in the price documents.) For titles in a single volume or multiple volumes not divided into cases, the number of items and number of subunits are the same. Ideally, it would be possible to use the individual volume as the subunit across all imported titles, but the number of volumes is rarely recorded for larger works.

Table 1.3 shows that average titles were not as expensive as the selections in tables 1.1 and 1.2. In fact, *all* of the selected titles in the preceding tables exceed the average fixed price of 21.0 *monme* ($684). At the same time, it is seen that the price increases incurred at auction for the selections in table 1.1 were hardly out of the ordinary. The price of the average item more than tripled at auction, rising to 68.9 *monme* ($2,130), while the numbers adjusted per unit still more than doubled, increasing from 11.0 *monme* ($359) to 27.0 *monme* ($840). Viewed in absolute terms,

62. As noted earlier, these documents are transcribed in Ōba, *Tōsen mochiwatarisho*, 453–656. The entries in the *shojaku motochō*, which Ōba transcribed from the copies at the Nagasaki City Museum, were supplemented and occasionally emended using those in the Waseda University Library collection.

68.9 *monme* per item may not approach the sums paid at auction for the works in table 1.1, but it remains a sizable amount. The figure, moreover, does not include a number of additional surcharges and fees that were added to the total, including brokerage commissions, packaging and shipping costs, and other administrative charges that were paid to the Customs Hall. These expenses, which were ordinarily recorded at the end of the *shojaku motochō*, routinely ran to between 30 and 50 percent of an item's fixed price. In light of this, it is safe to say that prices had roughly tripled by the time books emerged from auction in Nagasaki.

As books traveled onward from there and were dispersed across Japan, prices were rarely documented in bulk, and information must for the most part be cobbled together from disparate sources. One valuable exception is a set of notes the bookseller Kawachiya Kihē scrawled hastily on the back of the pages of a noh libretto at several auctions in Kyoto and his home city of Osaka in 1831 and 1832. These provide one of the only windows onto regional auctions of Chinese books, recording the titles of books along with the number of copies, the name of the winning bidder, and the amount of the successful bid. In total, the document provides price information for nearly two thousand items and points to the participation of no fewer than sixty-eight different booksellers.[63]

Kawachiya's notes make it possible to trace titles across three different stages—initial price-fixing, primary auction in Nagasaki, and secondary auction in Kyoto and Osaka—and to view the price increase incurred at each step, at least for the relatively small subset of titles for which data is available at all three stages. Table 1.4 traces the progress of a selection of titles from each of the four branches (*sibu*) according to which Chinese books were traditionally classified—classics (*jing*), histories (*shi*), masters (*zi*), and collections (*ji*)—as well as a substantial selection of fiction in both the vernacular and classical registers. The years for which data is available at each stage vary, but the inflation-adjusted dollar equivalents in parentheses allow for diachronic comparison. These

63. *Shinto Tōhon-ichi hikaechō*, in Yayoshi, *Mikan shiryō ni yoru Nihon shuppan bunka*, 2:343–404. A brief description of the document appears in Yayoshi, *Mikan shiryō ni yoru Nihon shuppan bunka*, 8:480, while a list of the entries by title is included in Yayoshi Mitsunaga, *Yayoshi Mitsunaga chosakushū* (Nichigai asoshiētsu, 1980–83), 3:272.

Table 1.4 Fixed Prices and Winning Bids for Selected Imported Titles, 1803–62

Title	Fixed price, 1803–54, *monme* (dollars)			
	copies	min.	avg.	max.
CLASSICS				
The Thirteen Classics (various editions)	21	50 ($1,560)	**145 ($4,800)**	250 ($8,580)
Peiwen yunfu 佩文韻府	9	400 ($14,500)	**772 ($26,200)**	1,200 ($39,300)
Kangxi zidian 康熙字典	133	35 ($1,250)	**47.2 ($1,550)**	60 ($2,010)
HISTORIES				
Dynastic histories 廿一史 (various editions)	16	200 ($6,250)	**494 ($16,600)**	1,180 ($36,900)
Siku quanshu zongmu tiyao 四庫全書總目提要	8	180 ($5,630)	**353 ($11,000)**	450 ($14,100)
Lienü zhuan 列女傳	2	2 ($63)	**2 ($63)**	2 ($63)
MASTERS				
Guangqun fangpu 廣羣芳譜	16	60 ($1,880)	**67.5 ($2,140)**	70 ($2,410)
Taiping yulan 太平御覧	1	270 ($8,440)	**270 ($8,440)**	270 ($8,440)
Rizhi lu 日知錄	46	12 ($375)	**14.6 ($462)**	20 ($654)
Tianzhong ji 天中記	1	40 ($1,250)	**40 ($1,250)**	40 ($1,250)
Jieziyuan huapu 芥子園畫譜	29	16 ($581)	**24.5 ($773)**	40 ($1,250)
COLLECTIONS				
Zhibuzuzhai congshu 知不足齋叢書	3	250 ($7,810)	**267 ($8,330)**	300 ($9,380)
Wang Yangming quanji 王陽明全集	31	40 ($1,380)	**44.7 ($1,430)**	56 ($1,750)
Dongpo quanji 東坡全集	4	45 ($1,410)	**45 ($1,440)**	45 ($1,550)
Quan Tang shi 全唐詩	2	90 ($2,810)	**90 ($2,810)**	90 ($2,810)
FICTION				
Taiping guangji 太平廣記	3	30 ($938)	**43.3 ($1,350)**	50 ($1,560)
Shuihu zhuan 水滸傳 (various recensions)	6	14 ($438)	**14.8 ($495)**	15 ($516)
Shuihu houzhuan 水滸後傳	—	—	—	—
Sanguozhi 三國志	2	22 ($710)	**22 ($710)**	22 ($710)
Jingu qiguan 今古奇觀	16	6 ($188)	**6.94 ($229)**	7.5 ($254)
Yetan suilu 夜譚隨錄	11	10 ($313)	**10 ($314)**	10 ($334)
Liaozhai zhiyi 聊齋誌異	2	12 ($376)	**12 ($376)**	12 ($376)
Xihu jiahua 西湖佳話	—	—	—	—
Jin Ping Mei 金瓶梅	1	6.5 ($229)	**6.5 ($229)**	6.5 ($229)
Hongloumeng 紅樓夢	5	3 ($108)	**4.2 ($138)**	5 ($161)
Zhiwen lu 咫聞錄	20	3 ($102)	**3 ($102)**	3 ($103)
Rulin waishi 儒林外史	2	5 ($156)	**5 ($156)**	5 ($156)
Xieduo 諧鐸	—	—	—	—
Jinghua yuan 鏡花緣	—	—	—	—

Winning bid at Nagasaki auctions, 1843–62, *monme* (dollars)				Winning bid at Osaka-Kyoto auctions, 1831–32, *monme* (dollars)			
copies	min.	avg.	max.	copies	min.	avg.	max.
11	40.5 ($1,270)	**324 ($10,100)**	461 ($14,400)	15	300 ($10,100)	**729 ($24,300)**	1,150 ($38,300)
1	1,710 ($51,600)	**1,820 ($55,700)**	2,180 ($68,100)	1	2,100.9 ($69,900)	**2,100.9 ($69,900)**	2,100.9 ($69,900)
9	74.6 ($2,180)	**115 ($3,510)**	230 ($7,190)	19	75 ($2,500)	**112 ($3,740)**	215 ($7,160)
2	520 ($18,600)	**975 ($30,300)**	1,430 ($42,000)	3	1,050 ($35,300)	**1,720 ($57,500)**	3,000 ($99,800)
9	520 ($16,300)	**603 ($18,700)**	856 ($26,800)	2	800 ($26,800)	**930 ($31,100)**	1,060 ($35,300)
1	36 ($1,060)	**36 ($1,060)**	36 ($1,060)	16	7 ($233)	**63.9 ($2,130)**	83 ($2,760)
14	90.1 ($2,820)	**121 ($3,760)**	160 ($5,000)	8	160 ($5,320)	**175 ($5,830)**	220 ($7,390)
1	570 ($17,800)	**570 ($17,800)**	570 ($17,800)	1	860 ($28,900)	**860 ($28,900)**	860 ($28,900)
10	38.5 ($1,200)	**47.4 ($1,430)**	80 ($2,220)	27	42 ($1,400)	**67.2 ($2,240)**	120 ($3,990)
1	58 ($1,510)	**58 ($1,510)**	58 ($1,510)	2	120 ($3,990)	**127.5 ($4,240)**	135 ($4,490)
24	60.7 ($1,900)	**69.2 ($2,130)**	100 ($3,130)	12	77 ($2,590)	**111 ($3,700)**	135 ($4,490)
4	345 ($10,400)	**399 ($12,300)**	550 ($17,200)	2	580 ($19,500)	**720 ($24,100)**	860 ($28,600)
22	103 ($3,220)	**133 ($4,000)**	500 ($13,000)	9	91 ($3,030)	**126 ($4,210)**	200 ($6,660)
6	50 ($1,560)	**245 ($7,270)**	386 ($11,300)	15	130 ($4,330)	**170 ($5,670)**	176 ($5,860)
—	—	—	—	2	430 ($14,300)	**515 ($17,100)**	600 ($20,000)
1	45.6 ($1,430)	**45.6 ($1,430)**	45.6 ($1,430)	1	100 ($3,330)	**100 ($3,330)**	100 ($3,330)
—	—	—	—	5 (70-ch.)	30 ($998)	**36 ($1,200)**	43 ($1,430)
				3 (120-ch.)	50 ($1,680)	**72 ($2,400)**	86 ($2,860)
				16 (unspec.)	12 ($399)	**25.9 ($867)**	30 ($998)
—	—	—	—	3	13 ($433)	**17.7 ($588)**	24 ($799)
1	34.5 ($1,080)	**34.5 ($1,080)**	34.5 ($1,080)	6	35 ($1,160)	**47.5 ($1,580)**	80 ($2,660)
23	11.8 ($369)	**14.0 ($438)**	20 ($625)	8	17 ($566)	**18.7 ($622)**	21.5 ($716)
14	11.3 ($353)	**15.4 ($483)**	25.8 ($806)	2	27 ($907)	**27 ($907)**	27 ($907)
—	—	—	—	8	29 ($965)	**36 ($1,200)**	43 ($1,430)
15	6.3 ($197)	**6.3 ($197)**	6.3 ($197)	9	10 ($336)	**11.9 ($397)**	16 ($532)
2	35 ($1,090)	**35 ($1,090)**	35 ($1,090)	5	2 ($67)	**21.1 ($713)**	30 ($1,010)
—	—	—	—	2	25 ($832)	**25 ($832)**	25 ($832)
—	—	—	—	5	20 ($666)	**20 ($666)**	20 ($666)
—	—	—	—	—	—	—	—
—	5.6 ($175)	**6.05 ($189)**	6.5 ($203)	—	—	—	—
—	—	—	—	7	14 ($466)	**19.6 ($654)**	21.5 ($716)

are calculated based on the specific year of importation of each copy and, for the aggregate figures, as weighted averages.

Several of the titles appear multiple times, in multiple years, across all three stages. The relative lack of variance in fixed prices offers evidence of stability and consistency in the determination of prices over time, suggesting that precedent, more than market forces, was the decisive factor as officials negotiated prices with Chinese merchants. Unsurprisingly, the Nagasaki auctions, where the market exerted more power through competitive bidding, introduced more volatility and fluctuation. The Kangxi Dictionary, which was imported almost continuously during the sixty-year period covered, affords the clearest view of both the stability of fixed prices and the variability of the market. The fixed prices oscillate within a narrow range of 35 to 60 *monme* ($1,250–$2,010), with the majority of copies clustered within 3 or 4 *monme* (~$100) of the average price of 47.2 *monme* ($1,550). It is only reaching back to 1784 (table 1.2) that we find a significantly higher price, 114 *monme* ($4,410); however, as discussed, this figure likely included an unknown premium on the fixed price.

At auction in Nagasaki, by contrast, prices varied widely. One copy of the Kangxi Dictionary was bid up by 283 percent in 1843, while another the very next year incurred a relatively modest increase of 80 percent. Conservatism in price negotiations assured the Customs Hall hefty profits in the aggregate, as can be easily seen by comparing the average fixed prices and average winning bids in both tables 1.3 and 1.4; auction almost always resulted in significantly higher prices. That said, reliance on precedent could at times work the other way, as can be gleaned from the figures for *Taiping guangji*, where the maximum fixed price was 50 *monme* ($1,560) but the highest winning bid only 45.6 *monme* ($1,430). These amounts are for the same copy, which arrived in 1844 and was auctioned in 1845. Still, even in this instance the Customs Hall came out ahead, as the fees assessed on the item came to 35 percent, bringing the total cost paid by the winning bidder to more than 60 *monme* ($1,880).

The far-right column in table 1.4 carries us onward to the last of the three phases, the regional auctions documented by Kawachiya Kihē. Some of the more expensive items fetched in the 300 to 500 *monme* range ($9,980–$16,800) and even, from time to time, well beyond, as exemplified by the winning bid of 3 *kan* ($99,800) for a Wanli (1572–1620) edition of the dynastic histories (*Wanli nianyi shi*). On the whole, the prices for a given title tend higher than at Nagasaki auction, but not exorbitantly so, especially factoring in the fees that Nagasaki bidders were required to pay.

Turning our attention to the bottom of the table, it is possible to make some observations about fiction specifically. The most immediately obvious point is that fiction was relatively inexpensive compared to other categories, with most works having fixed prices in the 5 to 15 *monme* range ($163–$489), only occasionally rising significantly higher. By contrast, the average for all imported books in the table is 21.0 *monme* ($684). Similarly, after auction in Nagasaki, fiction rose to the 10 to 35 *monme* range ($326–$1,140), while the average title across all categories fetched 68.9 *monme* ($2,130). The relative slightness of fiction in terms of its physical format may account for some of the difference, but it is still evident that fiction, as a less prestigious form of literature, was valued less than other genres.

Nevertheless, viewed in absolute terms even fiction can hardly be described as inexpensive. This is intimated by the present-day dollar equivalents, which begin in the hundreds at the fixed-price stage and rise into the high hundreds and thousands after auction in Osaka and Kyoto. Most readers could hardly imagine paying such sums for ordinary books today. Nor, for that matter, would Japanese readers have paid anything approaching this for domestic fiction. Typical titles of Japanese pictorial fiction sold for just a few coppers per volume (~$2–$4) into the early nineteenth century, while even somewhat later editions on high-quality paper with elaborate polychrome covers—much fancier than any imported edition of Chinese fiction—fetched 1 to 1.5 *monme* ($35–$52) for multiple volumes bound as one.[64] Which is to say, already at the first stage of the importation process, after fixed prices had been negotiated at the Customs Hall, Chinese fiction was many times more expensive than deluxe editions of domestic fiction.

There is, as mentioned, a paucity of information pertaining to the price of books in China before the modern era. That said, what evidence there is does not contradict the natural assumption that ordinary Chinese fiction would be less expensive in China than deluxe Japanese editions were in Japan.[65] In other words, at the same time that fixed prices

64. Utano, "Edo jidai no hon no nedan kō," 13.

65. See, for example, Shen, "Ming dai fangke tushu," 101–18.

underestimated the domestic Japanese market, assuring great profits for the Customs Hall, they were also many times higher than what those titles would have brought in China, assuring even greater profits for the Chinese merchants. Unsurprisingly, given the abundance of Chinese books at the point of origin and their scarcity in Japan, there was an enormous gulf between the market price for Chinese books in China versus that in Japan. Fixed prices occupied a middle point that was calibrated to assure a mutually beneficial arrangement. If the data were available, we might imagine an additional column on the left-hand side of table 1.4 carrying the story back to its origin, showing the purchase prices of titles in China. As it is, we observe prices rising from already expensive fixed prices to amounts at auction that were astronomical by the standards of the domestic book market.

Individual Buyers and Chinese Books on the Open Market

Following books onward, we at last arrive at sales to individual readers and collectors. Here, information about prices must be pieced together as best as possible from scattered sources. One relatively substantial record from the late seventeenth century is a list of titles that the Confucian scholar Kinoshita Jun'an, personal tutor to the shogun Tsunayoshi, purchased from the bookseller Tōhon'ya Seibē in 1687.[66] A later, more extensive record is provided by the daily calendar of the Sinologist Sawada Issai, who operated a major Kyoto bookstore under the name Fūgetsu Shōzaemon. Issai's calendar survives for a sixteen-month period between 1772 and 1773, offering a window onto his business operations, including the sale of many imported books.[67]

Jun'an's purchases were relatively modest in size, ranging from two to eighteen volumes. Nevertheless, they were by no means inexpensive:

66. Several titles are mentioned in Kinoshita Kazuo, "Kyōikushi to rinri: Edo jidai shoki rinri ni shuzai shite," *Kyōikugaku kenkyū* 21, no. 6 (January 1955): 15. The manuscript is reproduced in its entirety in Ōba, *Kanseki yunyū no bunkashi*, 259–61.

67. Yayoshi, *Yayoshi Mitsunaga chosakushū*, 3:252–53.

many were purchased for 5.5 *ryō* ($18,300), many more for 3 *ryō* ($10,000), and a few lesser works for around 1 to 2 *ryō* ($3,330–$6,670). Issai's sales include some heftier titles that fetched eye-popping sums, such as a copy of *Tongzhitang jingjie*, a 640-volume early Qing collection of classical commentaries, that sold for 3.6 *kanme* ($117,500). A pair of prefectural gazetteers went for 150 *monme* ($4,900) each; *True Records of Zhu Xi* (*Zhuzi shiji*), a twelve-volume set, fetched 1 *ryō* ($2,150)—a relatively modest price, perhaps because the title was available in a domestic edition. A copy of the Five Classics in a thirty-volume Imperial Academy edition (*jianben*) sold for 3.5 *ryō* ($7,540). Some prices reflect a considerable markup from the fixed-price and auction stages, as with the botanical treatise *Guangqun fangpu*, which at 30 *ryō* ($64,600) brought in more than nine times the 200 *monme* ($6,530) Issai had paid for it.[68] An even more extreme example is Chen Yaowen's *Tianzhong ji*, which he sold for 1.5 *ryō* ($3,230), a nearly seventy-fold increase on the modest 1737 purchase price of 68 coppers ($38).

The rare-book bubble only expanded as the eighteenth century drew to a close. Observers began to note the rise of a new breed of obsessive collector—typically daimyō and wealthy urban merchants—who sought books for rarity's sake and were willing to pay any price necessary to add to their collections. Wang Peng, a Chinese merchant-literatus who made several visits to Nagasaki in the 1780s, marveled at well-heeled collectors who "do not begrudge even the highest prices and buy them in bulk to wrap nicely and store away in a quantity that would make an ox break out in sweat and the house-eaves groan."[69] If ordinary books were expensive, genuinely rare or out-of-print works could fetch truly amazing prices. The physician and writer Tachibana Nankei gives the example of a copy of *Futian ji*, a posthumous collection by the poet-calligrapher Wen Zhengming (1470–1559), initially acquired in 1797 by a bookseller for 18 *monme* ($659) that he turned around and sold for 35 *ryō* ($78,700), outstripping even the profit margins enjoyed by Issai.[70] Even chance

68. Yayoshi, *Mikan shiryō ni yoru Nihon shuppan bunka*, 2:137.

69. Quoted in Hedberg, "Chinese Afterlives of Coxinga and the Forty-Seven Rōnin," 44.

70. Nankei's dating may be slightly off, as the Nagasaki documents record a copy of *Futian ji* as having arrived in 1798.

acquisitions could turn out to be savvy investments. A telling anecdote concerns not a book but a painting of a deer by the Fujianese artist Yang Zhou (fl. mid-eighteenth century). The item initially attracted little interest, but with the arrival of the miscellany *Zhiwen lu* (a particularly common and relatively inexpensive title, as seen in table 1.4), which features an entry on Yang Zhou that specifically mentions his paintings of deer, the buyer suddenly found himself with a treasure on his hands, and people thronged to see the painting.[71]

Examples like these illustrate why booksellers were willing to pay the high markups incurred at auction, as well as the benefits of a guild system that prevented auction prices from rising higher. The costs to booksellers were negligible compared to what could be obtained for the same items on the open market, and a single *Futian ji* could easily bring in more than the average Edoite would see in an entire year. Such sums naturally provided motivation for forgers and frauds. Around the turn of the century, Nankei described a recent catalog of dubious titles—many of which he surmised to be fakes—that one Chinese merchant was willing to import upon request for the right price.[72]

A few decades later, there is anecdotal evidence that the market had begun to cool. One incident involves an auction initiated by the celebrated author Kyokutei Bakin, who in 1836, ailing, losing his eyesight, and in desperate need of cash, was moved to sell off nearly forty boxes of books containing some seven hundred titles from his personal library. These included many Chinese titles. Given his fame, the auction, held at a bookstore near Nihonbashi in Edo, attracted a great number of booksellers who, in Bakin's colorful phrase, swarmed about "like ants." He looked on in horror as attendees tussled over items, even ripping one book apart in the process. However, this chaotic scene did not translate into high prices, and Bakin's Chinese books in particular sold at a significant loss. A copy of the hefty astrological compendium *Xieji bianfang shu* purchased from a Kyoto bookseller for 2.625 *ryō* ($5,660) sold for 85 *monme* ($2,980). The collection of vernacular tales *Slapping the Table in Amazement* (*Pai'an jingqi*), which he had bought for 2.5 *bu* ($1,350), sold for just 2 *shu* ($269), while a

71. *Momokusa*, in *Momokusa, Wagayadogusa, Guzasso, Shōtei manpitsu, Kōkyōrō manpitsu*, in *NZT* series 3, 9:132–33.

72. *Hokusō sadan*, in *NZT* series 2, 15:326–27.

copy of *Wondrous Tales New and Old* (*Jingu qiguan*) purchased for 200 *hiki* ($625) sold for 1 *bu* ($539), a relatively modest loss, but this in spite of Bakin having repackaged it in two custom-made cases at his own expense.[73]

Peter Kornicki cites this auction as evidence of a changing market, perhaps the result of a rise in supply of Chinese books or perhaps reflecting a decline in demand.[74] Certainly the steady stream of books coming through Nagasaki led to a cumulative increase in supply, and we can trace a decline in some market prices relative to the late eighteenth century. However, Bakin's sale came at a particularly inopportune moment, at the tail end of the Tenpō famine and a period of economic crisis, and we know little of the condition of the items in his library. Moreover, he expressed equal disappointment with the prices received for his Japanese books, among which many treasured volumes were treated "like wastepaper." Indeed, editions of Chinese fiction imported just a few years before and after Bakin's auction—as reflected in the prices paid at the auctions attended by Kawachiya Kihē in 1831 and 1832 and the prices set at the Nagasaki Customs Hall from 1839 onward—fetched much more robust sums even before they reached the open market. This includes *Wondrous Tales New and Old*, several copies of which were bought by bookstores in Kyoto and Osaka, and all of which sold for more than Bakin received for his copy. It is likely that, then as now, customers selling items back to retailers did so at a heavy premium. Booksellers sold high and bought low, and Bakin, in his particularly desperate straits, had no choice but to accept what he was offered.

A more significant decline in market prices seems to have come in the waning years of the Tokugawa shogunate. Writing in the mid-1850s, one observer noted that bookstores that had sold Chinese books just a decade earlier were instead selling domestically published sentimental fiction (*ninjōbon*). A bookseller informant explained the shift in simple economic terms, observing that while Chinese books had sold briskly into the 1830s, contemporary readers were only interested in "erotic prints and picture-books." Slackening demand and increased availability had

73. Bakin describes the auction and his losses in a letter to Tonomura Jōsai dated 1836.10.26, transcribed in Shibata Mitsuhiko and Kanda Masayuki, eds., *Bakin shokan shūsei* (Yagi shoten, 2002–2004), 4:225–27.

74. Kornicki, *The Book in Japan*, 177–78.

decreased profits on Chinese books to one-third of those on these other materials. Under the circumstances, it was only natural that many booksellers adjusted their inventory accordingly.[75] However, we must be careful not to confuse profit margins with prices. Sentimental fiction and erotica were not more expensive than Chinese books; they simply offered a better return on investment. Even if imported books were less expensive than in years past—a claim not supported by the limited data from the 1850s included in table 1.3—these figures still translated into considerable sums in the marketplace, and they were not inexpensive relative to domestic titles.

Chinese fiction never achieved the staggering prices recounted by Nankei, but throughout the early modern period it was imported in such small quantities that individual items consistently sold for the equivalent of hundreds or thousands of dollars. Collections like those of Nanpo and Bakin, which included hundreds of Chinese titles, represented enormous investments equivalent to hundreds of thousands of dollars today. And even if an individual title was not prohibitively expensive in and of itself, finding a copy to buy was another matter entirely. Bakin spent years unsuccessfully pursuing his own white whale: a copy of the 120-chapter recension of *The Water Margin*, a work that deeply informed his serialized masterwork *The Chronicle of the Eight Dogs of the Satomi of Southern Kazusa* (*Nansō Satomi hakkenden*, 1814–42).[76] When in the 1830s he finally tracked one down—a very poor impression at that—he happily forked over 2.5 *ryō* ($5,210), only to be forced to sell it off a decade later at a third of the price.[77] Buyers could of course seek out Chinese fiction in domestic editions, and before acquiring the 120-chapter recension Bakin owned the two available *wakokubon* editions of *The Water Margin*, which together reproduced the first twenty chapters.[78] But how many Chinese texts, and how much Chinese fiction in particular, were reproduced in such editions? This is one of the central questions taken up in the next chapter.

75. Hirose Kyokusō, *Kyūkeisōdō zuihitsu* (1855–57), in *ZNZT* 2:236–37.

76. Kanda Masayuki, "*Suikoden* no shohon to Bakin," in Suwa Haruo and Takada Mamoru, eds., *Fukkō-suru Hakkenden* (Bensei shuppan, 2008), 249–86.

77. Kanda, "*Suikoden* no shohon," 280, 282.

78. *Kyokutei zōsho mokuroku*, in Hattori Hitoshi, ed., *Bakin kenkyū shiryō shūsei* (Kuresu shuppan, 2007), 5:813.

CHAPTER 2

Wakokubon: *Chinese Books Printed in Japan*

In the preceding chapter it was shown that while Chinese books flowed quickly and in great quantities into early modern Japan, they often remained prohibitively expensive or nearly impossible to find for purchase. Enter the domestic reprint editions known as *wakokubon kanseki* ("Chinese books printed in Japan"), or *wakokubon* for short. *Wakokubon* brought down prices, increased accessibility, and facilitated the diffusion of Chinese texts. But how large a portion of imported texts was reprinted in such editions? What kinds of texts were most likely to be reprinted? How well was fiction represented? In other words, what selection of the Chinese literary imagination lay within easy reach of Japanese readers, and not hidden away in rare imported editions like the 120-chapter recension of *The Water Margin* that eluded Bakin for years? These are among the questions I will seek to answer in this chapter.

Before proceeding, it is important to pause to address the problem of terminology. A broad division is often made between *wahon* ("Japanese books," particularly those bound using traditional techniques) and *wakokubon* ("books printed in Japan" or, more precisely, "books [printed from woodblocks] carved in Japan"). On the surface, the distinction is an odd one. A significant portion of traditional Japanese books were woodblock-printed, and surely virtually all of these were prepared using blocks carved in Japan. Taken literally, not only do the two categories fail the test of mutual exclusivity, but they appear to overlap extensively.

In practice, however, the key lies in the added emphasis, and implicit contrast, contained in the character *koku* 刻 ("to carve"). On one side are Japanese books, on the other merely Japanese-*carved* books. Just as the words "American car" might refer to a Ford, Chevy, or Cadillac but not a Toyota, "American-*manufactured* car," at least with the added emphasis, seems unnatural unless singling out a vehicle that is only *made* in America—say, a Toyota assembled in Texas. The addition of the character *koku* serves a similar contrastive function. *Wahon* identifies books in traditional format with Japanese content, whereas *wakokubon*, by emphasizing the place of carving and not the content, is ordinarily reserved for domestic editions of foreign content—books that may have been made in Japan but were not Japanese in their ultimate origin. The present study uses the term in this sense, and generally in reference to Japanese editions of Chinese texts in particular, omitting the largely superfluous descriptor *kanseki*, as nearly all domestically printed foreign content was of Chinese origin.[1]

The history of *wakokubon* is in many ways the history of Japanese printing itself. After all, even into the 1600s, printing was reserved for texts with religious or cultural authority, and for much of Japan's history such authority was possessed mainly by texts from the continent. Indeed, Japan's earliest datable printed texts are of continental origin. Produced in the 760s, the *hyakumantō darani* ("dhāraṇī in one million pagodas") consisted of spells printed on narrow slips of paper that were then rolled up and placed inside small wooden pagodas. One million were ordered by Empress Shōtoku for distribution to temples across Japan, with those actually produced likely numbering in the hundreds of thousands.[2] Although they were not books, the *hyakumantō darani* at least fulfill the *wakoku* ("printed in Japan") half of *wakokubon*.

Following the return of the last Japanese mission to the Tang court in 839, there began a long period during which there was no formal con-

1. For overviews of *wakokubon* history, see Nakamura Yukihiko, "Wakokubon: kanseki no denrai to wakoku," in *Chūgoku bunka sōsho* 9: *Nihon kangaku* (Taishūkan, 1968), 260–71; and Ōba and Wang, *Tenseki*, 74–80. Isaka Kiyonobu's overview of the *wakokubon* editions in the collection of the National Diet Library in Tokyo also includes a short, accessible introduction to *wakokubon* history. Isaka, "Kokuritsu kokkai toshokan shozō no wakokubon kanseki gaikan," *Sankō shoshi kenkyū* 43 (September 1993): 1–17.

2. Peter Kornicki, "The *Hyakumantō Darani* and the Origins of Printing in Eighth-Century Japan," *International Journal of Asian Studies* 9, no. 1 (2012): 56.

tact with the continent. Nevertheless, there was an extensive inventory of Chinese texts that had already been imported. These were by no means limited to Buddhist texts, and a great many secular titles are recorded in Fujiwara Sukeyo's *Nihon-koku genzaisho mokuroku* (Catalog of Books Extant in Japan, likely compiled by 891), the oldest extant catalog of Chinese books in Japan.[3] However, Japanese printing continued to be confined to Buddhist materials through the Kamakura period, and the site of production was limited to temple complexes. Foremost among these was Kōfukuji, which published editions that later came to be referred to as "Kasuga editions" (*Kasuga-ban*) after the practice of presenting copies at the Kasuga Shrine, which was, like Kōfukuji, a tutelary religious institution of the Fujiwara clan. The earliest of these editions, the *Discourse on the Establishment of Consciousness-Only* (*Cheng weishi lun*), dates to 1088. Efforts followed at other Nara temples, including Hōryūji, Tōdaiji, and Saidaiji. Although the content remained religious, these were editions published for actual reading, not devotional practices such as those for which the *hyakumantō darani* were produced. As such, they can be seen to pave the way for secular texts. Still, more than two centuries would pass before the appearance of the first secular *wakokubon*.

As printing spread to other temples in Nara, Kyoto, and beyond, Zen monks at the Gozan ("five mountain") temples in Kamakura and Kyoto began to produce editions of Song and Yuan texts, known as "Gozan editions" (*Gozan-ban*), the earliest extant title being a 1287 edition of *Chanmen baoxun* (J. *Zenmon hōkun*), a collection of Zen teachings compiled by Dahui Zonggao and Zhu'an Shigui in the twelfth century. The first secular titles appeared a few decades later. Attesting to Zen interest in poetry, the earliest such book that survives is a collection of verse by the Tang recluse-poet Han Shan prepared in 1325, followed several decades later by the poetry manual *Shifa yuanliu* (J. *Shihō genryū*, 1359). The oldest Confucian text printed in Japan, an edition of *Lunyu jijie* (J. *Rongo shikkai*), was published in short order in 1364 by an otherwise obscure figure under the pseudonym Dōyū Koji in the city of Sakai.

3. The catalog also reveals the huge number of titles that have been lost today, with only one in ten extant. See Yajima Genryō, *Nihon-koku genzaisho mokuroku: shūshō to kenkyū* (Kyūko shoin, 1984).

Just as the content itself was of continental origin, much of the technical expertise for *wakokubon* editions was provided by skilled engravers who sought refuge in Japan during the turmoil of the late Yuan. Two of the most prolific, whose names are attached to numerous Gozan editions, were Chen Mengrong and Yu Liangfu, through whose labor texts such as the Tang primer *Mengqiu* and the poems of Du Fu were printed.[4] In general the practice was to reprint books using a process known as *kabusebori*, or *fukkoku*, in which a copy of the title to be reproduced was disassembled, the unfolded pages pasted upside-down on new blocks, and these blocks then carved as they would be for an ordinary woodblock-printed title. The same technique was later used to prolong the life of domestic editions after the blocks had begun to wear—or, less scrupulously, to prepare pirate editions. By sacrificing a single copy, a publisher could produce a run of hundreds of nearly identical reprints. With the arrival of a second wave of Chinese artisan-émigrés in the early Ming, the production of *wakokubon* editions continued unabated. Religious texts continued to constitute the bulk of production, but it has been estimated that by the end of the Muromachi period seventy-two secular titles in ninety-three different editions had been reprinted.[5]

The half-century from the 1590s to the 1640s witnessed a flourishing of innovative printing techniques, including the use of movable type to prepare around 400 known editions. Referred to today as *kokatsuji-ban* ("old movable-type editions") to distinguish them from later efforts, these include many Chinese texts that were reprinted using this new technology instead of the practice of *kabusebori*. Among the most famous *kokatsuji-ban* is a body of several dozen works known as Saga-bon, the product of a collaboration between the calligrapher Hon'ami Kōetsu and the publisher Suminokura Soan. These editions, prepared in Saga on the outskirts of Kyoto, were printed in limited runs using wooden movable type and are noted for their high production values. Although the Saga-bon are best known for reproducing Japanese classics, including literary landmarks such as *The Tales of Ise* (*Ise monogatari*) and Kenkō's *Essays in*

4. Kawase Kazuma, *Gozan-ban no kenkyū* (Nihon koshosekishō kyōkai [Antiquarian Booksellers Association of Japan], 1970).

5. Estimates by Nagasawa Kikuya, broken down by the four branches, are cited in Ōba, *Edo jidai ni okeru Chūgoku bunka juyō no kenkyū*, 15.

Idleness (*Tsurezuregusa*), they also include a Chinese text among their ranks: a 1599 edition of the *Shiji* (Records of the Grand Historian) in fifty volumes, bound in the so-called butterfly style (*detchōsō*). Long identified only tentatively as a Saga-bon, recent scholarship has made a more definitive case for the attribution of this edition.[6]

Although the *Shiji* is the only non-Japanese work known to have been published as a Saga-bon, Chinese texts are well represented among *kokatsuji* editions as a whole. The selection of nearly two hundred titles held by the National Diet Library reveals an almost even split between Japanese and imported texts, including Buddhist materials.[7] Broadly speaking, these movable-type editions fall into three categories: editions produced by temples, government-sponsored editions, and commercial editions. While imported texts are found in all three categories, temple editions are mostly limited to sutras and other Buddhist content and are not discussed further in the present study. Government-sponsored editions include the earliest movable-type editions, which were published at imperial decree. The first of these is an edition of the *Classic of Filial Piety* (*Guwen Xiaojing*) published at the order of Emperor Go-Yōzei in 1593; additional titles were published over the next decade, including the Confucian Four Books and *Kinshūdan*, a collection of Chinese poems compiled by the Zen monk Ten'in Ryūtaku for pedagogical purposes, and one further title appeared in 1621 under Emperor Go-Mizunoo.[8] Beginning in 1599, editions using wooden movable type were produced at the order of Tokugawa Ieyasu, first by the Zen monk San'yō Genkitsu at Enkōji Temple in Fushimi, south of Kyoto, where a set of several hundred thousand individual type pieces was produced for the task, then in Suruga using metal type after Ieyasu's relocation there in 1607. There is a fitting focus on military matters, with the reprinted texts including the *Liutao* (The Six Secret Teachings) and *Sanlüe* (The Three Strategies), then

6. Koakimoto Dan, "Saga-bon *Shiki* [*Shiji*] no shoshiteki kōsatsu," *Hōsei daigaku bungakubu kiyō* 49 (2003): 109–41.

7. Of 192 *kokatsuji* editions in the collections of the National Diet Library, nearly half reproduce imported texts: fifty-two (27 percent) are non-Buddhist Chinese texts, and a further forty-two (22 percent) are Buddhist materials. These figures are based on the catalog entries in Kokuritsu kokkai toshokan toshobu, ed., *Kokuritsu kokkai toshokan shozō kokatsujiban zuroku* (Kokuritsu kokkai toshokan, 1989).

8. See Suzuka Sanshichi, *Chokuhan shūei* (Rinsen shoten, [1930] 1986).

later all of the seven military classics (*wujing qishu*). Other titles were related to philosophy and governance, such as the *Book of Changes* (*Yi jing*), *Essentials of Government of the Zhenguan Era* (*Zhenguan zhengyao*), and *Selected Essentials of Rule* (*Qunshu zhiyao*).[9]

With the emergence of commercial publishing as a viable undertaking, movable-type editions also appeared on the commercial market. In the first decades of the seventeenth century, the Kyoto publisher Baijuken Sukeemon produced editions of around thirty Ming medical texts, including a 1608 annotated edition (based on a Chinese edition from 1586) of *Huangdi neijing Suwen zhuzheng fawei* (J. *Kōtei naikyō Somon chūshō hatsubi*), a commentary on the "Basic Questions" (*Suwen*) section of *The Yellow Emperor's Classic of Medicine* (*Huangdi neijing*).[10] Other publishers undertook editions of literature including the *Wenxuan* (Selections of Refined Literature), the collection of Bai Juyi's verse *Bai-shi wenji*, and, separately, his "Song of Everlasting Sorrow" ("Chang hen ge") and "Ballad of the Pipa" ("Pipa xing"). As can be seen in table 2.1 later in this chapter, fiction was also occasionally published in movable-type editions, but with the exception of Qu You's *New Tales by Lamplight* these likely date to later in the Edo period or even, in one instance, to the Meiji period.

As the commercial market expanded, movable type receded and woodblock-printing reasserted itself for reasons of convenience and economy. Accordingly, *kabusebori* regained its position as the primary technique used to prepare early modern *wakokubon* editions. To add value and enhance usability, it became common to annotate the texts before the blocks were carved, allowing commentary, marginal notes, glosses, reading marks, and other interpretive aids to be "hard-subbed" into the new edition. Such additions were relatively rare in *kokatsuji-ban* and pre-Edo editions. Along with annotation, Japanese editions also typically supplemented their sources with additional paratextual apparatuses including a new title page and colophon. Otherwise, the base text remained more or less identical to the original—although *kabusebori* did result in certain telltale traces (generally only discernable through careful comparison with the original), such as the subtle thickening of lines and other minor distortions.

9. Kawase Kazuma, *Kokatsuji-ban no kenkyū*, 3 vols., rev. ed. (Nihon koshosekishō kyōkai, 1967).

10. Kawase Kazuma, "Baijuken no isho kaihan ni tsuite," *Shoshigaku* 9 (1967): 1–10. See also Nakamura, "Wakokubon: kanseki no denrai to wakoku," 263.

The volume of *wakokubon* editions increased roughly in tandem with the publishing industry as a whole, with notable surges occurring at several points in the Edo period. The number of editions soon surpassed that of the preceding centuries, and as will be examined in detail, the available titles grew more diverse, ranging across all categories of literature. Commercial editions, moreover, were supplemented by official editions known as *kanpan*, the earliest being an edition of the *Liuyu yanyi* (J. *Rikuyu engi*) annotated by Ogyū Sorai. Domains published editions of their own, and from the end of the eighteenth century they were joined by the Shōheikō Academy. Although these official editions generally reproduced texts deemed worthy of propagation by those holding political power, they fed into the commercial market, as commercial publishers were granted permission to reproduce them separately at their own initiative.[11]

Given the scale at which Chinese texts were reproduced, there are many titles that survive only in their *wakokubon* editions, the originals having been lost or fragmented on the continent. These include the tenth-century rhyme guide *Yunjing*, first published in a Japanese edition in 1528, then again in revised form in 1564, and reissued many times subsequently. *Selected Essentials of Rule* (*Qunshu zhiyao*) survives not only in Ieyasu's Suruga edition but in later domainal editions as well. There are also works of fiction that fall into this category, including *A Visit to the Cave of the Immortals* (*Youxianku*, J. *Yūsenkutsu*), first reprinted early in the Edo period, and *The Cup That Reflects the World* (*Zhaoshibei*, J. *Shōseihai*), which was reprinted in 1765.[12]

Many works were preserved inadvertently by historical accident. Publishers had little way of knowing whether a given work had been lost on the continent, and this was not generally among their concerns. Titles were reproduced in commercial editions only with an eye to domestic readers. Nevertheless, certain titles *were* known to survive only in Japan, and in the eighteenth century Japanese Sinologists began to prepare editions of texts including commentaries (sometimes in partial form) on the

11. Kornicki, *The Book in Japan*, 144–45.

12. Both works were republished in China in the twentieth century in Chen Naiqian, ed., *Guyi xiaoshuo congkan* (Haining: Shenchutang, 1929). The collection includes a third title, *Sanguozhi pinghua*, that was preserved in Japan not as a *wakokubon* but in the original Chinese edition.

Five Classics, the *Analects*, the *Mencius*, and the *Classic of Filial Piety*.[13] As seems to have been the hope of many of the editors, copies were then exported back to China, where reactions ranged from over-the-top enthusiasm to skepticism about their textual authenticity. On the whole, however, the response was sufficiently positive that Japanese editions were among those included in the monumental *Siku quanshu* (Complete Writings of the Four Treasuries).[14] The most ambitious Japanese project was carried out between 1799 and 1810—too late for inclusion in the *Siku quanshu*—when Hayashi Jussai used wooden movable type to publish seventeen "lost" titles, mostly from the Tang and Song dynasties, under the title *Anthology of Extant Lost Books* (*Isson sōsho*, Ch. *Yicun congshu*).[15] These, too, were reintroduced to China, where within a few years several of the titles were included in Ruan Yuan's *Siku weishou shumu tiyao* (Overview of Books Not Included in the Four Treasuries, 1822). The collection as a whole was first republished in Shanghai in 1882.[16]

The Accessibility and Reach of Wakokubon *Editions*

My central concern in this chapter is to ascertain the extent to which *wakokubon* made Chinese texts accessible in Japan itself. In converting a single imported copy into a run of hundreds of copies, reprint editions made Chinese texts available to a much larger audience than that which could

13. The texts are Yamanoi Konron (d. 1728), edited by Ogyū Hokkei (1673–1754), *Shichikei Mōshi kōbun hoi* (Textual Study of the Seven Classics and the *Mencius*, with Supplement); *Guwen Xiaojing Kong-shi zhuan* (Kong Commentary to the Ancient Script Version of the *Classic of Filial Piety*), edited by Dazai Shundai (1670–1747); *Lunyu yishu* (Exegetic Commentary to the *Analects*), edited by Nemoto Bui (1699–1764); and *Xiaojing Zheng zhu* (Zheng Commentary to the *Classic of Filial Piety*), edited by Okada Shinsen (1737–99). See Laura E. Hess, "Qing Reactions to the Reimportation of Confucian Canonical Works from Tokugawa Japan," in Fogel, ed., *Sagacious Monks and Bloodthirsty Warriors*, 126–57.

14. Hess, "Qing Reactions to the Reimportation of Confucian Canonical Works," 132–36.

15. On *Isson sōsho*, see Ōba and Wang, *Tenseki*, 158–64.

16. *Yicun congshu* (Hushang: Huang shi muhuozi yinben qianyin, 1882).

be reached by a handful of imported originals. Indeed, although most titles were never reprinted, *wakokubon* and Japanese manuscript copies together account for the majority of extant Chinese texts in Japanese collections.[17] Reflecting supply, reprints also brought Chinese texts within reach of ordinary readers in terms of price. In the preceding chapter I showed that ordinary Chinese titles were ten times more expensive *at the first stage of importation* than even relatively high-quality editions of domestic fiction. Edo-period books were not printed with their retail price, and there is little evidence concerning the pricing of *wakokubon* specifically. In the early eighteenth century, one of the few periods for which limited information is available, it seems *wakokubon* were not especially inexpensive: a revised edition of the *Yunjing* sold for 2 *monme* ($110), Xie Zhaozhe's *Wuzazu* for 28 *monme* ($1,540), *Visit to the Cave of the Immortals* for 8 *monme* ($439), and *Biographies of Exemplary Women* (*Lienü zhuan*) for 9 *monme* ($494).[18] However, these prices are very much in line with those for domestic titles; Ihara Saikaku's fiction, among the cheaper titles available, sold in the 2 to 4 *monme* range ($110–$220), while heftier works could easily cost 10 *monme* ($549) or more. In other words, prices for commercial editions were roughly the same regardless of content. On this basis, we would expect later *wakokubon* to cost around the same as the lower-end domestic fiction discussed in the previous chapter, and less than the deluxe editions whose higher prices owed mainly to their use of higher-quality paper and polychrome printing, elements absent in *wakokubon* editions.

Ordinary readers and less wealthy institutions, such as many private academies, were likely to own more *wakokubon* editions than imported books. That said, even well-heeled individual and institutional collectors relied heavily on affordable reprint editions to fill out their collections. Of roughly 3,200 titles from former domain collections accessioned by the Tokyo Library (the precursor to the Imperial Library) between 1875 and 1878, more than a quarter were Chinese texts, and these ranged across all of the classifications in the conventional *sibu* "four branches" system.[19]

17. Isaka, "Kokuritsu kokkai toshokan shozō no wakokubon kanseki gaikan," 2.

18. Prices are taken from Maruya Genbē, *Zōeki shojaku mokuroku* (Kyōto: Maruya Genbē, 1709), in the collection of the National Diet Library.

19. See Nishimura Masamori and Sano Chikara, *Tōkyō shojakukan ni okeru kyūhan zōsho no shūshū*, in *Toshokan kenkyū shirīzu* 15 (Kokuritsu kokkai toshokan, 1973).

A significant portion were domestic reprints. Although contemporary catalogs rarely distinguish format or provide much bibliographic information, modern scholarly catalogs—at least the more careful ones—enable further investigation into the place of *wakokubon* in Edo collections. The extensive library of the Owari Tokugawa branch family, which later became the core of the Hōsa Bunko in Nagoya, included many rare titles bequeathed by Ieyasu. Even in this elite collection, *wakokubon* make up a sizable portion of titles: holdings of Chinese classical fiction are evenly divided between imported editions and copies produced in Japan, of which half are in manuscript and half are printed.[20] Smaller domains with more limited resources were likely to be more dependent on *wakokubon* editions. The modest holdings of the Chidōkan, the domainal academy of the northern Shōnai domain, break down fairly evenly between original Chinese editions, of which there are ninety-seven titles (55 percent), and *wakokubon*, which number eighty (45 percent).[21]

Some Chinese texts in institutional collections were printed by the domains themselves, or by the Shōheikō, which published nearly two hundred editions between 1799 and 1867. The primary aim was to make important texts affordable and accessible to academy students, but these editions were available more widely, often at subsidized prices, and might circulate far beyond academy walls.[22] In 1787, for example, the Owari domain published an edition of *Selected Essentials of Rule*, copies of which spread to other domains—one was among the eighty *wakokubon* titles held by the Chidōkan—and are today scattered in institutional collections across Japan.

For the most part, it was classics, histories, and works related to governance that were deemed worthy of reproduction in official editions. There are, however, notable exceptions—works that, like the earlier Gozan editions of poetry, reproduced content that was tangential to the primary institutional mission yet still seen to have didactic utility. Even fiction

20. Nagoya-shi Hōsa bunko, ed., *Nagoya-shi Hōsa bunko kanseki bunrui mokuroku* (Nagoya: Nagoya-shi kyōiku iinkai, 1975), 99–102.

21. For a catalog of the academy's holdings of Chinese texts, see Takahashi Satoshi, "Shōnai-han Chidōkan kyūzō kanseki ni tsuite," *Shidō bunko ronshū* 49 (2014): 49–95. A pair of titles in manuscript are excluded from the total figures.

22. Kornicki, *The Book in Japan*, 147.

could be reproduced given a sufficiently compelling rationale. In the first decade of the nineteenth century, Tsusaka Tōyō (1758–1825) began work on a legal casebook that would later be published by the Yūzōkan, the academy of the Tsu domain (modern-day Mie Prefecture) he had helped found and at which he served as an instructor. The finished product, titled *A Collection of Legal Cases* (*Chōkō ian*, 1831; preface dated 1806), includes excerpts from dynastic histories and other official sources, but also from miscellanies and story collections including Tao Zongyi's *Records after Plowing the Fields* (*Chuogeng lu*), Feng Menglong's *Pouch of Wisdom* (*Zhinang*, 1626), Zhang Chao's *New Tales of Yu Chu*, Ji Yun's *Record of a Summer at Luanyang* (*Luanyang xiaoxia lu*, 1789), and Wang Jian's *Collected Tales by the Autumn Lamp* (*Qiudeng conghua*, 1791). All of Tōyō's selections are concerned with the administration of justice and were thus deemed to possess sufficient curricular merit. A similar rationale surely underlies the three editions of fictional titles published by the Shōheikō (which are among those included in table 2.1).

Still, Chinese fiction was in general more likely to be reprinted in commercial editions. The availability of such an edition could greatly enhance the permeation of a text not only by disseminating it to a wider audience but by providing guidance in the form of annotation. For particularly challenging vernacular texts, reading marks and glosses might only go so far in steering readers toward a comprehensible Japanese rendering of the original. In the absence of detailed annotations explaining unfamiliar vernacular vocabulary, Okajima Kanzan's 1728 *wakokubon* edition of the first ten chapters of *The Water Margin*, which included reading marks, could at most help amateurs get a "foot in the door"; instead, *The Water Margin* gained its status as one the most popular and influential works of Chinese literature in the late Edo period through a gradual process, unfolding over many decades, of more careful explication and assimilation, through which it slowly became readable.[23]

For slighter vernacular narratives, basic annotation could be sufficient to push readers over the interpretive hump. In the 1740s and 1750s, Oka Hakku (1692–1767) and his student Sawada Issai (1701–82) prepared three *wakokubon* editions of selected vernacular stories, complete with reading marks and Japanese glosses. The collections are *Vernacular Tales: Essential*

23. Hedberg, *The Japanese Discovery of Chinese Fiction*, 41.

Words (*Shōsetsu seigen*, 1743) and *Vernacular Tales: Wondrous Words* (*Shōsetsu kigen*, 1753), both prepared by Hakku, and *Vernacular Tales: Elegant Words* (*Shōsetsu suigen*, 1758), prepared by Issai. As a group, these came to be popularly known as the "Japanese *Sanyan*" (*Wakoku Sangen*, lit. "*Sanyan* Printed in Japan"), after Feng Menglong's three *Sanyan* collections, even if they did not represent a complete annotated edition of Feng's collections, nor were their selections drawn exclusively from his work.[24] Hakku and Issai's editions played an important role in making the Chinese vernacular story accessible not just to general readers but also to elite scholars such as the writer Morishima Chūryō, who read a number of vernacular tales in the available *wakokubon* editions and adapted two of them into Japanese in the decade after he completed *Tales from the Withering Wind*, his collection of strange tales that drew heavily on *Liaozhai*.[25]

Classical fiction benefited the most from standard annotation techniques, given that it still presented interpretive difficulties but was written in a register that could be more readily decoded using conventional *kundoku* procedures. Qu You's *New Tales by Lamplight* circulated narrowly in manu-

24. *Essential Words* presents four tales drawn from *Constant Words to Awaken the World*; *Wondrous Words* consists of three from *Wondrous Tales New and Old* (*Jingu qiguan*) and one each from *Constant Words to Awaken the World* and *Fine Tales from West Lake* (*Xihu jiahua*); and *Elegant Words* presents two tales each from *Wondrous Tales New and Old* and *Common Words to Caution the World* (*Jingshi tongyan*), along with one from *Slapping the Table in Amazement*. (*Wondrous Tales New and Old*, of course, contains tales culled from the earlier collections of Feng Menglong and Ling Mengchu, but Hakku and Issai drew their versions from this "anthology of anthologies," rather than directly from the originals.)

25. Chūryō's adaptations from Chinese vernacular fiction are *An Elegant Tale by Moonlight* (*Gekka seidan*, 1798) and *The Jeweled Branch: Ink Spilled Playfully by Lamplight* ([*Tōka no geboku*] *Tama no eda*, 1802). The source for the former is "Scholar Qian's Accidental Marriage" ("Qian xiucai cuozhan fenghuang chou"), the seventh story in Feng Menglong's *Constant Words to Awaken the World* (and among those included in Hakku's *Wondrous Words*, by way of *Wondrous Tales New and Old*). See Aoki Masaru, "Kaidai," in *Tsūzoku Kokon kikan, fu Gekka seidan* (Iwanami shoten, 1932), 7–9. The latter is based on "A Thing Done in Jest Comes True in the Garden of the Seven Pines" ("Qisongyuan nong jia cheng zhen"), the first story in Zhuoyuan's early Qing collection *The Cup That Reflects the World* (*Zhaoshibei*, ca. 1661). See Masuda Wataru, ed., *Gen Kōran* [*Ruan Jianglan*] *shussetan: Shina shōsetsu, hoka nihen*, in *Kindai bungei senshū* 5 (Kenbunsha, 1926); a more detailed comparison of Chūryō's and Zhuoyuan's stories appears in Ishizaki Matazō, *Kinsei Nihon ni okeru Shina zokugo bungakushi* (Kōbundō, 1940), 243–48.

script form among Gozan monks after the collection first reached Japan in the early sixteenth century, but wider readership only came with the reprinting of the Korean annotated edition *Chŏndŭng sinhwa kuhae* (J. *Sentō shinwa kukai*) in 1648 by the Kyoto publisher Tawara Jinzaemon. Not only did the domestic edition make numerous copies available at a relatively modest cost, but it aided readers with its inclusion of Japanese reading marks and the occasional gloss, which were added on top of the classical Chinese annotation by the Korean scholars Im Ki (dates unknown) and Yun Ch'un-nyŏn (1514–67). These additions facilitated direct engagement with the text, and not just for readers of average literacy. When Chūryō reread Qu You's classical tales shortly before his death, he recalled with dismay how little he had understood when he had bought a copy and begun to read it in his mid-twenties three decades earlier. He had been, in his own words, "a rabbit fording a river."[26] No doubt the task would have been harder still had his copy not been the Kyoto edition of 1648, with its annotation and reading aids.

Tawara Jinzaemon's edition was reissued at least twice, and copies remained available for purchase throughout the Edo period.[27] Japanese adaptations began to appear already in the second half of the seventeenth century, most famously in Asai Ryōi's collection *Talisman Dolls* (*Otogibōko*, 1666). Familiarity with the stories was further magnified by the availability of related works including Li Changqi's "sequel" *More Tales by Lamplight* (*Jiandeng yuhua*, 1420), published in a *wakokubon* edition in 1692, and the secondary anthology *Collected Tales by Lamplight* (*Jiandeng conghua*), which was available in scattered imported copies. In the early eighteenth century, a lesser-known successor to *Talisman Dolls* titled *The Jeweled Curtain* (*Tama sudare*, 1704) presented a half-dozen adaptations from *New Tales by Lamplight* among its twenty-seven stories.[28] Most famous of all in the Japanese context was Qu You's story "The Pe-

26. Quoted in Okada Kesao, "Morishima Chūryō bannen tansaku: arui wa ichibunjin no gengo uchū," *Nihon bungaku* 32, no. 1 (1983): 69.

27. Fumiko Jōo, "'The Peony Lantern' and Fantastic Tales in Late Imperial China and Tokugawa Japan: Local History, Religion, and Gender" (PhD diss., University of Chicago, 2011), 119.

28. Kigoshi Osamu, "Kaidai," in Kigoshi, ed., *Ukiyozōshi kaidan shū*, in Takada Mamoru and Hara Michio, eds., *Sōsho Edo bunko* 34 (Kokusho kankōkai, 1994), 338–40.

ony Lantern" ("Mudan deng ji"), which attained enormous popularity not just through Ryōi's adaptation in *Talisman Dolls* (or *The Jeweled Curtain*, which contained its own version), but as it was rewritten and retold across a wide range of genres and media including oral storytelling.

Quantifying Wakokubon*: The Big Picture*

In the remainder of this chapter I move beyond individual texts and the anecdotal to consider *wakokubon* as a whole. We have established that many thousands of titles, including the majority of fiction printed in China, were imported to Japan over the course of the Edo period, often with startling speed. How much of this corpus was made more widely available through reprinting for the Japanese market? How much fiction was reprinted? How did the types of work selected for reprinting change over time? Previous scholarship has neglected such large-scale quantitative questions around the permeation of Chinese texts in early modern Japan, and not without reason. However fundamental such questions may be, there are enormous challenges that must be overcome in order to answer them. Peter Kornicki has gone so far as to declare it "impossible to quantify or to characterize the reprinting of Chinese works in the Tokugawa period," while further noting that much fundamental research remains to be done.[29]

If we are to attempt the impossible, we must first identify some of the obstacles that lie in the way. Most obvious is the fact that titles sometimes changed in the course of reprinting, as did the texts themselves. The example of Tsusaka Tōyō's collection of legal cases illustrates how subsections of larger works could be excerpted, rearranged, and reissued under a new title. This was not uncommon in domainal publications, which often took the form of "digest" editions, anthologies, or excerpted readers.[30] Such transformations were in keeping with the pedagogical aims that often underlay their production, much as scholarly editions today might excerpt primary sources without reproducing them in their entirety or in their

29. Kornicki, *The Book in Japan*, 155.
30. Ōba and Wang, *Tenseki*, 78–79.

strict original form. Similar examples can be found in commercial editions. Selections from Feng Menglong were reproduced in Issai and Hakku's three editions, but in spite of their popular moniker of the "Japanese *Sanyan*," we cannot even loosely consider them to constitute a Japanese edition of the *Sanyan*, as the great majority of tales were omitted, while tales were also interspersed from other collections by different authors.

Further nontrivial challenges stem from the survival rates of primary texts. There are known editions that are no longer extant, and there are surely others, unknown to us, that are also lost. Perhaps the most fundamental challenge to large-scale analysis is the absence of a comprehensive catalog even of those *wakokubon* that do survive. The best individual resource is the Zenkoku kanseki dētabēsu (Japan-Wide Database of Chinese Texts) maintained by the Institute for Research in Humanities at Kyoto University.[31] However, there are significant collections whose holdings are not represented (including, as the name suggests, all those located outside Japan), and the fact that the bibliographic data is provided by the owning institution yields entries that do not follow a standard format and for which important fields are often missing. In addition, the database's coverage includes both Chinese and Japanese editions, as well as modern facsimile and reprint editions, meaning that *wakokubon* editions must be identified on a case-by-case basis.

Nagasawa Kikuya's remarkable *Wakokubon kanseki bunrui mokuroku* (Classified Catalog of Chinese Books Printed in Japan), the most extensive catalog in print, is more narrowly focused on *wakokubon* but presents challenges of its own.[32] As the work of a single scholar, it inevitably falls short of comprehensiveness. Entire fields and categories of text are omitted, such as medical and Buddhist literature, and significant titles are missing in other areas as well. Among titles of fiction, for example, there is no entry for *The Cup That Reflects the World*, which as mentioned earlier

31. Zenkoku kanseki dētabēsu (Japan-Wide Database of Chinese Texts), Institute for Research in Humanities, Kyoto University, http://kanji.zinbun.kyoto-u.ac.jp/kanseki.

32. Nagasawa Kikuya, ed., *Wakokubon kanseki bunrui mokuroku*, rev. ed. The revised edition, published in 2006, consists of a reprint of the original handwritten edition (Kyūko shoin, 1976) accompanied by a typeset version of the corrections previously published separately as *Wakokubon kanseki bunrui mokuroku hosei* (Kyūko shoin, 1980).

was lost in China and survives only in the Japanese edition of 1765. Nagasawa is also inconsistent in his inclusion of reorganized or reanthologized editions such as the *Wakoku Sangen*, which is excluded from coverage. At the same time, the catalog's scope is in other ways too broad for our purposes. Most obviously, the entries extend to woodblock and facsimile editions from the Meiji, Taishō, and early Shōwa periods, all of which are presented alongside those from the Edo period and before.

Whatever the limitations and difficulties inherent in these resources, it is nevertheless possible—by coupling them with the Nagasaki import records and Chinese bibliographic scholarship discussed in chapter 1—to use them to approach the quantification of the reception of imported Chinese texts from several angles. These approaches converge around similar conclusions, allowing us to derive an informed estimate of the domestic reprint rate of Chinese texts that is the stronger for having been obtained through partly orthogonal methods. Although the estimation of this reprint rate is by no means the final word in reception history, it provides the larger context for chapter 3, where quantitative analysis gives way to qualitative study. The estimation process itself, moreover, involves a number of detours and digressions through which further details emerge and additional questions present themselves for consideration.

We can begin the process of interpolation by establishing a rough upper bound on the reprint rate. For this it is necessary only to compare the total number of unique titles in the Nagasaki import records with those in Nagasawa's *wakokubon* catalog.[33] The raw numbers—8,073 titles in the former versus 1,987 in the latter—point to a reprint rate of just below 25 percent. There are several factors that necessitate revising this figure downward. On the *wakokubon* side, Nagasawa's inclusion of editions postdating the Edo period skews the estimate of the number of reprint editions high. However, this effect is canceled out by the exclusion of certain genres as well as the presumed existence of editions that no longer survive. A sample of one hundred titles from Nagasawa suggests that less than 10 percent were first printed in the Meiji period or later; as will be discussed, the rate of disappearance for entire editions is estimated

33. Unique titles are drawn from the indices to Ōba's *Tōsen mochiwatarisho no kenkyū* and *Hakusai shomoku*.

to be about the same. The most important factor, then, is the incomplete and fragmentary nature of the import records, which, as noted in chapter 1, plausibly exclude half or more of actual imported titles. In light of this, the reprint rate likely lies somewhere below 12 percent.

This off-the-cuff estimate is confirmed by exhaustive, brute-force analysis: the careful examination, one by one, of known imported titles. For the data set, the 8,073 titles in the extant Nagasaki documents were lowered slightly to 7,674 by excluding certain types of materials, such as reproductions of inscriptions and books in album format, that were with rare exceptions not amenable to reprinting. Using an automated script, the results of which were exhaustively verified manually, these were then individually cross-referenced with both the Kyoto University database and Nagasawa's catalog to ascertain the existence of a *wakokubon* edition.[34] A total of 723 titles were determined to have been reprinted one or more times in the Edo period, corresponding to a reprint rate of 9.62 percent, with a margin of error of ±0.05 percent owing to a handful of incomplete and/or ambiguous entries.[35]

34. Although I did not have access to the back-end data, it was possible to automate the query process using a script. The script retrieved all hits for each of the 7,674 imported titles, flagging those that contained keywords strongly correlated with Edo-period *wakokubon*, including "Nihon," "Edo," and all of the Edo-period reign periods (*nengō*). The term *wakoku* itself was excluded, as only Edo-period editions were desired, not Meiji and twentieth-century *wakokubon* or undated *wakokubon* editions in modern anthologies. The keywords were designed to be liberal (as suggested by the example "Nihon"), but the number of false hits was reduced by adding a second list with common false positives. For example, "Keiō dai" and "Keiō daigaku" were included in this list so that hits for "Keiō" only returned books dating to the Keiō period (1865–68), not modern Chinese and Japanese editions held by the Keiō University library. Hits were separately flagged as potential manuscript copies, as opposed to *wakokubon*, if they included any of several terms (*sha*, *shōhon*, etc.) associated with manuscript reproduction.

All flagged entries were then examined individually to determine whether in fact they indicated the existence of a *wakokubon* edition of the title in question. Abridged editions with the same title that reproduced more than half of the original were counted. Several hundred false positives were manually removed through this final careful examination of the data. Finally, titles from Nagasawa's print catalog were run against non-hits to find additional hits, and these were examined individually to exclude any that were reprinted in the Meiji period or later.

35. The figure of 9.62 percent largely conforms with my earlier estimate of 8 percent, which was based on a relatively small sample of two hundred randomly selected titles and, accordingly, included a margin of error of several percentage points. A

Given the large sample size, this result is limited mainly by the survival rate of reprint editions. One way to estimate this survival rate would be to compile contemporary references to reprint editions and cross-reference these with the extant titles in Nagasawa and the Kyoto University database. In his study of missing Italian polyphony from the late fourteenth and early fifteenth centuries, Michael Cuthbert successfully employs a similar approach; by scouring contemporary verse for mentions of song titles and determining which are attested by extant manuscripts, he makes the case that the majority of the repertory is in fact extant.[36] Unfortunately, gathering contemporary references to *wakokubon* editions is no straightforward task, given that Edo mentions of Chinese texts rarely give detailed information concerning format or edition. Nor are there sizable Edo-period bibliographies or catalogs that reliably distinguish Japanese reprints from Chinese editions or manuscript materials.

In the absence of a substantial body of contemporary references or catalogs, the most straightforward way to estimate survival rates for editions is by using statistical methods—that is, estimating what is lost based on the number and distribution of copies of editions that *do* survive. Nagasawa's catalog is unsuitable for such a task, as it provides information only on extant editions and not on individual copies. The Kyoto University database, however, is composed of entries for individual items. The fact that many titles are represented by a small number of extant copies suggests a nontrivial disappearance rate. That is to say, if a significant number of editions are represented by a small handful of surviving copies—in some cases only one or two—there must also be a significant number for which *no* copies survive (or, more precisely, for which no copies are attested in the database—but determining the completeness of the database achieves the same end where our analysis is concerned).

We can attempt an initial estimate of this disappearance rate using a simple probabilistic model. If for a given title in an original print run of y copies the number of extant copies is x, then the probability of a given

small part of the upward revision is accounted for by the exclusion of inscriptions and other materials. See William D. Fleming, "Strange Tales from Edo: *Liaozhai zhiyi* in Early Modern Japan," *Sino-Japanese Studies* 20 (2013): 79.

36. Michael Scott Cuthbert, "Tipping the Iceberg: Missing Italian Polyphony from the Age of Schism," *Musica Disciplina* 54 (2009): 39–74.

copy having survived is $\frac{x}{y}$, and the probability of no copies having survived is, accordingly, $(1-\frac{x}{y})^y$. In spite of the incompleteness of the Kyoto University database, the majority of titles are attested by multiple copies, with those surviving in three or fewer copies comparatively rare. This suggests that the disappearance rate, while not trivial, is fairly low. In fact, even assuming a very low average number of surviving copies—lower than that suggested by the data—the disappearance rate is likely in the single digits. An average of three copies surviving out of an original print run of three hundred yields a survival rate of no less than 95.1 percent, while an average of 2.5 copies yields a rate of 91.9 percent. A still more conservative scenario of two copies lowers the estimated survival rate to 86.6 percent. In each scenario, the estimate of the print run matters relatively little, with the disappearance rate converging within 90 percent of the given values for a run of only a few dozen copies.

Although the conservative scenario of two surviving copies likely overstates the disappearance rate, there are some significant problems with this rudimentary model. For one, the average number of surviving copies is heavily skewed by certain titles that survive in large quantities, many of which were reprinted and reissued multiple times. This makes the task of estimating the average number of surviving copies less straightforward than it initially appears. More fundamentally, any such "average" is the average only of *extant* titles and does not include titles for which zero copies survive—the very lost titles we are trying to estimate. In other words, the model is subverted by the circular nature of the problem: to estimate the disappearance rate we need to know the average including lost titles, but to determine that average we must know the disappearance rate. Assuming the disappearance rate is relatively low, we can partly account for lost titles by plugging the first-order estimate back into the calculation and deriving a revised, second-order estimate. Depending on the scenario, this lowers the estimated survival rate to between 82.4 and 94.3 percent. We may be fairly confident that the lower figure provides a solid lower bound on the disappearance rate. However, to the extent that our scenarios of between two and three copies were arbitrary, the resulting window leaves much room for doubt. Surely it is possible to improve on this result.

Fortunately, others have devoted considerable attention to problems of a similar nature, in the process developing more sophisticated models and statistical methods. The locus classicus, a 1943 article by Ronald Fisher, A. Steven Corbet, and C. B. Williams, sought to use the number of individual butterfly specimens from several small Malayan islands (in what are now Indonesia and Malaysia) to estimate the number of species that remained unobserved.[37] Others soon recognized that this so-called unseen species problem could be generalized to any situation where the objective is to ascertain, based on the number of known specimens, the number of "species"—and, by extension, distinct words in a corpus, editions of printed texts, and so forth—for which there are *no* recorded specimens. In the 1970s, Bradley Efron and Ronald Thisted tabulated the number of appearances of each word used by Shakespeare in his collected works—tallying the number attested just once, the number used twice, three times, and so on—to estimate the number of words the playwright knew but did not use. Developing several models, their conclusions vary over a wide range; however, their proposed lower bound for unused vocabulary (35,000 words) exceeds that attested in the collected works (31,534 words).[38]

The possibility that unobserved species might outnumber the observed—seemingly borne out by Efron and Thisted's analyses—has led many scholars to imagine great bodies of lost texts, hidden from sight like the hulking mass of an iceberg submerged beneath the water's surface. Cuthbert, observing the prevalence of such a view in the field of medieval and Renaissance musicology, sets himself to the task of "tipping the iceberg" by means of a multipronged analysis. Complementing his investigation of references in contemporary verse, he applies statistical methods to the distribution of the number of surviving copies to show that even though many extant songs in this repertory survive in just a single source, the intuition that this implies an extensive lost body of work is not necessarily warranted. On the contrary, analysis suggests that upward of 75 percent of the repertory survives—a figure that largely accords with estimates made using other methods.[39]

37. R. A. Fisher et al., "The Relation between the Number of Species and the Number of Individuals in a Random Sample of an Animal Population," *Journal of Animal Ecology* 12, no. 1 (May 1943): 42–58.

38. Bradley Efron and Ronald Thisted, "Estimating the Number of Unseen Species: How Many Words Did Shakespeare Know?" *Biometrika* 63, no. 3 (December 1976): 435–47.

39. Cuthbert, "Tipping the Iceberg," 47.

Turning from manuscript to print, we might expect higher rates still, given the presumably greater number of copies produced in the first place. Again, however, intuition has the potential to lead astray. In their study of lost incunable editions, Jonathan Green and Frank McIntyre estimate a survival rate across all formats within a range of only 5 to 51 percent, with a mean of 38 percent. Nevertheless, the intuition that having a higher proportion of texts in a single source implies a higher loss rate *is* generally borne out. More specifically, as can be gleaned from Green and McIntyre's graph of surviving editions by format, the key feature of a corpus is the drop-off rate of the number of editions as a function of the number of surviving copies. A precipitous decline suggests a relatively high proportion of single-source texts, and we may also imagine extrapolating the line backward to arrive at a relatively high number of zero-source texts, which is to say lost texts; where the graph drops off less rapidly, by contrast, the loss rate is accordingly lower. The difference is evident in the case of folio editions, the graph of which shows the least precipitous drop-off, and which also have the highest estimated survival rate, in a narrow range between 92 to 93 percent.[40]

Where *wakokubon* are concerned, there are several factors that might lead us to expect a relatively high survival rate. They are of relatively recent origin compared to incunabula or Renaissance polyphony, and they are characterized by physical heft in terms of both format and page count; certainly, the corpus excludes ephemera analogous to the broadsheets that compose a large portion of incunabula. All the same, there are many other factors involved in an edition's survival, and the preceding discussion makes it clear that it is ultimately the distribution of editions versus surviving copies that determines the survival rate. To arrive at a concrete figure, we may rely on the improved statistical methods developed by Shahar Boneh, Arnon Boneh, and R. J. Caron in their 1998 treatment of the unseen species problem (methods that suggest considerably less missing Shakespearean vocabulary than claimed by Efron and Thisted, and that Cuthbert applies to his corpus with similar effect). In particular, there are two formulas we can bring to bear on our data set. First, to derive an

40. Jonathan Green and Frank McIntyre, "Lost Incunable Editions: Closing in on an Estimate," in Flavia Bruni and Andrew Pettegree, eds., *Lost Books: Reconstructing the Print World of Pre-Industrial Europe* (Boston: Brill, 2016), 62–64.

initial estimate U_0 of the number of unseen species (or lost editions), we use the exponential sum

$$U_0 = \sum_{k=1}^{k_{\max}} N_k e^{-k},$$

where N_k denotes the number of species in the sample (or corpus) attested by k individual specimens. To reduce the bias in this formulation, we then employ a second equation,

$$U(1 - e^{-N_1/U}) = U_0,$$

where U is the corrected number of unseen species.[41]

Applying this method to the *wakokubon* corpus for $k = 1$ to 15 (higher terms having a vanishingly small effect), we obtain a value of $U_0 = 48.2$. Given a total of 395 titles attested by 15 or fewer copies, this points to a survival rate for editions of 91.0 percent. Solving computationally for U, the result revises downward slightly to 89.1 percent—very much in line with our earlier rudimentary estimate. Survival rate in hand, we are now able to revise our earlier determination of the percentage of imported titles that were reprinted domestically, shifting the figure upward from 9.62 percent to 10.8 percent.

As the quality of the available bibliographic data improves, future efforts will no doubt be able to improve on this result. The ability to account for texts excerpted or partially reproduced in anthologies and digests, moreover, might edge the reprint rate slightly higher. Nevertheless, it is possible to assert with some confidence that across all genres, around one in nine imported Chinese titles were available to Japanese readers in reprinted form. In absolute terms, this represents a huge corpus of literature that was widely available to the public. At the same time, this is a situation where the iceberg metaphor *is* apt. No matter how large this corpus of reprint editions was, it represents only a small fraction of the vastly larger body of texts that made it to Japan in the first place. That

41. Shahar Boneh et al., "Estimating the Prediction Function and the Number of Unseen Species in Sampling with Replacement," *Journal of the American Statistical Association* 93, no. 441 (1998): 372–79.

which was available in reprinted form was dwarfed by that which loomed out of sight, accessible only in its original format.

The Availability of Chinese Fiction in Wakokubon *Editions*

Turning from Chinese texts at large to fiction specifically, we are able to apply a similar approach, beginning with a rough initial estimate and progressing toward a more refined result. Here an upper bound can be quickly established by turning to the catalog of one of the most voluminous early modern Sinological collections, that of the Shōheikō, whose extensive holdings extended to a strong selection of Chinese fiction. Limiting the scope of inquiry to works classified as *xiaoshuo* under the "masters" (*zi*) division of the four-branches classification, one counts 219 titles, as opposed to fifty-three in Nagasawa.[42] That is to say, this single collection by itself held more than four times as many titles of fiction as the total number known to have been printed domestically over the entire duration of the Edo period. As in the preceding section, we thus begin with a conservative, but firm, upper bound: at most, one-quarter of imported fiction was reprinted.

To close in on a more nuanced estimate, we can begin by turning again to Yuan and Hou's catalog of Chinese classical "fiction" (recognizing, as in chapter 1, that the traditional category of *xiaoshuo* does not map tidily onto our modern notions of fiction). Limiting ourselves to Ming-Qing titles predating 1850, we find twenty-eight titles that were reprinted in Japan according to either Nagasawa or the Kyoto University database. These are shown in table 2.1. The number of titles is fewer than the total of fifty-three in Nagasawa because of the exclusion of pre-Ming texts. Table 2.1 also incorporates Ōba's Nagasaki import records, making it possible to trace the journey of these titles across three stages: first their

42. See Ogawa Takehiko and Kanai Yasushi, eds., *Tokugawa bakufu zōshomoku*, in *Shoshi shomoku shirīzu* 16 (Yumani shobō, 1985), 10:54–59; and Nagasawa, *Wakokubon kanseki bunrui mokuroku*, 144–51.

Table 2.1 Ming-Qing Classical Fiction Reprinted in Japanese Editions

	Title	Year(s) of edition(s) given in Yuan and Hou	Printed acc. to Y+H?	Year(s) title appears in import records	Year(s) of ***wakokubon*** edition(s)*
1	*Caomuzi* 草木子	1456, 1522–66, 1609, 1762	Y	–	1669 (+)
2	*Jiandeng xinhua* 剪燈新話	1467, 1791	Y	1794 (title given as 剪燈)	Keichō period (1596–1615) (movable type) (K), 1648 (+, +) (but based on Korean edition of 1549)
3	*Jiandeng yuhua* 剪燈餘話	1467, 1791	Y	–	1692 (+)
4	*Chuogeng lu* 輟耕錄	1474	Y	1772	1652 (+, +, 1823)
5	*Mochi suolu* 墨池瑣錄	1522–66	Y	–	1793
6	*Yilin fashan* 藝林伐山	1572, 1606, 1607	Y	–	1716
7	*Mingshishuo xinyu* 明世說新語	1572–1620	Y	1760 (title given as 皇明世說新語)	1754 (1771), 1823 (K)
8	*Shishuo xinyu bu* 世說新語補	1585, 1762	Y	1754, 1760, 1843, 1844, 1845	date unknown (1694, +, 1779, +, +)
9	*Wenhai pisha* 文海披沙	1609	Y	–	1759 (+)
10	*Wuzazu* 五雜俎	1616	Y	–	1661 (+), 1795 (+, 1822)
11	*Qunsui lu* 群碎錄	Ming	N	–	1698, 1721 (K)
12	*Gujin yan* 古今諺	Ming	N	–	1775 (K), 1777 (K), 1784 (K), 1818 (K), 1846 (K)
13	*Kaopan yushi* 考槃餘事	Ming	N	1801	1803 (1823 [N], +)
14	*Qianbainian yan* 千百年眼	Ming	N	–	1767 (+)

15	*Taiping qinghua* 太平清話	Ming	N	–	1865 (Shōheikō)
16	*Xude lu* 畜德錄	Ming	N	1693, 1841	1834 (Shōheikō) (1856)
17	*Tingyu jitan* 聽雨紀談	Ming	N	–	1689, 1833 (K)
18	*Xichao leshi* 熙朝樂事	Ming	N	–	1772 (+)
19	*Zhuyu* 麈餘	Ming	Y	–	1796 (K) (1798, 1818, 1846)
20	*Zhinang* 智囊	Ming	Y	1760	date unknown (Shōheikō), 1821 (+, +, +)
21	*Jin shishuo* 今世說	1683	Y	1783, 1801, 1845	1803
22	*Yuchu xinzhi* 虞初新志	1700, 1760, 1803	Y	1762	1823 (+, 1851, +, +)
23	*Huachanshi suibi* 畫禪室隨筆	1720, 1768	Y	–	1840 (+, +) (title given as 畫禪隨筆 in Nagasawa)
24	*Shuyiji* 述異記	Qing (Chan: 1701)	N	–	1716 (1749, 1753, 1775 [N])
25	*Huaniao chunqiu* 花鳥春秋	Qing	N	–	date unknown (wooden movable type) (N)
26	*Dunbi suiwen lu* 盾鼻隨聞錄	Qing	N	–	late Edo date unknown (+)
27	*Banqiao zaji* 板橋雜記	Qing	N	1791	date unknown (wooden movable type), 1772, 1803 (K)
28	*Yanpu zaji* 簷曝雜記	Qing	N	1829	1829 (K)

* The letters N and K in parentheses indicate a *wakokubon* edition given only in one resource (Nagasawa or the Kyoto University database), not both. Years in parentheses indicate known later reissues of the same edition, while the symbol + indicates an undated later reissue of an edition included in Nagasawa.

publication in China, then their importation to Japan (where known), and finally their reprinting in one or more *wakokubon* editions.

That only eleven of the twenty-eight titles appear in the import records again reminds us of the incompleteness of these documents and the only partial window they provide onto what was available during the Edo period. Early *wakokubon* in particular were likely to have been reprinted from editions that predate official recordkeeping. This is uniformly the case for editions predating 1693, such as *New Tales by Lamplight*, which reached Japan in the 1500s and was first reprinted in 1648. Even some later *wakokubon* editions reproduce titles that first appear in the import records only at a later date. *Miscellaneous Records of the Wooden Bridge* (*Banqiao zaji*), for example, was published in a Japanese edition in 1772 but does not appear in the import records until 1791. That is to say, even when a title is attested in the records, additional copies may well have slipped through the cracks.

The incompleteness of the record notwithstanding, we observe examples of titles that were reprinted for the Japanese market very quickly, including one, Zhao Yi's *Yanpu zaji* (Miscellaneous Notes from under the Eaves), that was reprinted the very same year. Wang Zhuo's *Jin shishuo* (Tales of the Present Day) was imported in 1783, then again in 1801 along with *Kaopan yushi* (Remarks on the Abode of a Retired Scholar; attributed to Tu Long). Both were reprinted just two years later. The 1652 Japanese edition of Tao Zongyi's *Records after Plowing the Fields* (*Chuogeng lu*) reproduces a "Qing edition" (one that is not included in Yuan and Hou) that could have been published no more than eight years earlier.[43] Just as market forces and demand incentivized Chinese merchants to import newly published titles, similar incentives presumably played a role in determining which texts publishers chose to reprint. Books that reached Japan often did so fairly quickly, and they could sometimes be reprinted just as fast; at the same time, some earlier books only hit the Japanese market much later, with the importation of a new edition.

Of the sixty-nine pre-1850 Ming-Qing titles in Yuan and Hou that are attested in the import records, seven, or just over one in ten, were reprinted in *wakokubon* editions. However, using the estimate of the in-

43. *Chuogeng lu*, in Nagasawa Kikuya, ed., *Wakokubon kanseki zuihitsu shū* 2 (Kyūko shoin, 1972), unnumbered p. 1.

completeness of the import record developed in chapter 1 allows us to expand our sample to all twenty-eight titles in table 2.1. Recalling that 328 published titles were estimated to have been imported, this yields a reprint rate of 8.5 percent. Correcting for probable lost editions (using the estimated survival rate of 89.1 percent) raises the figure to 9.6 percent. In other words, fiction was reprinted at a marginally lower rate than the average across genres. Recalling from chapter 1 that around two-thirds of published Chinese fiction was imported, this suggests that somewhat more than 6 percent of Chinese fiction was republished in Japan. This figure puts a different spin on the "availability" of the Chinese literary imagination where Japanese readers at large were concerned. While virtually the entire fictional output of late imperial China may have *reached* Japan, nearly all of it was then secreted away in institutional and private collections, with only a tiny subset readily available to the reading public in printed form.

Historical Trends in the Wakokubon *Market*

Even the figure of 6 percent—the portion of printed Chinese fiction that was reprinted in Japan in the Edo period—overstates the true accessibility of Chinese fiction, as it represents the amount reprinted over the entirety of the Edo period and elides the question of historical change. Not only might a title published early in the Edo period have become difficult or impossible to obtain decades or centuries later, but the types of text chosen for reprinting also changed over time in response to a range of factors—commercial, cultural, political, and otherwise. In this final section of the chapter I approach the problem of historical change from several interrelated perspectives centered on the visual representation of the publication of *wakokubon* editions by decade.

Figure 2.1 shows the number of editions published across five categories each decade from the 1620s through the 1860s using raw data drawn from Nagasawa's *wakokubon* catalog. A database was created by inputting published editions year by year under each of the four-branches categories (weighting those for which only a reign period is given), omitting non-Edo-period editions (with the exception, in the interest of consistent

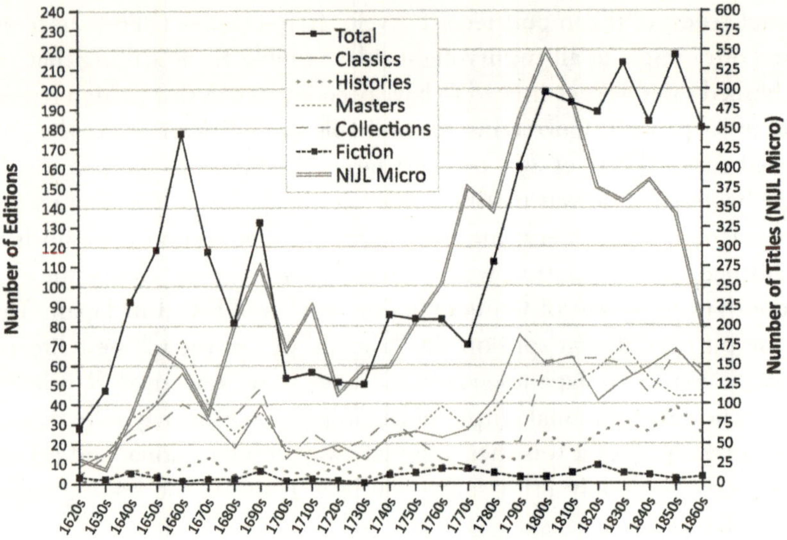

FIGURE 2.1 *Wakokubon* production by decade, 1620s–1860s

decade-long divisions, of a small number of titles from late 1868 and 1869, published at the dawn of the Meiji era), and incorporating the extensive list of errata and additions included in the revised edition. As is evident even from the relatively short list of titles in table 2.1, many *wakokubon* editions were reissued at least once. Nagasawa's catalog includes known reissues, revised editions, and *kabusebori* recarvings as separate entries, and figure 2.1 includes these where the year is known, adding greater nuance to the visualization of publication trends over time. It follows that a portion of the total in later decades consists of reprinted earlier titles, and that this portion grows steadily in tandem with the total number of titles that had been cumulatively reprinted.

In addition to the four-branches categories, "fiction" is included as a separate (albeit overlapping) fifth category composed of titles that appear under the heading *xiaoshuo* in both the "masters" (*zi*) and "collections" (*ji*) branches. This definition includes vernacular fiction but excludes certain miscellany-type works (for example, Xie Zhaozhe's *Wenhai pisha*) that fall elsewhere in the four branches, resulting in slightly different coverage from Yuan and Hou. Finally, to contextualize trends from the perspective of the publishing industry as a whole, the number of titles avail-

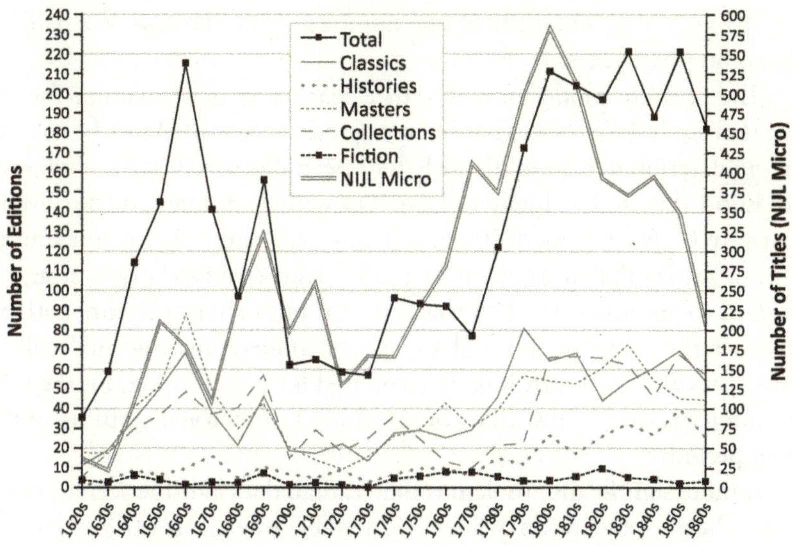

FIGURE 2.2 *Wakokubon* production by decade, 1620s–1860s, corrected for estimated survival rates

able on microfilm at the National Institute of Japanese Literature (NIJL) is included as a gray double line, with this series ("NIJL Micro") corresponding to the secondary y-axis scaling on the right-hand side.[44] These figures serve as a proxy for the total output of the early modern Japanese publishing industry.

Figure 2.2 offers a modified visualization of the same data, building on the statistical methods used earlier to account for the problem of survival rates. In his quantitative study of woodblock-printed titles on microfilm in the NIJL collections (many of which have been digitized in the intervening decades), Yamanaka Kōichi employs a fairly straightforward mathematical model for survival rates assuming a "half-life" for titles.[45] In the course of revising initial estimates of the number of titles published per decade in the Edo period, Yamanaka presents two scenarios,

44. The number of microfilmed titles is based on Yamanaka Kōichi, "Kokubungaku kenkyū shiryōkan zō maikuro shiryō mokuroku dēta kara suikei sareru kinsei no shuppan no henka," *Kokubungaku kenkyū shiryōkan kiyō* 12 (March 1986): 138.

45. Yamanaka, "Kokubungaku kenkyū shiryōkan zō maikuro shiryō mokuroku dēta," 145.

the first assuming a half-life of one hundred years, the second a half-life of two hundred years.

The half-life model provides an elegant way of correcting for the fact that early Edo titles that once existed are less likely to be extant, having deteriorated, been discarded, or been destroyed in fires, whereas late Edo titles are less likely to have met with such fates and survive in relatively higher numbers. There are, however, some significant limitations in Yamanaka's implementation. One issue that is relatively straightforward to address is the fact that survival rates change significantly as we enter the Meiji period and the era of modern institutional collections. This historical transition is accounted for by assuming, for the sake of simplicity, that all lost titles were already lost by the beginning of the Meiji period.

A more significant problem is that Yamanaka's half-life scenarios appear to be entirely arbitrary. Here we are able to use our earlier approximation of the survival rates for *wakokubon* editions—89.1 percent—to arrive at a more informed estimate. Given a survival rate of p for editions, the half-life h is given by the relation $p^{\frac{h}{124}} = 0.5$, where 124 is half the duration of the period of analysis in the figures—that is, the average time from publication to the end of the period. As the Meiji transition has been taken as the end point, the assumption is that editions surviving at that time, regardless of their age, have an equal probability of having been lost subsequently. Taking $p = 0.891$ and solving for h, we find an estimated half-life of 745 years, much longer than the scenarios modeled by Yamanaka.

The scale factor for year y, then, is $0.5^{\frac{y-1868}{745}}$. For 1860, on the historically proximate end of the graph, the scale factor approaches 1, meaning that the original number of titles is virtually the same as the extant number of titles (again, this is a model in which there are no further losses post-Meiji). At the far end of 1620, the scale factor is approximately 1.26. The change is subtle, but when we adjust the graph of *wakokubon* production to account for titles that once presumably existed but have been lost, the figures for earlier years become relatively more pronounced, while there is little change in the distribution for late Edo titles. For consistency, the NIJL microfilm numbers are adjusted using the same half-life; a more accurate estimation of the half-life of woodblock-printed books as a whole, using the same statistical methods applied above, is beyond the scope of this chapter, and in any event these figures are provided only for general comparative reference.

Figures 2.1 and 2.2 both show an obvious early surge in production peaking in the 1660s, as the publishing industry at large was coming into maturity. The relative weakness of the NIJL microfilm curve through much of the seventeenth century suggests that *wakokubon* editions occupied a comparatively large portion of overall publication during the early development of commercial publishing. In the wake of a second, smaller peak coinciding with the Genroku era (1688–1704), there are several decades of retreat followed by a sustained crescendo that begins in the mid-eighteenth century and builds through the end of the Edo period. The scaled numbers in figure 2.2 show that the early peak in the 1660s matches in magnitude the sustained publication rates of the nineteenth century, while the drop-off of the NIJL microfilm curve on the righthand side of both figures suggests that *wakokubon* editions again reasserted themselves in number relative to the industry as a whole in the late Edo period. As the availability of *wakokubon* increased, prices declined accordingly. Writing in 1770, the Ise scholar Minamikawa Kinkei (1732–81) marveled at the steady, large-scale production of domestic reprints in his lifetime—particularly histories, classics, and dictionaries, but also across other fields—and observed that prices had come down considerably compared to a half-century earlier.[46]

Within the small portion of *wakokubon* publication represented by fiction, there are swells independent of overall production, particularly in the second half of the eighteenth century, a period that coincided with the rise of what is often referred to as the "early *yomihon*"—that is, the strange tales of Tsuga Teishō, Ueda Akinari, and others, works that were deeply informed by their Chinese counterparts. Another swell occurs during the literary efflorescence of the Bunka-Bunsei period (1804–29) in the early nineteenth century. We will recall that Nanpo's appointment to Nagasaki occurred at the beginning of this period, and that he arrived in time to witness the early phase of a sustained influx of Chinese fiction. Recent work by Tokuda Takeshi has shed light on growing interest

46. *Kansan yoroku* (manuscript completed 1770; published 1777), in *Seiken chidan, Kansan yoroku, Orokaoi, Tadaima no owaraigusa, Natsuyama zatsudan, Ginkei issui nanka no yume, Saru chomonjū*, in *NZT* series 2, 20:85.

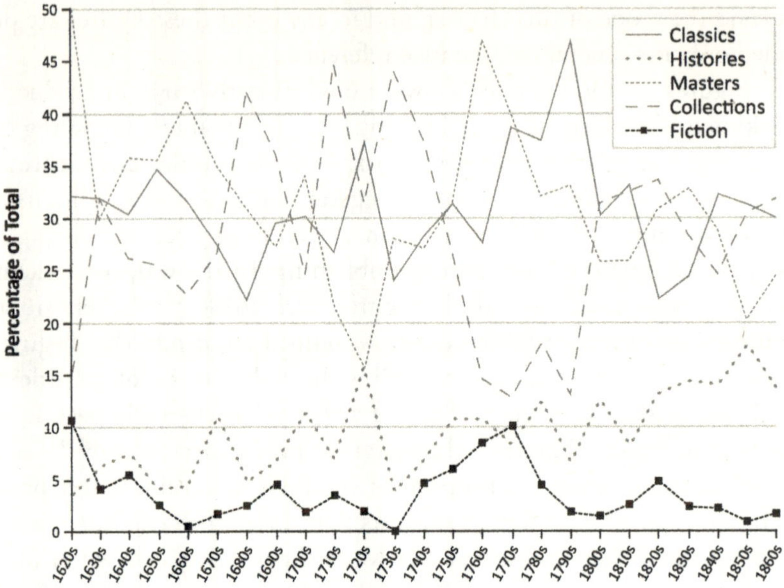

FIGURE 2.3 *Wakokubon* production by genre, 1620s–1860s

in Chinese *biji xiaoshuo*—collections of short stories and fictionalized historical anecdotes written in the classical register—among Japanese intellectuals in the early decades of the nineteenth century.[47] The increasing number of reprints during this period offers further evidence of this movement.

There is a largely inverse relationship between fiction and classics, which generally move in opposition to each other, as can be seen most clearly in figure 2.3, which shows each category as a percentage of the total. This trend is pronounced in the wake of the Kansei Reforms, a series of edicts issued by the bakufu between 1787 and 1793 that sought to address a perceived decline in public morals and promote traditional virtues and scholarship. Major figures in the world of popular fiction were singled out for punishment, including the publisher Tsutaya Jūzaburō, half of whose assets were confiscated, and the author-illustrator Santō

47. For example, Tokuda Takeshi, "Yomihon to Shinchō hikki shōsetsu: *Kinko kidan, Tsūzoku Haimonroku* ni tsuite" (1989), in *Edo kangaku no sekai* (Perikansha, 1990), 267.

Kyōden, who was handcuffed and placed under house arrest for fifty days. The fallout is also visible in the reprinting of Chinese fiction, with *wakokubon* editions dwindling during the 1790s and the first decade of the 1800s at the same time that editions of the masters and classics skyrocketed, followed shortly thereafter by histories. This decline in editions of fiction coincided with the publication of a wave of strange-tale collections on the continent in the 1790s. As is evident in figures 1.2 and 1.3 in the preceding chapter, many of these titles were imported to Japan almost immediately; however, amid a conservative political climate few were reprinted until later decades.

The reprinting of fiction was supplemented by Japanese translations (a topic returned to in chapter 4), which were often published with the label *tsūzoku* ("vernacular," lit. "reaching the masses") in their titles. The National Institute of Japanese Literature's *Union Catalogue of Early Japanese Books* contains entries for around forty unique *tsūzoku* editions of Chinese fiction published in the Edo period. About a dozen of these date to the late seventeenth and early eighteenth centuries, with the remainder appearing in a steady stream from the late 1750s through the early decades of the nineteenth century.[48] Some contained translations of texts—or, more typically, selections of texts, as they generally featured a limited selection from much longer narratives or anthologies—that were already available in reprinted form. Others presented texts that were otherwise unavailable, extending the range of what was accessible to readers in something close to its original form. By way of example, the six tales from Feng Menglong's *Constant Words to Awaken the World* (*Xingshi hengyan*, 1627) that were available in reprinted form in the *Wakoku Sangen* were supplemented by two later publications: a translation of the individual tale "The Oil Peddler Wins the Queen of Flowers" ("Maiyoulang duzhan huakui") under the title *Tsūzoku sekijō kien* (A Vernacular Translation of a Strange Marriage Tale, 1761), and Ishikawa Masamochi's *Tsūzoku Seisei kōgen* (A Vernacular Translation of Tales from *Xingshi hengyan*, 1789), which presented an additional four tales in translation. These two *tsūzoku*

48. The word *tsūzoku* appears commonly in the titles of other types of material with a didactic intent, including simplified religious texts, primers (*ōraimono*), and vernacular rewritings of the Confucian classics. These materials are unrelated to the translation of Chinese fiction and are not included in the total figure.

editions nearly doubled the number of tales from Feng's collection that were available to the general reader. Of course, the faithfulness of such translations varied. "The Oil Peddler Wins the Queen of Flowers" was retranslated by Sawa Tansai a half-century later in his collection *Tsūzoku Kokon kikan* (A Vernacular Translation of Tales from *Jingu qiguan*, 1814), but the later effort does little to improve on its predecessor and in some ways strays further from the original.

Although vernacular translations presented texts in a highly accessible form, in quantity they added only marginally to the much larger amount of Chinese fiction that was reprinted in *wakokubon* editions. Reprints facilitated readership and familiarity, and there are even significant works that survived in Japanese editions but were lost in China. Yet for every title that was reprinted, more than nine were not. We must be cautious, then, as we make sense of the wholesale importation of Chinese fiction to early modern Japan. Chūryō's reminiscences of reading *New Tales by Lamplight* as a young man are a valuable reminder that even annotated reprint editions could present challenges to readers. The obstacles to readership for the vast body of unreprinted works—works of which there might only be one or two copies, and rarely more than a handful, in the entirety of Japan—were far greater. In the chapters that follow, the focus increasingly narrows around the case of *Liaozhai zhiyi*. Although *Liaozhai* reached Japan in the middle of the eighteenth century amid a swelling resurgence in the publication of *wakokubon* fiction, it was to remain part of the large majority of texts that were never reprinted. But the story does not end there. As evidenced by a trail of printed adaptations, translations, and other rewritings, these works furtively continued their onward journeys, reaching a steady stream of new readers not through the printed medium of the *wakokubon* but by means of the less visible practices of manuscript culture.

CHAPTER 3

Hidden Practices

Collectors, Borrowers, and Manuscript Culture in the Age of Woodblock Print

The interconnected large-scale analyses developed in the preceding chapters offer detailed evidence that the literary imagination of late imperial China was transported almost wholesale to early modern Japan. By the close of the eighteenth century, the flow of texts was often nearly contemporaneous, with many works of fiction arriving within a year or two of their publication on the continent. At the same time, the great majority of imported titles were never reprinted in domestic editions. Given that these editions played such an important role in the absorption of texts from Qu You's *New Tales by Lamplight* to the vernacular collections of Feng Menglong, the situation raises obvious questions. What was the fate of imported fiction that was not reprinted? Were these books consigned to obscurity, doomed to gather dust in the libraries where their travels came to an end? Given the small number of copies involved, such a fate seems plausible, perhaps even inevitable. And yet, as this chapter demonstrates through a central, but not exclusive, focus on the case of *Liaozhai zhiyi*, the richness of book culture, borrowing, and above all manuscript practices ensured that this was not the case. The availability of texts in the commercial market was not the definitive, determining factor it first appears.

It is not known for certain when *Liaozhai* first reached Japan or in what form. Pu Songling prepared his tales over a roughly thirty-year period from around 1675 to 1705, and they circulated in manuscript form for decades before first appearing in print in Zhao Qigao's Qingketing edition of 1766. The possibility that one of these manuscripts reached Japan prior to 1766 therefore cannot be excluded. However, the timing of the first recorded copy, which arrived in 1768, suggests that it was the Qingketing edition. Three more copies arrived several decades later, in 1800, and the next two recorded copies arrived more than half a century later, in 1854, a decade after the appearance of two significant new editions: one with commentary by Dan Minglun, the other annotated by Lü Zhan'en.[1] In addition, there were copies that arrived but are not recorded in the fragmentary surviving import records. Kawachiya Kihē's notes from the auctions he attended in Kyoto and Osaka, for instance, record five additional copies that were bid on in 1831.[2] Another copy was among the personal effects onboard a distressed Chinese vessel that came ashore in Tōtōmi Province in 1826.[3] Still, the total number of copies that were imported was undoubtedly small, and the text was never reprinted in a Japanese edition.

In light of this, it is not surprising that until fairly recently *Liaozhai* was thought to have been almost completely unknown in Edo Japan and to have essentially disappeared into the void, exerting no discernible influence on writers of the period.[4] Certainly the tales never attained the wide readership or general familiarity enjoyed by earlier collections of classical tales such as *New Tales by Lamplight* or the early Song collection

1. For the relevant entries, see Ōba, *Edo jidai ni okeru Tōsen mochiwatarisho no kenkyū*, 253, 575, 687.

2. *Shinto Tōhon-ichi hikaechō*, in Yayoshi, *Mikan shiryō ni yoru Nihon shuppan bunka*, 2:356, 384.

3. The presence of two titles on the ship—*Liaozhai* and *Wondrous Tales New and Old* (*Jingu qiguan*)—was discussed during the scholar Noda Tekiho's "brush-conversations" with the captain and two others who were on board. Noda Tekiho and Zhu Liuzhu, *Tokutai-sen hitsugo* (Brush Conversations aboard the *Detai*), 2 vols. (Ki-han: Hyōyōkan, ca. 1826), 1:15a–15b.

4. See, for instance, the view expressed by Masuda Wataru and his collaborators in one of the major postwar translations. Masuda Wataru et al., trans., *Ryōsai shii* [*Liaozhai zhiyi*], in *Chūgoku koten bungaku zenshū* 21 (Heibonsha, 1958), 434. While prewar scholars such as Sasagawa Taneo and Fujii Otoo pointed to *Liaozhai* as an example of the sort of collection of supernatural tales that was avidly read and adapted in the Edo period, they did not give any actual examples of engagement with *Liaozhai* specifically, and it was not until much later that studies began to trace direct connections. See Sasagawa Taneo, *Kinsei bungeishi* (Meiji shoin, 1931), 139; and Fujii Otoo, *Edo bungaku sōsetsu* (Iwanami shoten, 1931), 514.

Taiping guangji (Extensive Records of the Taiping Era), or even, for that matter, earlier vernacular fiction such as *The Water Margin* or the tales of Feng Menglong—material that, in addition to being variously translated, annotated, and commented on, became known to an enormous readership through a large body of adaptations. *Liaozhai*'s relative newness may have been partly to blame. After all, any reception history begins at the earliest with the arrival of the first copy in 1768.

And yet *Liaozhai*'s apparent obscurity in early modern Japan turns out to have been just that: *apparent*. Beginning in the 1960s and continuing through the present, scholars have steadily identified more than a dozen literary adaptations of Pu Songling's tales, beginning possibly as early as 1773 but certainly no later than 1786.[5] In addition, several tales were translated into vernacular Japanese in the early nineteenth century—albeit indirectly, by way of a later Chinese anthology—and a smattering of individual tales were even reprinted in new contexts. These adaptations, translations, and reprintings sprouted up in diverse locations, including not only Edo and Osaka but also Nagoya and the small city of Takaoka on the Japan Sea coast. In other words, there is no doubt that a variety of readers in multiple locations *were* seriously engaged with Pu Songling's collection.

How is it possible, in the absence of a reprint edition, that a handful of imported copies should translate into wide readership and a rich array of adaptations? Where, how, and in what form did readers encounter *Liaozhai* and other titles that were unavailable in Japanese editions? The history of literary reception is often presented through print: on one side, the Chinese books that trickled into Japan; on the other, the published adaptations that surfaced downstream. But between these visible bookends is a story that takes place through practices mostly hidden from sight, one that underscores the importance of manuscript in an age of

5. Bakin, however, seems to have been the only adapter to acknowledge his source by name. The earlier date is the year of publication of Seita Tansō's (1719–85) *Two Tales from Medieval Times* (*Chūsei nidenki*, 1773), the second story of which possibly draws on "The Painted Skin" ("Hua pi"), while the later date corresponds to Tsuga Teishō's *Leaves of Crabgrass* (*Hitsujigusa*, 1786), the third story of which draws on "Hengniang." See Tokuda Takeshi, ed., *Shōseihai, fu Chūsei nidenki* (Yumani shobō, 1976), 472; and Tokuda, "Teishō to *Seiko kawa* [*Xihu jiahua*], *Ryōsai shii*," in *Nihon kinsei shōsetsu to Chūgoku shōsetsu*, 230.

print. Imported books were dispersed to collections across Japan, from the Momijiyama Library on the grounds of Edo Castle and the Shōheikō Academy a mile to the northeast to daimyō collections in the more than two hundred domains across Japan and the libraries of wealthy collectors in urban centers. Would-be readers leveraged their status and social connections, borrowing, reading, and copying texts with remarkable rapidity. These copies in turn gave rise to other copies, and texts multiplied, as did the uses to which readers put them. In the case of *Liaozhai*, some treated the collection as they did many other Chinese texts, approaching it as a reference work to be mined for vocabulary, cultural knowledge, case studies, or didactic insights. Others read for pleasure or literary inspiration, with some coming to feel a deep emotional bond with Pu Songling and seeing themselves as fellow "historians of the strange." A few were moved to adapt certain tales and publish versions of their own, through which the collection's hidden reception history emerges once more into the visible realm of print.

Surface Traces: The Reception of Liaozhai zhiyi *in Print*

The work of a handful of scholars over the past sixty years has gradually shed light on the existence of numerous adaptations and other rewritings of *Liaozhai* that were published in the Edo period. Table 3.1 synthesizes this work and makes several new additions, presenting a dozen titles that together draw on nearly thirty individual tales. Although these numbers are modest compared to the dozens upon dozens of adaptations of works like *The Water Margin* or *New Tales by Lamplight*, they are striking relative to the small number of imported copies of *Liaozhai* and the absence of a *wakokubon* edition. Many of the adaptations, moreover, date to the eighteenth century, when only one or two copies are known for sure to have reached Japan. Yet *Liaozhai* was hardly the only work that found its way into adaptations under such circumstances. Zhang Chao's *New Tales of Yu Chu* (preface dated 1700), another celebrated collection of classical tales, was first adapted in 1717, over a century before the publication of the earliest *wakokubon* edition in 1823—and also, in a reminder of the significant gaps in the documentary evidence, predating the first entry in the import records by nearly half a century.[6]

The earliest Japanese narratives to show the influence of *Liaozhai* were partial, loose adaptations. In his collection *Leaves of Crabgrass: Strange Stories Old and New* ([*Kokon kidan*] *Hitsujigusa*, 1786), Tsuga Teishō presents three legends explaining a group of burial mounds at Unai in Settsu Province. The final version, narrated by a local ascetic, incorporates elements from Pu Songling's "Hengniang," including its central story about a woman who instructs a friend in the art of seduction to help her edge out a rival for her husband's affection.[7] Even before this, one of the stories in a 1773 collection titled *Two Tales from Medieval Times* (*Chūsei nidenki*) shows possible awareness of the *Liaozhai* tale "The Painted Skin" ("Hua pi").[8] After a man's wife dies following an encounter with the vengeful ghost of the tenth-century warrior Taira no Masakado's son Yoshikado, her spirit returns to tell her husband that he must swallow his pride and go ask a seer figure named Old Man Reed-Bearer to help bring her back to life. The husband dutifully obeys, and after enduring abuse he is taken to the underworld, where the old man confines the spirit of Yoshikado and uses secret techniques to resurrect the wife.

The earliest nearly full adaption from Pu Songling is a story titled "How a Fox-Spirit and a Ghost Accused Each Other of Insincerity" ("Kosei kirei enshō o uttauru hanashi"), which appears in Bun'eidō Hōgusai's collection *Bedtime Ghost Stories, Round One* (*Kaii zenseki yawa*, 1790). The story reworks much of the *Liaozhai* tale "Lianxiang," omitting the very beginning and diverging from the original about two-thirds of the way through.[9] Both narratives describe strange love triangles in which a fox-spirit and a ghost, each in the guise of an attractive young woman, alternate

6. Tokuda Takeshi, "*Min Shin gundan* to *Gu Sho shinshi* 'Gonin den,'" *Kokubungaku: Kaishaku to kyōzai no kenkyū* 50, no. 6 (2005): 30.

7. Tokuda Takeshi, "Teishō to *Seiko kawa* [*Xihu jiahua*], *Ryōsai shii*," in *Nihon kinsei shōsetsu to Chūgoku shōsetsu*, 230.

8. In Tokuda, *Shōseihai, fu Chūsei nidenki*, 417–44. On the similarity to "The Painted Skin," see p. 472 in the accompanying "Kaisetsu."

9. Inoue Keiji, "*Kaii zenseki yawa* ron, fu honkoku: zenki yomihon, zenki kokkeibon kenkyū (5)," *Shūjitsu ronsō: Jinbun hen* 19 (February 1990): 24. Inoue's article includes the full transcribed text of the story.

Table 3.1 Published Edo-Period Adaptations, Translations, and Reprintings of Tales from *Liaozhai zhiyi*

Year	Work	Author (illustrator)	Genre (relationship with source)	Source tale(s)
1773	"The Tale of Old Man Reed-Bearer" ("Ashininai no okina no hanashi" 蘆擔翁話), second story in *Two Tales from Medieval Times* (*Chūsei nidenki* 中世二傳奇)	likely Seita Tansō 清田儋叟 (illustrator not credited)	*yomihon* (adaptation)	Possibly "The Painted Skin" ("Hua pi" 畫皮)*
1786	"Variants of the Legend of Motomezuka, in the Form of a Dialogue with the Spirit There" ("Motomezuka zokusetsu no idō tsuka no kami no rei mondō no koto" 求冢俗説の異同冢の神霊問答の話), third story in *Leaves of Crabgrass* (*Hitsujigusa* 莠句冊)	Tsuga Teishō 都賀庭鐘 (possibly Shitomi Kangetsu 蔀関月)	*yomihon* / *kidan* (adaptation)	"Hengniang" 恆娘*
1790	"How a Fox-Spirit and a Ghost Accused Each Other of Insincerity" ("Kosei kirei enshō o uttauru hanashi" 狐精鬼霊寃情を訴ふる話), second tale in *Bedtime Ghost Stories, Round One* (*Kaii zenseki yawa* 怪異前席夜話)	Bun'eidō Hōgusai 文栄堂反古斎 (illustrator not credited)	*yomihon* / *kidan* (adaptation)	"Lianxiang" 蓮香

1792	*Tales from the Withering Wind* ([*Hakushō kidan*] *Kogarashi zōshi* 拍掌奇談凩草紙): stories 2, 3, 5, 6, 7, 8, and 9	Morishima Chūryō 森島中良 (Kitao Masayoshi 北尾政美)	*yomihon* / *kidan* (adaptation)	"The Painted Skin" (2) "The Drinking Companion" ("Jiuyou" 酒友) (3) "The Gentleman from Fengyang" ("Fengyang shiren" 鳳陽士人) (5) "The Cricket" ("Cuzhi" 促織) (6) "Master Longfei" ("Longfei xianggong" 龍飛相公)* (7) "The Daoist Priest" ("Daoshi" 道士) (8) "Zhicheng" 織成 (9)
1797	*The Wag-Tale of a Celebrated Fool's Education* (*Oshiedori ahō no kōmyō* 押絵鳥癡漢高名)	Kyokutei Bakin 曲亭馬琴 (Kitao Shigemasa 北尾重政)	*kibyōshi* (adaptation)	"The Bookworm" ("Shu chi" 書痴)
1797	*A Tale of Chance Encounters* (*Wakuraba monogatari* 邂逅物語)	Unpukan Tenpo 雲府観天歩 (Katsukawa Shunzan 勝川春山)	*yomihon* (adaptation)	"Da'nan" 大男
1807	*Excursions in the Arts* (*Geien nisshō* 執苑日涉)	Murase Kōtei 村瀬栲亭	*zuihitsu* (reprinting)	"Performing Mice" ("Shu xi" 鼠戲) reproduced in its entirety; several other tales excerpted
1818	*Tales of Unrivalled Strangeness* ([*Katakiuchi*] *Kōsei kidan* 復讐曠世奇談)	Shinrotei 振鷺亭 [actually Chūryō] (Gekkōtei Bokusen 月光亭墨僊)	*yomihon* / *kidan* (adaptation)	(new edition of *Tales from the Withering Wind*; reprinted in 1833)
1819	*Pearls from Reishū* (*Reishū yoshu* 蛎洲餘珠): selected tales	Terasaki Reishū 寺崎蛎洲	*kanbun* essays and tales (commentary and loose adaptation)	various
1826	*Lost in Love for Doubled-Up Wives* (*Tsuma gasane omoi no rangiku* 棲重思乱菊)	Kantei Denshō 関亭傳笑 (Keisai Eisen 渓斎英泉)	*gōkan* (adaptation)	"Lianxiang," by way of *Kaii zenseki yawa* (see entry above)

(*continued*)

Table 3.1 (*continued*)

Year	Work	Author (illustrator)	Genre (relationship with source)	Source tale(s)
1828–29	*Paimen lu: A Vernacular Translation* (*Tsūzoku Haimonroku* 通俗排悶録): 14 stories out of a collection of 132	Ishikawa Masamochi 石川雅望 (Keisai Eisen 渓斎英泉)	*yomihon* (translation)	"Yu Jiang" 於江 (title given as "于江") "Coral" ("Shanhu" 珊瑚) "The Wife Lin" ("Lin shi" 林氏) "Zhang Cheng" 張誠 "Qiu Daniang" 仇大娘 "Poems as Evidence" ("Shi yan" 詩讞) "Rouge" ("Yanzhi" 臙脂) "Vice Censor Yu" ("Yu zhongcheng" 于中丞) "Solving Cases" ("Zheyu" 折獄) (translated as "費公") "A Case from Taiyuan" ("Taiyuan yu" 太原獄) (title given as "大原獄") "Cui Meng" 崔猛 "The Chivalrous Bird" ("Qin xia" 禽俠) (translated as "The Great Bird" ["Da niao" 大鳥]) "Yang Dahong" 楊大洪 (translated as "Loyal Yang" [楊忠烈]) "The Woman from Bo'xing" ("Boxing nü" 博興女)
1831	*A Collection of Legal Cases* (*Chōkō ian* 聴訟彙案): 6 case studies out of 94 total	Tsusaka Tōyō 津阪東陽	legal casebook (reprinting with reading marks)	"A Case from Taiyuan" (appears under title "A Woman Accused by Her Lustful Mother-in-Law" [淫姑誣婦]) first half of "Solving Cases" (under title "A Silver-Wrapper as Evidence of Adultery" [銀袱認姦]) "Poems as Evidence" (under title "A Villain Identified through Poetry" [姦賊詩讞]) second half of "Solving Cases" (under title "The Difficult Case of the Dry Well" [眢井疑獄]) "A False Verdict" ("Yuanyu" 冤獄) (under title "A Joke Leads to a False Verdict" [戲謔宪獄]) "Rouge" (under title "The Suspicious Case of the Bored Hole" [鑚隙疑案])

* An asterisk denotes a work or individual tale within a collection that shows the influence of the source story, but is not primarily an adaptation thereof.

nights with the male protagonist. The fox and ghost warn the man of each other's true identity—the fox-spirit out of genuine devotion, the ghost out of jealousy—and when the ghost saps the man's vitality, the fox-spirit helps restore him to health using a medicine with magical properties.

The most substantial engagement with Pu Songling in Edo literature followed two years after Hōgusai's effort, when Morishima Chūryō published a collection of strange tales titled *Tales from the Withering Wind* (*Kogarashi zōshi*) that, both structurally and stylistically, was heavily informed by the earlier collections of Teishō and Akinari.[10] Seven of the nine stories constitute full or partial adaptations of tales from *Liaozhai*, including two of the most enduringly popular: "The Painted Skin" and "The Cricket" ("Cuzhi"). Two more adaptations followed before the close of the eighteenth century. Unpukan Tenpo's *A Tale of Chance Encounters* (*Wakuraba monogatari*, 1797), like "Da'nan," the story from which it is closely adapted, tells of an unhappy family that falls apart one member at a time, then is reunited one by one into a more auspicious arrangement through a series of coincidences.[11] The same year, Bakin published a short satire in comic-book form based on "The Bookworm" ("Shu chi"), Pu Songling's story of a young man who naïvely (but not entirely mistakenly, as it turns out) believes books to hold the answers to all of life's challenges.

The early eighteenth century saw the publication of two secondhand adaptations: an extended work of pictorial fiction (*gōkan*) titled *Lost in Love for Doubled-Up Wives* (*Tsuma gasane omoi no rangiku*, 1826), based on the earlier adaptation of "Lianxiang" in *Bedtime Ghost Stories, Round One*, and an 1818 collection titled *Tales of Unrivalled Strangeness*

10. The full extent of Chūryō's debt to Pu Songling was first explored in Tokuda Takeshi's article "*Kogarashi zōshi* to *Ryōsai shii* [*Liaozhai zhiyi*]" (1980), in *Nihon kinsei shōsetsu to Chūgoku shōsetsu*, 336–70, and was not recognized as an influence in earlier discussions, such as that of Mizutani Futō. See "Sentaku kosho kaidai" (1937), in Mizutani, *Mizutani Futō chosakushū* (Chūō kōronsha, 1973–77), 7:140.

11. The work and its source material are mentioned in Mukai Nobuo, "Kansei nendai ni okeru Bakin chosaku no ni san ni tsuite," *Biburia* 61 (October 1975): 24–25. The most detailed discussion appears in Chen Beinkuen, "Edo bungaku to *Ryōsai shii*," *Shokō* 12 (2001): 58–63. Chen's article also includes treatment of *The Wag-Tale of a Celebrated Fool's Education* and *Tales from the Withering Wind*.

([*Katakiuchi*] *Kōsei kidan*).[12] Although it makes no mention of its true origins, the latter was in fact a reprint of *Tales from the Withering Wind* carved from an original copy onto new blocks (using the technique of *kabusebori*) with new illustrations by the artist Gekkōtei Bokusen.[13] Chūryō's name appears nowhere, and the tales are instead credited to the writer Shinrotei. While this may indicate Tamenaga Shunsui (1790–1843), the writer of sentimental fiction who assumed the penname Shinrotei II within a few years of the death of the first Shinrotei (d. 1815), it seems more likely that the unscrupulous publisher chose to attach the name of a well-known (and recently deceased) author as a way of capitalizing on his name recognition.[14] In any event, the pirate edition is of more than passing interest for Bokusen's striking, skillfully executed illustrations, which are more numerous than those in the 1792 original.

Table 3.1 also documents the fact that it is not, strictly speaking, correct that *Liaozhai* was never reprinted—at least not where a small selection of the tales is concerned. Some fourteen tales appeared in Japanese translation, by way of Sun Zhu's (1711–78) anthology *Paimen lu* (preface dated 1770), in Ishikawa Masamochi's (1754–1830) *Paimen lu: A Vernacular Translation* (*Tsūzoku Haimonroku*, 1828–29). Four of the same stories, plus one more—all depicting the administration of justice—were also reproduced two years later in their original form, with reading marks added, in Tsusaka Tōyō's (1758–1825) *A Collection of Legal Cases* (*Chōkō ian*, 1831; preface dated 1806).[15] Given the largely overlapping selection, it is possible

12. Inoue, "*Kaii zenseki yawa* ron, fu honkoku," 34. On *Tsuma gasane omoi no rangiku*, see Suzuki Jūzō, "Gōkan-mono no daizai tenki to Tanehiko," *Kokugo to kokubungaku* 38, no. 4 (April 1961): 64–65.

13. Yamazaki Fumoto early recognized the relationship between the two works, describing the later version as "a revised edition of *Tales from the Withering Wind* passed off as an original work." See Yamazaki, ed., *Nihon shōsetsu shomoku nenpyō*, in *Shoshi shomoku shirīzu* 6 (Yumani shobō, 1977) (revised edition of his 1929 *Nihon shōsetsu nenpyō*), 115.

14. Shinrotei's year of death is often given as 1819, but this is corrected in Tanahashi Masahiro, "Shinrotei nenpu kō," *Yomihon kenkyū* 10, no. 2 (1996): 49.

15. Although several *Liaozhai* stories included in *Paimen lu* are omitted, Masamochi's collection still contains fourteen translated tales from *Liaozhai*. For the full list of stories translated by Masamochi, as well as their original sources, see Tokuda Takeshi, "Yomihon to Shinchō hikki shōsetsu: *Kinko kidan*, *Tsūzoku Haimonroku* ni tsuite" (1989), in *Edo kangaku no sekai*, 260–64.

that Tōyō's decision to include tales from *Liaozhai* was inspired by an encounter with Masamochi's translations.

Reading Liaozhai zhiyi *in Early Modern Japan*

One of the few works in table 3.1 to acknowledge its source material directly is *The Wag-Tale of a Celebrated Fool's Education* (*Oshiedori ahō no kōmyō*, 1797), the preface to which relates Bakin's unflagging enthusiasm for Pu Songling's collection and his decision to turn out an adaptation. That so few writers identified *Liaozhai* as their source is not to suggest that they were trying to pull the wool over readers' eyes or pass off the material as entirely their own. On the contrary, adaptation was a widespread and recognized practice in what was a deeply intertextual literary tradition. To spell out one's sources was a gratuitous, unsubtle gesture that risked denying readers the pleasure of identifying those intertextual layers themselves. Indeed, as we begin to probe beneath the traces *Liaozhai* left in print, it becomes clear that at least by the nineteenth century the title *was* widely known and widely read. Writing to his younger brother in the autumn of 1801, Ōta Nanpo mentioned the "recent" collection—its author referred to only as "a man of Qing," perhaps suggesting that Pu Songling himself had not yet attained wide name-recognition—as an example of a text by a man of letters interested in the supernatural, placing it alongside the *Zuo Commentary* (*Zuo zhuan*), *In Search of the Supernatural* (*Soushen ji*), and *Records of the Hidden and the Visible* (*Youming lu*).[16] A few decades later, when the scholar Doi Gōga (1818–80) jotted down several dozen "must-have" titles at the request of a student, *Liaozhai* was among them.[17]

Readers approached Pu Songling's collection from a variety of perspectives. For some it was a source of linguistic knowledge to be mined like any other. The dictionary *Shōsetsu jii* (A Glossary of Vocabulary from

16. The letter is reproduced in Hamada, ed., *Ōta Nanpo zenshū*, 19:40.

17. The list, titled *Gōga's List of Essential Texts* (*Gōga-ō hissu shomoku*), was likely written around the mid-1840s. The text is reproduced in *Shinagaku* 2, no. 10 (1922): 70–75.

Chinese Fiction), first published in 1791, drew its entries from a corpus of around 160 titles, *Liaozhai* among them, and vocabularies and dictionaries through the bakumatsu period similarly pored through the collection for citations.[18] Tsusaka Tōyō's *A Collection of Legal Cases* (1831) includes five tales depicting the administration of justice as part of a larger casebook compiled for use by students at the Yūzōkan Academy in the Tsu domain in what is now Mie Prefecture. Essayists leafed through the tales in search of moments that offered a window onto continental cultural practices, just as they did on a grander scale with narratives such as *The Water Margin*. The Kyoto Sinologist Murase Kōtei (1746–1818) selected a handful of passages illustrating diverse forms of performance and entertainment for inclusion in his wide-ranging miscellany *Excursions in the Arts* (*Geien nisshō*, 1807), including the full text of a brief story (one of the shortest in *Liaozhai*) about a troupe of performing mice.[19] In his popular encyclopedia *For Your Enjoyment* (*Kiyū shōran*, 1830), Kitamura Intei (1783–1856) uses the tale "White Autumn Thread" ("Bai qiulian") to illustrate the practice of divination by opening a book to a random passage, comparing the practice to the Japanese custom of *utauranai*, or using a randomly chosen poem to tell one's fortune.[20] The Mito scholar Komiyama Fūken (1764–1840) compares "The Painted Horse" ("Hua ma"), which tells of an exceptional steed acquired by the King of Jin that is discovered to have escaped from a painting by the Song artist Zhao Mengfu (1254–1322), to similar legends involving the artist Kanō Motonobu (1476–1559).[21]

18. *Shōsetsu jii*, 4a, in Nagasawa, *Tōwa jisho ruishū*, 15:5. For a later dictionary, see Kaneuchi Kakuzō, *Tokō jii* (Edo: Suwaraya Mohē et al., 1860).

19. Murase Kōtei, *Geien nisshō* (1807), in Kokumin tosho kabushiki kaisha, ed., *Nihon zuihitsu zenshū*, vol. 1 (Kokumin tosho, 1927), 361–699.

20. *Kiyū shōran*, in *NZT bekkan*, 9:352. The passage is not included in the Seikadō bunko manuscript, which is the basis for the widely available Iwanami bunko edition of the text. The writer Kita Seiro (1765–1848) cites the same passage, likely drawing it secondhand from Intei. See Kita Seiro, *Baien nikki* (1845), in *NZT* series 3, 12:17.

21. *Kaihō nissatsu* (1811–21), in Mori Senzō, ed., *Zuihitsu hyakkaen* 3 (Chūō kōronsha, 1980), 251–52. Legends circulated about Motonobu's paintings of horses, most famously one on a votive tablet at Sensōji Temple in Asakusa that was popularly attributed to him and that was said to come to life each night to roam the temple grounds and fill itself on crops from neighboring fields. To prevent further incidents, the temple

There were others whose engagement with Pu Songling went much deeper, including some who saw themselves as kindred spirits or even fellow "historians of the strange." One of the places furthest afield where it is possible to trace the circulation of *Liaozhai* is the castle town of Takaoka, a center of learning in the Kaga domain on the Japan Sea coast. Tucked away on Toyama Bay south of the Noto Peninsula, it was here that Ōtomo no Yakamochi was stationed for several years in the middle of the eighth century, with the area providing the setting for a number of his poems in the *Man'yōshū*. A millennium later, Takaoka was home to two of *Liaozhai*'s most enthusiastic Japanese readers. One was a relative of the eminent Sinologist Hattori Nankaku by the name of Hattori Shukushin (1773?–1805), who in 1802, while serving as city elder (*machidoshiyori*), erected a stele commemorating the *Man'yōshū* that still stands today on the grounds of Fuse Shrine to the northwest of the city. The other was Shukushin's close friend Terasaki Reishū (1761–1822), a scholar and writer who had studied in Kyoto with Murase Kōtei and Minagawa Kien (1734–1807) before returning home and taking up a teaching position at a local private academy.

Shortly before his death, Shukushin wrote a passage extolling the unique pleasures of Pu Songling's prose. Characterizing *Liaozhai* as the most popular of the many "rare collections and strange volumes" that had made the rounds in recent years, he underscored the tales' strange power through reference to a famous legend recounted in Zhao Qigao's prefatory notes to the Qingketing edition. According to Zhao, Pu had initially titled his manuscript "Tales of Foxes and Ghosts," but after finding himself mobbed by angry foxes and ghosts during one of his unsuccessful attempts at the civil service examination—the creatures resented him for having depicted them in such exquisite detail—he gave the collection its new title. Shukushin then illustrates Pu Songling's "intoxicating" effect on two readers who appear in the pages of the collection itself. The first is the author's friend Bi Yi'an, who, as told in "Fox Dream" ("Hu meng"), became smitten with Pu's fox paramour Qingfeng after reading her eponymous story, which appears in an earlier volume. After Yi'an succeeds in

commissioned another artist to add lead ropes to the painting. See the entry for Sensōji in Saitō Gesshin et al., *Edo meisho zue* (Edo: Suwaraya Mohē, 1834–36), 6:2a, 7b.

securing a fox lover of his own, she becomes jealous of Qingfeng and demands a story of her own from Pu Songling.

Shukushin concludes his passage by recounting an exchange with Reishū:

> "Tales like 'Chang'e' and 'Fengxian' are simply perfect in their construction," my friend Reishū once said. "Whenever I read them I am filled with awe, overwhelmed by their rich tapestry of life and emotion. I find myself desperately wanting to share my feelings with someone over a cup of tea or saké. But when I put the book down, it is as though a mirage has faded before my eyes, and I am plunged into gloom."
>
> "That is because you, too, are drunk on his prose," I replied. "This isn't the sort of thing anyone else could understand. It's just something for the two of us to have a laugh over."
>
> Ah, but those of us who read Liuxian's tales have no business laughing at Yi'an. We are just like him ourselves![22]

Fourteen years after Shukushin wrote these words, Reishū compiled a two-volume collection of strange tales in literary Sinitic under the title *Pearls from Reishū* (*Reishū yoshu*, 1819). The second volume opens with a story titled "Pu Liuxian," which reproduces Shukushin's passage in its entirety before carrying the story forward. Echoing Pu's encounter with foxes and ghosts after the completion of his draft manuscript, Reishū relates Shukushin's own supernatural encounter, which occurred as he dozed off after putting his musings down on paper:

> Just then, two petty officials appeared and hauled Shukushin away to a government office. In the middle of the hall sat a man in a scholar's cap. He called Shukushin forward. "I am Pu Songling," he said. "Because you take such pleasure in letters, I have asked Enma that you be reborn in the house of court historian Cao. With the Complete Library of the Four Treasuries piled around you, by the age of sixteen you will be appointed to the Hanlin Academy. This is not just my hope for you, it is decreed as your destiny. Now hurry up and get your affairs in order!"

22. *Reishū yoshu*, in Isobe Yūko and Moriga Kazue, *Toyama bungaku no reimei*, 2:5.

> Shukushin listened respectfully and accepted his charge. The two petty officials escorted him home, and he awoke with a start. Sure enough, he died a few days later.
>
> My own family is poor, and my debts to Shukushin are like those of Guan Zhong to Bao Shuya.[23] I haven't repaid even a tiny fraction of what he has given me. If only he had some masterwork in progress that I could help ready for publication. But when might Pu Songling come for me? Shukushin was just thirty-three years old.[24]

The story concludes with Reishū waxing rhapsodic on the story "Lianxiang," which he praises for its immediacy and stylistic playfulness.

As traced by Isobe Yūko and Moriga Kazue in their annotated edition of *Pearls from Reishū*, *Liaozhai*'s reach extends throughout the text. Readers regularly encounter vocabulary and turns of phrase lifted directly from Pu Songling. In one story, Reishū describes a terrifying spectacle (later revealed to have been produced with professional help) conjured one evening by a fabulously wealthy eccentric for the entertainment of his friends. The parade of phantasms includes a mysterious and alluring beauty (in fact the renowned kabuki female impersonator Segawa Kikunojō) who saunters across the stage only to vanish suddenly before the audience's very eyes. The swooshing sound that accompanies her disappearance is rendered with the unusual onomatopoetic phrase *liuliuran*—the same phrase used in "The Painted Skin" to describe the moment the Daoist priest sucks the malignant spirit into a magical bottle-gourd.[25]

Reishū also occasionally emulates Pu Songling's use of appended commentary as a means of reflecting on stories, their origins and significance, and similarities with other narratives. These commentaries are not as frequent as those by Pu's "Historian of the Strange" (*yishi shi*)—Pu appends remarks to nearly two hundred of his tales altogether—but they serve a similar function, enhancing the narratives' verisimilitude, distancing the author from his literary creation, and reinforcing the perception of the writer as collector and transmitter but not originator or fabricator. One such story presents itself as

23. Bao Shuya is best remembered for his close friendship with Guan Zhong, whom he helped attain his position as minister in the state of Qi in the early seventh century BCE.

24. *Reishū yoshu*, in Isobe Yūko and Moriga Kazue, *Toyama bungaku no reimei*, 2:5.

25. *Reishū yoshu*, in Isobe and Moriga, 1:84–94.

a factual account of an 1803 rescue in a Kyushu village. Readers are told of a man who was found semiconscious after a flood swept away a section of river embankment, revealing the remains of a house that had collapsed in an earthquake years before. In his appended commentary, Reishū speculates that this must have been an earthquake known to have occurred in 1792, meaning that the man had survived underground for more than a decade. The scenario brings to mind that of Pu Songling's "Master Longfei" ("Longfei xianggong"), and Reishū draws on Pu's commentary on that tale both in describing the event itself and in his own commentary, in which he reiterates Pu's assessment of the plausibility of surviving for an extended period underground by noting the slowed metabolism of snakes and other animals in underground hibernation.[26]

Liaozhai may have been Reishū's favorite work of classical Chinese fiction, but it was far from the only collection of strange tales with which he was intimately familiar. A close reading of *Pearls from Reishū* attests to wide reading that encompassed many other eighteenth-century collections, including *Chibei outan* (Casual Tales from North of the Pond, published in 1701 and imported in 1762), *Yetan suilu* (Informal Record of Nighttime Stories) and *Ershi lu* (Stories as I Heard Them) (both published in 1791 and imported that same year), and *Xieduo* (The Bell of Humor, published in 1792 and imported in 1794). Like *Liaozhai*, none of these titles was ever reprinted in a *wakokubon* edition. Nevertheless, all managed to reach a small castle town on the Japan Sea coast, where they left their mark on the literary endeavors of a little-known writer and instructor at the local academy.

Beneath the Surface: Collectors, Borrowers, and Manuscript Culture

If this sizable body of adaptations and wide readership arose in the absence of a reprint edition or vernacular translation (excluding the modest, relatively late selections documented in table 3.1), we must look elsewhere

26. *Reishū yoshu*, in Isobe and Moriga, 1:28–31.

to understand how Pu Songling's tales circulated. Few if any of those who adapted the tales appear to have owned copies of their own. Instead, the story begins with the institutional and individual collectors with the financial means to amass substantial libraries of imported books. Foremost among these were the collections of the Momijiyama Library and the Shōheikō Academy. Although fiction was not a primary emphasis of either, the former nevertheless held just over seventy titles of fiction in the nineteenth century, while the more extensive fictional holdings of the latter encompassed an astounding 219 works, including *Liaozhai* and many other late imperial collections of strange tales.[27] (Given that the bakufu ordinarily had right of first refusal for newly arrived titles, it is likely that the Shōheikō copy of *Liaozhai* was the one that arrived by itself in 1768.[28]) Domainal academies generally had at least modest representation in fiction, with a few boasting more substantial holdings.[29] Some of the most impressive collections belonged to daimyō themselves, including not only the wealthy Tokugawa branch families but many others scattered across the archipelago, such as Matsudaira Sadanobu (1758–1829), who in spite of his aggressive stance against popular fiction during the Kansei Reforms had dabbled in satirical fiction only a few years earlier and owned a respectable selection of thirty works of Chinese fiction.[30]

An examination of diverse forms of evidence—including early modern catalogs, references in letters and journals, and physical copies that

27. The catalog of the Momijiyama Library *Jūtei goshojaku mokuroku* (1836), in the collection of the National Archives of Japan, lists seventy-one titles of Chinese fiction. Only one new title was added in the three decades before the production of the later catalog *Genji zōho goshojaku mokuroku* (1864), also held in the National Archives. The latter is reproduced in Ogawa and Kanai, *Tokugawa bakufu zōshomoku*, vols. 1–7.

28. See Kornicki, *The Book in Japan*, 381, on the bakufu's preference for books that did not have previous Japanese owners.

29. A valuable bibliography of catalogs of daimyō and domainal academy collections available in modern editions appears in Takahashi Satoshi, *Umi o watatte kita kanseki: Edo no shoshigaku nyūmon* (Nichigai asoshiētsu, 2016), 200–203.

30. For Sadanobu's holdings in Chinese fiction, see Asakura Haruhiko, ed., *Matsudaira Sadanobu zōsho mokuroku* (Yumani shobō, 2005), 1:167–69. On a piece of satirical fiction he likely wrote in 1784, see Haruko Iwasaki, "Portrait of a Daimyō: Comical Fiction by Matsudaira Sadanobu," *Monumenta Nipponica* 38, no. 1 (Spring 1983): 1–19.

survive in collections today, which often include ownership seals or are in some instances traceable through other means, such as accession records—suggests that most copies of *Liaozhai* imported in the Edo period went to these elite collections. In addition to the copy held by the Shōheikō, several more were owned by daimyō across Japan. These include the Matsudaira of the Hamada domain and the Mōri of the Tokuyama domain, both in far western Japan. Hotta Masaatsu (1755–1832), daimyō of the Katata domain along Lake Biwa and junior councilor under Sadanobu during the Kansei Reforms, owned a copy as part of his substantial collection of fiction. Another was possibly held by the Akimoto clan in the Tatebayashi domain north of Edo.[31]

This is not to suggest that privately owned copies did not exist outside such rarified circles. In 1778, while traveling in northern Kyushu, the iconoclastic intellectual Miura Baien (1723–89) met many local scholars, among them a retainer of the Nakatsu domain named Kuranari Ryūsho (1748–1812), who showed off some of the highlights of his personal library, including a copy of *Liaozhai*.[32] Assuming that the copy imported in 1768 had been acquired by the bakufu, Baien's encounter points to the importation of additional copies not attested in the import records already by this early date. Other owners included Koga Tōan, a prominent bakufu scholar and instructor at the Shōheikō, and Hirade Jun'eki, a prosperous

31. The Tokyo Shojakukan (one of the precursors to the Imperial Library) accessioned a large number of books from former domainal collections in 1875 and 1876, including a copy of *Liaozhai* from what had been the Hamada domain. See Nishimura and Sano, *Tōkyō shojakukan ni okeru kyūhan zōsho no shūshū*, section 2 ("kōfu shomoku"), 15. The Mōri clan's copy, recognizable from the ownership seals impressed on the volumes, is one of two held today in the collection of the Archives and Mausolea Department of the Imperial Household Agency (Kunaichō shoryōbu). On Hotta Masaatsu's collection of Chinese fiction, see Isobe Akira, "*Saiyūki* to *Tsūzoku Saiyūki*," in Wakan hikaku bungakukai, ed., *Wakan hikaku bungaku sōsho 7: Kinsei bungaku to kanbungaku* (Kyūko shoin, 1988), 147n22. The collection of the Akimoto clan is now housed in the Tatebayashi City Library in Gunma Prefecture; new titles were added through 1917, and examination of the copy of *Liaozhai* in the collection yielded no evidence concerning when the item was acquired. (Indeed, inspection of many other copies in Japanese collections today revealed that most are either later editions or copies that were acquired after the Edo period.)

32. *Kizanroku sōkō*, in Saigusa Hiroto, ed., *Miura Baien shū* (Iwanami bunko, 1953), 85.

Nagoya physician.[33] Still, these were hardly ordinary readers but instead represented cultural elites. Although inspection of those copies that survive today reveals little about the transactions that took place between Nagasaki and their final owners, five copies of *Liaozhai* were purchased at auction by two different Osaka booksellers in 1831 for 29 and 43 *monme* ($974 and $1,430) per copy. The price paid by collectors would have been considerably higher, beyond the means of many readers.

Books in the most elite private collections were likely to be inaccessible to all but a few. In his search for a copy of the 120-chapter recension of *The Water Margin*, Bakin learned that Mōri Takasue, the daimyō of the Saiki domain in northern Kyushu and a prolific collector, owned some seventeen different editions of the text, but in the end he was never able to access them.[34] For other collections, however, accession represented only the final stop of books as objects, not of the texts they contained. Volumes did not simply gather dust on library shelves but continued onward on their journeys as they were actively read, borrowed, and copied. Institutional collections played an important role because of both the size of their holdings and their accessibility to a relatively large number of readers. The Shōheikō in particular was an obvious first destination, and knowledge of its holdings spread not just through word of mouth but in written form through manuscript catalogs.[35]

Granted, it was often insiders who leveraged their access to greatest effect. Consider the scholar Suzuki Tōya (1800–1852), whose enthusiasm for Chinese fiction was encouraged at a young age by his father, Suzuki Hakutō (1767–1851), who often read to him from the *wakokubon* edition of *New Tales by Lamplight*.[36] Hakutō held posts at the Shōheikō and the Momijiyama Library, and in 1839 Tōya followed in his footsteps and

33. An additional copy earlier thought to have belonged to a late Edo haikai poet writing under the name Mugean (see Fleming, "*Liaozhai zhiyi* in Early Modern Japan," 80) was on further examination found to have been owned instead by the art historian Imaizumi Yūsaku (1850–1931), who also used the pseudonym Mugean and who, while born in the Kaei era, likely acquired the set in the Meiji period at the earliest.

34. Kanda, "*Suikoden* no shohon to Bakin," 250.

35. Nanpo was among those writers who owned a copy of the Shōheikō catalog. See *Shokusanjin zōsho mokuroku*, 370.

36. Tokuda Takeshi, *Kinsei kindai shōsetsu to Chūgoku hakuwa bungaku* (Kyūko shoin; 2004), 180.

became an instructor at the academy, where he was able to sate his appetite for fiction amid its vast holdings. His reading encompassed many of the same collections of strange tales enjoyed by Reishū and Shukushin, including *Liaozhai*, *Yetan suilu*, *Yu Chu xinzhi*, and *Xieduo*. References to these works appear in Tōya's own manuscript collection of some eighty-five strange tales titled *Writings on the Back of Scrap Paper* (*Hogo no uragaki*, 1848–50), which he prepared, according to the text's introduction, for the private amusement of his friends. The subject matter encompasses crime, sorcery, and the supernatural, including a number of stories about foxes and ghosts; two of these feature comments that directly reference *Liaozhai*, which was in his view the finest Chinese collection of strange tales.

Borrowing books was an important part of Tōya's reading practice. As an instructor at the Shōheikō, he was allowed to check out titles from the academy library to read in the comfort of his own home.[37] Similar policies at the Momijiyama Library allowed bakufu officials and daimyō to borrow books, although they might be recalled at any moment if requested by a reader higher up the political hierarchy. A wider range of bakufu and daimyō retainers, including Shōheikō students, were allowed to read materials on site.[38] Meanwhile, those with less ready access to institutional collections made the most of their personal networks. Around 1683, long before Feng Menglong's *Constant Words to Awaken the World* had been partly reprinted in Hakku and Issai's mid-eighteenth-century *Wakoku Sangen* editions (and even before it appeared in the Nagasaki records in 1727), the Confucian scholar Itō Jinsai (1627–1705) recorded in his diary borrowing a copy from a seller of Chinese books.[39] Such borrowing was often reciprocal and could even take place through organized networks of readers.[40] Tōya, for his part, may have had access to *Liaozhai* through personal connections even before his appointment at the Shōheikō: his

37. Books loaned out from the Shōheikō collection were recorded in a ledger known as the *oshikirichō*. The years 1849 to 1868 are held in the special collections of the University of Tsukuba library. For borrowing rules, see Monbushō, ed., *Nihon kyōikushi shiryō* 7 (Monbu daijin kanbō hōkokuka, 1892), 117–19, 177–83, 502–3.

38. See Kornicki, *The Book in Japan*, 379, and "Manuscript, Not Print," 30.

39. On the entry in Jinsai's diary, see "Kogidō no shōsetsuka-tachi," in Nakamura, *Kinsei sakka kenkyū*, 132.

40. Kornicki, *The Book in Japan*, 405.

brother-in-law Koga Tōan, also an instructor at the academy, owned a complete edition of his own.[41] When the Chinese ship *Detai* floundered ashore south of what is now the city of Shizuoka in 1826, Tōan recommended Noda Tekiho (1799–1859), one of his favorite students at the Shōheikō, for the task of interviewing the crew. Remarking on the copy of *Liaozhai* that was found aboard, Tekiho informed his Chinese interlocutors that he was familiar with the collection and, echoing Tōya, that it was his favorite work of Chinese fiction. Presumably he had read and perhaps copied the text either at the Shōheikō or using his teacher's copy.

Lending out one's books was not without risks. The Confucian scholar Minagawa Kien recalled having twice acquired copies of *The Water Margin* only to have friends borrow but then refuse to return them.[42] Nevertheless, many considered lending a scholarly obligation, the expectation being that borrowers would copy the items, thereby ensuring the propagation and survival of rare texts. The nativist scholar Motoori Norinaga (1730–1801) viewed this duty in moralistic terms, chastising greedy scholars with "defiled hearts" who kept prized manuscripts squirreled away for private enjoyment.[43] In return for access, borrowers were expected to treat borrowed books with care and to read them quickly. The Genroku-era educator Kaibara Ekiken (1630–1714) recommended one day per volume, allowing an extra day for particularly hefty volumes.[44]

Flouting Walter Benjamin's assertion that borrowers are unlikely to return a borrowed book and even less likely to read it, early modern Japanese not only read but copied the books they borrowed (even if they did on occasion fail to return them). The replication of texts by hand was hardly a lost art in contemporary Europe; the excerpting of passages in reading journals was widely, enthusiastically practiced, and

41. Tōan's copy, identifiable from its ownership seals, survives today in the collection of the Archives and Mausolea Department of the Imperial Household Agency.

42. William C. Hedberg, "Reclaiming the Margins: Seita Tansō's *Suikoden hihyōkai* and the Poetics of Cross-Cultural Influence," *International Journal of Asian Studies* 12, no. 2 (2015): 196n9. One of the two copies was taken by Seita Tansō.

43. Norinaga, *Tamakatsuma*, trans. in John R. Bentley, *Tamakatsuma: A Window into the Scholarship of Motoori Norinaga* (Ithaca, NY: Cornell East Asia Program, 2013), 33–34.

44. Ekiken, *Kadōkun*, in Ekiken-kai, ed., *Ekiken zenshū*, vol. 3 (Ekiken zenshū kankōbu, 1911), 457.

scribal reproduction remained the primary mode of dissemination for certain categories of text (including not only amateur verse but also that of certain luminaries such as John Donne), even retaining commercial viability in some contexts.[45] All the same, those who hand-copied entire books, like the schoolmaster Maria Wutz in Jean Paul's eponymous 1793 novella, were seen as rare, if charming, oddities who did so owing presumably to their financial circumstances.[46] In early modern Japan, by contrast—whatever the image of the period as a golden age of print culture—scholars and readers at all levels of the social hierarchy copied books by hand as part of their daily practice.

Manuscript remained commonplace in many other contexts as well. Vast quantities of literature were composed privately with no eye to commercial publication but circulated exclusively by hand. There could be a gendered element to such production; with the exception of a few tales anthologized by a male contemporary, Arakida Reijo's (1732–1806) fiction was read only in manuscript form until the modern period. Others wrote for personal enjoyment or for their friends, as Suzuki Tōya did with his strange tales (although, as seen in the next chapter, doing so also allowed him to write in a more reportage-like fashion and skirt conventions that required distancing such material in the historical past). For certain types of public literary production, such as playscripts and other texts for the theater, manuscript remained the norm out of both convention and practical concerns, while for other genres, such as underground vernacular histories (*jitsuroku*) or castaway accounts of foreign lands (*hyōryūki*), it was necessitated by regimes of censorship and political con-

45. Ann M. Blair has documented the compilation of textual excerpts and related bibliographic data in early modern Europe; such reference materials, prepared often but not always with an eye to eventual publication, multiplied in response to the daunting, ever-increasing abundance of printed knowledge. See Blair, *Too Much to Know: Managing Scholarly Information before the Modern Age* (New Haven, CT: Yale University Press, 2010), in particular the introduction and chapter 2, "Note-Taking as Information Management." For an overview of manuscript practices and the multifaceted concept of "scribal publication" in early modern England, see Harold Love, *Scribal Publication in Seventeenth-Century England* (Oxford: Clarendon Press, 1993).

46. On his experience of the borrowing and acquisition of books, as well as his passing mention of the "poor little schoolmaster Wutz," see Walter Benjamin, "Unpacking My Library" (1931), in Benjamin, trans. Harry Zohn, *Illuminations* (New York: Harcourt, Brace & World, 1968), 61–62.

trol. In specific contexts, manuscript books even remained viable in the commercial sphere and were available for purchase or rented out by the period's numerous lending libraries.[47]

Many catalogs of private and institutional collections—catalogs that were themselves written and circulated in manuscript form—distinguish between manuscript and print holdings, and it is apparent from these that a significant portion of many private collections was composed of handwritten materials. One in four titles owned by Bakin (totaling as many as eight thousand volumes at his collection's peak around 1832, just a few years before he was forced to sell most of them off) were hand-copied. For Nanpo the figure was even higher: more than one thousand titles altogether, or nearly 40 percent of his collection.[48] The Tōhoku merchant and nativist scholar Uchiike Nagatoshi (1763–1848) had large quantities of manuscript among his 2,500 volumes, and in at least one instance possessed manuscript and print copies of the same work, having first acquired the text in manuscript form, then purchased it again with the publication of a revised print edition.[49]

In other words, hand-copied books were everywhere, and they proliferated rapidly. Ekiken's admonition to borrowers that they return books within a day or two per volume might have challenged even the fastest early modern scribes, but they were still remarkably quick and prolific. When Nagatoshi lent two volumes of current scholarship to an acquaintance in the Nihonmatsu domain for copying, the man returned the items several months later with an apology for his lateness. In the interim, however, his letter explained, "everyone else in the domain" had copied them as well.[50]

47. On manuscripts as commodity, see Nakajima Takashi, "Hanpon jidai no 'shahon' to wa nani ka," in *Kokubungaku: Kaishaku to kyōzai no kenkyū* 42, no. 11 (1997): 49–53.

48. The figures are based on the entries in "Bakin shozōbon mokuroku (1): honkoku *Chosakudō haisho mokuroku* narabi ni *Kyokutei zōsho mokuroku*," in Hattori Hitoshi, ed., *Bakin kenkyū shiryō shūsei* (Kuresu shuppan, 2007), 5:793–814, and on those in *Shokusanjin zōsho mokuroku*. The figure of eight thousand volumes is given in Takada Mamoru, *Takizawa Bakin: momotose nochi no chiin o matsu* (Kyōto: Mineruva shobō, 2006), 218.

49. Takahashi Akinori, "'Hanpon' no 'shahon' o tsukuru no wa naze ka: Tōhoku no kokugakusha Uchiike Nagatoshi o rei ni," *Nao de la China* 6 (2004): 27–28.

50. Takahashi, "'Hanpon' no 'shahon' o tsukuru no wa naze ka," 28.

And yet, in spite of the commonness of copying by hand, there were those who felt nostalgia for what they saw as a vanished age of manuscript culture. One such figure was the nativist scholar and waka poet Katō Enao (1692–1785), who complained that his contemporaries simply acquired printed editions of the canonical poetry anthology *Kokinshū* (Collection of Poems Old and New, early tenth century) without ever copying out the poems by hand themselves. Following the example of the Confucian scholar Ogyū Sorai (1666–1728), who was said to have copied out the *Wenxuan* in its entirety three times on the back of sheets of scrap paper, Enao copied the *Kokinshū* three times by hand.[51] Similarly, in his memoir *An Account of My Self-Cultivation* (*Shugyōroku*, ca. 1823), senior councilor Matsudaira Sadanobu recounts with pride the many copies he had produced of great works of literature, including *The Tale of Genji*, *The Tales of Ise*, the *Man'yōshū*, and all of the twenty-one imperial anthologies of poetry.[52]

Esteem for the artistry of accomplished calligraphers of the past was an important part of what made manuscript so precious to Enao. An episode from Ihara Saikaku's *Great Mirror of Female Beauty* (*Shoen ōkagami*, 1684) colorfully illustrates this perspective. After an argument erupts between two brothelgoers about whether a specific phrase appears in the "Kashiwagi" chapter of *The Tale of Genji*, the men ask a courtesan to lend them her copy of the text. She presents them Kitamura Kigin's *Kogetsushō*, a widely available printed edition with commentary. One of the men then reminisces about the days when no courtesan was without copies of classic texts in the hand of celebrated calligraphers. To be confronted with a printed edition was almost too much to bear, a reminder of how standards and aesthetic sensibilities had declined.[53]

51. In fact, Enao's remarks on copying the *Kokinshū* appear appended to what we may assume to have been his third copy of the anthology. See Suzuki Jun, "*Kōya-gire* no Edo," in *Waka ga kakareru toki*, vol. 2 of Asada Tōru et al., eds., *Waka o hiraku* (Iwanami shoten, 2005), 80.

52. Matsudaira Sadamitsu, ed., *Uge no hitokoto, Shugyōroku* (Iwanami shoten, 1942), 195, 213.

53. Ihara Saikaku, *Kōshoku nidai otoko* [*Shoen ōkagami*], in Fuji Akio, Inoue Toshiyuki, and Satake Akihiro, eds., *Kōshoku nidai otoko, Saikaku shokoku banashi, Honchō nijū fukō*, in *SNKBT* 76 (Iwanami shoten, 1991), 211. The episode is also discussed in Emmerich, *The Tale of Genji*, 426n125.

Such perspectives anticipate the twentieth-century critiques of mass culture and mechanical reproduction of Adorno and others. However, aesthetic concerns were not the only reason traditionalists favored manuscript. Copying by hand was also a technique of discipline, religious devotion, and, as the very title of Sadanobu's memoir suggests, self-cultivation. Manuscript was not the means to an end but the end itself, a process that was seen to have intrinsic value. The physical act of rewriting a text demanded careful word-by-word engagement and was an integral part of studying the classics and improving one's own compositional skill.[54] Printed editions may have brought the canon to a much wider readership, but they were also seen, paradoxically, as distancing readers from the texts. The easy availability of literature gave traditionalists cause for concern and led them to reaffirm the importance of manuscript.

Even those enamored with the *idea* of print often felt reservations in practice. In a lengthy reflection on the relative merits of print and manuscript in his miscellany *Tamakatsuma* (A Jeweled Basket), written mostly in the final decade of the eighteenth century, Motoori Norinaga praises print for its convenience and availability.[55] He also saw in its relative permanence and fixedness—qualities achieved through sheer power of numbers—a remedy for the ephemerality and variance of manuscript. Like much of Norinaga's scholarship, his views are informed by a desire for an authentic "original," premised on the belief that such a thing exists and can be recovered. Print, as he saw it, held at least in theory the power to propagate true, authentic versions of all texts: a vast library of definitive editions.

Although Norinaga recognized that the availability of a print edition might hasten the neglect and even disappearance of manuscript versions of a text, he does not seem to have considered this a problem so long as the printed version was, as his ideal scenario held, a definitive edition reconstructed through painstaking scholarly labor. In practice, however, the decision of which manuscript version to reproduce in print was often

54. The retention benefits of writing by hand have attracted renewed attention in our own digital age. For one study that drew widespread coverage in the popular media, see Pam A. Mueller and Daniel M. Oppenheimer, "The Pen Is Mightier Than the Keyboard: Advantages of Longhand over Laptop Note Taking," *Psychological Science* 25, no. 6 (June 2014): 1159–68.

55. Bentley, *Tamakatsuma*, 28–34.

made out of convenience, and those doing the choosing were seldom experts; even when they were, errors were not infrequently introduced in the production process.[56] However much he despised variation, seeing it as a reflection of the degradation of the original, it was better to retain a profusion of manuscript variants, holding out the possibility of reconstructing the desired authentic original, than to have a flawed print edition and risk losing those manuscripts.

In the end, worries about the demise of manuscript were overstated. Manuscript practices continued to thrive in many contexts, and the numerous hand-produced copies of the classics that survive from the Edo period should give pause even with regard to the conservatives' area of greatest concern. Still, it is true that the center of gravity of manuscript culture changed. Early modern scribes worked with an efficiency scarcely fathomable today, but copying by hand nevertheless required a significant investment of time and labor. While they may have reproduced literary classics as a form of self-improvement, as a diversion, or for artistic reasons, they had less incentive to expend resources on texts that were readily available for purchase. Where manuscript remained dominant was as a medium for reproducing and circulating texts that were rare or hard to find—whether because they were prohibited, out of print, unpublished, or otherwise unavailable on the market.

This includes many of the Chinese texts stored away in bakufu and domainal collections. While those with status were able to borrow books and copy them at their own desks, others labored away on site and took their own copies home with them instead. Once freed from the restrictions of institutional collections, these titles were then free to propagate more widely. Peter Kornicki offers the example of Tanaka Joan, an obscure provincial samurai from what is now Gunma Prefecture who spent many days copying books by hand at the Shōheikō and the Momijiyama Library over the course of several years in the 1830s—an early-modern counterpart to the graduate student in the archives perched over documents with a camera or parked at the copy machine.[57] Another prolific copier in the

56. Norinaga expands on the heightened risk of errors in manuscript, as well as the desirability of legible handwriting, later in *Tamakatsuma*. See Bentley, *Tamakatsuma*, 162–63.

57. On Joan, see Kornicki, "Manuscript, Not Print," 27–32.

bakufu collections was the noted bibliophile Suzuki Hakutō, father of Suzuki Tōya and father-in-law of Koga Tōan, who spent more than twenty years in administrative roles in the collections. First assigned to the Shōheikō in 1800, he was appointed as one of the directors (*shomotsu bugyō*) of the Momijiyama Library several years later, in 1807. Hakutō was noted for his breadth of learning, which ranged from Chinese and Japanese classics to popular literature and theater; he is perhaps best known today for his manuscript of Tsuruya Nanboku's *Ghost Stories at Yotsuya on the Tōkaidō Highway* (*Tōkaidō Yotsuya kaidan*, premiered 1825), which served as the basis for the most widely read modern edition of the play.[58]

In his miscellany *Reminiscences by Winter Lamplight* (*Kankei satetsu*, 1871), Asano Baidō (1816–80) offers a roughly contemporary perspective on Hakutō's erudition, prolific reading, and acquisition of books on all manner of subjects. Hakutō is depicted as a frugal scholar, although not stingy—he seems to have been quite generous with his friends—whose eccentric habits included writing letters on carefully ironed candy-wrapping paper. At any given moment he had large quantities of books on loan from his wide circle of acquaintances, but he kept careful track of borrowed items and never failed to return them promptly. This punctiliousness was no doubt helped by an efficient regimen wherein he copied dozens of pages each day.[59]

One telling anecdote concerns Hakutō's acquisition of an incomplete set of Sima Guang's monumental history *Comprehensive Mirror for Aid in Government* (*Zizhi tongjian*, 1084), a work that in its entirety comprises some 294 volumes and more than three million characters. By systematically borrowing the missing volumes from acquaintances scattered far and wide, then quickly copying them by hand, Hakutō eventually succeeded in producing his own complete version of the text. It is unclear how many volumes were missing from his original purchase, but Baidō's emphasis of Hakutō's persistence and repeated borrowing makes it clear that he copied a significant portion of the massive compendium by hand.

This was just one title among countless others that he added to his library through his own manual labor. Many of Hakutō's manuscripts were

58. See Satoko Shimazaki, *Edo Kabuki in Transition: From the Worlds of the Samurai to the Vengeful Female Ghost* (New York: Columbia University Press, 2016), 259–65.

59. *Kankei satetsu* (sometimes read *Kankei sōtetsu*), in *ZNZT* 3:232.

copied from books in the bakufu collections he was charged with overseeing, and it has been speculated that his dismissal from the Momijiyama Library in 1821 was because he had copied some titles that were off-limits. Unfortunately, his personal collection was later lost in a fire, and the whereabouts of the only known manuscript copy of its catalog are unclear.[60] Knowledge of which works he copied is therefore fragmentary and largely speculative, but certainly a manuscript copy of the Shōheikō's copy of *Liaozhai*—at sixteen volumes, a quite modest text in comparison to the *Comprehensive Mirror for Aid in Government*—seems easily plausible given his interest in Chinese fiction and his speed, stamina, and prolificness.

Selections from Hakutō's own literary Sinitic poetry were in turn recorded by another indefatigable copier, Yamazaki Yoshishige (1796–1856), an Edo pharmacist who together with Bakin and others was a member of the short-lived Tankikai Society, a group that met monthly in the mid-1820s to share and investigate historical artifacts and rare manuscripts.[61] Yoshishige's illustrated minutes show the focus to have been largely, although not exclusively, on Japanese materials.[62] However, outside of the society, his obsessive gathering, reading, and copying of rare materials extended to many Chinese texts. Yoshishige's routine was to copy often substantial passages from his daily reading, interspersed with his own musings, into an ongoing reading journal that grew over time to comprise hundreds of volumes in all. Some of this material was then used in his published miscellanies, while other content he deemed worth saving he compiled into a self-selected set of twelve volumes of the finest entries, which included Hakutō's poems. Buried in the tenth volume is an observation on the recent importation of Chinese single-sheet prints depicting characters from *The Water Margin*, *Journey to the West*, and other vernacular narratives as faithful dogs. Yoshishige explains the cultural significance of the trope through

60. On Hakutō's dismissal, see Mori Junzaburō, *Momijiyama bunko to shomotsu bugyō* (Shōwa shobō, 1933), 607. The manuscript copy of Hakutō's catalog was produced by Junzaburō himself. (Junzaburō was the younger brother of Mori Ōgai.)

61. On the Tankikai, see Margarita Winkel, "Entertainment and Education: An Antiquarian Society in Edo, 1824–25," in Anna Beerens and Mark Teeuwen, eds., *Uncharted Waters: Intellectual Life in the Edo Period* (Leiden: Brill, 2012), 13–34.

62. *Tanki manroku* (meeting minutes recorded by Bakin and Yoshinari), in the National Diet Library collection.

reference to the *Liaozhai* tale "The Faithful Dog" ("Yi quan"), which he copies out in its entirety.[63]

The compulsion to copy and excerpt by hand was arguably amplified, paradoxically, by the proliferation of print—further complicating any lingering notion that manuscript yielded to new technologies in a steady, one-directional progression. Ann Blair has documented a version of this phenomenon in early modern Europe, where the accumulation of printed texts created a state of information overload that anxious scholars sought to manage by gathering and organizing excerpts into various types of reference material.[64] Japanese readers like Hakutō and Yoshishige felt the same acute need to preserve and compile as much as they could from the unprecedented abundance of texts that passed, often momentarily, through their hands.

Copying had the further advantage of allowing scholars to add to their collections at little or no cost. For rare titles, the financial incentives were obvious, as such texts were likely to be prohibitively expensive if available for purchase at all. However, attesting to their frugality (and endurance), large numbers of readers routinely copied even titles that were widely and inexpensively available. It has been noted, for example, that readers were more likely to borrow works of domestic popular fiction from a lending library and make their own copy than to buy a printed copy.[65] No matter how inexpensive the edition, it was still more cost-effective to write out the text by oneself, especially if one did so using repurposed waste-paper, as did Hakutō, Tōya—whose best-known work was, after all, titled *Writings on the Back of Scrap Paper*—and many other frugal collectors. Of course, while scholars of modest means readily traded their time for financial savings, they were unlikely to see it primarily in such terms, as they also considered copying an intrinsically valuable part of their scholarly regimen.

A corollary of the trade-off between time and money is that manuscript and the labor it entailed were products that could be bought and sold like any other. As a young man, Bakin prepared manuscripts both for personal use and to sell to others to supplement his income. In later years, when he had attained literary success and financial stability, he

63. Yamazaki Yoshishige, *Kairoku* [1820–37] (Kokusho kankōkai, 1915), 477–78.

64. Blair, *Too Much to Know*.

65. Nakamura Yukihiko, *Kinsei shōsetsu shi*, in *Nakamura Yukihiko chojutsu shū* 4 (Chūō kōronsha, 1987), 186.

would borrow rare books that were unavailable for purchase and pay others to copy them for him. In an 1835 letter, he recounted the large quantity of manuscripts he had copied in this way, including an average of one hundred per year in the early 1830s, observing that "this has cost a good deal of money over the years, but for an old man like me there is no greater pleasure than reading books."[66] When his financial situation soured shortly thereafter, he was forced to sell off more than six thousand manuscript volumes from his library.[67]

Prices suggest that business for professional copyists was fairly lucrative. In 1833 Bakin paid to have around sixty to seventy volumes copied at a total cost of 7.5 *ryō* ($16,000, or about $250 per volume).[68] Commercial manuscripts varied in price according to many factors—including size, quality, and content—but the price of manuscript copies of nativist scholarship purchased by Uchiike Nagatoshi from Norinaga's successor Motoori Ōhira in the 1810s and 1820s was comparable to what Bakin paid. Nagatoshi was initially quoted a price of six *rin* ($2.10) per leaf in 1817, a figure that rose to one *bu* ($3.27) a decade later. Depending on the length of the manuscript, this put the cost of a single volume anywhere from 1.5 to 6 *monme* ($49–$210).[69] These figures suggest that commissioned manuscripts were roughly comparable in price to ordinary imported Chinese books, and that those hoping to acquire rare texts on a budget were advised to do the copying themselves.

Following Liaozhai*'s Trail in Nagoya*

We are able to observe many of the elements discussed in the preceding section in the circulation of *Liaozhai* specifically by turning our attention to another place the text resurfaces in early modern Japan: the castle city of Nagoya. With a population of around 100,000 by the late Edo period, Nagoya was Japan's largest publishing center outside of the three

66. Bakin, letter to Tonomura Jōsai, 1835.2.21, in *Bakin shokan shūsei*, 4:25.
67. Takada, *Takizawa Bakin: momotose nochi no chiin o matsu*, 27–28, 218.
68. Takamaki Minoru, *Bakin ikka no Edo-gurashi* (Chūō kōron shinsha, 2003), 126.
69. Takahashi, "'Hanpon' no 'shahon' o tsukuru no wa naze ka," 25–26.

major cities of Edo, Osaka, and Kyoto. In addition, the city boasted early modern Japan's largest lending library, that of Ōnoya Sōhachi (known in abbreviated form as the Daisō), whose collections of upward of 20,000 volumes filled three storehouses by the mid-eighteenth century.[70]

Nagoya was also home to a sizable community of scholars, artists, collectors, and readers who regularly borrowed, traded, and copied books among themselves. On the tenth day of the first month of 1853, a group of these bibliophiles gathered a few blocks south of Nagoya castle for an evening of socializing and book-viewing at the residence of a domain retainer named Kamiya Kizaemon (1788–1871). Kizaemon had spent twenty-five years in Kyoto in the service of one of daimyō Tokugawa Munechika's daughters following her marriage to a courtier, and he had acquired a great number of books during his time there.[71] Back in Nagoya, he passed his days copying out rare books in his study, which was crammed from floor to ceiling with his enormous, ever-expanding personal library.[72]

Kizaemon's guests that evening were all equally enthusiastic copiers and collectors. They included the physician Hirade Jun'eki (1809–61), the local historian and chronicler of Nagoya life Kodera Gyokuchō (1800–1878), and, at Gyokuchō's invitation, his friend Hosono Yōsai (1811–78), an instructor at the domainal academy, the Meirindō. All three consumed large quantities of fiction and kept ongoing reading journals into which they regularly copied lengthy excerpts. In his early twenties, Jun'eki excerpted passages from eighty-odd medieval and early Edo tales, and in the two decades that followed he went on to fill fifteen volumes with selections from some 532 titles.[73] Gyokuchō kept a similar reading journal in which he excerpted passages from more than 240 literary titles, with

70. On the Daisō, see Andrew Markus, "The Daisō Lending Library of Nagoya, 1767–1899," *Gest Library Journal* 3, no. 3 (Winter 1989–90): 5–34.

71. Kishino Toshihiko, *Owari-han shakai no bunka, jōhō, gakumon* (Ōsaka: Seibundō shuppan, 2002), 198.

72. Hosono Yōsai, *Kankyō manpitsu*, in Nagoya-shi kyōiku iinkai, ed., *Nagoya sōsho*, vol. 20: *Zuihitsu hen 3* (Nagoya: Nagoya-shi kyōiku iinkai, 1961), 44.

73. Dylan McGee, "Hirade Jun'eki no *Daisui manshō* kara ukagaeru bassui shōroku to Daisō-bon no kashidashi," *Gengo bunka ronshū* 37, no. 1 (October 2015): 36–37.

an emphasis on popular fiction and collections of haikai verse.[74] Yōsai, for his part, kept a detailed account of his reading, borrowing, and interactions with fellow bibliophiles, as well as his proclivity for copying passages and entire texts that appealed to him.[75]

That evening at Kizaemon's house, Jun'eki extended an invitation to his companions to gather again in a few days' time to view his own extensive collection of rare books. Six days later, the same group stood in Jun'eki's study and looked on as, at Yōsai's request, Jun'eki laid out his personal library of Chinese fiction: some thirty-seven rare titles, nearly all unavailable in Japanese editions. These included *Wondrous Tales New and Old* (*Jingu qiguan*), *The Scholars* (*Rulin waishi*), *Dream of the Red Chamber*, and, last but not least, a complete sixteen-volume set of *Liaozhai*.[76] This impressive collection continued to grow in the years that followed. The catalog of Jun'eki's personal library (which includes titles added through his death in 1861) lists around 4,000 titles, including many additional works of Chinese fiction in both *wakokubon* and imported editions.[77]

At least a half-century before Jun'eki showed off his collection to his friends, another instructor at the Meirindō had placed a copy of *Liaozhai* on his desk and copied out a selection of tales. He also wrote a short inscription describing Pu Songling's collection as a "masterpiece of fiction" in spite of its often vulgar subject matter, and explaining his selection of tales as representing those he considered relatively refined and elegant. The scholar was Suzuki Akira (1764–1837), and the catalog of his personal library lists a number of works of Chinese fiction in diverse formats—*wakokubon*, Chinese editions, and manuscript—including this manuscript selection of tales, as well as his own notes on the collection.[78] Un-

74. Gyokuchō, *Nan no tame ka wa*, in Mitamura Engyo, ed., *Mikan zuihitsu hyakushu* 12 (Chūō kōronsha, 1978).

75. Hosono Yōsai, *Kankyō manpitsu*, in Nagoya-shi kyōiku iinkai, ed., *Nagoya sōsho*, vol. 19: *Zuihitsu hen 2* (Nagoya: Nagoya-shi kyōiku iinkai, 1960), 273, 285. Mentioned in passing in Kornicki, 263–64. Yōsai's catalog of his personal library is held in the National Diet Library collection.

76. *Kankyō manpitsu*, in *Nagoya sōsho*, 20:48.

77. Wakayama Zenzaburō, ed., *Hirade-shi zōsho mokuroku* (Nagoya: Bunkōdō shoten, 1939).

78. See Suzuki Akira, *Hanareya zōsho mokuroku*, and the table of contents of *Hanareya kenmonroku* in Okada Minoru and Ichihashi Taku, *Suzuki Akira: hyakusanjūnenki kinen* (Nagoya: Suzuki Akira kenshōkai, 1967), 243–60, 174–79.

fortunately, many of Akira's materials were destroyed in the firebombing of Nagoya in World War II, and neither his manuscript nor his reading notes survive today. As a result, it is not possible to determine whose edition he relied on to prepare the manuscript, although it is conceivable that it was the same copy that later came into Jun'eki's hands. Jun'eki was more than forty years Akira's junior, but the two men's network of friends and acquaintances overlapped considerably.

Whatever its origins, Akira's manuscript illustrates the power of borrowing and manuscript practices to facilitate the proliferation of a text that was rare in printed form. Akira was generous with his personal library, and after making his own copy of the tales from *Liaozhai* he in turn lent the manuscript to at least nine acquaintances and family members over the period from 1801 to 1832, as can be traced through reference to his meticulous lending ledger.[79] Among these was his student Ryūtei Senka (1804–68), who borrowed the manuscript along with three other titles in 1824 and did not return them until five years later. Senka's encounter with *Liaozhai* came at a key moment in his early literary development. He was struggling financially, having recently lost most of his inheritance, and had not yet become the follower (and eventual successor) of the literary giant Ryūtei Tanehiko (1783–1842), the author of one of the nineteenth century's runaway bestsellers, *A Fraudulent Murasaki's Rustic Genji* (1829–42).[80]

In 1826 Senka began to compile a manuscript of his own containing many of Akira's unpublished writings, including the inscription on the *Liaozhai* manuscript he had in his possession.[81] That same year he wrote the first entries in an ongoing reading journal that documented his encounters with a wide swath of Japanese and Chinese popular fiction, from Ihara Saikaku and Hiraga Gennai to *Journey to the West* and *Fine Tales from West Lake* (*Xihu jiahua*). Amid his extensive notes and excerpted passages appears an entry from 1827 listing the thirteen tales contained in Akira's manuscript, along with the names of several of the protagonists.[82]

79. Mizuno Kiyoshi, "Suzuki Akira no shakushobo," in *Bunbaku* 4 (1979): 47–125.

80. Ishikawa Ryō, "Shodai Ryūtei Senka nenpu kō: sono ichi," *Ōtsuma joshi daigaku bungakubu kiyō* 11 (1979): 27–28.

81. Ryūtei Senka, *Hanareya sensei bunshō*, 5:13a. The manuscript is in the collection of the National Diet Library.

82. Ryūtei Senka, *Oshibana*, 8:10b. The manuscript is in the collection of the National Diet Library. The tales Akira had copied are scattered across twelve of the sixteen

Senka would periodically turn to this journal as he wrote tales of his own, which notably include adaptations from the fiction and drama of Li Yu.[83] Although he does not appear to have adapted any material from *Liaozhai*, he did reference the collection in a piece of pictorial fiction published in 1847, comparing his own storyline to that of "Ruiyun," which he summarizes as follows: "The famous Hangzhou courtesan Ruiyun was temporarily disfigured in an attack by a villain, but with the generous help of an immortal was able to regain her beauty and win the man she loved."[84] "Ruiyun" was one of the longer tales included in Akira's manuscript.

The many Edo writers who adapted, translated, or otherwise rewrote Pu Songling's tales each had their own individual encounters with the text. While the details of these encounters are mostly lost to time, we may surmise that they resembled those of Akira or Senka in their broad outlines. As readers borrowed the tales, reading journals were filled with notes and excerpts, new copies were prepared, and these were in turn lent out to others who repeated the process. Through a series of such individual actions, a handful of imported copies reached a steadily growing readership even in the absence of a domestic reprint edition. Only a few years after the first copy was unloaded in Nagasaki, adaptations began to appear, and these continued to be published in a steady stream throughout the nineteenth century and beyond. Although this chapter has centered on the case of *Liaozhai*, the same practices lie behind the pervasive reach of many other texts, and indeed of Chinese fiction at large. Bakin's comic book, Chūryō's historical fiction, and Reishū's tales in literary Sinitic represent but the tidy, printed surface under which churned a vast and messy world of manuscript.

---

volumes of the Qingketing edition, suggesting that he had access to a complete set. The entry in *Oshibana* is mentioned in Suzuki Jūzō, *Ehon to ukiyoe* (Bijutsu shuppansha, 1979), 51.

83. On Senka's adaptations from Li Yu in particular, see the extensive treatment in Xiao Hanzhen, "Li Yu yu Jianghu wenyi: Ryūtei Senka de *Seidan Tokiwa no iroka* ji *Mimeyori sōshi*," *Minsu quyi* 189 (September 2015): 119–55.

84. Ryūtei Senka, *Mimeyori sōshi* (Edo: Yamamotoya Heikichi, 1847), 2:15a–b. Quoted in Suzuki, "Gōkan-mono no daizai tenki to Tanehiko," 65.

CHAPTER 4

Kidan: *Strange Tales from Japan*

In the remaining chapters, our central concern shifts from the material to the textual. Having examined imported books as physical objects, both as vessels for the text and as objects for reproduction, we now follow *Liaozhai* through its afterlife in Japanese adaptation. In other words, we shift from literal rewriting to rewriting in its more abstract sense, considering how writers and critics conceived of the process of literary adaptation, how notions of the strange were reconfigured in new linguistic, literary, cultural, and political contexts, and the new uses to which Chinese strange tales were put in Japan under shogunal rule. At the center of this wide-ranging examination sits Morishima Chūryō's *Tales from the Withering Wind* (1792), a collection of nine strange tales that constitutes the single most extensive engagement with *Liaozhai* in early modern Japanese fiction. It is a work with certain inherent contradictions. Imbuing its source tales with a deep intertextuality, it augments their strange qualities in some ways while diminishing them in others; pervaded by gestures of deference toward the Tokugawa regime, it also affords a veiled glimpse of subversion and resistance to authority.

As the forms of rewriting ascend to a higher level of abstraction, they continue to reflect many of the same underlying processes discussed in the preceding chapters. Adaptation may be a more distant form of rewriting, but it complemented other practices as a form of textual preservation and propagation. Indeed, precisely *because* of the greater remove from the ultimate "source," adaptation magnified the reach of more proximate practices of reprinting and manuscript copying; distance allowed texts to encounter many new readers, ever widening their reach. Readers who knew nothing of Feng Menglong were familiar nonetheless with the tale of a man who returns from the dead to fulfill a promised rendezvous with his dearest friend. Others who had never heard of Pu Songling had still read the story of a man torn between two competing supernatural lovers—one a fox, the other a ghost—or another who was bewitched by a demon wrapped in the skin of an alluring young woman. All of which is to say that while the framework of "rewriting" may encompass diverse practices that can be unruly and disjointed, it is not an arbitrary nomenclatural convenience.

Before proceeding, it is useful to situate ourselves in genre, establishing the sources for Japanese adaptations and the terminology that was applied to these texts. The conventional division in Chinese classical tales, first introduced by the Ming scholar Hu Yinglin (1551–1602) in the late sixteenth century, is that between the *zhiguai* and the *chuanqi*.[1] The distinction is one of both length and quality. Where *zhiguai* denotes the terse, no-frills anomaly accounts that emerged as a category in the early Six Dynasties period, *chuanqi* refers to the lengthier, more elaborated narratives that developed from the mid-Tang. As has been noted, to view the former as a nascent form of fiction is a problematic teleology. *Zhiguai* not only present themselves as "factual" accounts of strange events observed firsthand but were largely read as such by contemporary readers.[2] *Chuanqi*, by contrast, are distanced from their subject matter, often through the intermediation of named informants, provide a greater level of biographical detail and characterization, and betray deeper concern with style. As suggested by the character *qi* 奇—which will be touched on further—they are also broader in scope, encompassing any material that might elicit wonder or amazement, including but not limited to the anomalous. Nevertheless, and in marked contrast with the early modern Japanese strange tales treated in this study, the situation of the *chuanqi*

1. On Hu's six-part division of *xiaoshuo*, see Laura Hua Wu, "From *Xiaoshuo* to Fiction: Hu Yinglin's Genre Study of *Xiaoshuo*," *Harvard Journal of Asiatic Studies* 55, no. 2 (December 1995): 339–71.

2. See, for example, Robert Ford Campany, *Strange Writing: Anomaly Accounts in Early Medieval China* (Albany: State University of New York Press, 1996), 156–59.

within a larger tradition of anecdotal literature still renders their retroactive classification as fiction problematic and anachronistic.[3]

Nearly all extant Tang *chuanqi*, along with some Six Dynasties *zhiguai*, are preserved in the massive early Song collection *Taiping guangji* (Extensive Records of the Taiping Era), copies of which reached early modern Japan in considerable quantity and were read by Sinologists including Hayashi Razan and Seita Tansō as well as writers of popular fiction from Ryōi to Chūryō and Bakin.[4] Although the *chuanqi* is closely associated with the Tang, longer classical tales continued to be written through the late imperial period, with *New Tales by Lamplight* and its "sequel" *More Tales by Lamplight* among the most widely read. Indeed, the former gained popularity not only in Japan, as discussed in chapter 2, but also in Korea, where Im Ki and Yun Ch'un-nyŏn prepared the annotated edition that would serve as the basis for the Japanese reprint edition of 1648, and in Vietnam, where the text was introduced in the late fifteenth century and quickly began to be rewritten and emulated in the vernacular.[5]

Renewed interest in *zhiguai* and *chuanqi* in the late Ming coincided with the republication of earlier narratives, including the *Taiping guangji*, which was reprinted in a new edition in 1566.[6] A steady stream of new strange tales continued to be written through the nineteenth century and

3. Roland Altenburger, *The Sword or the Needle: The Female Knight-Errant (Xia) in Traditional Chinese Narrative* (New York: Peter Lang, 2009), 19–22.

4. Adaptations from the *Taiping guangji* appear in Razan's *Kaidan zensho* (Compendium of Strange Tales, completed ca. 1627 and first published in 1698), and the collection's influence is evident in *Two Tales from Medieval Times* (tentatively attributed to Tansō). On the latter, see Nakamura Yukihiko, *Kinsei bungei shichōron*, in *Nakamura Yukihiko chojutsu shū* 1 (Chūō kōronsha, 1982), 205. One of the stories in Chūryō's *Tales from the Withering Wind* features passages describing cockfighting and uses language inspired by the *Taiping guangji* story "The Old Man of the Eastern Wall" ("Dongcheng laofu zhuan"), which tells of Emperor Xuanzong's construction of a special facility for elaborate cockfighting tournaments. On Ryōi and Bakin's reliance on the collection (and Bakin's probable copying of selections thereof), see Tokuda, *Kinsei kindai shōsetsu to Chūgoku hakuwa bungaku*, 140, 198.

5. On *New Tales by Lamplight* in Vietnam, see Nam Nguyen, "Writing as Response and as Translation: *Jiandeng xinhua* and the Evolution of the *Chuanqi* Genre in East Asia, Particularly in Vietnam" (PhD diss., Harvard University, 2005).

6. Allan H. Barr, "The Later Classical Tale," in Victor H. Mair, ed., *Columbia History of Chinese Literature* (New York: Columbia University Press, 2001), 685.

beyond. Yet the application of the labels *zhiguai* and *chuanqi* to these later texts can be problematic. Some tales, such as those in Yuan Mei's *Zi bu yu*, display a straightforwardness and simplicity that resonates strongly with the *zhiguai* tradition. Other collections are more ambiguous—none more than *Liaozhai*, which draws on both modes, and regarding which different critics have highlighted different aspects. Lu Xun, in his 1930 history of Chinese fiction, notably describes the collection as "*zhiguai* told in *chuanqi* fashion."[7] Rania Huntington views it as containing both types of narrative separately.[8] Judith Zeitlin emphasizes the *zhiguai* qualities, although not to the exclusion of others, while Wilt Idema and Lloyd Haft shy away from the term *zhiguai*, describing it instead as a collection of "*chuanqi* and brief notes on unusual matters."[9]

It is precisely the impossibility of pinning down Pu Songling's tales as either *zhiguai* or *chuanqi* that invited criticism from Ji Yun (1724–1805), the author of the later collection of strange tales *Yuewei caotang biji* (Notes from the Cottage of Close Scrutiny).[10] For modern readers, the difficulty of assigning *Liaozhai* to received categories is less likely to detract from the reading experience than to contribute to the work's appeal. We might instead question the categories themselves and their usefulness in many contexts. Perhaps surprisingly, we would be joined in this by Hu Yinglin himself, who described the categories he had identified as "extremely fluid genres" that "readily move from one . . . to the other. . . . In some cases there are both types of tales in one work . . . in other cases there are features befitting both genres in one tale."[11]

Although the *zhiguai-chuanqi* division is often preserved in literary histories, there are other terms of modern provenance that skirt the issue and provide useful alternatives. *Wenyan xiaoshuo* would seem to be the

7. Lu Xun, *Zhongguo xiaoshuo shilüe* (Shanghai: Shanghai guji chubanshe, 1998), 148.

8. Rania Huntington, *Alien Kind: Foxes and Late Imperial Chinese Narrative* (Cambridge, MA: Harvard University Asia Center, 2003), 26–27.

9. Zeitlin, *Historian of the Strange*; Wilt Idema and Lloyd Haft, *A Guide to Chinese Literature* (Ann Arbor: Center for Chinese Studies, University of Michigan, 1997), 189.

10. Allan H. Barr, "Pu Songling and *Liaozhai Zhiyi*: A Study of Textual Transmission, Biographical Background, and Literary Antecedents" (PhD diss., University of Oxford, 1983), 192.

11. Wu, "From *Xiaoshuo* to Fiction," 353.

most straightforward, and it is the nearest equivalent to the English "classical tale."[12] In its narrowest definition, as employed for example by Allan Barr, it comes close to a stand-in for the "strange tale," identifying the *zhiguai* and *chuanqi* without resorting to those labels.[13] However, others employ a more expansive definition. As acknowledged in the quantitative analyses earlier in this study, Yuan and Hou's bibliography of *wenyan xiaoshuo*, for example, encompasses other varieties of classical prose, including *biji* miscellanies, or "jotted notes"—short, casual sketches that vary widely in character by writer. The *biji* tradition provides another common term of modern origin applied to strange tales: the *biji xiaoshuo* (J. *hikki shōsetsu*). Here, too, the boundaries are nebulous. The term can single out narratives (*xiaoshuo*) scattered among the entries of *biji* miscellanies. It can also refer to collections consisting exclusively of narratives that might individually be characterized as *zhiguai* or *chuanqi*. Some later writers of strange tales, such as Ji Yun, positioned their own collections in the *biji* tradition, emphasizing their casualness and lack of pretense.

The term *biji xiaoshuo*, however, is of modern origin. In some instances the net is cast wide, as reflected in the series *Biji xiaoshuo daguan* (Compendium of *Biji Xiaoshuo*, 1960) and its shorter supplement *Biji xiaoshuo daguan xubian* (1962), which together feature some three hundred titles from the Han through the Qing, the largest by far being the *Taiping guangji*.[14] Others reserve the term primarily for later collections of strange tales, including *Liaozhai*, as represented by Tokuda Takeshi, who defines the genre as comprising "short stories and fictionalized historical anecdotes written in the classical style by [Qing] intellectuals."[15] In any event, more than 40 percent of the titles in the *Biji xiaoshuo daguan* and its supplement date from the Qing. These include many of the collections that poured through Nagasaki in the late eighteenth and early nineteenth centuries, among them *Yu Chu xinzhi* (New Tales of Yu Chu),

12. See, for example, Hou Zhongyi and Liu Shilin, *Zhongguo wenyan xiaoshuo shigao* (Beijing: Beijing daxue chubanshe, 1993).

13. Barr, "The Later Classical Tale."

14. *Biji xiaoshuo daguan* (Taibei: Xinxing shuju, 1960); and *Biji xiaoshuo daguan xubian* (Taibei: Xinxing shuju, 1962).

15. Tokuda, *Edo kangaku*, 260.

Ershi lu (Stories as I Heard Them), *Xieduo* (The Bell of Humor), *Chiwen lu* (An Account from a Hand's Length), *Yetan suilu* (Informal Record of Nighttime Stories), and *Zi bu yu* (That of Which the Master Did Not Speak). Although the term is less commonly encountered in reference to the strange tale in Western scholarship, surely the *biji xiaoshuo* is what Idema and Haft have in mind when they describe *Liaozhai* as containing *chuanqi* and "brief notes."

Chinese strange tales in the vernacular were also an important source for Japanese writers. Feng Menglong's three *Sanyan* collections were among the most widely read, with selections republished as *wakokubon* and in Japanese translation (*tsūzoku*) much as they were reprinted many times in China. Alongside the four major long-form vernacular narratives (*Romance of the Three Kingdoms*, *The Water Margin*, *Journey to the West*, and *Jin Ping Mei*), these were among the most frequently adapted vernacular Chinese texts in early modern Japan, with versions produced by many of the period's leading writers.[16] The vernacular tale's status as fiction is less ambiguous than that of the *zhiguai* or *chuanqi*, filled as they are with narratorial intrusions, direct appeals, and other devices to remind readers that they are in the hands of a storyteller.[17] In terms of subject matter, however, there is extensive overlap with earlier *zhiguai* and *chuanqi*. Feng's collections include tales of foxes, ghosts, karmic entanglements, and deeds carried out from beyond the grave, and as Hanan notes, nearly all of his sources were classical tales and anecdotes.[18] Thus the *Sanyan* provided Japanese readers an alternative source for many tales included in the *Taiping guangji* and other classical collections, whether that of Wu Bao'an's friendship in *Stories Old and New* (*Gujin xiaoshuo*,

16. Among the many writers who adapted Feng Menglong's tales were Tsuga Teishō, Ueda Akinari, Morishima Chūryō, Kyokutei Bakin, Shikitei Sanba, Ishikawa Masamochi, Unpukan Tenpo, Saeda Shigeru, and Itami Chin'en.

17. Patrick Hanan terms the pretense wherein the author purports to be addressing a live audience the "simulated context" of vernacular fiction, although we might equally describe it as the author's acknowledgment of the actual context of the reader's engagement with the text. Hanan, "The Nature of Ling Meng-ch'u's Fiction," in Andrew Plaks, ed., *Chinese Narrative: Critical and Theoretical Essays* (Princeton, NJ: Princeton University Press, 1977), 87.

18. Patrick Hanan, *The Chinese Vernacular Story* (Cambridge, MA: Harvard University Press, 1981), 104.

1620–21), the version of the legend of the white snake in *Common Words to Caution the World* (*Jingshi tongyan*, 1624), or the retelling of Dugu Xiashu's strange dream in *Constant Words to Awaken the World*.[19]

Japanese Strange Tales as Genre

With the exception of the broadest category, *xiaoshuo* (J. *shōsetsu*), the terms applied to the strange tale in China saw infrequent use in Japan outside the confines of Sinology. *Zhiguai* was hardly used at all, *chuanqi* only somewhat more so.[20] A pair of Japanese "*chuanqi*" (J. *denki*) from 1773, both adaptations of Tang *chuanqi* contained in the *Taiping guangji*—one of the two being Li Chaowei's *Tale of Liu Yi* (*Liu Yi zhuan*)—are likely the work of the Sinologist Seita Tansō.[21] Bakin's *Kyokutei denki hanakanzashi* (1804), one of the only works by a major writer to self-identify as a *chuanqi*, was written with the other use of the word in mind, which is to say in reference to *chuanqi* drama; Bakin draws on Li Yu's *The Jade Clasp* (*Yu saotou*), adding language and conventions from

19. On the probable source for Feng Menglong's story of Wu Bao'an, see Maria Franca Sibau, *Reading for the Moral: Exemplarity and the Confucian Moral Imagination in Seventeenth-Century Chinese Short Fiction* (Albany: State University of New York Press, 2018), 145.

20. Bakin uses the terms *haishi* (Ch. *baishi*, "unofficial history") and *shōsetsu* (Ch. *xiaoshuo*) in reference to narrative fiction in Japanese, both alone and in such combinations as *haishi shōsetsu*, *kokuji shōsetsu*, and *shōsetsu denki*. Yokoyama Kuniharu, *Yomihon no kenkyū: Edo to Kamigata to* (Kazama shobō, 1974), 46. However, the last of the three, which includes the term *chuanqi* (J. *denki*), seems to have been very uncommon. When *chuanqi* does appear, it is usually limited to discussion of Chinese tales; for instance, in the marginal notes Chūryō wrote in his copy of Feng Menglong's *Common Words to Caution the World*. On the content of these notes, see Tokuda Takeshi, "Morishima Chūryō no *Keisei tsūgen* [*Jingshi tongyan*] kakiire ni tsuite" (1985), in *Nihon kinsei shōsetsu to Chūgoku shōsetsu*, 371–86.

21. On the sources for Tansō's adaptations, which were published as *Two Tales from Medieval Times*—a work that appears in table 3.1 for its possible additional use of material from *Liaozhai*—see Nakamura Yukihiko, "Kakuretaru hihyōka," in *Kinsei bungei shichōron*, 205. Although Nakamura is reluctant to credit the tales to Tansō, later scholars have come down more decisively in their attributions.

the Japanese popular theater.[22] Given its modern origins, *biji xiaoshuo*, the last term discussed in the preceding section, was not used by Edo writers. *Biji* (J. *hikki*) by itself was not uncommon, but was used in reference to a wide range of written records without any sense of situating those works within a specific tradition.

How, then, did Japanese writers classify their rewritings of Chinese tales? As is clear from the list of *Liaozhai* adaptations in table 3.1, these works were produced across a range of genres. That said, among these the body of works conventionally referred to as the *yomihon* stands out as the most frequent site for adaptation. In particular, most adhere to the model of the so-called early *yomihon* (*zenki yomihon*), collections of tales that were first published in the western cities of Kyoto and Osaka in the middle of the eighteenth century. Although these works developed their own structural and stylistic conventions, in subject matter they cover much of the same territory as the Chinese strange tales from which many (although by no means all) of the individual tales were indeed adapted.

In contrast to later *yomihon*, which were shaped by the increasing commercialization of the publishing industry, these earlier collections were mostly produced in the literati milieu. The two best-known authors are Tsuga Teishō and Ueda Akinari, with Teishō's *A Garland of Stories* (*Hanabusa sōshi*, 1749) conventionally positioned as the progenitor of the form and Akinari's *Tales of Moonlight and Rain* given pride of place as the pinnacle of the genre, its place in the literary canon secure. However, there were others writing in a similar vein. In western Japan, these included lesser-known figures such as Sōkan Sanjin (fl. 1770), whose name is attached to a single collection, and Itami Chin'en (ca. 1752–81), who was by contrast very prolific.[23] As the center of gravity of literary pro-

22. Tokuda, "Kaisetsu," in Tokuda Takeshi and Yokoyama Kuniharu, eds., *Shigeshige yawa, Kyokutei denki hanakanzashi, Saibara kidan, Toribeyama shirabeno itomichi*, in *SNKBT* 80 (Iwanami shoten, 1992), 527.

23. Early readers, including the late-Edo critic Kimura Mokurō, speculated that Sōkan Sanjin was none other than Tsuga Teishō himself. This theory, which was later abandoned, has recently been revived on the basis of closer textual analysis and the publication history of his collection. Nevertheless, in the absence of more decisive evidence, the attribution remains tentative. See "Kaisetsu," in Iikura Yōichi, ed., *Zenki yomihon kaidanshū*, in Kigoshi Osamu, ed., *Edo kaidan bungei meisakusen* 2 (Kokusho kankōkai, 2017), 354.

duction shifted eastward in the late eighteenth century, these writers were succeeded by Edo natives such as Morishima Chūryō and Shinrotei, who began to produce collections of their own that preserved many of the same features.[24]

It should be apparent that the "early *yomihon*" is a category of modern origin; after all, the early phase of a phenomenon can be distinguished only after the fact. However, the term *yomihon* is itself a retroactive description. The word first appears only in the early nineteenth century, long after the publication of many of the works it describes, and its use as a bibliographic category developed later still, in post-Edo literary scholarship. More problematic than the appellation's anachronism is its lack of generic cohesion. *Yomihon* is not a particularly descriptive term to begin with—it means simply "books for reading"—and in practice it is applied to a number of very different types of fiction. Dividing the *yomihon* into early and late phases resolves some of this imprecision, but the designation "early *yomihon*" tends to be reserved for historical fiction written in western Japan and does not encompass the stylistically similar works by slightly later Edo authors including Chūryō and Shinrotei. Compounding the problem, longer-form narratives such as the many mid-eighteenth-century adaptations of *The Water Margin* are often also categorized as early *yomihon*. Simply put, division by time period instead of generic quality involves inevitable limitations, while alternatives such as *tanpen yomihon*, meaning "short-form *yomihon*," resolve some of the ambiguity but give no sense of the characteristic features of these narratives aside from their length.

A more suitable term appears in the very subtitles (*tsunogaki*) to the collections under consideration. Teishō's three collections—*A Garland of Stories*, *A Thicket of Tales* (*Shigeshige yawa*, 1766), and *Leaves of Crabgrass*—are all self-described as "strange tales old and new" (*kokon kidan*), while Akinari's *Tales of Moonlight and Rain* are "strange tales recent and old" (*kinko kidan*). Chin'en's *Tales from the Deep Mountains* (*Miyamagusa*, 1782)

24. Although all of the authors mentioned here wrote under literary pen names, only Sōkan Sanjin and Shinrotei are identified using these pen names. In Sōkan Sanjin's case, this is because his true identity remains unknown. Shinrotei's identity, by contrast, is known—his name in real life was Ikari Teikyo—but his pen name is more widely recognized.

features several variant subtitles, depending where one looks: "strange stories new and old" (*konko kitan* on the title slip and *konko kaidan* in the internal title, or *naidai*), or simply "strange tales" (*kidan*, as given in the table of contents). Chūryō's *Tales from the Withering Wind* proclaims itself a collection of "strange tales to make you clap your hands [in amazement]" (*hakushō kidan*), while Shinrotei's *A Handful of Tales* (*Hitofutagusa*, 1795) comprises "strange tales for all seasons" (*kan'on kidan*).

Where the label *yomihon* is imprecise, overinclusive, and anachronistic, the term *kidan*, translated as "strange tales" in the preceding examples, was not only the most common way authors themselves described these collections but has the additional virtue of foregrounding the most salient generic feature—strangeness—in a way *yomihon* does not. The term also resolves some of the limitations of finer subdivisions such as "early *yomihon*." While the *kidan* includes much of the early *yomihon*, given its absence of temporal or geographic associations it also encompasses similar works written by later authors, as well as those active outside of western Japan. Although he limits the label more decisively to earlier works, the cohesiveness of the *kidan* corpus has led Yokoyama Kuniharu to position the *kidan-mono*, as he terms it, as one of four subdivisions within the early *yomihon*.[25] Others have subsequently probed the boundaries and uses of the term *kidan* in contemporary sources.[26]

Kidan is not to be confused with *kaidan* (often translated as "ghost stories"), a term more familiar to modern readers and with greater currency in recent popular culture. While not quite as common as *kidan*, *kaidan* was also widely used in the Edo period, most famously in the title of Tsuruya Nanboku's kabuki play *Ghost Stories at Yotsuya on the Tōkaidō Highway*. Familiarity with the term in the West owes largely to Lafcadio Hearn's 1904 collection *Kwaidan: Stories and Studies of Strange Things* and Kobayashi Masaki's 1965 film adaptation of four of its tales. Unlike *kidan*, *kaidan* has seen some use as an organizing category in modern scholarly anthologies, from the early *Kaidan meisaku shū* (1927) through its more recent successors *Shoki Edo yomihon kaidan shū* (2000)

25. Yokoyama, *Yomihon no kenkyū*, 100–101.

26. Iikura Yōichi, "Kinsei bungaku no ichiryōiki to shite no 'kidan,'" *Nihon bungaku* 61, no. 10 (October 2012): 24–35.

and *Zenki yomihon kaidan shū* (2017), and has been advanced as a category in some Western-language scholarship as well.[27]

In choosing to characterize their contents as both *yomihon* and *kaidan*, the two recent anthologies highlight the insufficiency and ambiguity of each term by itself. *Yomihon* is less a designation of content than of format, while *kaidan* denotes content distributed across a wide range of generic and pseudogeneric categories, including but not limited to the *yomihon*. The titles of both anthologies position their contents at the intersection of the two. The 1927 anthology, which does not limit itself to works that fall under the rubric of the *yomihon*, illustrates some of the breadth of the *kaidan* through its inclusion of several late seventeenth-century *kanazōshi* (kana booklets). This breadth is also seen in the recent anthology *Ukiyozōshi kaidan shū* (1994), which contains three *ukiyozōshi* (tales of the floating world) collections of *kaidan* from the first decade of the eighteenth century.[28]

A further distinction between the *kidan* and the *kaidan* lies in the different nuances of the characters *ki* 奇 (Ch. *qi*) and *kai* 怪 (Ch. *guai*). Both denote the strange, but *ki* is the more expansive, encompassing not only the uncanny and otherworldly—the territory of *kai*—but also strange content with no connection to the supernatural. In its breadth, it is arguably the better fit with the English words "strange" and "anomalous," at least in their strict etymological senses: strange as that which is outside or foreign (from the Latin *extraneus*), anomalous as that which is not regular (from the Greek *anṓmalos*). At its broadest, *ki* denotes anything that elicits a response of wonder, as captured in the title of Ling Mengchu's *Slapping the Table in Amazement* (*Pai'an jingqi*)—which, as explained in the author's preface, refers to the reaction of his friends as they sat listening to his stories—or the subtitle to Chūryō's collection, which promises an experience that will have readers clapping their hands in wonder and delight. Indeed, the Edo enthusiasm for strange tales was

27. *Kaidan meisaku shū*, in *Nihon meicho zenshū: Edo bungei no bu* 10 (Nihon meicho zenshū kankōkai, 1927); Ōtaka Yōji and Kondō Mizuki, eds., *Shoki Edo yomihon kaidan shū*, vol. 1 of Takada, ed., *Edo kaii kisō bungei taikei*; and Iikura Yōichi, ed., *Zenki yomihon kaidan shū*. For an example of the use of *kaidan* as a category in English-language scholarship, see Reider, "Emergence of *Kaidan-shū*."

28. Kigoshi, *Ukiyozōshi kaidan shū*.

part of a larger cultural phenomenon, as new material culture, oddities, and spectacles such as *misemono* side-shows fueled intense curiosity and a desire for new and strange experiences—a history that underlies the modern Japanese word for curiosity, *kōkishin*, denoting literally the "love of *ki*," or the yearning for the strange and wondrous.

This breadth is reflected in the early modern application of the term *kidan*. Perhaps influenced by Teishō's use of the term in his first collection of tales, *kidan* gained prevalence in the book trade around the middle of the eighteenth century as a new conceptual framework comprising material as diverse as seventeenth-century kana tales, the "floating world" fiction of Ihara Saikaku, and the mock-didactic and satiric "sermons" known as *dangibon*—which generally emphasized the *dan*, or "telling," half of *kidan* over the *ki*, or "strange."[29] However, in terms of self-identification the term did not reappear until the publication of Teishō's second collection in 1766. As a steady stream of collections in the same mold similarly presented themselves as *kidan*, the term also began to appear from time to time in the subtitles of works in markedly different genres, from Yūkokushi's satirical travel fantasy *Wasōbyōe* (*Wasōbyōe*, 1774) to Tachibana Nankei's travelogue-miscellanies *Journey to the East* (*Tōyūki*, 1795) and *Journey to the West* (*Saiyūki*, 1795).[30]

This study uses *kidan* in its narrow sense to denote the mid- to late eighteenth-century collections of Teishō and his successors. These texts delineate a relatively coherent genre of fiction with many common characteristics. The basic plots are often Chinese in origin, drawing heavily on the *zhiguai*, *chuanqi*, *biji xiaoshuo*, and vernacular tales discussed in the preceding section, but also on medieval Japanese anecdotal literature (*setsuwa*).[31] Accordingly, the uncanny realms of ghosts and spirits, foxes

29. See Iikura Yōichi, "'Kidan' no ba," *Gobun* 78 (May 2002): 22–32. As Iikura notes, *kidan* appears as a category in the Kyoto bookseller Nagata Chōbē's 1754 catalog *Shinzō shojaku mokuroku*, which includes nearly sixty titles under the heading.

30. *Wasōbyōe* (also read *Wasōbē*) is subtitled "strange tales from distant lands" (*ikoku kidan*), while Nankei's miscellanies are "strange tales from the various provinces" (*shokoku kidan*).

31. My focus is primarily on tales with Chinese sources, but the boundary can be obscure. Still, although many of the formal structures are otherwise the same, some scholars attempt to distinguish between *setsuwa*-derived collections (of which *Hitofutagusa* is an example) and Chinese-derived collections. See Inoue Keiji, "*Morokoshi no*

and demons, and karma and destiny predominate, although authors at times turned elsewhere for the wondrous or strange, reflecting the breadth of *ki* as a conceptual category.

Like other genres, these collections were granted their own characteristic physical presence, helping them carve out their niche among the abundant offerings of the early modern Japanese book market. Almost all were printed as five fascicles in the relatively large *hanshibon* format (approximately 16 by 23 centimeters). They also shared with nearly all Edo popular fiction the inclusion of illustrations—generally one or two per fascicle—by leading *ukiyoe* artists of the day. Following the model of *A Garland of Stories*, the number of tales in each collection was commonly nine, but with some variance, as with the seven in *A Handful of Tales* or the thirteen in Sōkan Sanjin's *Fenceside Tales* (*Kakinegusa*, 1770). Certain diffuse large-scale structures can be discerned in the ordering of the tales, but they are otherwise independent and self-contained. The geographic settings are similarly diverse: collections rarely concentrate on a single region but feature settings strewn far and wide across the Japanese archipelago.

Reflecting the erudition of their authors, *kidan* are filled with learned disquisitions on topics ranging from history, medicine, and the natural world to music, poetry, and the arts, not to mention occasional baser pursuits such as drinking and cockfighting. They are also densely intertextual. Although many have one or two antecedents that can be identified as the primary sources for adaptation, this material is woven and transformed into a complex tapestry, with new meanings imparted through allusions to texts ranging across the full breadth of the Chinese and Japanese tradition. Particularly in those instances where *zhiguai* and *biji xiaoshuo* provide the outline for the plot, the resulting narrative is often many times longer than the source text.

Another difference that emerges when reading *kidan* alongside their Chinese sources concerns the temporal setting. Granting certain exceptions, particularly for earlier tales such as those in the *Taiping guangji*,

---

Yoshino joron, fu honkoku: zenki gesaku kenkyū (2)," *Shūjitsu ronsō* 16 (February 1987): 85–134; Makiyama Masayuki, "'Setsuwa-kei kidan' no isō josetsu: Shinrotei *Kan'on kidan hitofutagusa* no hōhō," *Kokusai bunka kenkyūka ronshū* (Tōhoku daigaku) 5 (December 1997): 23–29; and Iikura, "'Kidan' no ba."

many Chinese strange tales are set against an indeterminate historical backdrop reflecting their more ambiguous status as fiction. Pu Songling's stories are often presented with the conceit of having been shared with the author by a friend or acquaintance; in some cases a specific informant is mentioned, giving a feeling of recentness and authenticity but also, through the omission of overt historical markers, of timelessness.[32] Even where scholarship has unearthed evidence of a textual lineage reaching back to earlier sources, as in the two dozen or so stories rooted in Tang tales, Pu is known to have made changes to situate the narrative, at least apparently, in his own time.[33] Feng Menglong's tales, for all the ways in which they are more overtly fictional, are similarly ambiguous. While they invariably establish their geographic settings with great precision, they provide few historical markers, conveying a vague impression that the events happened in the recent past.

The general absence of datable events extends to mentions of warfare and unrest, which are relatively rare in the *Taiping guangji* and *Liaozhai* or, for that matter, in Feng Menglong. The few *Liaozhai* tales set amid rebellion or upheaval, such as "The Wild Dog" ("Ye gou") and "Wailing Ghosts" ("Gui ku"), or in which such events are mentioned in passing, as in "Zhang Cheng" and "Gongsun Jiuniang," are among the only ones to break with this general rule by referencing specific historical incidents. Warfare features more prominently in *New Tales by Lamplight*, reflecting the historical context in which Qu You wrote. His tales exude a sense of timeliness, in contrast to *Liaozhai*'s timelessness, and the tumult and hardship of the Yuan-Ming transition cast their shadow across many of the tales—notably "The Tale of Aiqing" ("Aiqing zhuan"), which, as will be explored, was a source for both Ryōi and Akinari. In general, however, *Liaozhai* is the more representative collection in this regard. For all of Yuan Mei's protestations concerning the distinctions between Pu Songling's collection and his own, the tales in *Zi bu yu* are quite similar with respect to their apparent timelessness and the general backdrop of

32. For a discussion of what he terms "factual framing" in *Liaozhai*, see Charles E. Hammond, "Factual Framing in *Liao zhai zhi yi*," *Acta Orientalia Academiae Scientiarum Hungaricae* 59, no. 2 (2006): 205–30. On the perceived "authenticity" of the tales, see Barr, "Pu Songling and *Liaozhai Zhiyi*," 252.

33. Altenburger, *The Sword or the Needle*, 164–65.

social and political stability. Stories such as "General-in-Chief Zhao Stabs a Ghostly Visage" ("Zhao dajiangjun ci pilian guai") or "The Thunder God Is Tricked" ("Leigong bei dai") are the rare exceptions, and of these the former is set not during conflict but in its aftermath. This in spite of the natural association of disorder (*luan*) and the strange (*guai*) reflected in the line from Confucius directly quoted in the title: "That of which the master did not speak (*zi bu yu*): the strange, feats of strength, disorder, and spirits."[34]

Kidan display a marked departure from such conventions. They are mostly set with careful precision in the distant past, generally during a reign period specified within the opening lines of the story. The context is often one of unrest, with tales set against the backdrop of many of the major conflicts in Japanese history. In many collections the majority of tales unequivocally fit this description. This is certainly true of Akinari's *Tales of Moonlight and Rain*. Chūryō's *Tales from the Withering Wind*, for its part, contains four tales that unambiguously fit this description, but the figure rises to six if we include one that features vengeful spirits slain in an ancient battle and another recounting a succession struggle and the vendetta that ensues. Even the otherwise celebratory final story is set against the backdrop of the Hideyoshi invasions and includes an encounter with the Heike dead near the Straits of Shimonoseki. Conflict features less prominently in the tales of Teishō, who, perhaps not coincidentally, hews relatively closely to his source texts. Nevertheless, warfare is a stronger presence in *A Thicket of Tales* than in the earlier *A Garland of Stories*, suggesting a progression in the development of the genre. And at least one setting of historical unrest—the turmoil of the Southern and Northern Courts period—features in all three of his major collections.

If not quite foregrounded, then, violence and instability provide the broader context more often than not. This is not only a general distinction between the Chinese strange tale and its Japanese counterpart but a difference that can be observed in individual source texts and their adaptations. Warfare is routinely introduced into narratives in which it was originally absent. All of this raises an obvious question: Why would authors born into one of the great ages of peace in world history actively rewrite strange tales against the backdrop of the warfare of the past?

34. Confucius, *Analects* 7.21.

Chapter 5 considers the role of political pressures and other external factors in shaping this convention. In the final section of this chapter, we will examine instead the function of historical recontextualization *within* the tales, including the narrative and affective value of warfare, as well as its implication in complex webs of intertextual association that further enhance the very strangeness of the Japanese strange tale.

Tales from the Withering Wind

Much of our attention for the remainder of the book will be devoted to *Tales from the Withering Wind*, a neglected jewel of the *kidan* genre that, as noted, represents the most extensive engagement with *Liaozhai* in all of early modern Japanese literature. The titular "withering wind" carries multiple meanings, evoking the spine-tingling quality of the otherworldly tales themselves, as well as the bitter weather of early winter, when the author, Morishima Chūryō, wrote the preface to the collection—not to mention his tongue-in-cheek desire that the book might "sell copies as numerous as leaves scattered amidst the withering wind."[35] Chūryō also promotes his stories as "good bedtime reading for autumn nights when the withering wind gusts fiercely," suggesting that *Tales for the Withering Wind* might serve as an equally appropriate rendering of the title.

Chūryō came from a long line of scholars with close ties to the Tokugawa elite. His older brother, Katsuragawa Hoshū (1754–1809), was an accomplished scholar of Dutch learning and medicine who served as personal physician to the shogun, a post inherited from three generations of Katsuragawa before him. As the second son, Chūryō was unencumbered by official duties and pursued a path largely of his own choosing. His formal occupation was as a physician, in which capacity he cared for

35. *Kogarashi zōshi*, in Ishigami Satoshi, ed., *Morishima Chūryō shū* (*MCS*) (Kokusho kankōkai, 1994), 144. Page references to Ishigami's edition of the text are given throughout. However, in the case of several minor inconsistencies, translations refer to the original edition: Morishima Chūryō, (*Hakushō kidan*) *Kogarashi zōshi* (Edo and Ōsaka: Kazusaya Rihē et al., 1792).

numerous patients, apparently with a specialization in Western medicines and techniques.[36] He was also an active participant in a network of Dutch studies scholars that included his brother, the physician Ōtsuki Gentaku (1757–1827), the polymath-author Hiraga Gennai (1728–80), the daimyō Kutsuki Masatsuna (1750–1802), and many others. Chūryō's involvement with this circle yielded some of the most widely read nonfiction writing of the Edo period, essay collections in which he introduced diverse aspects of Western culture, society, and learning in an easily digestible form aimed at mass readership.

His greatest legacy, however, is as a writer of popular fiction. Chūryō's literary career began at a young age, when he came under Gennai's tutelage and collaborated with him on several plays for the puppet theater. In the 1780s he emerged onto the Edo literary scene as an active figure in his own right, writing comic verse, pictorial fiction, and several pieces in the genre known as the *sharebon*—witty, urbane, dialogue-heavy narratives set most often against the backdrop of the urban pleasure quarters. It was in this last genre that Chūryō made one of his greatest contributions to Edo fiction. In a piece titled *A Provincial Production* (*Inaka shibai*, 1787), he offered a polemical denunciation of the excesses of the genre—which had come to emphasize unflattering, sharp-edged exposés of courtesans and brothel life—and established a template for dialogue-based fiction set outside the brothel districts, with humor derived instead from gentle caricature. This novel approach paved the way for two of the masterpieces of Edo comic fiction: Jippensha Ikku's (1765–1831) *Hoofing It along the Tōkaidō* (*Tōkaidōchū hizakurige*, 1802–22) and Shikitei Sanba's (1776–1822) *Bathhouse of the Floating World* (*Ukiyoburo*, 1809–13). Indeed, both Ikku and Sanba cherished Chūryō as a literary

36. Sakai Tadahiro (the daimyō of Himeji), Shikitei Sanba, and others wrote of medicine as Chūryō's primary occupation, praising him as a talented physician whose services were much in demand. See *Keirin manroku*, in *NZT* series 1, 2:279; and *Inaka shibai Chūshingura*, in Aeba Kōson, ed., *Chūshingura hinikuron, Chūshingura henchikiron, Inaka shibai Chūshingura*, in *Shūchin meicho bunko* 48 (Fuzanbō, 1912), 118. Chūryō's notebooks hint at the nature of his practice, with lists of Western ingredients, materials, and techniques. See, for example, *Daishin manshō* (unpaginated manuscript, National Diet Library), 21a–23b; and the scrapbook *Sekijichō* (Album of Treasured Texts; owned by the Waseda University Library).

mentor, seeing him as the principal stylistic successor to Gennai, even if this influence waned as Chūryō achieved his mature style.[37]

By 1788 at the latest, Chūryō had set his sights on writing a collection of strange tales, as evidenced by the publisher Fushimiya Zenroku's catalog of fiction for the upcoming year, which includes an advertisement for a forthcoming work under Chūryō's name titled *The Plum Blossom Collection* (*Konohana zōshi*). The accompanying text describes the collection as "an entertaining book bringing together a number of tales of the supernatural in the manner of [Teishō's] *A Garland of Stories* and *A Thicket of Tales*."[38] Although no work by the title *The Plum Blossom Collection* is extant, the collection undoubtedly shared a common origin with *Tales from the Withering Wind*, which appeared in 1792 with illustrations by Kitao Masayoshi.[39] Over the next decade, Chūryō would publish two further adaptations from Chinese sources: *An Elegant Tale by Moonlight* (*Gekka seidan*, 1798) and *The Jeweled Branch: Ink Spilled Playfully by Lamplight* ([*Tōka no geboku*] *Tama no eda*, 1802), adaptations of vernacular tales from Feng Menglong's *Constant Words to Awaken the World* and Zhuoyuan's *The Cup That Reflects the World*, respectively.

With the rise of modern scholarly interest in Edo literature in the early twentieth century, *Tales from the Withering Wind* attracted a measure of notice and was even nearly canonized in a formative anthology: the twenty-eight-volume *Nihon meicho zenshū: Edo bungei no bu* (Complete

37. See, for instance, the eulogy Sanba wrote for Chūryō the year after his death, and the memoirs of Hoshū's great-great-granddaughter Imaizumi Mine, in which she describes Ikku's visits to the Katsuragawa residence. Sanba, *Inaka shibai Chūshingura*, 118; and Imaizumi Mine, *Nagori no yume: ran'i Katsuragawa-ke ni umarete*, in *Tōyō bunko* 9 (Heibonsha, 1963), 109–10.

38. Quoted in Ishigami Satoshi, *Manzōtei Morishima Chūryō no bunji* (Kanrin shobō, 1995), 716. Although the characters are written incorrectly, the second work is almost certainly intended to read *A Thicket of Tales*. The two works, then, would be Teishō's *A Garland of Stories* (1749) and its sequel *A Thicket of Tales* (1766).

39. It is possible that *The Plum Blossom Collection* was originally an early version of *Tales from the Withering Wind*. However, the colophon of the latter contains an advertisement for a sequel titled *The Plum Blossom Collection*, and another advertisement for a work by the same title appeared in 1806. See Ishigami, *Manzōtei Morishima Chūryō no bunji*, 586. This suggests either that the title had been transferred to the sequel volume, or that the two works were envisioned as companion volumes from the beginning. Given the existence of multiple references over an extended period, it is conceivable that the book was in fact published but does not survive today.

Masterworks of Japan: Edo Literature Series, 1925–29). One of the earliest and most voluminous anthologies of Edo literature, the series begins with Saikaku, Bashō, and Chikamatsu and continues with volumes organized mostly by genre.[40] Appended to each volume is a catalog of the entire series, including the contents of forthcoming installments. Several of the early catalogs show ambitious plans for the tenth volume of the series, titled *Kaidan meisaku shū* (Collected Masterpieces of Supernatural Fiction). Some twenty-four works were slated for inclusion, beginning with Ryōi's *Talisman Dolls* and continuing more or less chronologically through the eighteenth century, covering several of the aforementioned *kidan* collections and ending with none other than *Tales from the Withering Wind* (its title rendered phonetically to avoid the unusual domestic character for "withering wind" used in the original orthography).[41]

When the tenth volume appeared late in 1927, however, the scope was decidedly less grand, with only ten titles included, along with a facsimile of a picture scroll depicting a demonic procession (*hyakki yagyō*) attributed to the artist Tosa Tsunetaka. The best-known works remained, including those by Ryōi, Teishō, Akinari, and Takebe Ayatari (1719–74), but most of the less-familiar works originally planned for transcription, including *Tales from the Withering Wind*, did not make the final cut. It may be that the editors' plans were simply too ambitious, as even in its truncated form the volume totals more than one thousand pages. Had the original list of titles all been included, the page count would have run to more than twice that. Although many of the excluded works were synopsized by Mizutani Futō a decade later, most would have to wait many years for modern editions, and some continue to be accessible only in their original format.

As a result, attention to *Tales from the Withering Wind* remained largely limited to mentions of the collection's preface, in which Chūryō offers a concise overview of the history of the strange tale in China and Japan. Echoing the lengthier history of Chinese fiction presented in Feng

40. *Nihon meicho zenshū: Edo bungei no bu*, 28 vols. (Nihon meicho zenshū kankōkai, 1925–29).

41. See, for example, "*Nihon meicho zenshū* (dai-ikki shuppan): *Edo bungei no bu* (zen nijūrokkan oyobi tsuika hen nikan) shomoku yotei ichiran," 2, included as a supplement to volume 26, *Senryū zappai shū* (June, 1927).

Menglong's preface to *Stories Old and New*, Chūryō traces a grand progression from early Ming *chuanqi* and Feng's vernacular tales through their Japanese adaptations in the hands of Ryōi and Teishō.[42] As such, the passage is sometimes cited for its value in tracing the lineage of Edo strange tales back to their Chinese predecessors, and for demonstrating contemporary awareness of this progression.[43] The opening lines read as follows:

> The book *New Tales by Lamplight* and its companion volume were rendered in our own vernacular as *Talisman Dolls*, while the four works *Stories Old and New*, *Wondrous Tales New and Old*, *Common Words to Caution the World*, and *Slapping the Table in Amazement* were drawn on in the creation of *A Garland of Stories* and *A Thicket of Tales*. These three collections are the parents of recent popular tales.[44] Their strange conceits and alluring style are such that each reading is like the first. Readers take the volumes in hand and never grow tired of them. Recently I have followed their example, writing up a slew of utter fictions in a realistic manner.[45]

42. In Shuhui Yang and Yunqin Yang, trans., *Stories Old and New* (Seattle: University of Washington Press, 2000), 5–6.

43. See, for example, Yamaguchi Takeshi, "Yomihon no hassei: Teishō to Akinari to no kankei" (1926), reprinted in Konoe Noriko, ed., *Akinari kenkyū shiryō shūsei* 11 (Kuresu shuppan, 2003), 103; or Nakamura Yukihiko, *Kinseiteki hyōgen*, in *Nakamura Yukihiko chojutsu shū* 2 (Chūō kōronsha, 1982), 307.

44. In context, it is clear that Chūryō uses the term *otogizōshi* (lit. "companion books"; translated as "recent popular tales") not in reference to medieval stories, as the term is now commonly used, but to indicate the many imitators and successors to Teishō: that is, the sorts of works planned for inclusion by the editors of the *Kaidan meisaku shū* or contained in recent anthologies such as Ōtaka and Kondō's *Shoki Edo yomihon kaidan shū*.

45. *Kogarashi zōshi*, in *MCS*, 144. The works mentioned are (1) Qu You's *New Tales by Lamplight* (ca. 1380) and (2) its "sequel," Li Changqi's *More Tales by Lamplight* (1420); (3) Asai Ryōi's *Talisman Dolls* (1666); (4) *Stories Old and New* (1620–21) (also known by the title *Clear Words to Instruct the World* [*Yushi mingyan*]) and (5) *Common Words to Caution the World* (1624), two of Feng Menglong's *Sanyan*; (6) Ling Mengchu's *Slapping the Table in Amazement* (1628), which was followed by the sequel volume *Slapping the Table in Amazement, Part Two* (*Erke Pai'an jingqi*, 1633)—together with Feng Menglong's collections these are called the *Sanyan erpai*; (7) Baoweng Laoren's ("The Urn-Bearing Old Man") *Wondrous Tales New and Old* (ca. 1640), which anthologized a selection of stories from the *Sanyan erpai*; and (8) Tsuga Teishō's *A Garland of Stories* and (9) *A Thicket of Tales*.

Aside from occasional references to this passage, *Tales from the Withering Wind* attracted scant interest until many years later. It was among the nearly 250 works overviewed by Mizutani Futō in his 1937 survey of Edo fiction, but his discussion of the collection's source texts is limited to two of the tales that were based on medieval Japanese sources.[46] Three years later, Ishizaki Matazō quoted the preface but otherwise noted only what was already obvious from the lineage in which Chūryō had positioned himself: that the ultimate origins of many of the tales must lie in some undetermined Chinese collection.[47] It was only in 1980 that Tokuda Takeshi first identified this source as being *Liaozhai*, with six of Chūryō's nine stories being primarily adaptations from Pu Songling (see the entry in table 3.1). Tokuda also offered a reappraisal of the tales, positioning them as worthy of comparison with those of Teishō and Akinari, or the longer historical narratives of Ayatari.[48] This favorable assessment prompted a broader shift wherein *Tales from the Withering Wind* has slowly risen in critical estimation and attracted somewhat more attention. Ōtaka Yōji sees the work as one of the only collections of strange tales published in the city of Edo with literary merits uniquely its own, as opposed to being primarily derivative of the Kamigata (Kyoto-Osaka) tradition.[49] Ishigami Satoshi, who in 1994 published the first and only modern edition of the text, deems the work a "masterpiece" that ranks among Chūryō's finest efforts.[50]

Indeed, *Tales from the Withering Wind* shows a more creative engagement with its sources than Chūryō's other adaptations, which are comparatively straightforward and have not enjoyed the same newfound critical esteem. Its relative strength is perhaps not unrelated to the fact that it was, if we are to take his often tongue-in-cheek prefaces and afterwords at their word, the only one of his four *yomihon* undertaken at his own initiative and not at the request of the publisher. Contemporary

46. Mizutani, *Sentaku kosho kaidai* (1937), in *Mizutani Futō chosakushū*, 7:140.

47. Ishizaki, *Kinsei Nihon ni okeru Shina zokugo bungaku shi* (1940), 244.

48. Tokuda, "*Kogarashi zōshi* to *Ryōsai shii*," 336–70. In addition to the sources identified by Tokuda, borrowings from or resonances with other *Liaozhai* tales can be observed elsewhere in *Tales from the Withering Wind*.

49. Ōtaka Yōji, "Edo yomihon no tenkai: Kansei, Kyōwa nenkan," in Yokoyama Kuniharu, ed., *Yomihon no sekai: Edo to Kamigata* (Sekai shisōsha, 1985), 10.

50. "Kaidai," in *MCS*, 381, 386.

readers seem to have assessed the tales favorably as well. Writing a decade after the collection's initial publication, Chūryō claimed with some apparent surprise that *Tales from the Withering Wind* remained "as popular as the day it was written."[51] We may question the impartiality of this assertion, but it is true at least that the tales achieved sufficient success that they were reissued with new illustrations in 1818 (and again in 1833) in a pirated edition titled *Tales of Unrivalled Strangeness* ([*Katakiuchi*] *Kōsei kidan*), through which later generations of readers came to enjoy them as well.

From Translation to Adaptation: The Spectrum of Rewriting Practices

Chūryō's activities as de facto scribe for his brother and the circle of Dutch studies scholars who frequently gathered at the Katsuragawa residence in Edo ensured that numerous remarkable anecdotes that would otherwise have been lost were not only preserved but made their way into print. Many were included in *Various Tales from the Dutch* (*Kōmō zatsuwa*, 1787), an accessible collection of short essays on the Dutch and topics related to the West, and its sequel *New Tales of Myriad Lands* (*Bankoku shinwa*, 1789), which similarly drew on Dutch sources but focused its attention primarily on the people and customs of Asia. Both collections were reprinted multiple times and enjoyed wide readership. Chūryō also wrote or planned studies of Ryūkyū, Korea, and rural Japan, compiled the first published Japanese-Dutch dictionary, gathered castaway reports of foreign lands, and maintained a scrapbook into which he pasted imported merchandise seals, snippets of foreign text, and other ephemera.

All of these efforts paint a picture of Chūryō as an avid collector of tales. He was in this regard not unlike Pu Songling or Feng Menglong. They, too, were tireless collectors—revising, rewriting, and anthologizing, but not always "originating" their stories. Chūryō's manuscript compilation of castaway narratives *Strange Reports from Overseas* (*Kaigai ibun*,

51. Ishigami Satoshi, "Honkoku (*Tōka no geboku*) *Tama no eda*," *Yomihon kenkyū* 8, no. 2 (September 1994): 116.

ca. late 1780s–1809), which features nearly sixty oral accounts of foreign lands dating back to the late sixteenth century, is particularly striking for its broad parallels to *Liaozhai*. These extend not only to its title, structure, and to some degree the content itself, but to the work's afterword, which like Pu's preface paints a scene of the author-compiler seated at his desk with a voluminous body of strange tales scattered before him.[52]

A similar act of collecting the strange underlies *Tales from the Withering Wind*. Although Chūryō does not explicitly identify Pu Songling as the primary source for many of his tales, the preface's characterization of the collection as a "rare book" (*chinsho* 珍書) suggests both the strangeness of its source material and the literal rareness of *Liaozhai* as a printed text in Japan. Even at its most straightforward, the act of appropriating a text is, as Linda Hutcheon observes, also the act of salvaging it.[53] The art of the rewriter, collector, or anthologizer preserves and rescues material from obscurity and potential loss. This notion had a foundational place in the East Asian tradition, where it was often framed in terms of ensuring the survival of valuable texts for posterity, and was a common conceit among Chinese authors of tales of the strange who, borrowing the words of Confucius, often claimed to "transmit but not create."[54] Of course, even mere transmission is not a passive process but involves gathering, selecting, revising, rewriting, and anthologizing—that is to say, choosing what to pass on (as well as what not to) and in what form.

As a transmitter, Chūryō's selections resonate with modern preferences, with his source texts including two *Liaozhai* stories that are among the most familiar today: "The Painted Skin" and "The Cricket." That said, the writing of *kidan* was more than simply an exercise in salvaging that which was available elsewhere. *Kidan* were obviously fictionalized in a way that *zhiguai* and even *chuanqi* were not, and they made no claim merely to pass on that which had been received. As such, they existed at the far end of a spectrum of practices for the cross-cultural transmission of texts, or what we might characterize as forms of transla-

52. The preface and afterword to *Kaigai ibun* are reproduced in Okada Kesao, "Morishima Chūryō no mita kaihi no bunka: *Kōmō zatsuwa*, *Bankoku shinwa* o chūshin ni," *Kokubungaku kenkyū* 151 (2007): 69–70.

53. Hutcheon, *A Theory of Adaptation*, 8.

54. Confucius, *Analects* 7.1.

tion. They rewrote texts for a new readership in a different language, but in a way we would evaluate as among the least "faithful" to their sources. Indeed, because of the liberties it allows, adaptation is often viewed as a practice entirely apart from translation. There is some irony, then, that when considered in its own right, adaptation is regularly evaluated precisely for its faithfulness.

At the opposite end of the spectrum of translation practices sits *kundoku*: the reading of Chinese texts directly using Japanese pronunciation and the rules of Japanese grammar. By providing (to varying degrees) reading marks, glosses, and other forms of annotation, *wakokubon* editions equipped readers with the basic tools to engage in *kundoku*. In some sense, this was arguably the most faithful form of translation. After all, what could be more faithful to the original than to leave it intact on the page? Yet *kundoku* presupposes a large body of knowledge and leaves much of the actual labor to the reader. Depending on the level of annotation, texts could still present great challenges, and even the successful navigation of a *kundoku* edition resulted in a sort of decoded or deciphered Chinese, the meaning of which could be quite opaque to readers not already equipped with a solid command of the language. In this regard, much like adaptation at the opposite extreme of the spectrum, it is questionable whether *kundoku* can be considered a form of translation at all. More than "faithful," the appropriate term might be "conservative," and contemporary critiques of *kundoku* often targeted precisely this conservatism, positing that texts could not be at once Chinese and Japanese but were to be accessed either in the original or, for those without the necessary preparation, in vernacular translation. Many Japanese Sinologists memorably compared the limited effectiveness of *kundoku* to "scratching an itch through one's shoe," while Chūryō saw the task of reading Qu You's *New Tales by Lamplight* in annotated form as that of a "rabbit fording a stream."

In between these two poles—*kundoku* at the conservative end and adaptation at the "free" end—lies a middle ground encompassing practices that we may more readily characterize as "translation" without reservations or caveats. These range, as Rebekah Clements has traced, from "partial transcription of *kundoku*" (that is, reordering characters and writing out inflections instead of requiring readers to perform these procedures themselves) through "loose renderings in classical Japanese" and "freer translation."[55] One of the most common labels for translation into vernacular Japanese was *tsūzoku*, meaning literally that which could "reach the masses." Often the word was appended before the title of the translated text, as with Sawa Tansai's *Tsūzoku Kokon kikan* (A Vernacular Translation of Tales from *Jingu qiguan*, 1814), or Ishikawa Masamochi's *Tsūzoku Seisei kōgen* (A Vernacular Translation of Tales from *Xingshi hengyan*, 1789) and *Tsūzoku Haimonroku* (A Vernacular Translation of *Paimen lu*, 1828–29), to name just three of many such translations from classical and vernacular Chinese fiction. These translations were rarely complete. Among the preceding examples, the first two included only a handful of stories from the original collections, while the third, a substantially larger collection of 131 relatively brief tales, still omitted several dozen stories from its even larger source text.

Tsuzōku translations varied in their conservativeness. Masamochi's *Tsūzoku Haimonroku* hews close to the original, but not slavishly so; certain passages resemble *kundoku* transcription at first glance, but closer inspection reveals adjustments or rewritings for the sake of clarity. Masamochi's translations of Feng Menglong in *Tsūzoku Seisei kōgen* deviate further from *kundoku* transcription. Yet here, too, initial impressions can mislead. The preservation of key features of vernacular Chinese, such as its question words, counters, and personal pronouns—albeit with glosses in standard Japanese—as well as the use of katakana for Japanese particles and inflections, combine to create the appearance of *kundoku* transcription and impart an exotic "vernacular Chinese" flavor to the translation. However, virtually none of the text can properly be termed *kundoku* transcription. *Kundoku* was ill-equipped to tackle vernacular Chinese given its key differences with the classical register, and Masamochi's translations diverged out of sheer necessity. Some passages stray from the original meaning, while other sections are omitted altogether, including the embedded commentary and poems. In spite of this, by imbuing his translation with the "flavor" of the original and concerning himself with meaning instead of gloss, and doing this in mostly natural, readable prose, Masamochi's effort comes close to fulfilling our modern ideal of faithfulness. *Kundoku* may be more faithful insofar as it preserves the source,

55. Rebekah Clements, *A Cultural History of Translation in Early Modern Japan* (Cambridge: Cambridge University Press, 2015), 223.

but it falls short of well-executed *tsūzoku* translations when judged by readability and the conveyance of textual meaning *as Japanese*.

In addition to *tsūzoku*, there were many other terms used to describe what we would now collectively label "translation." Clements, who enumerates more than twenty distinct words for different forms of translation, asserts that "this plethora of terminology suggests there was no one overarching mental category of 'translation' in early modern Japan."[56] But we might view this proliferation in a different light. At the same time that it points to a finely partitioned set of distinct techniques, in practice there was extensive overlap in the way these terms were used and the methods they described. This suggests less the absence of any larger conceptual framework than a framework composed of a fluid spectrum of techniques.

This fluidity is seen in the varied application of many of the individual terms for translation. *Tsūzoku* editions ranged even beyond the preceding examples, with some constituting little more than *kundoku* transcriptions and others—perhaps precisely because of the availability of *kundoku* as a form of "faithful" translation—taking considerable liberties with the text. Another of the most common words, *yaku*, saw even wider deployment, appearing on the title page of each of the three preceding examples to describe the roles of Masamochi and Tansai as translators, but also used in reference to Oka Hakku and Sawada Issai's roles as annotators in their *kundoku* editions of tales from Feng Menglong's *Sanyan*.

Other descriptors were still more fluid in their application. One common expression for the rendering of Chinese fiction in Japanese was *kokuji ni yawaragu* (or *kana ni yawaragu*), meaning "to soften into Japanese writing." (The verb *yawaragu*, which means literally "to soften," carries an additional layer of significance in that it is often written with the character *wa* 和, also used to mean "Japanese.") Itami Chin'en employs this phrase in reference to *tsūzoku*-style translation, while others, including Chūryō and Bakin, use it to describe the process of adaptation—the rewriting, or "softening," of Chinese texts into Japanese fictional narra-

56. Clements, *Translation in Early Modern Japan*, 11.

tives.[57] In other words, although it was perfectly possible to make a distinction between translation and adaptation as forms of rewriting, in practice there was often a blurry boundary between the two that can be observed in a tendency not to carefully distinguish between the practices, as well as in the use of language that does not always map neatly onto retroactive conceptions.

Anxieties and Influences in Kidan *Adaptations*

If, as descriptions like "softening [a text] into Japanese" suggest, adaptation was conceived of as part of a spectrum of overlapping translation practices, it occupied not only the far extreme but also the most expansive swath of territory, receding endlessly into a mist of increasing distance from the source text. Rewriting Chinese tales as *kidan* required not only interlingual translation but also intermedial and intercultural translation. Some generic conventions, such as the use of verse prevalent in Feng Menglong's tales, could be overcome in various ways that conformed to *kidan* norms. Poems were often dropped altogether in adaptation, but they could also be converted into Japanese verse, as in the tale that opens Teishō's *A Garland of Stories*, or simply naturalized into the prose narrative, as in Akinari's "The Chrysanthemum Vow." More fundamentally, vastly different geographic, cultural, and literary landscapes needed to be transposed and rewritten for a new audience. In practice, this was often accomplished by weaving the plot into a familiar domestic historical setting and its associated sources. In the preface to an adaptation of a tale by Feng Menglong, one early nineteenth-century Japanese author

57. Itami Chin'en, *Chin'en zatsuwa*, in *Edo kaii kisō bungei taikei*, 2:699. Preface to *Kogarashi zōshi*, in *MCS*, 144. *Wakae no hato* (1805), in Suzuki Jūzō and Tokuda Takeshi, eds., *Wakae no hato, Sangoku ichiya monogatari*, in *Bakin chūhen yomihon shūsei* 2 (Kyūko shoin, 1995), 6–7. For a brief comparison of Bakin's work with one of its sources, Langxian's tale "The Siege of Yangzhou" ("Jiangdu shi xiaofu tushen"), see Ellen Widmer, "Tragedy or Travesty? Perspectives on Langxian's 'The Siege of Yangzhou,'" in Eva Hung, ed., *Paradoxes of Traditional Chinese Literature* (Hong Kong: Chinese University Press, 1994), 197–98.

succinctly described his process as that of "mixing an imported story (*xiaoshuo*) with an old tale (*monogatari*) from our own country."[58]

Informed by Romantic notions of the heroic author as a vessel of pure, spontaneous inspiration, modern readers are inclined to view adaptations with suspicion or even contempt, as derivative and inferior versions of the "original." Linda Hutcheon observes the distinct moral dimension inherent in this view.[59] Yet for much of literary history, both in the West and in East Asia, adaptation was an entirely respectable endeavor. In Japan this was perhaps not unrelated to, or even a corollary of, the general subordination of the author to the text, a tendency reflected in the tradition of anonymous authorship and tentative attributions.[60] The ability to work skillfully within the confines of tradition was not merely acceptable but indeed a key measure of literary value, with no small portion of the canon composed of works that to one degree or another draw from other texts. Even into the early modern period, as their Western counterparts were increasingly burdened by Bloomian anxieties of influence, Japanese writers continued to embrace the inherent intertextuality of all literary production. Besides, to privilege the "original," imagined or otherwise, is to reduce literature to plot alone. *Kidan* writers transformed and wove together storylines, adding a profusion of detail and often recasting the spare plots of their sources as frames on which to spin allusive tapestries that draw upon the full breadth of the Chinese and Japanese literary tradition. Like modern adaptations, the best *kidan* are enhanced by the additional layers of meaning accessible through familiarity with the source, but were read and enjoyed by all readers, not just those few able to apprehend the intertextual palimpsest in its entirety.

58. Saeda Shigeru, *Jūninmae sara no yakitsugi* (1812), quoted in Suzuki, "Gōkanmono no daizai tenki to Tanehiko," 64. Although Suzuki describes this as Saeda's only piece of fiction, he was in fact the author of nearly two dozen known works.

59. Describing attacks on film adaptations of literature in particular, Hutcheon documents a range of "moralistic" words applied to such efforts, including "tampering," "violation," "betrayal," "perversion," and "desecration." Hutcheon, *A Theory of Adaptation*, 2. To these one might add the view of adaptation as an act of intellectual "laziness" or, worse still, one of "appropriation" or "theft."

60. See the discussion in Adam L. Kern, "The Writer at His Desk: The Professionalization of Authorship in Eighteenth-Century Japan," in Wilt L. Idema, ed., *Books in Numbers* (Cambridge, MA: Harvard-Yenching Library, 2007), 275–79.

The intertextuality of the genre is foregrounded in the preface to *Tales from the Withering Wind*, in which Chūryō positions himself within a literary lineage reaching back to Feng Menglong and Qu You by way of Teishō and Ryōi, as well as in the very pseudonym under which he published the collection: Master Shinra (Shinrashi 森羅子), a shortening of one of his often-used comic pen names, Shinra Manzō, that can also be taken phonetically to mean "a new Master Luo" (Shin Rashi 新羅子). In other words, Chūryō slyly positions himself as a modern-day Luo Guanzhong (J. Ra Kanchū), the author to whom *Romance of the Three Kingdoms* and *The Water Margin* were conventionally attributed. The preface's closing lines align him with Teishō as well. "The words and phrases that here blossom forth are clumsy, and you may privately consider them unrefined," Chūryō writes, "but profit would bring the publisher happiness."[61] This self-deprecatory appeal to the reader parodies the preface to *A Garland of Stories*, in which Teishō addresses his readers to request their forbearance: "All you gentlemen who read this, you will find that our unadorned phrases do not do justice to the word 'garland,' but if you would overlook this it would bring us great happiness."[62]

Amid these overt and veiled references to his predecessors, there are two writers of particular relevance whom Chūryō does not mention. Especially glaring is the omission of Pu Songling himself. Although at first glance this may appear an effort to pass off the relatively unfamiliar plots as the author's own, the reasons are likely more mundane. To spell out one's sources—which, it should be noted, include several other works in addition to *Liaozhai*—would be to mar the subtlety of the tales' allusivity and spoil the enjoyment readers derived from making such connections themselves. It would also have broken with an established convention that Chūryō openly recognizes by positioning his work, in its very preface, within the tradition of Japanese adaptations from Chinese fiction. Ryōi, Teishō, and others had similarly refrained from naming their sources, and their doing so did not prevent readers from identifying them.

61. *Kogarashi zōshi*, in *MCS*, 144.

62. *Hanabusa sōshi*, in Nakamura Yukihiko, Takada Mamoru, and Nakamura Hiroyasu, eds., *Hanabusa sōshi, Nishiyama monogatari, Ugetsu monogatari, Harusame monogatari*, in *SNKBZ* 78 (Shōgakkan, 1995), 20. Ōtaka Yōji notes the parallel in "Edo yomihon no tenkai," 11.

Liaozhai was, as we have seen, read widely enough that the source tales would have been identifiable to learned readers (and of little concern to more casual readers). Just in case, Chūryō drops additional hints along the way, although nothing quite so obvious as the advertised title of a planned sequel, *The Fox's Fur Robe* (*Kitsune no kawagoromo*), which borrows a colorful metaphor from Pu Songling's own preface, where he describes his approach to writing *Liaozhai* as one of "piecing together patches of fox fur to make a robe."[63]

The other author Chūryō leaves out of his lineage is Akinari. Given that *Tales of Moonlight and Rain* had not yet achieved the canonical status it enjoys today, the omission is perhaps understandable. Nevertheless, *Tales from the Withering Wind* shows awareness of Akinari's tales both in occasional resonances in setting and in glancing allusions in the prose itself.[64] The two authors also deploy historical recontextualization to similar effect, using moments of conflict and unrest from Japanese history as a backdrop that heightens the mood of strangeness and uncertainty that pervades their narratives. While this is a technique observed more broadly across the *kidan* genre, the similarities are particularly striking between Chūryō and Akinari. Strange things often occur as the result of excessive desire, obsession, or otherwise anomalous emotions, and warfare introduces an anomalous context to match. It is also a convenient plot element in stories that hinge, as many of them do, on separation, establishing a compelling external source of uncertainty that extends beyond the mere fickleness or unfaithfulness of the characters themselves.

We observe such a transformation in "The Chrysanthemum Vow" ("Kikuka no chigiri"), Akinari's tale of the male lovers Samon and

63. An 1809 advertisement for the sequel described it as a collection of "stories left over from *Tales from the Withering Wind*." Reproduced in Satō Satoru, "Honkoku *Izumi no Chikahira monogatari*," *Jissen kokubungaku* 42 (September 1992): 166. Although the advertisement indicates that an illustrator, Utagawa Toyohiro (1774–1830), was already lined up, there is no evidence that the work was ever completed. For Pu Songling's 1679 preface, see Zhang Youhe, ed., *Liaozhai zhiyi: huijiao huizhu huiping ben* (*LZ*), 3 vols. (Beijing: Zhonghua shuju, 1962), 3.

64. For a discussion of several parallels with Akinari in Chūryō's tales, see Sonoda Yutaka, "*Kogarashi zōshi* to *Ugetsu monogatari*," *Sōsho Edo bunko geppō* 32 (accompanying *MCS*) (July 1994): 5–8. Beyond his clear familiarity with *Tales of Moonlight and Rain*, Chūryō was, as Sonoda notes, possibly the first to attribute the collection to Akinari.

Sōemon. After Sōemon suddenly takes ill on the road, Samon, a stranger, nurses him back to health. The two men form a fast bond. When it comes time for Sōemon to continue onward on his journey, he promises to return on the day of the autumn Chrysanthemum Festival. However, circumstances conspire to prevent this promised reunion. At times Akinari hews very close to his source, "A Meal for Fan Juqing, Friend in Life and Death" ("Fan Juqing jishu sisheng jiao") from Feng Menglong's *Stories Old and New.* His opening lines, which establish the central theme of the tale by comparing superficial friendship to the willow that is verdant in spring but soon succumbs to the winds of autumn, are a nearly character-by-character rendering of the Chinese source text into Japanese. Other passages are not as clear-cut but nevertheless evoke a hybrid Sino-Japanese character that is reminiscent of *kundoku* style even if not directly traceable to such practices.

Elsewhere the source text is left far behind. As Dennis Washburn has observed, Akinari substantially lengthens the scene depicting Samon as he awaits Sōemon's promised return on the evening of the Chrysanthemum Festival, thereby enhancing the feeling of impatience.[65] Just as significant as the change in quantity is the change in quality. Snippets of conversation from passersby impart an eerie mundanity that increases the feeling of tension and uncertainty and heightens the contrast with the otherworldly encounter that follows. However, the most fundamental departure from Feng Menglong has to do with the reasons for Sōemon's inability to appear in the flesh. In the earlier telling, Sōemon's counterpart, Fan, simply forgets. Distracted by family obligations and trivial business concerns, he becomes precisely the sort of fickle friend warned of in the story's opening lines. Accordingly, his decision to take his own life seems impulsive and capricious, even implausible. In "The Chrysanthemum Vow," the historical setting resolves this narrative weakness. Samon and Sōemon are unshakably devoted, and there is never a moment's wavering or negligence. Instead, the forces that prevent their promised reunion lie beyond their control, as Sōemon is held captive in Toda Castle in Izumo Province, far from Samon's hometown in Harima Province, following the capture of the castle by the daimyō Amako Tsunehisa. In

65. See the discussion in Dennis Washburn, *Translating Mount Fuji* (New York: Columbia University Press, 2007), 60–61.

resituating the plot in a time of war, Akinari strengthens the bond between the two protagonists.

The meanings that result from this sort of recontextualization are not always constructed anew, as in this example, but are often negotiated instead through webs of associations with other texts, frequently within the *kidan* genre itself. Sometimes this intertextuality takes the form of secondary adaptation. The final sections of one tale in Shinrotei's *A Handful of Tales*, for example, closely retread parts of an earlier tale from Chin'en's *Chinese Brocade* (*Kara nishiki*, 1780). Yet as Makiyama Masayuki argues, Shinrotei was not simply trying to pass off Chin'en's narrative as his own. Rather, given that the similarities extend even to the naming of the respective protagonists (Hagimoto in Chin'en and Hagiwara in Shinrotei), Shinrotei appears to have been intentionally conjuring the associations of a story that, as part of a well-known collection, would have been closely familiar to his audience.[66]

The fifth tale of *Tales from the Withering Wind*, titled "How Three People Were Strangely Wounded in a Dream" ("Muchū no kai sannin kizu o etaru koto"), presents a more complex intertextual web, the untangling of which exposes deeper meanings and transforms the interpretation of what is on the surface a deceptively simple narrative. To trace the tale's "origins," if such a thing is possible, we must reach back at least to Xue Yusi's Tang *zhiguai* collection *Hedong ji* (Records from East of the River), which includes a tale titled "Dugu Xiashu." The narrative opens with the eponymous scholar homeward bound after more than two years in a far-off region. His final night on the road, less than a half-day's journey remaining, Dugu takes shelter at an abandoned temple. Tying up his donkey, he settles down to rest beneath the bright light of the moon. He finds himself unable to sleep. Before long a strange scene materializes in front of him. A large group of revelers enters the courtyard, and Dugu is startled to see his wife among them. As she begins to perform a song for her companions, his amazement gives way to jealous anger and he hurls a brick into their midst. The vision vanishes as strangely as it began. The next morning Dugu arrives home to learn that his wife had an identical dream.

66. Makiyama, "'Setsuwa-kei kidan' no isō josetsu," 24–25.

Xue's tale was subsequently included in the *Taiping guangji*, and adaptations were produced by both Feng Menglong and Pu Songling.[67] Pu's version, titled "The Gentleman from Fengyang" ("Fengyang shiren"), makes a number of significant changes, including shifting the vision from the husband to the wife, introducing the wife's brother as a character, and reducing the group of merrymakers into a single figure: an attractive girl who appears before the wife by moonlight and promises to reunite her with her husband.[68] As the pair sets out into the night, their progress is slow, and the girl gives the wife her shoes, which allow her to travel as if flying. They come to the husband, who is headed home atop a white donkey, and the girl leads the couple to a banquet in a nearby house. There the wife looks on helplessly as her husband and the girl grow intimate over cups of wine. In desperation, she flees and chances upon her brother. When she tells him what has happened, he storms off and hurls a rock into the house, killing the husband. The wife awakens in terror to find that it was all a dream. The next morning, the husband returns home atop a white donkey identical to that in the dream. A short time later the brother appears, and it is discovered that all three experienced the same dream. Separated in space, they have been joined in the dream-world through sheer force of longing, albeit under inauspicious circumstances that reflect their unspoken anxieties.

Chūryō transforms this *Liaozhai* source by overlaying numerous interconnected associations and allusions to Chinese and Japanese classics, as well as to earlier *kidan* narratives. The result is a confluence of intertextualities, shaped at once by Akinari, Ryōi, and the poetic tradition before them, but retaining many of the central aspects of the version of the narrative presented in "The Gentleman from Fengyang." Like many *kidan*, the story opens with a learned discussion of a topic of relevance to the narrative, in this case the nature of dreams. The Chinese tradition has much to say about the often blurry boundary between dream and

67. Feng Menglong's adaptation, titled "Dugu Has a Strange Dream as He Journeys Home" ("Dugu sheng guitu nao meng"), is included in *Constant Words to Awaken the World* (1627).

68. Allan Barr and Judith Zeitlin both offer their own discussions of Pu Songling's changes to the source story. See Barr, "Pu Songling and *Liaozhai Zhiyi*," 273; and Zeitlin, *Historian of the Strange*, 157–58.

reality. Among the most celebrated passages is Zhuangzi's parable of the butterfly, in which he awakens uncertain whether he has just dreamed he was a butterfly, or whether he is a butterfly dreaming he is Zhuangzi. Chūryō opens with a proverb derived from elsewhere in the *Zhuangzi*: "It is said that sages do not dream." However, this assertion is quickly contradicted as he draws together other musings on the subject of dreams from the Chinese tradition, building a case for their deep significance. Touching on the Duke of Zhou's office of dream divination, the Yellow Emperor's obtainment of the Way in a dream, Confucius's mention of no longer meeting the Duke of Zhou in dreams, and the *Liezi*'s interpretation of dreams, the passage builds to its conclusion: "It is readily apparent that sages *do* dream," Chūryō declares. "Our personal unhappiness, the things that lie hidden in our hearts—these appear in sleep as apparitions, amidst the wild fancy of dreams."[69]

The merging of dream and reality early established itself as a poetic conceit in the Japanese literary tradition as well. Here the counterpart to Zhuangzi in influence and sheer quantity of later allusions is arguably the sixty-ninth episode of *The Tales of Ise*, which recounts the protagonist Narihira's pursuit of the Ise Shrine Virgin. After a single nocturnal encounter in which the virgin and a young girl attendant visit his bedchamber by moonlight, Narihira's amorous thoughts keep him awake until she sends him a poem: "Did you come to me or was it I who went to you—I cannot even think / Was it a dream, or was it real; were we sleeping, or awake?"[70] When their desired reunion is frustrated the following night, she writes once more, this time sending an incomplete verse. Narihira finishes the missing lines with little subtlety, writing that he shall "once more cross the Ōsaka Barrier"—a reference to the barrier station between the capital and the eastern provinces that, owing to its name (Ōsaka means literally "the slope of meeting"), appeared frequently in poems of longing and desire.

69. *Kogarashi zōshi*, in *MCS*, 191.

70. *Kimi ya koshi / ware ya yukikemu / omōezu / yume ka utsutsu ka / nete ka samete ka*. *The Tales of Ise*, episode 69; also *Kokinshū* 13:645. The translation is adapted from Edwin A. Cranston, *Grasses of Remembrance*, in *A Waka Anthology*, vol. 2 (Stanford, CA: Stanford University Press, 2006), part A, 72.

Beyond its general depiction of separated lovers, there are a number of details in Chūryō's tale that conjure this episode in *The Tales of Ise.* Following the short discourse on dreams, the narrative proper begins with the husband, a horseman named Tsuzuki Oribe, setting off from his home near Kyoto to acquire some wild horses in the east. Leaving his wife, Shizu, at home, he has instructed her younger brother to look after her in his absence. Months pass without word, and Shizu is hardly able to endure the pain of separation. Then one autumn night, as she gazes out at the full moon rising in the east, a lovely young girl appears at her side in flowing white robes and promises a reunion with her husband. Like the Ise Virgin and her young attendant before them, Shizu and the girl step out into the bright, moonlit night. After they have gone some distance, Shizu's wooden sandals cause her foot to bleed, and she stops to bind the wound. The girl then takes her by the hand, and the two fly rapidly over the landscape until they come to the Slope of Meeting.

It is the night once a year when foals are led into the capital from the provinces. Beneath the full moon, the director of the imperial stables and his retinue process past with dozens of horses. Among the crowd following behind is Oribe, resplendently attired atop a chestnut steed and wearing a wide lacquered bamboo hat. Following a tearful reunion, the girl leads the couple to a nearby house where a banquet awaits. Elegant women provide musical entertainment, and with each cup of wine Oribe and the girl grow increasingly intimate. At length the two retire to an adjacent room, while Shizu looks on helplessly, only now realizing that the house is in fact a brothel. In great distress, she runs until she comes to a nearby river. As she is about to throw herself in, a man pulls her back. Thinking it is Oribe, Shizu struggles with him and sinks her teeth into his shoulder. It is her younger brother, Tōhachi. Having discovered her missing at home, he divined her location and raced in pursuit. She tells him everything that has happened, and they rush back to the brothel, where Tōhachi curses the girl and hurls a rock at her. He strikes Oribe instead, killing him. Shizu collapses to the floor.

A moment later she awakens in bed. The dream is over, yet the pain lingers in her foot. She discovers that it has been tightly bound with her sash, and the flesh underneath is bloody and torn. In the morning, a servant rushes in to announce Oribe's return. Shizu hurries outside and finds him seated astride a chestnut horse, wearing a wide lacquered bamboo hat. As he removes the hat, her eye is drawn to a large wound on his forehead. Marveling at this strange coincidence, she relates her dream, and he reveals that he had the very same dream the night before at an inn by the Ōsaka Barrier. Moments later Tōhachi appears, having heard of Oribe's return. He, too, shared the same dream, and he slips his robe down past his shoulder to reveal the spot where Shizu's teeth tore the flesh.

Chūryō's story heightens the elegant confusion between dream and reality in ways that reach beyond the conventional associations from classical verse and *The Tales of Ise*. The addition of the telltale wounds shared by the three principal characters establishes a physical connection among them, material evidence of their shared dream that further blurs the line between dream and reality. Although not part of "The Gentleman from Fengyang," similar reminders of past experience are found elsewhere in *Liaozhai*. In the tale "Le Zhong," the eponymous hero cuts flesh from his own thigh to feed his dying mother, and the scars later reappear, transformed, when his courtesan traveling companion rubs the same spot.[71] Scars also serve as evidence of events that are forgotten or whose truth is doubted, as in "Zhicheng" (the source for the final story in *Tales from the Withering Wind*), in which bite marks affirm the reality of an otherworldly encounter whose truth is doubted. Although the central events in Chūryō's adaptation of "The Gentleman from Fengyang" unfold within a dream, the scars assert the deeper reality of shared emotional distress that underlies the ordeal.

The seamlessness with which the narrative enters the dream sequence further blurs the boundary between waking and dreaming. It is significant that this shift occurs as Shizu gazes out at the moon, a site of longing and desire in Japanese verse. As an object that does not change from place to place, the moon has the power to link lovers separated by distance. Surely Oribe, too, must be looking up at its light:

> Soon the summer he had promised to return came and went, and it was halfway through autumn. Yet still there was no trace of a letter, no hint of

71. In his translation of the tale, John Minford reads the protagonist's name as "Yue Zhong." Minford, trans., *Strange Tales from a Chinese Studio* (New York: Penguin Books, 2006), 436–45.

news. And so his wife, Shizu, lay alone in their bedchamber, filled with longing.

One autumn night, her sleeves drenched with dew, she gazed eastward at the clear, full moon, thinking *he* must be out there, beneath the distant sky. Would that news might arrive, borne on the wings of the first geese of autumn![72]

The unusual brightness of the full moon, which further amplifies Shizu's longing, is an important element in "The Gentleman from Fengyang." But Chūryō imparts further significance to the scene through resonances with Akinari. Indeed, his immersion in the world of his *kidan* forebears is nowhere more apparent than in this tale, with its deep allusivity, mystery, and poetic qualities. These are all evident in his description of Shizu, which, as Sonoda Yutaka observes, shows a marked affinity to that of Miyagi, the faithful wife in "The Reed-Choked House" ("Asaji ga yado") in *Tales of Moonlight and Rain*, whose mounting anxiety for her husband, Katsushirō, is narrated as follows:

> Katsushirō's wife, too, thought to seek refuge somewhere, but she took heart in her husband's instructions to wait until the fall. She remained at home, anxiously counting each day. When the autumn winds blew in and brought no tidings with them, she composed the following, despondent to find him as inconstant as the world itself: *I cannot convey my bitter sorrow— tell him, cock of the Ōsaka Barrier, that autumn will soon pass.* But many provinces separated her from her husband, and there was no way to send word.[73]

"The Reed-Choked House" is a relatively rare example of a *kidan* tale in which warfare is not introduced in the process of adaptation but is an important feature of the source text itself, in this case "The Tale of Aiqing" from Qu You's *New Tales by Lamplight*. The contours of the original will be largely familiar even to modern readers who have only encountered Akinari's version. The narrative begins with the faithful

72. *Kogarashi zōshi*, in *MCS*, 191.

73. *Ugetsu monogatari*, in Nakamura Yukihiko, ed., *NKBT* 56 (Iwanami shoten, 1959), 60–61. See Sonoda, "*Kogarashi zōshi* to *Ugetsu monogatari*," 6.

and beautiful wife Aiqing remaining at home in Jiaxing, in Zhejiang Province, while her husband heads north to the capital to attend to family business. As his return is delayed month after month, the chaos of the Red Turban Rebellion (1351–68) spreads across the region, and Aiqing hangs herself rather than succumb to the advances of a lustful enemy commander. When at last the husband returns, he finds his hometown ravaged almost beyond recognition. His own house is overgrown with weeds. With the help of an elderly former manservant, he gives his wife a proper burial, and her ghost visits him for one final happy reunion. Freed from her lingering, unfulfilled desire, Aiqing is reborn as a baby boy in the nearby city of Wuxi, a living memento of the love she and her husband shared.

Akinari's retelling involves substantial changes to the plot. Notably, at the time of their joyous reunion, Katsushirō has not yet realized that Miyagi is dead. It is, moreover, a poem, not a child, that she leaves him as keepsake. Where the broader historical context is concerned, however, a simple transposition is all that is necessary. In place of Zhang Shicheng's capture of Suzhou, Akinari sets his tale against the early skirmishes of the Kyōtoku disturbances (1455–83). As conflict envelops Japan's eastern provinces, Miyagi anxiously awaits her husband's return from the distant capital. She considers fleeing, but taking heart in his promise that he will return by summer's end, she remains at home, counting the days as they pass. In addition to dwelling on the passages devoted to her waiting, thereby heightening the sense of anxiety, Akinari extends the duration of the husband's absence from six months to seven years.

Both Chūryō and Akinari's adaptations tell of husbands who leave home on business that takes them past the Ōsaka Barrier, and the wives who experience intense longing during what proves an unexpectedly long separation. When at last the couples are briefly reunited, the experience turns out to have been an illusion (although in *Tales from the Withering Wind* a genuine reunion follows shortly thereafter). Both tales also conclude with an encounter with a wise seer figure of the sort frequently encountered in the *kidan*. This figure, endowed with privileged vision that allows him to discern what the protagonists themselves cannot, puts events in context through reference to ancient legend. In *Tales of Moonlight and Rain*, it is an elderly villager who recounts the story of the maiden Tegona of Mama, whose tragic fate is told in verse in the *Man'yōshū*. In

Tales from the Withering Wind, the role is assumed by a diviner the family summons to make sense of their ordeal. Relating the story of a prostitute named Kane who long ago plied her trade near the Ōsaka Barrier, he reveals that Oribe must have unwittingly trampled the woman's neglected grave as he passed on horseback, prompting her spirit to lead them astray. The legend of a prostitute from Ōmi named Kane, renowned for the physical strength she displayed when she restrained a wild horse by stepping on its reins with her wooden clogs, appears in the thirteenth-century *setsuwa* anthology *A Collection of Anecdotes Old and New* (*Kokon chomonjū*). Beyond merely dropping her name into his narrative, Chūryō's choice of setting, as well as prominent physical details including Oribe's horse and Shizu's wooden clogs, offer further resonances with this legend from a collection that numbered among Chūryō's favorite sources.[74]

The evocation of still other texts imparts further allusive significance to Chūryō's tale. The reference to "the distant sky" (*sonata no sora*) in the passages depicting Shizu's suffering in her husband's absence conjures scenes of longing in earlier texts, among them the noh play *Lady Han* (*Hanjo*), whose forlorn protagonist passes her nights "gazing out at the distant sky where *he* must be," holding out for word from a courtly lover who vowed "to return before autumn without fail."[75] There are also echoes of Ryōi. In a tale in *Talisman Dolls* that, like "The Reed-Choked House," takes "The Tale of Aiqing" as one of its principal sources, Ryōi tells the story of a young woman who dies far from home whose ghost writes a letter to her parents in distant Ōmi Province, beyond the Ōsaka Barrier. The letter begins with an account of days spent gazing off at "the distant sky," her sleeves drenched with an unceasing stream of tears, and—in an evocation of the legend of Su Wu, the commander who sent word to the Han emperor Zhaodi after his defeat in battle by affixing a letter to the wing of a wild goose—hoping in vain that the autumn geese might bring tidings.[76]

74. The same visual elements feature prominently in a later kabuki dance piece based on the legend, titled *The Woman Washing Cloth* (*Sarashime*, 1813).

75. *Hanjo*, in Nishino Haruo, ed., *Yōkyoku hyakuban*, in *SNKBT* 57 (Iwanami shoten, 1998), 216.

76. "Yūrei sho o bumo ni tsukawasu" (A Girl's Ghost Sends a Letter to Her Parents), in Matsuda Osamu, Watanabe Morikuni, and Hanada Fujio, eds., *Otogi bōko*, in *SNKBT* 75 (Iwanami shoten, 2001), 354.

The significance of these intertextual threads is multifold. Certainly convention is at play in a literary tradition that emphasized allusion and rewriting—practices through which the author situated himself in a lineage both preceding and continuing beyond him—over unconstrained originality. Allusion additionally facilitates subtlety and concision, allowing meanings and associations to go unspoken as they are instead borrowed from the world of texts beyond the individual text at hand. The reader's encounter with particular details, whether Shizu's wooden clogs or the girl's white robes flowing in the moonlight, is inevitably informed by these resonances. But intertextuality casts an even wider shadow, imbuing the text with the affective weight of earlier depictions and transforming the reader's perception of the very context within which the tale unfolds.

Like Pu Songling's "The Gentleman from Fengyang," Chūryō's rewriting features little that might tie the narrative to a specific historical setting beyond, in deference to generic convention, the mention at the outset of a specific reign period: the Kyōroku era (1528–32). There is no explicit reference to events of the period, which included fierce battles both near the capital, where Shizu remains, and in the eastern regions to which Oribe travels. Nevertheless, the intertextual strands come together to underscore not merely the sense of distance, anxiety, and separation experienced by the two, but also this historical context. As in "The Tale of Aiqing," it is conflict that keeps Katsushirō and Miyagi apart in "The Reed-Choked House." Similarly, Ryōi's adaptation unfolds amid the turmoil of the late sixteenth century, with the protagonist's death coming after she is taken prisoner by Oda Nobunaga's men and separated from her family. Even the trope of the wild goose has its origin in a time of war—an association reinforced in Japan through its retelling at the end of the second chapter of *The Tale of the Heike* (*Heike monogatari*).

Allusion is employed to similar effect elsewhere in *Tales from the Withering Wind*, even where the mood is otherwise less anxious. In the collection's sole comic tale, a generally lighthearted account of an improbable friendship between an old man and a tanuki (raccoon dog) that sprouts from their shared fondness for drink, Chūryō deviates from convention and follows the indeterminate world of his source, Pu Songling's "The Drinking Companion" ("Jiuyou"), by not specifying a historical period at the outset. However, the time period becomes clear in the final lines when, in a departure from the *Liaozhai* version of the tale, warfare abruptly intrudes on the action. As the forces of Satomi Yoshihiro and Hōjō Ujiyasu clash at Kōnodai—a real-life battle that occurred in 1564—the tanuki and his friends repay the old man's generosity by rescuing him and his family from the pillaging troops.

Although the intrusion of this historical setting seems to appear out of nowhere, it is subtly anticipated in the story's opening lines. Following a brief discourse on wine replete with allusions to the Chinese classics, Chūryō begins the narrative proper by drawing, as in his dream tale, on Akinari's "The Reed-Choked House." In this instance, he presents a loose rewriting of the opening lines of the earlier tale, specifying the same geographic setting—the village of Mama in Katsushika—and introducing the character of the old man with a series of phrases that echo Akinari's description of Katsushirō. As Sonada Yutaka has argued, these resonances serve as a subtle foreshadowing of the battle that intrudes at the end of the story.[77] Throughout *Tales from the Withering Wind*, a stream of allusions to antecedent texts set against the backdrop of conflict serves a similar function, signaling a layer of uncertainty and danger that lurks beneath the surface, and heightening the mood of tension and unease that pervades these strange tales.

77. Likewise, the old man's excited preparations for the tanuki's arrival recall Samon's hasty arrangements when Sōemon appears at the climactic moment in "The Chrysanthemum Vow." The resonances are observed in Sonoda, "*Kogarashi zōshi* to *Ugetsu monogatari*," 6–7.

CHAPTER 5

Taming the Strange

Anomalies and the Tokugawa Order

Among the qualities shared by both Chinese and Japanese collections of strange tales is the wide geographic diversity of their settings. Just as the tales of Qu You, Pu Songling, and the *Taiping guangji* transport readers to locations scattered across the continent, *kidan* settings span nearly the full length of the Japanese archipelago. Akinari's *Tales of Moonlight and Rain* begins with the poet-monk Saigyō's journey from the capital to the remote mountains of Shikoku, proceeds through the shores of Lake Biwa and the rural fringes of Edo, and concludes in a samurai household in the far north. Chūryō's *Tales from the Withering Wind* covers terrain that stretches from the remote northern landscape traversed by Bashō in *The Narrow Road to the Interior* (*Oku no hosomichi*) to the northern coast of Kyushu. The collections of Teishō, Chin'en, Shinrotei, and others are similarly varied in their settings.

Amid this geographic diversity there is, however, one space that is only rarely encountered: the city. Although it is not uncommon to find characters from the capital, or who travel to cities to sell their wares, it is nearly always *outside* the city that they confront the strange. In Akinari we observe this in Saigyō's encounter with the ghost of Emperor Sutoku far from the capital, where his journey begins, as well as with Katsushirō's reunion with his departed wife, which occurs in his rural home village after he returns from a seven-year stay in the capital. The physical remove from Edo, Kyoto, and other urban centers places the strange at a remove from the lived, everyday experience of many contemporary readers who, like most *kidan* authors and the publishing industry that sustained them, were based in the major cities.

The geographical distancing in Chinese strange tales reflects an ideological binary that divides space into an ordered, sacred center and a periphery that is the site of disorder and the anomalous. At the same time, as an act of collecting and bringing in the strange, the compilation of anomaly accounts can be seen as an effort to assimilate and impose a measure of order on the margins.[1] These dynamics and their directionality are partially reconfigured in the Japanese context. Writers of *kidan* were also collectors, but rather than bringing in and taming the margins of their own domestic space, they gathered much of their material from Chinese sources and, through the process of rewriting, cast the strange outward into the Japanese periphery. Still, the effect remains to affirm the binary between center and periphery, positioning urban centers as spaces of order and control at a safe remove from the disorder at the margins.

In fact, the *kidan* goes further in holding the strange at bay. As observed in the previous chapter, many of the Chinese strange tales that serve as the source texts for Japanese rewritings feature little by way of historical contextualization, with a reliance on "factual framing" such as the use of named informants positioning events in a vaguely conceived present.[2] The *kidan* renounces such temporal ambiguity. Narratives are pinpointed in time, with reign periods regularly specified within the first few lines. These reign periods fall almost without exception before the close of the sixteenth century. Teishō and Akinari each wrote just one story set unambiguously in the Tokugawa era, both taking place in the early seventeenth century. Only two of Chūryō's tales are not given precise historical settings, but even these include passages that set the action long before the author's own time. It is as if the strange ceases to exist with the onset of Tokugawa rule.

1. It has been noted that many of the strange events narrated in the *Taiping guangji* occur as characters are in transit, often "between the center (i.e., the capital and China) and the peripheries (i.e., provinces and foreign lands)." "Introduction," in Alexei Kamran Ditter, Jessey Choo, Sarah M. Allen, eds., *Tales from Tang Dynasty China: Selections from the Taiping Guangji* (Cambridge, MA: Hackett Publishing, 2017), 26. On the "collection" of the strange, see Campany, *Strange Writing*, 8–14.

2. On Pu Songling's use of informants and similar "factual" devices, see Hammond, "Factual Framing in *Liao zhai zhi yi*."

There is an element of literary convention in such historical distancing. In response to Tokugawa edicts forbidding the depiction of contemporary events, scandalous or otherwise, authors and playwrights came to rely on the literary device of *mitate*, a form of parodic double-vision in which historical settings stood in for the contemporary world. As a strategy for circumventing regulations, *mitate* lent itself to subversive application, and some authors actively tested the limits of official forbearance. In the early eighteenth century, Chikamatsu's satirical puppet play *The Sagami Lay Monk and the Thousand Dogs* (*Sagami nyūdō senbiki no inu*, premiered 1714) pushed the bounds of acceptability by positioning the fourteenth-century regent Hōjō Takatoki, a frequent literary exemplar of the unvirtuous tyrant, as an unambiguous stand-in for Tokugawa Tsunayoshi, whose efforts at promoting animal welfare earned him the moniker "the dog shogun." In pictorial fiction, historical figures were associated with contemporary government officials through the use of the likenesses of popular kabuki actors who were read as their proxies.[3] But subversion and satire carried the risk of serious punishment. In the late 1780s, after a number of authors published *kibyōshi* satires set in the past to obscure their intended targets, the bakufu responded with a vigorous clampdown on popular fiction as part of the wider conservative agenda known as the Kansei Reforms.[4]

A focus on resistance and subversion has come to be seen as outmoded in certain quarters, and not without some justification. Chikamatsu's satire of Tsunayoshi, for example, was the subject of a meticulous close reading by Donald Shively already nearly seven decades ago.[5] In his relatively recent study of Edo popular culture and its relationship with

3. For the most extensive treatment of the use of actors' likenesses, see Takahashi Noriko, *Kusazōshi to engeki: yakusha nigaoe sōshiki o chūshin ni* (Kyūko shoin, 2004).

4. A discussion of several of these "protest pieces" appears in Adam L. Kern, *Manga from the Floating World: Comicbook Culture and the Kibyōshi of Edo Japan* (Cambridge, MA: Harvard University Asia Center, 2006), 202–12. Anne Walthall's discussion of riots in the city of Edo briefly touches on another piece that was quickly banned for satirizing the political failures surrounding the Great Tenmei Famine of the 1780s. Walthall, "Edo Riots," in James L. McClain, John W. Merriman, and Ugawa Kaoru, eds., *Edo and Paris: Urban Life and the State in the Early Modern Era* (Ithaca, NY: Cornell University Press, 1994), 417–18.

5. See Donald H. Shively, "Chikamatsu's Satire on the Dog Shogun," *Harvard Journal of Asiatic Studies* 18, no. 1/2 (June 1955): 159–80.

power, Katsuya Hirano dismisses the concept of cultural resistance as "facile" and undertakes to complicate a "reductive" model of state oppression and popular subversion.[6] His effort at reframing the terms of analysis draws on Bakhtin's conception of the dialogic—the polyphonic interaction of diverse voices and perspectives—coupled with a positioning of the body as a central site of contestation between official and popular discourses. The approach is further guided through sustained reference to the Althusserian concept of overdetermination. Insofar as overdetermination views politics as a mediation among practices, it offers a theoretical alternative to "idealist" conceptions of individual action, or individual acts of resistance—providing, in Hirano's view, the potential to ascribe equal weight and agency to cultural production as not just an effect of ideological contradiction but something that precipitates it.[7] The danger, however, is that the conclusion is predetermined by the methodology. It is also a model that is difficult to sustain empirically. Hirano hedges against this limitation at the outset by largely rejecting the value of empiricism, proclaiming instead a preference for developing the theoretical framework. Nevertheless, the inevitable result, with evidence in the form of textual reading relegated to secondary status, is that the texts are not allowed to speak for themselves.

This disconnect is evidenced by the largely orthodox readings of mostly canonical texts in Edo literary studies—an assortment of usual suspects that meanders from Chikamatsu's love suicides through Gennai's greatest hits and Kyōden's *Playboy Roasted à la Edo* (*Edo-umare uwaki no kabayaki*, 1785) en route to Shikitei Sanba's *Bathhouse of the Floating World* (*Ukiyoburo*, 1809–13). Along the way we build a typology of familiar forms of literary *resistance*, including parody, social satire (*ugachi*), and the inversion of hierarchies and centering of the margins, as well as variations on familiar arguments about the (re)appropriation of "high" forms by the "low."[8] The aim is to combine these pieces into a larger structure,

6. Katsuya Hirano, *The Politics of Dialogic Imagination: Power and Popular Culture in Early Modern Japan* (Chicago: University of Chicago Press, 2014), 3.

7. Hirano, *Politics of Dialogic Imagination*, 24–25.

8. With one or two minor exceptions, the discussion of these topics does not engage with the nuanced treatments by prominent scholars of Edo literature such as Nakano Mitsutoshi, Hino Tatsuo, and others; the earlier, foundational work of Nakamura Yukihiko is touched upon only in passing. By way of example, the discussion of the

to show such cultural resistance as pervasive, ongoing, and *productive*—as opposed to scattershot or self-indulgent escapism. But the very notion of "idle" resistance is a straw man. Setting aside the innovative theoretical scaffolding, the characterization of popular culture as a sphere of ongoing political negotiation and productive contestation is strikingly reminiscent of another Shively article of midcentury provenance, "Bakufu versus Kabuki," which details the ongoing negotiations between authority and popular culture that yielded what was arguably the dominant form of popular cultural expression in early modern Japan.[9] Shively's work, along with that of many others, is difficult to square with Hirano's claim that previous studies "have failed to provide a cogent explanation of how and why the putatively apolitical realms of play and pleasure . . . were a constant source of concern for officials and intellectuals."[10]

The question of resistance is revisited from a novel perspective in the epilogue. This chapter, for its part, charts another alternative course, taking as its starting point the observation that any view of popular culture as existing in a contradictory, constitutive relationship with authority—much like the view of writers engaged in escapism or idle resistance such a model seeks to transcend—similarly risks obscuring another essential quality of that culture, namely the ways in which it could serve equally as a tool of the status quo. Eschewing a focus on subversion altogether, this chapter examines instead the ways writers performed obeisance to authority, a stance that at times verged on complicity.

The use of historical disguises offers a point of entry. Such disguises were certainly deployed at times for satirical effect, but more often they

---

reordering of status distinctions in popular culture dusts off one of Gennai's most frequently cited passages, from *Rootless Grass* (*Nenashigusa*, 1763), in which he depicts the vibrant, heterogenous crowd at Ryōgoku Bridge in Edo. No mention is made of the many readings of this same passage dating back at least to the work of Haga Tōru, who singled it out for its colorful depiction of a "kaleidoscope of the masses" and held it up as representing the very essence of Gennai's style. See Haga Tōru, *Hiraga Gennai* (Asahi shinbunsha, 1981), 237. Instead, the primary reference point for a supposed canonical view of Edo popular culture is intellectual historian Masao Maruyama's *Studies in the Intellectual History of Tokugawa Japan* (Princeton, NJ: Princeton University Press, 1974).

9. Donald Shively, "Bakufu versus Kabuki," *Harvard Journal of Asiatic Studies* 18, no. 3/4 (December 1955): 326–56.

10. Hirano, *Politics of Dialogic Imagination*, 3.

represented an act of submission, as authors obligatorily performed their compliance with the limitations placed on their creative output. One of the best-known examples is the play *Chūshingura*, whose playwrights resituated the sensational Akō vendetta of the early eighteenth century in the distant fourteenth-century world of the *Taiheiki*. Although the thinly disguised subtext remained immediately obvious to theatergoers, the letter of the law was observed. In exchange for such displays of deference, the bakufu was generally willing to look the other way. After all, popular entertainment helped keep the public content. Besides, in the case of *Chūshingura*, the events dramatized in the play were already nearly a half-century in the past by the time of its 1748 premiere, and the central themes of honor and duty were unlikely to invite censure. The response to the satirical *kibyōshi* clearly demonstrated that the authorities were not afraid to clamp down more forcefully when writers overstepped their bounds. And yet even in these pieces, the use of historical settings can be seen to reflect a degree of submission: however subversive the subtext of their satires, they dared not *directly* challenge the regime.

In any event, the question remains: why should historical settings have become the norm in the *kidan*? Such recontextualization may have been customary for material inspired by real-life events or possessed of political significance, but the Chinese strange tales the *kidan* drew on were hardly timely or sensitive, and indeed had little apparent connection at all to contemporary Japan. One clue comes from the separate body of regional strange tales and anomaly accounts that were also widely read in early modern Japan. These tales, which like *zhiguai* presented themselves as ostensibly true accounts, circulated not as printed volumes but in manuscript form.[11] In this regard, they occupied a similar space to *jitsuroku* accounts of real-life rebellion and unrest, which were discreetly copied and circulated underground throughout the period. *Kidan* may have drawn on sources that originated outside the sphere of Tokugawa control, but given the verisimilitude and historical indeterminacy of those texts—the qualities that complicate their status as fiction—to map such narratives directly onto the Japanese context would have been a risky endeavor, one that suggested the possibility of disorder in the Tokugawa

11. A selection of such tales is included in Tsutsumi and Sugimoto, *Kinsei minkan ibun kaidan shūsei*.

realm, even if only at the margins. The subversive power of the strange necessitated both distance and manifest fictionalization, the delineation of a clear boundary between fact and fiction.

In an analysis guided by Robert Campany's reading of Chinese anomaly accounts, Anthony Chambers has noted the caution evident in Akinari's use of distant settings in *Tales of Moonlight and Rain*.[12] The observation obtains equally to the *kidan* as a whole. By positioning the strange at a remove in space and time, authors inoculated themselves against the perception of any link between their subject matter and the present regime. More than that, their depiction of disorder as a phenomenon of the margins, indeed one that had been banished altogether from the present world, can be read as an implicit celebration of the Tokugawa order. Locating the strange in this way can be seen to collapse ambiguity and uncertainty, representing a conflicting impulse from the many ways in which the genre seeks to draw out these qualities. This tension is evident in the use of warfare, explored in the previous chapter for its affective functions—its potential to enhance feelings of strangeness and unease—as well as its value in strengthening narrative logic. At the same time, the prevalence of warfare can be seen as a form of cautious reassurance. To some extent, conflict goes hand in hand with historical distancing, given the violence and bloodshed that runs through Japanese history prior to the early modern era. Yet the sheer pervasiveness of warfare in the *kidan* points to political value in depicting the past as an endless succession of political and social instability, and of implicating such unrest as among the conditions that give rise to the strange. Readers are constantly reminded of the strange wonder of the Tokugawa peace itself.

Attunement to political concerns is further evidenced by the delicate approach taken on those rare occasions authors venture into more proximate historical settings. Chambers has noted the way in which "The Owl of the Three Jewels" ("Buppōsō"), the only story in *Tales of Moonlight and Rain* set in the Tokugawa period, compensates for such uncomfortable closeness with an opening passage that effusively praises the regime. Such rhetoric is often positioned where it is unlikely to be overlooked. Akinari lays down casual references to the Tokugawa peace in the preface, then

12. See Campany, *Strange Writing*, 9; and "Introduction," in Chambers, *Tales of Moonlight and Rain*, 20–21.

once more at the end of the final tale, thereby bookending his collection with gestures of deference to authority. Once again, we can observe a similar tendency across the *kidan* genre. The opening tale of *A Thicket of Tales* is set at a relatively safe historical distance, nearly a century before the dawn of Tokugawa rule. Still, as the most recent tale in the collection, Teishō is careful to conclude with a passage overtly celebrating the Tokugawa peace, lest his intentions be misconstrued. Other writers signaled their loyalties even amid more distant historical settings. Chūryō opens *Tales from the Withering Wind* with a narrative whose final scene depicts a ceremony honoring the establishment of the Kamakura shogunate under Minamoto no Yoritomo, complete with songs celebrating the pacification and unification of Japan under shogunal rule. At least in this instance, temporal distancing serves not to circumvent authority but to extol it.

There is also a moral component to the *kidan*'s conservatism. As in the Chinese strange tale, vulnerability to the strange is regularly associated with unmoderated obsessions and uncontrolled desires. One common archetype is the protagonist from hardworking, respectable stock who neglects familial duties to pursue his individual wants. Readers encounter three such figures in Akinari alone: Katsushirō, the merchant in "The Reed-Choked House" who leaves his family behind to seek fortune in the capital; Shōtarō in "The Kibitsu Cauldron" ("Kibitsu no kama"), who forgoes farming in favor of women and wine; and Toyoo, the protagonist of "The Serpent's Lust" ("Jasei no in"), who dreams of sophistication beyond his station as the son of a provincial merchant. For Samon and Sōemon in "The Chrysanthemum Vow," it is the relentless ambition of others that wreaks havoc on their friendship. At times writers demonstrated didactic restraint, finding it sufficient merely to illustrate the strange effects of obsession, impropriety, and bloodshed. Elsewhere the lessons implicit in such narratives are spelled out in no uncertain terms, as when Toyoo at last grasps that he has been seduced by a serpent and pauses to consider the moral shortcomings that led to his predicament. "It is because of the lack of virtue in my heart," he reflects, "that I have been bewitched by the creature these months and years."[13]

13. *Ugetsu monogatari*, in *NKBT* 56:115.

This chapter illuminates the many ways in which the *kidan* tames the strange, branding its sources with a more overt moralism and rewriting them to the concerns of its own day and age. The primary focus remains on *Tales from the Withering Wind* and its *Liaozhai* adaptations. Chūryō's decision to move on from the subversive genres in which he had made his literary reputation represented a decision rooted in judicious caution. Amid the chill winds of the Kansei Reforms, the *kidan* presented itself as a safe space for literary expression. In *Tales from the Withering Wind*, we see him building on the genre's inherent conservatism and formalizing its didactic techniques. Many of the tales are bookended by moralistic passages that signal the intended lesson at the outset, then debrief readers on the far side. At the same time that he transplants the lessons of the source tales largely intact, Chūryō magnifies and transforms them, layering on new meanings and redirecting them toward different targets. And there are moments when the collection goes further still, evincing a conservatism that crosses into the territory of complicity, promoting ideas and perspectives specifically advocated by the Tokugawa authorities as part of the reform agenda of the day.

Dangerous Obsessions

Several of Chūryō's stories hinge on unexpected encounters with apparitions that appear as the manifestation of unrestrained obsessions, anxieties, and desires. While the consequences are sometimes benign—as in the tale of the old man whose abnormal fondness for wine leads to an encounter with a tanuki who is able to match him cup for cup—more often they are far more serious. Chūryō's longest narrative concerns a samurai whose all-consuming passion for poetry leaves him vulnerable to a bloodthirsty demon that appears in the guise of a beautiful girl whose name, Uta, means literally "poem" or "song." In her illuminating study of Pu Songling's tales, Judith Zeitlin devotes a chapter to the theme of obsession, which she positions as the site of boundary-crossing between subjects and objects, that which bridges the gap between the world of ordinary experience and the realm of spirits, ghosts, and the supernatural.[14] Chūryō brings the didacticism implicit in this association to the surface, more clearly marking the failure to moderate one's emotions and appetites as a form of moral deficiency that invites harm from without. A further layer of didacticism comes in the form of his frequent disquisitions on the particular obsession central to a given tale. Much as Pu drew on specialized manuals to bring himself up to speed and add detail to his depictions of cricket-fighting, pigeons, rocks, and flowers, Chūryō scours a range of classics and histories, as well as more specialized texts, in search of relevant, often cautionary, examples for his brief lectures on wine, dreams, cockfighting, and other topics.[15]

In the story of Shizu and the dream she shares with her husband and brother, the thin line between the desirer and the object of their desire is further obscured by the confusion of waking and dreaming. After Oribe's departure for the eastern provinces, Shizu is gripped by deepening longing that culminates, in a moment of particularly intense desire, in the appearance of a mysterious girl who guides her into her strange dream. In his mid-nineteenth-century commentary on "The Gentleman from Fengyang," the *Liaozhai* source from which the tale is adapted, Dan Minglun (1782–1853) offers a straightforward interpretation of the dream, seeing it as a manifestation of the wife's mental state, a vision in which we can discern both her longing and her anxiety.[16] Indeed, while her desire is fulfilled by the reunion with her husband, we see her subconscious fears play out in the encounter that follows, in which he flirts with the beautiful girl while she looks on helplessly. Chūryō intensifies this shift from desire to anxiety by relocating the pivotal scene to a brothel—a site for male infidelity, but also a physical space that mirrors Shizu's internal psychological state. Having begun her dream gazing out at the moon and a seemingly endless horizon, she nears its conclusion trapped in a confined, claustrophobic room. While the wife's own disordered mental state plays a role in leading her into the clutches of a malicious spirit, at the very end of the tale Chūryō shifts the blame, with a diviner revealing the dream to have been caused by Oribe's inadvertent trampling of

14. Zeitlin, *Historian of the Strange*, 61–97.

15. On Pu's use of manuals and guidebooks, see Barr, "Pu Songling and *Liaozhai Zhiyi*," 278–79; and Zeitlin, *Historian of the Strange*, 71–72.

16. *LZ*, 190.

an unmarked grave on his homeward journey. The lesson carried over and magnified from the source text comes into conflict with Chūryō's desire to tame the strange, to explain it away. The effect is to dissipate the carefully constructed mood of uncertainty, offering a moment of clarity that externalizes the source of the dream.

The consequences of obsession and emotional disorder for Shizu and her family are, in the end, relatively benign, the only lasting damage the telltale scars that serve as evidence of their shared experience. Elsewhere the results are far more gruesome. In the tale immediately preceding this one, strange events are again set in motion through a chance encounter. It is the mid-sixteenth century, and Japan is wracked by the turmoil of the Warring States period. We find ourselves at the mansion of the warlord Imagawa Yoshimoto. One day, after catching a glimpse of a beautiful maid in his wife's service, Yoshimoto instructs his wife to set the girl up as his mistress. This she does, dutifully supplying the girl, whose name is Narumi, with elegant robes and helping polish her manners. As Narumi is transformed from an attractive maid into a sophisticated beauty, Yoshimoto's wife grows jealous and hatches a devious scheme that eventually results in nothing less than the demise of the Imagawa clan.

The ruler whose obsession with a woman gives rise to disaster is a familiar theme from Chinese antiquity—one thinks of "castle topplers" from Bao Si to Yang Guifei. To this Chūryō adds the figure of the jealous wife. Two specific Chinese sources can be seen to lie behind his narrative. The first is an episode from *Strategies of the Warring States* (*Zhanguo ce*) in which the King of Wei sends an alluring beauty to the King of Chu. The King of Chu's wife, Zheng Xiu, attends to the girl's needs and provides her with lavish garments and accessories. However, she is secretly jealous and executes a scheme to eliminate her rival. Informing the girl that the king, while otherwise captivated by her beauty, finds her nose unsightly, she instructs her to cover her nose in his presence. When the girl does as instructed, the king asks Zheng Xiu about this puzzling behavior and is told that the girl finds his odor unpleasant. The enraged king orders the girl's nose cut off as punishment. Chūryō closely retraces this earlier episode, but with an even more gruesome resolution. After Yoshimoto himself viciously slices off Narumi's nose and limbs, he orders his men to dump her body in the servants' latrine. This additional detail shows the influence of Sima Qian's account of Empress Lü—who, in one of the most heinous acts recounted in the *Shiji*, cuts off Lady Qi's hands and feet, plucks out her eyes, cauterizes her ears, forces her to drink a potion that renders her mute, and, calling her the "human pig," has what is left cast into the latrine.[17]

Zheng Xiu and Empress Lü were often paired as archetypes of the "poisonous woman," as when the compilers of the *Book of Tang* (*Jiu Tang shu*) sought worthy comparisons for the alleged cruelty of Empress Wu: "Long ago, the ancients observed the poisonous slander of the nose-covering incident, and the realm recognized the unjustness of the cruel incident of the human pig. In plotting to assume the position of principal wife, Empress Wu strangled her own infant child; that she would crush her own flesh and blood demonstrated the utmost perversion."[18] Although Chūryō's rewriting of the two episodes distributes vice between husband and wife, he is more concerned with the wife. She is, to be sure, the more complicated character. While Yoshimoto is merely an impetuous pawn, slave to his fickle emotions, his wife is the conniver pulling the strings behind the scenes. She is also the one who pays more dearly for her misdeeds. Unable to cope with the consequences of her actions, she is haunted by visions of Narumi. The night after the murder, as the wife sits playing games with her attendants, the girl materializes in front of her. She unsheathes her dagger and slashes at the phantom, while her attendants, who have seen nothing, cry out in alarm. Unnerved, she hastily retires for the night. Moments later, Narumi appears before her once more, her torso and lower body seated side by side, severed along the dagger's path. The wife gasps and faints. In the coming days, she suffers terrible pain in her nose and extremities—the sites of Narumi's injuries—and steadily descends into madness. She dies ten days later.

The gruesomeness of this sequence anticipates similar moments on the nineteenth-century kabuki stage, where the figure of the vengeful female ghost was to make regular appearances. One discerns parallels with both Narumi and Yoshimoto in the figure of Oiwa in Tsuruya Nanboku's blockbuster *Ghost Stories at Yotsuya on the Tōkaidō Highway*, premiered

17. The parallels with the episodes in *Strategies of the Warring States* and the *Shiji* are noted in Tokuda, "*Kogarashi zōshi* to *Ryōsai shii*," in *Nihon kinsei shōsetsu to Chūgoku shōsetsu*, 364.

18. *Jiu Tang shu* (Beijing: Zhonghua shuju, 1975), 6:133.

in 1825. Poisoned by her husband, Iemon, Oiwa suffers horrible disfigurement and dies in agony. Later, Iemon casts her body into the Sumida River and curses her to be pecked apart "by kites and crows."[19] Even as he continues to display no remorse, Iemon is haunted by Oiwa's bloodied, disfigured ghost, which reappears repeatedly as a gruesome reminder of his wrongdoing. Yoshimoto's wife has a further counterpart in Lady Macbeth. Modern readers encountering Chūryō's tale having first seen Kurosawa Akira's 1957 film adaptation *Throne of Blood* (*Kumonosu jō*) may envision Yamada Isuzu's chilling performance as Lady Asaji, the film's version of Lady Macbeth. Set, like Chūryō's tale, against the backdrop of Japan's Warring States period, Asaji sets in motion the bloodshed perpetrated by her husband and is haunted by her complicity to the point of delusion and madness, represented memorably in the scene in which she desperately attempts to wash the invisible blood from her hands.

It is tempting to read Yoshimoto's wife's vision of Narumi and her severed body as a similar delusion, the manifestation of her guilt and disordered mental state. However, the second half of the tale complicates this interpretation. As the narrative continues, the focus shifts to a new maidservant who enters the service of one of Yoshimoto's ladies-in-waiting some years later. Her first night on duty, before she has heard of the events surrounding Narumi's death, she unknowingly passes along the corridor near the latrine where the body was cast. Here she crosses paths with an elegant, noble-looking woman who greets her warmly and welcomes her into the household with a gift: a beautiful, lavishly embroidered robe. The woman insists that this act of kindness remain a secret, so that the girl's mistress does not feel obligated to reciprocate. When a robe is later found to be missing from the lady-in-waiting's chests, it is discovered among the girl's belongings, and she is called in for questioning. As she begins to describe the woman who gave it to her, she lets out a cry. Blood spurts from her mouth, and purple marks appear at her throat where the flesh has been crushed by Narumi's invisible hands. Nor does Yoshimoto escape punishment of his own. In the coming months, the Imagawa clan falls into ruin, and each night in the courtyard a woman's voice is heard singing a portentous, sorrowful song. Not long thereafter, Yoshimoto dies

19. Suwa Haruo, ed., *Tōkaidō Yotsuya kaidan*, in *Kabuki on sutēji* 18 (Hakusuisha, 1999), 173.

on the battlefield at Okehazama, "near the post town of Narumi"—tying his historical death to his fictional obsession with a girl by the same name, and joining him with his wife as the victim of his uncontrolled desires.

The details of the story, particularly those in the second half, are sufficient to suggest the "realness" of Narumi's ghost, that she is not solely the manifestation of the wife's guilty conscience. Both she and the maidservant experience bodily harm that leaves observable, physical marks, and the ominous song—presumably in the voice of Narumi—is similarly heard by all. Far from being symptoms of a delusion, then, the visions experienced by Yoshimoto's wife represent quite the opposite: her status, at least prior to her descent into madness, as the sole possessor of truth. In other words, there is a peculiar form of subjective vision at play in which it is only Narumi's victims, with their access to privileged knowledge, who are able to see her and apprehend the truth of the situation.

Such individualized vision and subjective distortion of sight is a trope that occurs widely across the Chinese strange tale and Japanese strange tales informed by them. It is a form of seeing that contrasts sharply with other ways of experiencing the supernatural in the Japanese tradition, such as the spectacle of demonic processions—what Michael Dylan Foster terms "pandemonium on parade"—or the communal experience of the strange in regionally circulating supernatural tales such as *An Account of Inō Heitarō's Spirit Encounters*. In the latter, a text roughly contemporaneous with the heyday of the *kidan*, the strange is a spectacle shared first among the protagonist's friends, then more widely with the community at large, as villagers travel from around the surrounding region to Heitarō's home north of Hiroshima to marvel at the anomalies appearing there.[20]

One form of subjective vision regularly encountered in the Chinese strange tale and its *kidan* adaptations is that of the male protagonist who, unable to rein in his sexual desires, falls victim to foxes, ghosts, and other

20. For representations of Heitarō's supernatural encounters as regional spectacle in two picture-scroll (*emaki*) versions of the narrative, see the illustrations in Sugimoto, *Inō mononokeroku emaki shūsei*, 110–11. Scenes of Heitarō experiencing his encounters alongside his friends appear throughout these picture-scrolls; one particularly compelling example, which offers an elegant juxtaposition with the individualized "fence-peeping" discussed later in this chapter, occurs in a scattering of moments in which Heitarō and his friends peer out, as a group, from gaps in the sliding screen. See, for example, Sugimoto, 126–27, 148–49.

malevolent spirits in the guise of women. In Qu You's "The Peony Lantern," the protagonist Qiao, having recently lost his wife, is instantly smitten by a mysterious, elegant beauty who passes his house during the New Year's lantern festival. He pursues his target and invites her into his home, where the two commence a sexual relationship. She continues to visit him each night for half a month, at which point, through the intervention of a neighbor, Qiao learns that his vital essence has been nearly depleted. His life is in grave danger. The woman, it turns out, is the deceased daughter of a local official, her body interred at a temple not far from Qiao's home.

The characteristic reversal in which the male aggressor becomes the victim reflects a deep-rooted anxiety toward women. Encounters with women are always fraught with danger. Beneath the alluring surface, they may be foxes or demons out to supplement their energy and achieve immortality through sexual vampirism, sucking the life essence (*jing*) from their male victims and ultimately killing their hosts. Rania Huntington, in her study of foxes in late imperial Chinese fiction, observes the development of this trope from its first intimations in Tang fox lore through its codification in the Qing.[21] Even mortal women who were not foxes presented a danger to be navigated with care, as evidenced by the large corpus of texts devoted to sexual techniques through which male practitioners might conserve their vitality and turn female sexuality to their own advantage.[22]

In male encounters with foxes and ghosts in the strange tale, privileged sight is often afforded to a seer figure who is able to see through surface appearances and alert the victim to his predicament. In "The Peony Lantern," this role is played by an elderly neighbor who peers through a hole in the wall and observes Qiao seated by lamplight next to a skeleton adorned with makeup and jewels. (This moment is the subject of a striking illustration in Asai Ryōi's 1666 rewriting of the tale in *Talisman Dolls*.) The old man returns the next day to warn Qiao that his life

21. Huntington, *Alien Kind*, 178–83.

22. On Chinese sexual practices aimed at the preservation and supplementation of vital energy, see Douglas Wile, *Art of the Bedchamber: The Chinese Sexual Yoga Classics, Including Women's Solo Meditation Texts* (Albany: State University of New York Press, 1992).

is in danger, and refers him to a Daoist priest who gives him a pair of protective talismans that keep the woman at bay. However, after an evening of drinking more than a month later, Qiao lets down his guard and ambles off to the temple where the body is interred. The woman's maidservant comes out to greet him and guides him inside, where the woman takes him by the hand and pulls him into her coffin. Their bodies are found side by side the following day.

Often the roles of seer and savior are combined in a single person. In Akinari's "The Serpent's Lust," Toyoo encounters this figure during a flower-viewing outing in the mountains of Yoshino. As he and his party lay out their picnic boxes beside a crashing waterfall, they are approached by a mysterious figure. Although he is initially identified, as in "The Peony Lantern," only as an "old man" (*okina* 翁, Ch. *weng*), it is evident in context that he is a practitioner of shugendō, the syncretic belief system centered on mountain-worship and itinerant ascetic practice: he navigates the difficult mountain terrain with ease and is encountered beside a pounding waterfall along the Yoshino-Kumano pilgrimage route where he was presumably practicing austerities; he is later revealed to be affiliated with a shrine some distance to the north. As he encounters Toyoo's party, the old man glares at Manago and her maidservant and curses them beneath his breath: "Evil spirits! Why must you guide men astray? Do you think you can sit there right before my very eyes?" The women plunge into the falls, and water boils up around them. In spite of ample previous evidence of her true nature, it is only after this encounter that Toyoo grasps that he has been seduced by a serpent and reflects on the lack of virtue that rendered him vulnerable in the first place.[23]

A similar lesson lies at the heart of one of Pu Songling's best-known tales, which foregrounds the role of vision, surface appearances, and illusion in its very title: "The Painted Skin." The narrative wastes no time on framing or otherwise setting the scene but begins immediately with the encounter between the male protagonist and the alluring femme fatale. On the road early one morning, a gentleman named Wang is passed by a young woman carrying a heavy load, and he hurries after her to strike up a conversation. He is immediately taken by her physical beauty, and after learning of her precarious situation—she relates that she is fleeing

23. *Ugetsu monogatari*, in *NKBT* 56:114–15.

an abusive household where she was sent as a concubine—he offers to shelter her in his private study. She accepts, and the two become intimate. When Wang reveals the arrangement to his wife, Lady Chen, she warns that there may be trouble if the girl turns out to have fled a prominent household. In spite of her words of caution, he refuses to send the girl away. Several days later, in the marketplace, Wang has his encounter with the tale's seer figure. A Daoist priest stops him, peering into his face, and warns that his life is in grave danger. The encounter gives Wang pause, but he refuses to believe that the girl has cast a spell on him. Instead, he convinces himself that the priest's words are merely a ploy to coax him into paying for an exorcism.

Wang returns to his study to find the door bolted shut. Creeping up to the window and peering inside, he looks on in horror as a hideous demon touches up a human pelt laid out across the bed, wraps it around itself, and transforms back into the form of the young girl. Wang flees in terror and locates the priest, who gives him a protective talisman to hang above his door. But it is of little use. That night, as he lies in bed with his wife, the girl storms into the bedroom. Trading sexual vampirism for the literal sort, she decries the priest for attempting to thwart her—"Does he think I would spit out what is already in my jaws!?"—then tears out Wang's heart and disappears into the night with her bloody prize. The following day, Wang's younger brother tracks down the priest to enlist his help once more. Sensing the girl's presence at the brother's family compound, the priest discovers her in the guise of an old woman and dispatches her with a swing of his wooden sword. Lady Chen then begs him to bring her husband back from the dead. The priest ponders the request and informs her that while he is unable to help, there is a beggar in the marketplace who may be able to bring back her husband, provided she accepts whatever abuse he throws her way. She locates the man, who insults her and leers at her, then spits a lump of congealed phlegm into his hand and thrusts it into her face, demanding that she eat it. In spite of this unspeakable humiliation, she steels herself and swallows it, but with no apparent effect. She returns home in shame. Then, as she tends to her husband's body, she feels the lump of phlegm suddenly rise in her throat. Before she can turn away, it falls into his open chest cavity. The phlegm has become her husband's beating heart. She binds the wound, and overnight Wang regains consciousness and returns to health.

While Pu Songling and subsequent commentators acknowledge the unfortunate lot of Lady Chen, for male critics the central lesson of the story concerns the husband. The Daoist priest himself succinctly articulates this interpretation immediately after his encounter with Wang in the marketplace. "Poor fool!" he mutters to himself as he wanders off after failing to impress Wang with the seriousness of his situation. "Some men blind themselves to the truth even when death is staring them in the face!"[24] This truth, of course, concerns the danger of surface appearances. Pu again spells this out in his own commentary at the end of the tale. "How foolish men are," he writes, "to see nothing but beauty in what is clearly evil!" Similar interpretations accrued to the text as further commentaries were added in later editions. Among these, Dan Minglun's 1842 commentary offers a particularly blunt assessment of Wang's shortcomings: "A man who lets a ghost into his own room, ignores his wife's warning, and is blind to the advice of the Daoist priest, is clearly a man in the grip of a serious sexual delusion."[25] The consensus interpretation concerns the power of sexual obsession to distort vision and lead men astray.

Repainting "The Painted Skin"

"The Painted Skin" serves as the basis for the longest tale in *Tales from the Withering Wind.* Titled "How the Lesser Monk of Yokawa Vanquished an Evil Spirit" ("Yokawa no kohijiri akuryō o gōbuku suru koto"), the adaptation runs to some thirty-four pages in the 1792 edition and features two of the collection's ten illustrations. The average tale, by contrast, is under twenty pages with just one illustration. This relative length is more striking still when contrasted with the brevity of "The Painted Skin" itself, which fills just four pages in the 1766 Qingketing edition. While some of the discrepancy can be accounted for by the relative concision of Chinese orthography and the classical register, the difference remains pronounced in English translation, where Chūryō's rewriting runs to

24. *LZ*, 120. Translated in Minford, *Strange Tales from a Chinese Studio*, 127.

25. *LZ*, 120, 123. The comments are included in the notes accompanying the translation in Minford, 521.

nearly three times the length of the original.[26] This expansion is the result of several factors, including Chūryō's framing of the narrative with an introduction and conclusion, extensive elaboration and detail at the level of plot, and a wealth of allusions to texts ranging from the Confucian classics to *The Tales of Ise*. The result is not only the longest tale in the collection but one that is in many ways its thematic center of gravity as well. And yet, as will be seen, the nature of that theme is transformed in rewriting, as new meanings emerge into the foreground.

In place of Wang, the protagonist is a provincial samurai named Kuranuki Koyata, a resident of the northern province of Ōshū. One autumn evening, as Koyata sits by the window of his mountain cottage contemplating the sights and sounds of the season, his reverie is interrupted by the sound of crying outside the gate. He ventures out to investigate and discovers an elegant-looking girl about sixteen years of age, her sleeves soaked with tears. Koyata comforts her, and she relates the events that have brought her to his doorstep. Her name is Uta. Born in Kyoto, she was indentured to a cloth merchant several years earlier and traveled with him and his wife to the eastern provinces. There, far from home, the man made his true intentions known and forced himself on her, while the jealous wife took to beating her viciously. Having managed at last to escape, Uta is distraught and appears determined to take her own life in the nearby Abukuma River, that she might "vanish like the bubbles that froth upon its surface." However, she is heartened by Koyata's consoling words, and he offers to care for her until her wounds heal and they can find someone to take her back to the capital. As they pass the hours conversing by lamplight, the girl is overcome with gratitude toward her rescuer, while Koyata finds himself succumbing to her feminine charms. They pledge their love and pass the night in each other's embrace.

Some days later, as Koyata passes through town after a brief visit to his main residence to replenish his dwindling funds and retrieve clean robes for Uta, an itinerant monk—in this case he is explicitly identified as a practitioner of shugendō—approaches from the opposite direction. He is clad in tan robes and leg-guards, with snowy white hair flowing

26. "The Painted Skin" totals around 2,200 words in English translation, while Chūryō's tale runs to more than 6,100 words. See Minford, 126–32; and Fleming, "*Liaozhai zhiyi* in Early Modern Japan," 101–15.

disheveled from his head. As they pass each other, coming so close their faces nearly touch, the monk remarks in a low voice on the evil aura that shrouds Koyata. But his words hardly register. Koyata is so preoccupied with thoughts of Uta waiting alone in his secluded cottage that he hurries on without so much as a backward glance. Only after glimpsing Uta in her true demonic form does he retrace his steps and track down the monk to beg for his help. During this second encounter, the monk introduces himself as the "lesser monk of Yokawa"—Yokawa referring to one of the three complexes of Enryakuji Temple on Mount Hiei in Kyoto—and gives Koyata a protective talisman with text in cinnabar ink. However, the charm only serves to enrage Uta and fails to save Koyata from disaster.

For some readers, this series of events will bring to mind the strikingly similar sequence in Mizoguchi Kenji's 1953 film adaptation of Akinari's *Tales of Moonlight and Rain*. Toward the end of the film, Genjūrō, one of the two male protagonists, uses the profits from selling his pottery to purchase robes for Lady Wakasa, the evil spirit that has seduced him in the guise of an elegant noblewoman. As he hurries through town on his way back to her secluded estate, Genjūrō crosses paths with an itinerant monk. The man's clothing and distinctive twin-cylindered "lotus hat" (*renge-gasa*) mark him as a Tendai monk from Mount Hiei undertaking the ascetic practice of "circling the peaks" (*kaihōgyō*). At the sight of Genjūrō, the monk stops in his tracks and remarks on the shadow of death that lies on his face. Genjūrō initially refuses to believe that he is in danger, but the monk convinces him and attempts to help by writing protective spells in Sanskrit across his upper body. When Lady Wakasa discovers the spells she is infuriated by Genjūrō's betrayal, and he begs desperately to be spared.

Although this sequence closely parallels Chūryō's tale, it represents a significant departure from "The Serpent's Lust," the Akinari tale credited as the source for this narrative thread. Most conspicuously, in rewriting their source, Mizoguchi and screenwriter Yoda Yoshitaka resituated the encounter with the monk from a Yoshino waterfall to a street in the market town of Nagahama on the shores of Lake Biwa.[27] While the

27. Although Yoda's screenplay drew not directly on Akinari but on an adaptation by the novelist Kawaguchi Matsutarō, this scene is not part of Kawaguchi's novella, which was published the following year as the titular narrative in a collection of five

possibility cannot be entirely ruled out, it is unlikely that Mizoguchi or Yoda were aware of Chūryō's tale, which was not published in a modern edition until several decades later. Familiarity with "The Painted Skin" is more plausible, given that Shibata Tenma's translation, which first appeared in his banned 1933 edition of selected *Liaozhai* tales, had been reissued just one year before Mizoguchi's film as part of his long-delayed complete translation.[28] However, the close parallels recede in comparison with Pu Songling's sparer telling of this narrative sequence. Most likely, the resonances between Chūryō's and Mizoguchi's visions reflect an unconscious convergence. As it draws from the well of elements and tropes that constitute the strange tale, the film uncannily echoes one of Akinari's earlier successors.

At the same time that he looks forward to a landmark of Japanese cinema, Chūryō looks backward as he reconceives the key moment in which Koyata realizes Uta's true nature. Even after he passes the monk at the crossroads, Koyata remains blind to the danger. He returns to his cottage to find the door bolted shut. Suspecting (not entirely incorrectly) that Uta must be fixing her hair and makeup, he tiptoes up to the window to surprise her. He peers inside. Seated in the girl's place is a hideous demon with prickly hair, rows of disordered fangs, and fearsome, flashing eyes. As Koyata looks on in terror, the demon lays out what appears to be an animal hide, touches it up with powder and rouge, and then pulls the skin over its head, transforming into Uta before his very eyes. The scene is colorfully represented in the first of the two illustrations by Kitao Masayoshi that accompany the tale (figure 5.1). Depicting the moment Koyata first sees Uta without her human skin, the overall conception is similar to that of the illustration of "The Painted Skin" in the later 1886 Shanghai edition *Xiangzhu Liaozhai zhiyi tuyong* (*Liaozhai zhiyi* with Annotations, Illustrations, and Poems) (figure 5.2). Taking some liberties with the text, Masayoshi depicts Koyata standing outside the gate with one hand on his sword, the other covering his mouth in a gesture of shock. The inside of the cottage is exposed to view. Uta sits hunched near the veranda with a mirror in her hand. Although she is turned away from

works of historical fiction. See "Ugetsu monogatari," in Kawaguchi, *Ugetsu monogatari* (Tōgensha, 1954), 7–82.

28. Shibata Tenma, trans., *Ryōsai shii* [*Liaozhai zhiyi*], vol. 9 (Sōgensha, 1952), 64–71.

FIGURE 5.1 Illustration accompanying the story "How the Lesser Monk of Yokawa Vanquished an Evil Spirit," in *Tales from the Withering Wind* (*Kogarashi zōshi*, 1792). Courtesy of the Library of the Graduate School of Letters and Faculty of Letters, Kyoto University.

the viewer, her demonic features are reflected in a second, standing mirror. The result is a grotesque parody of the conventional, erotically charged image of a woman grooming herself at her dresser.

The text, for its part, reframes this scene through reference to the world of the Heian *monogatari*. When Koyata first glimpses the demon, his thoughts turn to the familiar sixth episode of *The Tales of Ise*, in which a demon devours a woman in a single gulp as a thunderclap muffles her cries. Thinking that the creature in front of him has devoured his beloved Uta, he shows momentary resolve, easing his sword from its sheath and preparing to avenge her death. However, he hesitates upon noticing Uta's garments lying nearby. Then, as the demon pulls the skin over its head, he recoils in terror. The demon has not devoured Uta; it *is* Uta. Both the narrative and Masayoshi's illustration evoke the act of *kaimami* (lit. "looking through a gap in the fence"), the illicit peeping that is central

FIGURE 5.2 "Hua pi" ("The Painted Skin"), in *Xiangzhu Liaozhai zhiyi tuyong* (*Liaozhai zhiyi* with Annotations, Illustrations, and Poems, 1886). Courtesy of the University of California, Berkeley.

to courtship in the world of *The Tales of Ise*, *The Tale of Genji*, and other Heian texts. In this ritual the man, often dressed as if embarking on a hunting expedition, preys on women trapped within walls that provide little defense. Here the conventional power imbalance is instantly flipped on its head. As Koyata peers in on the unsuspecting woman, he realizes in horror that *he* is the prey.

Any courage he might have possessed now dissolves completely. His legs give way beneath him, and he drags himself away on all fours. Now grasping the significance of his earlier encounter, he tracks down the monk and receives the protective charm, which he rushes off to affix to the gate of his main residence. He then locks himself inside and collapses on the floor, sweating and moaning in great distress, while his wife, Ayase, looks on in shock. As evening arrives, the onset of darkness is narrated in a passage not unlike that preceding Samon and Sōemon's reunion in "The Chrysanthemum Vow." Chūryō establishes an uneasy tension between the eerie mundanity of the cries of servants' children at play in the next room, pretending to fight off the demon by themselves, and the shadow of dread cast by the incipient supernatural encounter. The passage of time is captured in evocative turns of phrase, as the bustle of human activity gives way to ominous stillness:

> The servants' children in the next room began to shout in their rough eastern style. "If some sort of monster shows up here, we'll twist its horns, run a rope through its snout, and tie it up in the cowshed!" As they carried on cursing the demon, soon the lamps had burned low. By the time the drum sounded halfway through the hour of the ox, the men who had earlier chattered in excitement lay sprawled on the floor, heads to the west, pillows to the east. The night deepened further.[29]

Late that night, a violent storm blows up. Through the howling wind, Koyata and Ayase discern a faint knocking at the gate. It is Uta. Enraged by the charm, she tears down the earthen wall and circumvents the gate altogether. Moments later, she appears above their bed "like a raging whirlwind," her robes billowing in front of her. Ayase faints, and Koyata reaches for his sword. But Uta seizes him and pushes back his head. Slashing his chest with her raptor claws, she tears open a gash, thrusts in her hand, and pulls out his heart, which she devours "in a single gulp."

29. *Kogarashi zōshi*, in *MCS*, 169. "Halfway through the hour of the ox" (*ushi mitsu*) corresponds to around two o'clock in the morning but was commonly used with the more general sense of "the dead of night." All manner of frightening things were thought to happen at this time of night, as reflected in the expression "paying one's respects at the hour of the ox" (*ushi no koku mairi*), meaning to place a curse on someone or to pray for bodily harm to befall them. The unusual Chinese-style turn of phrase "heads to the west, pillows to the east" suggests that the men have fallen asleep in place without properly settling down for the night.

Then, smacking her lips, she vanishes into the night. In the next room, the other members of the household are roused by the noise, and the disoriented children resume their cries: "Hey, the demon's here! Run a rope through its snout and lead it to the cowshed!"

Morning comes. A crow caws in the trees, and crimson streaks appear in the eastern sky. The monk arrives at the door to inquire about the events of the night before. He then leads Ayase and her men deep into the forest, where they find Uta and he vanquishes her with a single blow from his staff. Impressed by his extraordinary powers, Ayase begs the monk to bring her husband back from the dead, but he sends her in search of another, described only as a "strange-looking seeker of the way" (*ayashige naru dōjin*), who will help her instead. She is cautioned not to let pride or anger get in the way. As she and her men near the banks of a raging river, they come across a leprous beggar sprawled amid urine-soaked filth in a place used as a dumping ground by the nearby villagers. Ayase is certain he must be the man they are looking for. Steeling herself, she accedes to his nauseating demands, sucking his festering sores to ease his pain and choking down a lump of filthy rice that glistens with his thick phlegm. In the end she is sent on her way with nothing to show for this humiliation. Back at home, however, as she tends to Koyata's body, she feels the rice begin to churn in her stomach:

> That very moment, she sensed once more the pus and blood, and the lump of filthy rice, still firmly lodged in her chest. As the stench of blood assaulted her nostrils, the lump rose into her mouth. She raised her hand to stop it, but out it came, dropping straight into the open wound. When she looked down, there was a pool of fresh, hot blood. In the middle was the lump of rice. It had landed right in Koyata's chest cavity, where it lay jumping about vigorously. As she stared at it, there could be no doubt. It was his heart.[30]

Ayase wraps the wound in cloth, and before long steam begins to rise from Koyata's skin. By the next morning he is fully recovered, the only physical trace of his ordeal a thin red scar that runs from his chest down to the abdomen.

30. *Kogarashi zōshi*, in *MCS*, 177.

Strange Bedfellows: Didacticism and the Politics of Fiction in the Kansei Era

Chūryō's rewriting of "The Painted Skin" remains to a degree a cautionary tale about the consequences of the failure to rein in one's sexual impulses. This lesson is reinforced by a number of parallels, at times quite close, between Koyata and Shōtarō, the protagonist of Akinari's "The Kibitsu Cauldron." Shōtarō's defining attribute is his fondness for pleasures of the flesh. Even after his parents attempt to rein in his behavior by marrying him into a respectable family, he persists in his ways. Like Koyata, he neglects his wife and takes up with a new woman, in his case a prostitute in a port town some distance away, whom he buys out of servitude and installs at a second home in the nearby village. The parallels are most striking in the passages leading up to the two men's deaths, which follow a nearly identical progression. There is a moment of fearful realization as they peer inside a house; an encounter with a religious seer figure, who recognizes the imminent danger; then the receipt of paper talismans with cinnabar ink. After this, both men lock themselves inside their homes, cowering in terror until the vengeful spirit appears at the gate in the dead of night (in "The Kibitsu Cauldron," it is his spurned wife, who dies after Shōtarō neglects her) and angrily denounces the charm that has been placed there. Finally, the protagonists meet their gruesome, bloody end. For Shōtarō this occurs on the last of his forty-two nights of confinement. Deceived by the brightening night sky, he believes morning to have arrived and opens the door. A scream of terror echoes from the eaves. His neighbor rushes to investigate but finds only Shōtarō's topknot and streams of fresh blood trickling down the walls.

At the same time that Chūryō retains the theme of sexual excess, and indeed draws attention to it through resonances with Akinari, in many other ways this theme is diminished in his telling. Koyata is a more passive figure than Wang or Shōtarō; rather than actively initiating his interaction with the girl, he has her unexpectedly show up at his door in evident distress. His culpability is further diminished by an emphasis on his altruistic motives for taking her in, which he explains through reference to the well-known allegory of the baby and the well from the *Men-*

cius. What good person would *not* help someone in mortal danger? When Koyata later succumbs to Uta's charms, the narrator assures us that he does so in spite of a moral fiber to rival that of Liuxia Hui, the wise, virtuous minister praised in the *Analects* for having embraced a woman to save her from freezing to death while resisting any temptation to take advantage of the situation.

Nor must Koyata overcome his wife's remonstrations. When Wang's wife learns of his new mistress, she urges him to end the arrangement lest she turn out to have run away from an influential family. He ignores her warnings and persists in the relationship. Ayase, by contrast, makes no attempt to intervene, as she only learns of the situation after it is too late. This is not, at least not initially, because Koyata seeks to deceive her. On the contrary, he proposes to Uta that they reveal their relationship and relocate her to his main residence. Ayase, he tells her, is eager for a child and has urged him to take a mistress. Far from ignoring his wife's wishes, Koyata is acting in accordance with them. Uta, however, dissuades him from revealing their secret by alluding to a familiar episode from *The Tales of Ise* in which a wife remains complacent as her husband sets off to visit his lover. "It is said," Uta explains, offering a novel interpretation of the episode, "that while she bore no resentment on her face . . . within her breast a kettle of water came to a boil."[31] There is no shortage of ironic foreshadowing in this reference. In the *Ise* episode, the wife's untroubled reaction makes the husband suspicious that she herself might have a lover, but his doubts are allayed after he secretly peers through the hedge and sees her reciting a poem of longing for him as she applies her makeup. A rather different realization awaits Koyata.

As the theme of sexual profligacy recedes into the background, a new one emerges in its place: that of the dangers of physical weakness and neglect of duty. Throughout his collection, Chūryō carefully introduces his protagonists, describing their appearances and backgrounds, giving pedigrees that at times reach back to actual historical personages, and nearly always placing them in specific historical and geographic settings. Koyata is introduced as follows:

31. *Kogarashi zōshi*, in *MCS*, 164–65. Uta's reference is to the twenty-third episode in *The Tales of Ise*, commonly known as the "well-curb episode."

> Long ago, in the district of Shinobu in the north country, there lived a rural samurai by the name of Kuranuki Koyata. An ancestor with the same surname had served with distinction for the duration of the Later Three Years' War and was rewarded with his own holding of land. The estate was passed down in uninterrupted succession to Koyata, now the thirteenth generation. Thus was his an exceedingly prosperous family.
>
> At twenty-seven years, Koyata was possessed of clear eyes and a graceful brow. Though born and raised in such a remote locale, in his elegant refinement he was the match of any samurai from the capital. And yet, with the realm long at peace and prosperity in abundance, he neglected the ways of archery and horsemanship, indulging himself solely in the pleasures of composing poetry. To this end, he had set up a second residence in the mountains of Shinobu, leaving the care of the main house to his wife, Ayase. Sequestering himself in this little cottage, he plumbed the depths of antiquity in pursuit of fragrant blossoms of poetry and traversed seldom-seen stretches of the Way of Shikishima gathering the grasses of verse.[32]

This background sets the stage for Koyata's encounter with the girl, whose name, Uta 歌—"poetry"—clearly marks her not only as an object of sexual desire but as the embodiment of the particular preoccupation that distracts Koyata from his duties. Two forms of obsession are merged into one.

The opening lines also position Koyata as an exemplar of a familiar archetype. Katsushirō in "The Reed-Choked House," Shōtarō in "The Kibitsu Cauldron," and Toyoo in "The Serpent's Lust" are all introduced with passages that similarly emphasize their neglect of familial obligations and distaste for the occupation through which their forebears made their livelihood. The parallels with Toyoo are particularly striking. Both show little inclination toward physically demanding labor (in Toyoo's case, the fishing business through which his family earns its living) and are naturally drawn to the elegant ways of the distant capital. For both men, the capital comes to them in the form of a deadly love interest, an

32. *Kogarashi zōshi*, in *MCS*, 162. Shikishima, the residence of two early emperors, was used first as a pillow word for the place name Yamato, then as an appellation for Japan as a whole. The expression "Way of Shikishima" denotes the art of classical Japanese poetry.

elegant beauty from the city met with hardship in the provinces. For Toyoo it is Manago, whom he first encounters as they seek shelter at the same hut during a sudden late-autumn downpour. Uta appears at Koyata's doorstep under still more desperate circumstances, a vulnerable maiden on the verge of taking her own life. These resonances with Akinari not only underscore Koyata's vulnerability and foreshadow his fate but also strengthen the attribution of their underlying cause: neglect of duty.

Chūryō spells out this causal link at the end of the first half of the narrative. When the monk reaches the scene the morning after Koyata's violent death, he offers the following explanation for the futility of his efforts to intervene:

> It seems that the unplacated spirits of the women who died at your ancestors' hands in the Later Three Years' War linger in this world. Who can say how many winters have come and gone as they have awaited vengeance? For many generations yours was a valiant clan, skilled in the way of archery. The flesh was firm, no tender region where they might inflict their wound. Yet in the present generation the warrior's arts have been neglected. Seizing on this gap, this weakness, they spun their disastrous web. Koyata became ensnared and met his untimely end. No technique could save him, for it was a thing he invited on himself.[33]

Lest the lesson be forgotten, Chūryō further complements the opening lines of the tale with a moralistic conclusion in which Koyata reflects on the meaning and causes of his ordeal. Tracing his experience not to a generalized "lack of virtue," as Toyoo does, or to uncontrolled sexual desire, he instead identifies the cause as neglect of duty and martial preparedness. Recognizing the error of his ways, he immediately rectifies his behavior:

> Koyata reflected on his situation. "It was because I was foolish and neglected the ways of archery and horsemanship that I died at the hands of an evil spirit. Surely it grieved the souls of my ancestors to see their line come to an end, and for that reason they brought me back to life."

33. *Kogarashi zōshi*, in *MCS*, 171.

> From that moment on he righted his ways, and with the brush at his left hand and sword at his right, he soon restored the luster to his clan's name.[34]

The framing of the narrative between a pair of tidy didactic bookends presents a marked contrast with the approach in many *Liaozhai* stories, including "The Painted Skin." Pu's characters regularly appear on the scene with little by way of introduction and are rarely given more than a surname.[35] Wang is no exception. Identifying him only by family name and place of origin in Taiyuan, the narrative immediately proceeds—within the very first line of text—to his encounter with the girl. Many stories end with similar abruptness. After he revives, Wang offers only a brief remark about the painful, dreamlike state he endured while he was "dead." Pu himself does offer occasional judgment—literary, moralistic, and otherwise—in the form of the appended commentaries that accompany over a third of his tales. These, however, are set apart from the narrative and, through their attribution to the "Historian of the Strange" (*yishi shi*), are presented in the voice of the compiler rather than the narrator.

Chūryō's framing comes at the expense of some of the very "strangeness" of his source material. For readers of *Liaozhai*, the abrupt immersion in Pu's narrative worlds was one of the collection's appeals. Feng Zhenluan (1760–1830) homes in on this in his 1818 *Liaozhai* commentary. Objecting to a reader's complaint that the protagonist of "The Daoist Priest" appears and disappears with no explanation whatsoever, Feng argues that it is precisely this that gives the story its otherworldliness.[36] In Chūryō's rewritings, uncertainty and lingering questions are at least in part resolved. Not only is Koyata's fate directly attributed to his own negligence, but Uta is explained away as the spirit of a woman killed at the hands of his ancestors. (The explanation sheds light on her cryptic declaration as she makes off with his heart: "At last I have achieved vengeance on an ancient foe!")

34. *Kogarashi zōshi*, in *MCS*, 177.

35. It has been observed that there may have been extratextual reasons for Pu Songling's reluctance to identify his characters more precisely. See, for example, Hammond, "Factual Framing in *Liao zhai zhi yi*," 208.

36. *LZ*, 301.

A similar transformation is evident in the rewriting of "The Gentleman from Fengyang." Pu concludes the tale with an enigmatic question: "But who was the beautiful girl? No one knew."[37] Chūryō provides an answer with the added scene in which a diviner reveals the girl to have been the spirit of a prostitute whose grave Oribe inadvertently trampled on his way home. The reader is afforded a moment of uncertainty, but it quickly dissipates as the reasons behind the anomaly are explained away.

To fully account for the didacticism of *Tales from the Withering Wind*—the way in which the text seeks to pin down moral ambiguity and impose certainty, taming the strange in ways that go beyond even the conventional historical and geographic distancing of the *kidan* genre—it is necessary to situate the text in its particular historical moment. Chūryō first conceived the collection around 1788, and it appeared in print in 1792. This gestation period closely coincides with the execution of a program of reforms under the shogun's new senior councilor, Matsudaira Sadanobu. Between 1787 and 1793, the series of edicts known collectively as the Kansei Reforms targeted a range of economic and social ills, including aspects of everyday life from gambling and prostitution to public bathing and fashion. A further target was the vibrant popular fiction scene that had flourished through the 1770s and 1780s and was seen to lie at the heart of broader social decay and cultural decadence.

Among the slogans advanced as part of this reform effort was the exhortation for samurai to uphold "the twin paths of the literary and martial arts" (*bunbu nidō*). So frequently was this phrase bandied about that it lent itself to ridicule as an empty platitude. Given the similarity of the phrase *bunbu* to the buzzing of a mosquito—*bun-bun*—one wag of the day (later said to have been Ōta Nanpo) composed a comic verse that mocked it as a *literal* buzzword, comparing the incessant droning on about the twin paths to the sound of a pesky mosquito in the middle of the night.[38] Authors of pictorial fiction quickly piled on with satires of their

37. *LZ*, 190.

38. The poem reads, *Yo no naka ni / ka hodo urusaki / mono wa nashi / bunbu to yūte / yoru mo nerarezu*. The attribution to Nanpo is tenuous, given that the verse was first cited by the daimyō Matsura Seizan several decades after the fact. Seizan, *Kasshi yawa*,

own, among them a piece by Chūryō's friend Hōseidō Kisanji titled *The Twin Paths Threshing Device* (*Bunbu nidō mangoku dōshi*, 1788) and Koikawa Harumachi's *Parroting the Twin Paths* (*Ōmugaeshi bunbu no futamichi*, 1789), which is reported to have been one of the most commercially successful works in the entire genre.[39]

This fun soon came to a halt as the bakufu trained its sights on popular fiction. In 1790 several edicts were issued restricting politically sensitive content and anonymous authorship, formalizing censorship regimes, banning the use of historical settings to mask satirical intent, and, more broadly, forbidding all works deemed injurious to public morals.[40] Severe punishments were meted out, with the authorities choosing high-value targets as a warning to others. Kyōden was among those punished during this period, first in the form of a fine for his role as the illustrator of Ishibe Kinkō's comic book *A Mirror of History in Black and White* (*Kokubyaku mizukagami*, 1789), which alluded to a fatal attack on senior councilor Tanuma Okitsugu's son Okitomo several years earlier, and later with fifty days in manacles for the publication of three *sharebon* that were deemed "depraved books" that violated the new regulations.[41] Amid this transformed literary climate, occasional resurgences of the subversive strain were met with swift action. In 1799 Shikitei Sanba published a *kibyōshi* set in the fourteenth-century world of the *Taiheiki* that lampooned the brawling antics of Edo's fire brigades. The humor was not well received by its objects, and a band of disgruntled firemen destroyed

---

vol. 1, in Nakamura Yukihiko and Nakano Mitsutoshi, eds., *Tōyō bunko* 306 (Heibonsha, 1977), 29. Several scholars have offered English translations of the verse, among which Adam Kern's is particularly effective in capturing its multiple layers of meaning: "Nothing in the world / Bugs in the quiet of night / So much as that buzz-buzzing / About the so-called 'Twin Arts' / You can hardly get to sleep!" In Kern, *Manga from the Floating World*, 219.

39. See Kern, 53.

40. The edicts are reprinted in Takayanagi Shinzō and Ishii Ryōsuke, eds., *Ofuregaki shūsei*, vol. 5: *Ofuregaki Tenpō shūsei* (*ge*) (Iwanami shoten, 1941), 809–10.

41. For the most substantial treatment of Kinkō's satire, see Tanahashi Masahiro, *Kibyōshi no kenkyū* (Wakakusa shobō, 1997), 109–22. The record of the official investigation of Kyōden's offending *sharebon* is translated in Peter F. Kornicki, "*Nishiki no Ura*: An Instance of Censorship and the Structure of a *Sharebon*," *Monumenta Nipponica* 32, no. 2 (Summer 1977): 157–59.

the home of the publisher and, according to some accounts, Sanba's as well. For his role in disturbing the peace, the authorities sentenced Sanba, like Kyōden before him, to fifty days in manacles—a punishment more severe than that meted out to the firemen themselves.[42]

As he watched the literary efflorescence of the previous decades shrivel beneath these withering winds, Chūryō responded with caution, turning away from the genres in which he had made a name for himself since his literary debut a decade earlier. He had already evidenced a distaste for some of the excesses of contemporary popular fiction. After publishing six *sharebon* of his own, in 1787 Chūryō launched a broadside against prevailing literary trends with the publication of *A Provincial Production*, a work that presented itself as a *sharebon* in form but rejected many of the qualities most closely associated with that genre—biting wit, urbanity, and behind-the-scenes glimpses of brothel life—in favor of a gentler, rustic humor and decidedly non-urbane setting, features that would be emulated by Ikku, Sanba, and many others. Chūryō's preface made clear his distaste for the sort of material that would get Kyōden into such trouble, memorably comparing the *sharebon*'s muckraking to the hoisting up of a female impersonator's robes during a kabuki performance. Having savaged the genre, Chūryō turned his back on it altogether, and with the intensification of the bakufu assault on popular fiction he took an extended hiatus from the *kibyōshi* as well, trying his hand at the genre again only in 1794.

Instead, he waited out the storm of the Kansei Reforms in safer harbors, collecting castaway reports, preparing reference works and essay collections including *Tales of Ryūkyū* (*Ryūkyū banashi*, 1790), and becoming one of the first Edo-based writers to turn to the *kidan*—a genre that was not worldly, contemporary, or subversive but *other*worldly, historical, and deferential toward authority. But Chūryō went further still, taking an approach that was cautious even by *kidan* standards. In the figure of Koyata, Akinari's neglectful commoner protagonists are replaced with a landed provincial samurai whose shortcomings as a husband are also

42. An annotated reproduction of Sanba's piece, titled *Front-Tied Headbands: A Chronicle of Urban Gallantry in an Age of Great Peace* (*Kyan taiheiki mukō hachimaki*), appears in Koike Masatane, Uda Toshihiko, Nakayama Yūshō, and Tanahashi Masahiro, eds., *Edo no gesaku [parodī] ehon* (Shakai shisōsha, 1980–85), 4:193–228.

shortcomings *as a samurai*, the failure to uphold the duties and norms expected of his social status. If the underlying lesson were not clear enough, it is spelled out again at the narrative's conclusion in the language of contemporary policy: the twin paths of the "brush" and "sword" to which Koyata commits himself in the story's final line.

Chūryō was in a tenuous position. Unlike many others in Edo's urban literary circles, he was not a townsman or low-ranking samurai but the son of an elite family with connections to the highest reaches of officialdom. As bakufu physician, his brother's duties included attending to the shogun himself. This proximity to power no doubt contributed to Chūryō's reluctance to challenge the status quo, and his position is said to have prompted him, on occasion, to give material he felt uncomfortable publishing under his own name to his younger townsman friend Jippensha Ikku.[43] In other words, his alignment with the bakufu agenda may have been merely perfunctory, a calculated strategy of self-preservation. That his true sympathies may have lain elsewhere is hinted at by a possible satirical subtext in *Tales from the Withering Wind* explored in the epilogue.

In a memorable passage in the preface to one of the installments of *The Chronicle of the Eight Dogs*, Bakin praises *The Water Margin* and other Chinese vernacular fiction for coating their didacticism in the "honey" of exciting plots and flawless style, coaxing readers into consuming virtuous fare through a practice he saw as a variation on Buddhism's "expedient means."[44] For many writers, however, it was the moralizing itself that was the expedient means. Coating their fiction in a healthy layer of didacticism rendered it palatable to the powers that be while allowing them to dish up servings of high-sugar content for their readers. Chūryō, too, seems to approach his lessons as afterthoughts, positioning them prominently but devoting most of his attention elsewhere.

43. Chūryō's relationship with Ikku is described in *A Lingering Dream* (*Nagori no yume*), the posthumously published oral memoir of Chūryō's great-great-grandniece Imaizumi Mine. See Imaizumi, *Nagori no yume*, 109–10.

44. *Hakkenden*, in Hamada Keisuke, ed., *Shinchō Nihon koten shūsei bekkan: Nansō Satomi hakkenden*, vol. 2 (Shinchōsha, 2003), 11–12. For a translation of the passage and a discussion of Bakin's views on didacticism in fiction, see Glynne Walley, "'I Would Rather Be a Faithful Dog than an Unrighteous Man': Virtue and Vice in Kyokutei Bakin's *Nansō Satomi hakkenden*" (PhD diss., Harvard University, 2009), 13–16.

All the same, the possibility of genuine complicity with the official agenda cannot be excluded. Chūryō's distaste for exposé and muckraking—which led to a reputed, if much debated, break with Kyōden—may have made him sympathetic to reining in at least the most egregious excesses of popular fiction, even if it is hard to imagine that he would have approved of the draconian punishments meted out to his friends and colleagues.[45] There is further circumstantial evidence in the fact that, within months of the publication of *Tales from the Withering Wind*, Chūryō entered the service of none other than Matsudaira Sadanobu.[46] Although the reasons for this employment are unclear, Sadanobu had recently commissioned the Dutch interpreter Ishii Shōsuke (1743–?) to translate Dononaeus's sixteenth-century botanical treatise *Cruijdeboeck*. In light of Chūryō's knowledge of Dutch studies and familiarity with Western medical techniques, which he employed in his own practice, it seems likely that he was brought in to collaborate on this project. His employment with Sadanobu lasted five years, during which he divided his time between Edo and Sadanobu's home domain of Shirakawa, two hundred kilometers to the north. His diminished output during this period includes only a few short works of fiction and a single nonfiction work: an illustrated collection of didactic maxims and edifying anecdotes titled *Lessons from a Provincial Capital* (*Hitokotogusa*, 1796). Written for parents to read with their children, the focus on edification, filial piety, and personal virtue resonates strongly with the themes explored in *Tales from the Withering Wind*, as well as its tendency to spell out its lessons in no uncertain terms.

Whether heartfelt, coerced, or a mere calculated strategy, the accentuated didacticism that emerged in the context of the Kansei Reforms dictated

45. According to two accounts by Bakin, both written decades after the fact, Kyōden perceived the preface to *A Provincial Production* as a personal attack and cut off all contact with Chūryō thereafter. However, there are reasons to question the reliability of Bakin's versions of events. For overviews and divergent interpretations of the controversy, see Sonoda Yutaka, "Manzōtei to Kyōden no zekkō ni tsuite: Bakin kyokuhitsu setsu e no ichi shiron," *Edo jidai bungakushi* 4 (November 1985): 23–37; Tanahashi, *Kibyōshi no kenkyū*, 249–371; and Nakano Mitsutoshi, *Gesaku kenkyū* (Chūō kōronsha, 1981), 369–70.

46. Chūryō's employment with Sadanobu lasted from late in 1792 through 1797. See Ōtsuki Nyoden, ed., *Shinsen yōgaku nenpyō* (Ōtsuki Shigeo, 1927), 77.

the terms on which Chūryō's tales were received in subsequent generations. In 1818 a *kidan* collection was published under the title *Tales of Unrivalled Strangeness*. Although the work presented itself as a selection of new strange tales by the late author Shinrotei, the body text was in fact an exact copy of *Tales from the Withering Wind* prepared using the facsimile technique of *kabusebori* described in chapter 2. Nevertheless, there were a few changes in the paratextual apparatus that can be seen to reflect shifts in the literary landscape in the intervening quarter-century. The most conspicuous of these was the replacement of the original illustrations by Kitao Masayoshi with new ones by the Nagoya artist Gekkōtei Bokusen, a student of Kitagawa Utamaro and Katsushika Hokusai, that better conformed to contemporary tastes. In addition to those that accompany the tales themselves, two illustrations preceding the body text depict a lineup of eight of the collection's protagonists—a sort of dramatis personae or cast call reflecting the ever-expanding influence of the kabuki stage in early nineteenth-century fiction.

The other substantial difference between *Tales from the Withering Wind* and *Tales of Unrivalled Strangeness* is the replacement of the original preface—in which Chūryō famously, if briefly, traces the history of the Japanese strange tale back to its Chinese forebears—with a shorter preface that, while still celebrating the strangeness and marvelousness of the tales, instead foregrounds didacticism as the text's principal attribute. Advancing a functional view of fiction, the new preface praises the collection for guiding readers toward moral enlightenment through allegory, singling out in particular its unwavering focus on the themes of loyalty, filial piety, and "promoting and chastising."[47] This last phrase is short for "promoting virtue and chastising vice" (*kanzen chōaku*), a catchphrase applied to didactic literature—through the writings of the Meiji critic Tsubouchi Shōyō it was later associated with Bakin's fiction in particular—that had become so familiar by the early nineteenth century that it could be deployed in abbreviated form, omitting reference to what exactly it was that was being promoted and chastised.

As flip sides of the same coin, the promotion of virtue and chastising of vice go hand in hand. At times the depiction of the gruesome conse-

47. Shinrotei, (*Katakiuchi*) *Kōsei kidan* (Ōsaka, Nagoya, Edo, and Kyōto: Akitaya Taemon et al., 1818), 1a–2a.

quences of obsession and other forms of unvirtuous behavior—such as the violence, jealousy, and scheming of Yoshimoto and his wife—serves as a cautionary tale, a warning that guides readers toward virtue. Elsewhere characters themselves are given the chance to rectify bad behavior, and virtue follows on vice. After Koyata's moral failures are punished and expiated through his violent death, he emerges on the far side to reap the benefits of his newly virtuous ways.

Chūryō's penultimate tale, titled "How Master Kyūgan Used His Daoist Arts to Deceive Two Men of Wealth" ("Kyūganbō ga senjutsu fumin o taburakasu koto")—one of two singled out for their didacticism in the preface to *Tales of Unrivalled Strangeness*—follows a similar moral arc and, in its denouement, offers a richly allegorical lesson. Echoing Pu Songling's "The Daoist Priest of Mount Lao" ("Laoshan daoshi"), the story begins by introducing Master Kyūgan, a simpleminded young man who becomes the laughingstock of his village after devoting himself to the study of Daoist techniques in hopes of achieving immortality and magical powers. However, Chūryō soon transitions to a rewriting of "The Daoist Priest" ("Daoshi"), anticipating a reversal in which the apparent fool gets the last laugh. One spring day, Kōzō and Yahei, a pair of wealthy men from the village, set out with a group of servants and entertainers for a banquet beneath the cherry blossoms. Stumbling upon Kyūgan's hut, they mock him for his misguided pursuit of otherworldly delights and tempt him with the delicacies afforded by their worldly wealth. Kyūgan greedily devours the food and wine set before him, and as he leaves he offers to return their hospitality the following evening. The men readily accept, expecting a further laugh at his expense.

When they arrive the next day, Kōzō and Yahei find that the door to Kyūgan's hut opens onto a lavish hall carpeted in soft felt and illuminated by gleaming silver lamps. Handsome servants bring forth trays piled high with rare delicacies and (affording a glimpse of Chūryō's abiding interest in all things Western) pour red wine from French carafes into cups of English crystal. Kyūgan welcomes his guests and thanks them for having opened his eyes to the folly of his ways. As the wine flows, two lovely maidens named Hotoke (meaning "Buddha") and Nanamoto (七本) are summoned to provide musical entertainment. After their performance, Kyūgan drapes his arms over the women's shoulders and withdraws with them to a private chamber. Kōzō and Yahei stumble in drunken pursuit, drive Kyūgan out of the room, and force themselves on the women. In Pu Songling's tale, the surname of the sisters, Shi (meaning "stone"), anticipates their true nature, which the men discover when they wake up the next morning—one beneath a set of stone steps, the other atop a filthy rock in a crumbling latrine. In similar fashion, Kōzō awakens to find himself sprawled beside a stone statue of the bodhisattva Jizō, while Yahei lies nearby clutching a set of seven memorial stupas (*shichihon* 七本 *sotoba*). Literally forced to embrace virtue, the men recognize the error of their ways and return home to lead virtuous lives.

Framing Virtue: The Auspicious Opening (and Felicitous Finale)

The preface appended to the unauthorized 1818 edition of *Tales from the Withering Wind* characterizes the collection's didacticism as a quality that shines through "from start to finish." It is particularly evident *at* the start and finish. Replicating at a larger scale the didactic frame that bookends many of the individual tales, the collection as a whole opens and closes with stories that present uncomplicated visions of virtue, their plots propelled by a straightforward moral calculus in which happiness and prosperity follow naturally from moral rectitude. In the opening tale, a young girl demonstrates exemplary filial piety as she travels hundreds of miles and endures hardship and privation to secure her mother's release from captivity. In the final tale, a courtier's remarkable poetic abilities, together with a well-timed act of bravery, earn him a divine wife and wealth beyond his wildest imagining. Readers are welcomed into the collection and sent on their way with narratives that are at once felicitous and transparently didactic.

The auspicious opening tale is a feature of many *kidan* collections. As a group, these tales share a number of qualities that set them apart from the remainder of the collections in which they appear. Many distance themselves altogether from the strange Chinese "other" that is otherwise such an important source, drawing instead on Japanese source material. They are often not particularly "strange," and the warfare that otherwise pervades the genre plays a less prominent role. There are exceptions, such as Akinari's "Shiramine," which opens *Tales of Moonlight and Rain* and relies heavily on Japanese martial epics and other native sources, or the first story of Shinrotei's *A Handful of Tales*, which shows the influence of "Shiramine" and features an extended disquisition on military history.[48] Yet both of these tales, while opening with passages that recount the sweep of violence in Japanese history, are not themselves set directly against a backdrop of war. They merely survey conflict at a remove in time.

The framing of collections filled with strange, at times violent, content with opening tales that are often neither can be seen as a further extension of the *kidan*'s cautious conservatism. The political implications are spelled out unambiguously in the tale that opens Teishō's *A Thicket of Tales*. A monk travels from his home temple to visit Shitennō Temple in Naniwa (modern-day Osaka) and shelters for the night on the top floor of the temple's five-story pagoda. As he begins to doze, a strange confluence of winds brings together clouds from the four directions in the skies overhead, and he listens intently as they expound at length on clouds and their significance. Their discussion culminates with a prediction of the felicitous clouds that will fill the skies "a hundred years hence"—which is to say, given the story's setting in the Daiei era (1521–28), at the dawn of Tokugawa rule:

> "An age of enduring peace will be upon us, and auspicious clouds will drift unceasingly through the heavens. Prosperity will fill the land, civilization will sprout thick, and the blessings of the east wind will be ever abundant. Even drifting clouds such as ourselves will flap our sleeves with joy as we endlessly float across the sky in marvelous formations—a fitting sight for a realm at peace. Do not forget this!"
>
> With this felicitous proclamation they slowly scattered in the four directions.[49]

Throughout the East Asian tradition, natural phenomena and human affairs were seen to be entangled as part of the larger system of correlative cosmology. If the human realm was ordered, then nature was ordered; conversely, misrule or illegitimacy might trigger strange heavenly phe-

48. See Gotō Tanji, *Senki monogatari no kenkyū* (Tsukuba shoten, 1936), 453.

49. "Unkon unjō o katatte hisashiki o chikau hanashi" (The Clouds Opine on Their Nature and Make an Eternal Vow), in *Shigeshige yawa*, in Tokuda and Yokoyama, eds., *SNKBT* 80:13–14.

nomena, natural disasters, unseasonable weather, or anomalous behavior in the animal world.[50] In Japan's martial epics, natural omens such as the color-coded white waves and clouds or red and white gamecocks in *The Tale of the Heike* foreshadow victory and defeat on the battlefield, as well as the legitimacy and illegitimacy of rulers. For his part, Teishō conjures an image of the natural world in perfect order—"auspicious clouds" in "marvelous formations"—to pay literary tribute to the Tokugawa order and the Great Peace. Positioning such displays of deference at the outset of *kidan* collections was yet another strategy for taming the strange. The laudatory tone further diminishes the possibility that the strange tales that compose the remainder of the collection might be perceived as subversive or otherwise critical of authority, while readers themselves are reassured that strange things do not happen in an ordered realm.

The opening tale in *Tales from the Withering Wind* similarly culminates in passages that can be read as an extended paean to the Tokugawa peace. The story announces its virtuous theme and auspicious outcome in its very title: "How Manju's Exemplary Filial Piety Rescued Her Mother from Captivity" ("Manju ga shīkō haha no kingoku o manukareshimuru koto"). Although there is little in the tale that is strange or otherworldly—aside, perhaps, from the extreme filial devotion of the title character, which can be seen as a sort of strange marvel—an element of mystery is imparted by the framing of the tale, which emerges from an encounter between a visitor to the ancient capital of Kamakura and a local resident who appears with uncanny timing to answer his questions. The noh-like qualities of this encounter invite comparison with Akinari, whose tales at times evoke the conventions and atmosphere of noh, and serve as a reminder that the "auspicious opening" is a technique with broader currency in the Japanese tradition, including the theater.[51]

As Chūryō's unnamed traveler roams the outskirts of Kamakura in search of traces of the past, he stumbles across a cavern in a recess in a

50. See, for example, Aihe Wang, *Cosmology and Political Culture in Early China* (Cambridge: Cambridge University Press, 2000), 109.

51. On Akinari and noh, see "Introduction," in Leon M. Zolbrod, trans., *Ugetsu Monogatari: Tales of Moonlight and Rain* (Vancouver: University of British Columbia Press, 1974), 74–75.

rocky hillside, at a place known as the Valley of the Buddha's Hall.[52] The rock surface is overgrown with ancient moss, and he feels a strange chill run through his body. Surely there must be a story behind the place. Just then, an old man happens by, and the traveler calls out to inquire about the site and whether there are any legends associated with it. The old man tells him that the cavern is known as "Karaito's dungeon." It was here, many years ago, that a woman by that name was imprisoned. The old man then proceeds to relate her story, "that it might be passed on to young people to make known the happy virtue of filial piety."

Here we exit the frame and enter the narrative proper, which is loosely adapted from the medieval companion-booklet (*otogizōshi*) *The Tale of Karaito* (*Karaito sōshi*), making it one of only two in the collection not based to any extent on Pu Songling. The year is 1183. At Minamoto no Yoritomo's palace in Kamakura, a lady-in-waiting named Karaito receives a letter from her husband, who is a loyal retainer of Yoritomo's rival Kiso Yoshinaka. Two years earlier, during a period of heightened tensions, Yoshinaka's son was sent to Kamakura as hostage, and Karaito joined his retinue under disguised identity. Now Yoritomo has turned his forces against Yoshinaka, and Karaito is ordered to assassinate Yoritomo. A dagger is enclosed with the letter. However, in spite of her fierce determination, her attempt on his life fails, and she is imprisoned in the hillside cavern that later comes to bear her name. Meanwhile, Karaito's eleven-year-old daughter Manju hears that her mother has been imprisoned in a pitch-black pit. Disguising herself as a *shirabyōshi* dancer in training, she journeys hundreds of miles to Kamakura with her father's stable hand Yosō, sleeping in fields and begging for food along the way. She arrives to find Karaito under close guard, the cavern so tightly secured she can only gaze at it from a distance. She passes the days in sorrow, praying for a chance to see her mother.

Manju is one of several filial children depicted in *Tales from the Withering Wind*. In the sixth tale of the collection, an eleven-year-old boy

52. Shakadō-ga-yatsu ("The Valley of the Buddha's Hall"), about a kilometer southeast of Tsurugaoka Hachiman Shrine, takes its name from the temple Hōjō no Yasutoki constructed there in memory of his father, Yoshitoki. The building stood only until the middle of the Muromachi period, but the place name survives today. See the entry in Miura Katsuo, ed., *Kamakura no chimei yurai jiten* (Tōkyōdō shuppan, 2005), 97–98.

dies but is still able to honor his father after Enma, the king of hell, is moved by his filial pleas and casts his spirit into a gamecock that racks up a series of cockfighting victories. In "The Cricket," the *Liaozhai* tale from which the story is adapted, the boy recovers from illness to reveal that he dreamed of being the cricket that brought his father glory in competition. It is unclear whether he actively controlled the cricket, fighting for his father's sake as an act of intentional filial piety. Chūryō's version resolves this uncertainty, rewriting the son as an unambiguous exemplar of filiality whose devotion is all the more extraordinary for being carried out from beyond the grave. This theme continues in altered form in the next tale, which also features a son who descends into hell as he seeks to honor his parents—in this case, by fulfilling his mother's dying words and waging a violent vendetta to avenge his father's death. In a sequence loosely inspired by Pu Songling's "Master Longfei" ("Longfei xianggong"), the boy falls down a deep crevasse into the underworld, where, in the manner of the medieval "tour of hell" (*jigoku meguri*) genre, he observes the many torments that await the unvirtuous, including his father's killer, and receives divine assistance in his mission as a reward for his own unimpeachable virtue.

In both of these tales, filiality sprouts like a rare flower amid the injustice of the wider world. Chūryō's adaptation of "The Cricket" in particular echoes its source's unvarnished depiction of peasant hardship at the hands of corrupt, self-interested officials—carrying with it an intriguing subversive subtext, as touched on in the epilogue. In Manju's story, by contrast, there is little to cloud the narrative's auspicious logic, which progresses toward a conclusion that complements its celebration of filial piety with an unsubtle homage to Tokugawa rule. As Manju waits, never losing hope that she will one day be rejoined with her mother, the months turn to years, and Yoritomo consolidates his control over the realm. A celebratory ceremony is planned at Tsurugaoka Hachiman Shrine, and he decrees that a dozen girls are to be chosen to perform dances as an offering to secure the god's continued favor. Manju's lovely singing voice and abilities as a dancer earn her the twelfth and final spot.

The day arrives, and the other dancers—all accomplished *shirabyōshi* with established reputations—rise to the occasion with performances that delight the audience. When it comes time for Manju's performance, they are shocked that an unknown has been chosen to join the others. She is met with cruel, derisive laughter. However, the jeers are quickly silenced as she lifts her face and begins to sing "in a voice as sweet as the bush warbler in the valley." By the time she finishes, the crowd is entirely on her side, and they excitedly hurl their swords and formal jackets into the air until a small hill has piled up in front of the stage. Yoritomo is delighted. He rewards Manju with a sizable holding of land and asks if there is anything else she desires. At last revealing her true identity, she begs for her mother's freedom. Karaito is brought forth, and after eight long years mother and daughter are reunited. Moved to tears by Manju's utter devotion, Yoritomo doubles his reward as a further act of magnanimity. Karaito and Manju move to their new estate with Yosō and his new wife, and together they build a prosperous, virtuous, and filial household.

Going further than other tales in the collection, the story's conclusion links personal virtue with good fortune not just for the individual but for the realm at large, as Manju's filial act and the achievement of political stability and peace unfold in parallel. The proceedings are further capped with a grand gesture of shogunal benevolence, as Yoritomo extends clemency to a former rival. The implications are spelled out in the two *imayō* songs Manju performs, whose lyrics read as paeans to the splendor of shogunal rule:

(1) *May a thousand years pass*
here upon the Hill of Cranes,
and in the Valley of the Turtle
let us rejoice at the promise
of myriad upon myriad reigns;
in the Valley of Pines ten times blooming
and the Valley of Plums to match those of Dayu Ridge,
here in this land at the height of splendor,
our lord ever flourishing.

(2) *At Kamakura Mountain, where the firewood is cut,*
the realm basks in your radiance, the sky above bright with stars.[53]

53. *Kogarashi zōshi*, in *MCS*, 159.

As in *Chūshingura*, Kamakura serves as a thinly veiled substitute for Edo, with the celebration of a realm at its height of glory, alongside references to cranes, turtles, pines, and other symbols of permanence and longevity, contributing to an unabashed celebration of Tokugawa rule.

The final story in *Tales from the Withering Wind* sends readers on their way in similarly felicitous fashion. A rewriting of Pu Songling's "Zhicheng," the action unfolds against the backdrop of the Japanese invasions of Korea at the end of the sixteenth century. As the scholar Gamō Yasusato races from the capital with a message for Hideyoshi, he faces unexpected supernatural encounters, first with the unsettled ghosts of the Heike dead near their resting place at Dan-no-ura, then, off the coast of northern Kyushu, with the Dragon King and his retinue. After inadvertently offending the latter, Yasusato announces himself as a descendant of Fujiwara no Hidesato, the tenth-century archer who, according to legend, came to the Dragon King's aid and defeated the giant centipede of Mount Mikami, a deed for which he was rewarded with a magical, inexhaustible rice sack. Like his ancestor before him, Yasusato impresses the Dragon King—first with his poetic abilities, then by risking his life to rescue one of the king's female attendants. At the end of the tale, he is given the girl's hand in marriage and receives magical gifts including a plate piled with treasure that, like Hidesato's rice sack, endlessly replenishes itself.

Replicating the framing of his individual tales, Chūryō packages his collection as a whole between bookends that are at once auspicious and didactic. Readers enter the world of ghosts, demons, and the uncanny with a staidly titled tale that holds the strange at bay not merely by banishing it to the past, but by having very little about it that is conventionally strange. The narrative makes no obvious gesture to the supernatural, and it traces its origins not to a Chinese strange tale but to a medieval Japanese companion-booklet. At the same time, Manju's unflagging devotion—her "extreme" or "unsurpassable" filial piety (*shikō*), as the title puts it—is itself a wonder that fits within the range of meanings contained in the category of *ki*. Obsessive behavior, so often the breeding ground for dangerous anomalies, can also be a virtue that gives rise to order and prosperity. Complementing this at the far end of the collection is a tale in which a Chinese source is again molded not only to *kidan* convention but to the political climate of the moment. In introducing himself to the Dragon King, Yasusato presents himself as a Koyata-like figure, remiss in his devotion to the twin paths: "Since I was a youth I have forsaken the martial arts and set off down the path of letters." Neglecting the archery through which his celebrated ancestor made his name, he has instead sought to perfect his poetry. Unlike Koyata, however, Yasusato self-corrects and proves his mettle when it is put to the test. There is plenty of strange, swashbuckling adventure in his encounters at sea, but his moral shortcomings are not purged through bloodshed or grotesque humiliation. Instead, the collection concludes with a mood of unabashed wonder and celebration.

EPILOGUE

As the Tokugawa period receded into distant memory, Japanese writers rediscovered Pu Songling's tales with little or no awareness that their forebears had done so many decades earlier. At times they retrod the same ground, as when Koganei Kimiko rewrote "The Painted Skin" in a studied classical style that, while generally spare, at times unknowingly evokes Chūryō's adaptation as much as Pu's terser presentation. Others molded the collection to the contours of new cultural and intellectual currents, from literary nationalism to the grotesque and the absurd. A brief detour into these later responses in this epilogue reframes the terms of engagement with the text and the Chinese strange tale at large, setting the stage to reenter the world of their Edo rewritings from a novel perspective.

Meiji authors regularly couched their responses to *Liaozhai* using a distinctly modern vocabulary. Some, such as Kunikida Doppo, saw supernatural tales as reflecting a national "essence." "Sometimes I wonder how it is I love ghost stories so much," Doppo mused shortly before his death in 1908. "Chinese ghost stories especially are unrivalled for their sheer eccentricity of thinking. We Japanese (*wa ga kokujin*) cannot compete." Strange tales, he concluded, represent "the most extreme manifestation" of a people's (*minzoku*) imagination, as well as their sense of humor, and "a people who don't talk about demons, ghosts, and the supernatural are a people just barely getting by, unable to see beyond mundane reality." Among the Chinese tales he so admired, *Liaozhai* was to him the pinnacle of achievement, imbued with "a richness and freshness of language that transcend the rest."[1]

During his travels on the continent in the spring of 1921, Akutagawa Ryūnosuke showed a similar determination to make sense of China through the lens of centuries-old literature, even in cosmopolitan Shanghai, where he spent the first segment of his journey. In this he was successful, albeit not in the way he had envisioned. In place of "Du Fu, Yue Fei, Wang Yangming, or Zhuge Liang"—his motley exemplars of the elegant, refined world of Chinese poetry and prose he had hoped to find—he found himself confronted instead at every turn with the "obscene, cruel, and greedy" world of *Jin Ping Mei* and *Precious Mirror for Ranking Flowers* (*Pinhua baojian*). Even at the temple of the city god, which he found suitably impressive, he still took recourse in fiction, writing that it was "just as though one were looking at the illustrations in books like *Liaozhai zhiyi* or [*Zi bu yu*]."[2]

Liaozhai was a touchstone for Akutagawa throughout his literary career. As a teenager he jotted down a number of ostensibly true strange tales in a notebook titled *Strange Tales of Jiao Tu* (*Shōzu shii*), and the short stories he wrote after achieving literary prominence are filled with many of the same characters as those of Pu: scholars and peasants, monks and sages, and the occasional supernatural creature. A number of his stories are, in fact, rewritings of *Liaozhai* tales. In "The Story of a Head That Fell Off" ("Kubi ga ochita hanashi," 1917), Akutagawa spins the grotesque conceit of "A Certain Man from Zhucheng" ("Zhucheng moujia")—a slight tale about a man who literally laughs his head off—into a commentary, alternately acerbic and moving, on the absurdity of

1. *Byōshōroku* (Notes from My Sickbed), in *Teihon Kunikida Doppo zenshū*, 9:68–69.

2. *Shanhai yūki* (Travels in Shanghai, 1921), in Akutagawa Ryūnosuke, *Akutagawa Ryūnosuke zenshū* (Iwanami shoten, 1977–78), 5:3–59. Akutagawa refers to *Zi bu yu* using its revised title *Xin qixie*. The travelogue was one in a series of four Akutagawa wrote during his travels in China, later published together under the title *Shina yūki* (Travels in China). A full translation by Joshua A. Fogel and Kiyoko Morita appears in *Chinese Studies in History* 30, no. 4 (Summer 1997): 10–55. William Hedberg has discussed the text from the perspective of its relationship with Akutagawa's interest in Chinese fiction and drama. See Hedberg, "Akutagawa Ryūnosuke's Uncanny Travels in Republican-Era China," *Japan Forum* 29, no. 2 (2016): 236–56.

war. "The Wine Worm" ("Shuchū"), published one year earlier, hews closely to the source tale by the same title (although perhaps not as closely as Akutagawa himself self-deprecatingly put it when he described the two as being "hardly any different"), but in addition to his characteristic attention to minute detail, Akutagawa shows a marked interest in *Liaozhai*'s use of appended commentary, concluding his version with three possible interpretations of the tale for the reader's consideration. Other stories borrow another of Pu's favored techniques, that of leaving the narrative unresolved. The final line of "Rashōmon," for example ("What became of the servant, nobody knew"), brings to mind that of "The Gentleman of Fengyang" ("But who was the beautiful girl? No one knew").

Above all, Akutagawa was drawn to the strain of resistance and subversion in *Liaozhai*, seeing Pu Songling as a kindred spirit, a fellow malcontent lobbing veiled critiques at contemporary politics and society. *Liaozhai* is often noted for its "trenchant social criticism," to borrow a phrase used by both Allan Barr and Wai-yee Li, with favorite targets including official corruption, injustice, and the inequities of an examination system that had repeatedly frustrated Pu Songling himself.[3] In a brief essay written not long before his departure for China, Akutagawa took his countrymen to task for failing to appreciate this satirical undercurrent in the collection. Seeing in Pu's denunciations of the Manchu authorities the same spirit of resistance as in *Los Caprichos*, Goya's late eighteenth-century series of satirical prints, Akutagawa offered his own satirical interpretation of an individual tale, reading "The Swordswoman" ("Xia nü")—the story of a young woman who avenges her falsely condemned father—as a veiled satire of the purported assassination of the Yongzheng emperor.[4]

Along with a fixation on the grotesque and the absurd, a similar satirical vein is among the defining characteristics of Akutagawa's own writing. While these qualities also run through large swaths of Edo popular literature, they are largely absent in the *kidan* strange tale. The distinction is evident in the way Akutagawa and Chūryō treat the *Liaozhai* tale

3. Barr, "The Later Classical Tale," 692; and Wai-yee Li, "Early Qing to 1723," in Kang-i Sun Chang and Stephen Owen, eds., *Cambridge History of Chinese Literature Volume 2: From 1375* (Cambridge: Cambridge University Press, 2010), 232.

4. Akutagawa, *Kottōkō*, in *Akutagawa Ryūnosuke zenshū*, 3:464–65.

"The Daoist Priest of Mount Lao." Both produced adaptations, and on the surface their versions bear some similarity to each other. Where Pu's protagonist, Wang, is the son of a prosperous family who aspires to become a Daoist sage but is humiliated in the process, Akutagawa and Chūryō both recast Wang as a humble provincial who, while humiliated during his naïve pursuit of sagehood, is ultimately vindicated. In the process, criticism is redirected toward his tormentors.

Akutagawa's version, titled "The Immortal" ("Sennin"), tells of a domestic servant named Gonsuke who walks into an Osaka job agency and tests the limits of their boilerplate guarantee ("We'll get you ANY job!") by demanding to apprentice as an immortal.[5] The proprietor is naturally caught off guard, but after consulting with the neighborhood doctor, whose cunning wife spies an opportunity for exploitation, he secures a position in the couple's household. For twenty years Gonsuke obligingly toils away, assured that when his indentureship is over he will learn the secret to becoming a sage. When the day comes and Gonsuke asks for his payout, the doctor's wife gestures toward a pine tree in the garden and orders him to begin climbing. As he reaches the top, she shouts for him to release his grip. Just as he appears poised to plunge to his death, he instead ascends into the heavens and disappears among the clouds. Where Akutagawa turns away from his *Liaozhai* source only in this final moment, after having depicted Gonsuke as a hapless, exploited fool throughout, Chūryō's "Master Kyūgan" veers in a different direction almost from the beginning, quickly diverting to another tale altogether (the similarly titled "The Daoist Priest"). The result is a narrative whose sharp edge is blunted, one in which satire gives way to didacticism as the predominant quality—a shift brought home by the moral redemption of Kyūgan's adversaries at the tale's conclusion.

Chūryō's apparent aversion to more sardonic, cutting fare did not preclude some measure of the irreverence and humor Doppo saw as essen-

5. The story is one of three Akutagawa wrote with the same title, the first in 1915, this one in 1922, the other undated. The 1922 story is reproduced in *Akutagawa Ryūnosuke zenshū*, 5:377–83. On the two dated stories and their relationship with *Liaozhai*, see Fujita Yūken, "*Ryōsai shii* no ichisokumen: toku ni Nihon bungaku to no kanren ni oite," in *Keiō gijuku sōritsu hyakunen kinen ronbunshū* (Keiō gijuku daigaku hōgakubu, 1958), 74–75.

tial to supernatural fiction. Certainly in giving free rein to his comic impulses in genres other than the *kidan*, he at times partook of the rich, frequently humorous tradition of *yōkai*—the diverse supernatural creatures of Japanese folklore. In fact, at the very moment that plans for *Tales from the Withering Wind* were taking shape, he collaborated with the artist Kitao Masayoshi on another piece, an illustrated collection titled *A Ghastly Picture-Book Classic* (*Ehon sangaikyō*, 1791) that presented a motley assortment of monsters—with each entry including an illustration, a brief description, and a comic verse by one of Chūryō's literary associates—many of which parodied, both visually and verbally, familiar creatures from folklore. The first hint of a similarly irreverent attitude toward his subject matter in *Tales from the Withering Wind* comes in the preface, where Chūryō repeatedly jests about his publisher's preoccupation with profitability and his hope that copies might fly off the shelves like leaves in the withering wind. Near the end of the preface, Chūryō combines these pleas with a close retreading of a line from the preface to Teishō's *A Garland of Stories*, looking backward at the very moment he looks forward to a broader shift wherein the *kidan* passed from the purview of *bunjin* literati like Teishō and Akinari into the hands of Edo authors less reluctant to recognize literature as a commercial product.

Although there are occasional moments of humor elsewhere in his collection, Chūryō's comic sensibility is most evident and sustained in his adaptation of "The Drinking Companion." Set near the village of Mama in Katsushika, the tale introduces an enthusiastic and prodigious drinker self-styled "Old Man Waterbird"—a playful reworking of the characters that make up one of Li Bai's pseudonyms, "the Sage amidst Wine."[6] Beneath walls adorned with famous verses on wine by Du Fu and Ōtomo no Tabito, the old man is endlessly at his cups, and when he retires for the evening his wife places an enormous ten-liter jug at his bedside to tide him over until morning. One night, after finding

6. The sobriquet Old Man Waterbird is formed by breaking the characters "wine" 酒 and "sage" 仙 into their left- and right-hand components: "water" 水 (氵), "bird" 鳥 (酉), "mountain" 山, and "man" 人 (亻). "Mountain man," a term denoting an ascetic or sage that was commonly used in literary pseudonyms, is translated for the sake of readability as "Old Man."

the jug unexpectedly empty, he lights a lamp and discovers a grimy-looking fellow passed out on the floor nearby. Momentary alarm gives way to mirth as it becomes apparent that the intruder is a tanuki disguised in human form. While the wife stifles her laughter with her sleeve, the old man gazes upon the creature in awe, marveling at its ability to polish off an entire jug of wine. He dotingly covers it with his own bedding.

When at length the tanuki comes to, it makes a frenzied effort to escape. The old man implores the creature not to be frightened, and the tanuki offers an apology—an impeccably polite one in spite of its hoarse voice and slurred speech—for having helped itself to the wine. The old man reassures the tanuki that far from being angry, he is delighted to have found his match in capacity for drink. Laughing, he invites the creature to call at his house whenever he pleases. They become fast friends and regular drinking companions, and the tanuki is able to repay the old man's kindness by teaching him secret farming techniques that make him a wealthy man. Some time later, when marauding soldiers appear at the old man's doorstep, the tanuki gathers a group of his friends and leads the old man and his family to safety. Apart from this sudden intrusion of violence at the very end—a test that serves as evidence of the depth of their friendship—the tone is primarily comic and lighthearted throughout. At least in this tale, the unexpected encounter with the supernatural is a benign one.

The scene in which the pair seals their friendship is also the comedic high point of the tale. The day after their initial encounter, the tanuki saunters up to the old man's door in a shabby pair of formal trousers, doing his very best to appear respectable. As inhibitions are washed away by cup after cup of wine, the old man asks his guest to provide some entertainment for him, his wife, and their servants using his shape-shifting abilities. The tanuki, mildly offended by the suggestion, proceeds to deliver a humorous speech in which he expounds on the differences between foxes, which are skilled at shape-shifting, and his own more humble species, which is not. This extended monologue constitutes a sort of comic parody of the scholarly disquisitions favored by the *kidan* genre—the tanuki draws on a range of classic texts, from the *Baopuzi* and the *Taiping guangji* to Kaibara Ekiken's *Yamato honzō* (A Japanese Materia Medica,

1709)—and can be further seen as a knowing nod to Pu Songling's tale, in which it is a fox in the role of drinking companion:

> Foxes and tanuki have been spoken of together since ancient times. Yet when a fox has lived a thousand years it transforms into a seductress, and at a hundred it takes the form of a beautiful maiden. It produces fire by striking its tail and assumes human form by placing a skull upon its head. A fox puts its ears to the ice before crossing a river, and in death it rests its head upon the hillside and shows compassion. All these things are written in ancient texts.[7]
>
> Foxes also throw themselves about on the coattails of mighty tigers and set the hundred beasts to flight. Their learning spans a wide range of texts—one once criticized Zhang Hua's abilities as a scholar—and their otherworldly nature allows them to communicate with the gods.[8] They work their way up to positions of the highest influence, where they deceive men and bring about their demise.
>
> We tanuki, on the other hand, are dimwitted creatures. We are unable to communicate with the gods, and we bring no harm to humans. We use abandoned fox dens as our own dwellings and wear people's old, discarded clothing. It's true that we change into human form, but we aren't especially skilled at it, and we certainly don't toy with people's hearts. Instead, we change our appearance the way I did last night and endure fresh pine needles for our trouble.[9]
>
> Really the only things we're particularly skilled at are expanding and contracting our testicles and drumming our bellies as an accompaniment

7. Similar descriptions of the lifecycle and capabilities of foxes appear in numerous Chinese sources, including the *Baopuzi* and the *Xuanzhong ji* (the latter nonextant, but cited in vol. 447 of the *Taiping guangji*). Kaibara Ekiken's *Yamato honzō* mentions the phenomenon of foxes listening to the ice on Lake Suwa in Shinano Province (modern-day Nagano Prefecture), as well as their reputed ability to produce fire by striking their tails. See Ekiken, *Yamato honzō* (Kyōto: Ono Zensuke, 1709), 16:19a.

8. The *Soushen ji* relates how the Jin scholar and statesman Zhang Hua, an early collector of tales of the strange, debated a fox that called upon him in the guise of a young scholar. Zhang Hua was suspicious of his guest's extensive learning, and after exposing the creature's true identity had it boiled alive. *Soushen ji* 18:421, in Kenneth DeWoskin and J. I. Crump, trans., *In Search of the Supernatural* (Stanford, CA: Stanford University Press, 1996), 216–18.

9. The smoke of green pine needles was used both to exorcise fox spirits and to drive the animals from their dens.

> for dance. Now, the art of expanding testicles is quite vulgar, but my belly-drumming has been celebrated in a verse by the monk Jakuren: *At an old temple, no one remains, neither the sound of the bell—only a tanuki beating the drum.* So, if you will indulge me, I shall perform.[10]

Seeming quite pleased with himself, the tanuki rubs his "sleek, furless gourd of a belly" and begins to beat an increasingly quick and lively rhythm. His audience is delighted at the novelty of this, and the old man works himself into a frenzy dancing, "reaching up toward the ceiling, then bending down to the ground, twisting around this way then that way, shouting vigorously all the while." Before long the entire group is doubled over in sidesplitting laughter.

While the story of Old Man Waterbird and his supernatural drinking companion complicates the picture of the *kidan* as a predominantly humorless genre, we are likely to find more subversive fare elsewhere. Unsurprisingly, the search for Pu Songling's social criticism and satirical edge in an Edo adaptation leads us to the unruly genre of the *kibyōshi* comic book and Bakin's 1797 adaptation *The Wag-Tale of a Celebrated Fool's Education*. Although couched in the mock-heroic language of didacticism—"The story may seem mere passing foolery," Bakin writes in the preface, "but even a cursory glance will provide moral guidance for a thousand years"—the tale is in fact a satirical send-up of flawed, over-indulgent parenting and naïve book-learning whose source is quickly recognizable as the *Liaozhai* story "The Bookworm."[11]

The action is set during the fifteenth-century reign of Ashikaga Yoshimasa, the shogun responsible for the building of Ginkakuji (the Temple of the Silver Pavilion). Kaneko ("Money Man") Tsukumo ("Ninety-Nine"), a moneylender from the Kyoto area, and his forty-year-old wife, Omomo ("One Hundred"), are childless and pray to various gods in hope

10. *Kogarashi zōshi*, in *MCS*, 180. The poem by Jakuren, a poet of the late Heian and early Kamakura periods, appears in the entry on tanuki in Terajima Ryōan's encyclopedia *Illustrated Account of the Three Realms in Japan and China* (*Wakan sansai zue*, 1712). See Shimada Isao, Takeshima Atsuo, and Higuchi Motomi, eds., *Wakan sansai zue* 6, in *Tōyō bunko* 466 (Heibonsha, 1987), 92.

11. *Oshiedori ahō no kōmyō*, in Seida, "Honkoku Kyokutei Bakin no kibyōshi (3)," 71.

of divine intervention. (The piece may have been conceived as a playful gift to Bakin's own wife, also named Omomo; the two had been married less than three years at the time and did not yet have a son, although one would be born within the year.) One day the couple's prayers are answered. A deity appears before Omomo in a dream, pulls thirty-two coppers from a string of one hundred (technically ninety-six under the standard system of tabulation), and hands them to her. In due course she gives birth to a son, whom she names Musoshirō ("Sixty-Four Boy").[12]

Musoshirō proves to be endowed with very limited natural abilities—he is, quite literally, not working with a full string of coins—but his coddling parents hire a tutor and pay strangers to lavish praise on his modest achievements. Consequently, he grows into a self-deluded fool, blissfully unaware of his own limitations. When his parents die, Musoshirō inherits their credit slips and learns that they can be used to exact payment. Amazed that just a few scraps of paper with writing on them can be converted into such large sums, he ponders the vast treasures that might lie hidden in books filled with page after page of words. He throws himself into reading. In a scene that humorously captures the gulf between his abilities and aspirations, he gathers up paper snow from a theatrical performance so that, in emulation of Sun Kang, he might read at night by the moonlight it reflects. Some time later, as he begins to run low on supplies, his neighbors play a trick on him by placing quantities of rice and miso atop his books while he is away. When he returns, he is delighted at this further evidence that books hold the answer to all of life's needs. He throws himself into reading with even more vigor in hopes that a beautiful woman might appear, too.

Then one day, as he uncomprehendingly leafs through the pages of yet another book, Musoshirō comes across an illustration of an attractive woman. He is smitten. Suddenly the woman materializes in the flesh before him, and the two are quickly married. After his bride fails to conceive

12. A mother's dream foreshadowing the conception and character of a child was a common conceit. According to popular legend, Li Bai's mother became pregnant with him after a dream in which she saw the white orb of Venus (*bai* meaning "white"). In a humorous vein more resonant with Bakin's piece, the mother of the farting man in Hiraga Gennai's *Hōhiron* (A Treatise on Farting, 1774) is said to have given birth after dreaming of a bellows. *Hōhiron*, in Nakamura Yukihiko, ed., *Fūrai Sanjin shū*, in *NKBT* 55 (Iwanami shoten, 1961), 237.

a child in their first year together, she eventually has to provide him a rudimentary sexual education, which she does with the help of a toy monkey that pounds rice with a pestle—filling in for the wagtail bird from which the deities Izanami and Izanagi learn the same.[13] In a few short months they have a son, Misojirō ("Thirty-Two Boy"). Misojirō makes up the missing thirty-two coppers, and Musoshirō is suddenly transformed into a competent, talented scholar. Yoshimasa hires him to prepare the official records of Ginkakuji and Kinkakuji (the Temple of the Golden Pavilion), and his masterly work earns him a post at the imperial academy.

Much as in "The Bookworm" itself, the lessons of Bakin's tale are partly sincere, partly tongue-in-cheek. At the same time that he satirizes parental indulgence, the primary focus is on the pitfalls of a certain kind of book learning. In this, the farcical elements of the source tale are taken to even greater heights, as Bakin constructs a *reductio ad absurdum* narrative of a young man completely absorbed in books, but foolishly and with no direction. The rewards of learning, he assumes, will fall in his lap, and reading is consequently undertaken not as a means of self-enrichment but in expectation of a straightforward payoff. And yet, in the central irony shared in both Pu and Bakin's versions of the story, the woman who ultimately guides the protagonist in the ways of the world is herself born of a book, and in spite of his deeply misguided motivations, persistence and devotion do indeed transform him into a worthy scholar.

Although historical settings, particularly in the *kibyōshi*, could be deployed to obscure commentary on the present—as seen in the previously mentioned pieces by Sanba, Harumachi, Kyōden, and others, whose targets ranged from Edo firefighters to bakufu policy and even a political assassination—there is little to indicate that Bakin chose to set his tale in the reign of Yoshimasa for such reasons. It is of course conceivable that he sought to critique a certain type of contemporary bourgeois household or the strictly utilitarian view of education he may have perceived among some of his contemporaries. However, the most compelling reason for his fifteenth-century setting appears simply to be the thematic suitability of

13. The *kometsukizaru* ("rice-pounding monkey") is a traditional Japanese toy that is operated by pulling a string.

the Golden and Silver Pavilions in a work about a family of moneylenders. If we are to find traces of *Liaozhai*'s more pointed satirical edge, we must continue our search.

This quest leads us back where we least expect it: the *kidan*. The remaining paragraphs advance a reading of Chūryō's rewriting of Pu Songling's "The Cricket" in *Tales from the Withering Wind* as a targeted satire of bakufu corruption and misrule in the author's own day, offering a rare complication—enabled by the same convention of historical distancing—to the complicity that otherwise pervades the genre. Remarkably, Chūryō's targets include none other than senior councilor Matsudaira Sadanobu, who was to become his employer just a few months later. It is a stunning act of resistance, well disguised but hard to deny in the face of compelling evidence. Even in the exceedingly cautious space of the *kidan* there was room for defiance, for the possibility of repurposing the forced submission of *mitate* as a weapon of resistance.

On the surface, there is little to suggest that the tale is anything other than innocuously didactic. The plainly descriptive title ("A Filial Son's Spirit Enters a Gamecock and Brings Fortune to His Parents") signals the dominant theme, and indeed filial piety emerges as the main focus in the second half of the tale, which builds to a tidy moralistic conclusion. The setting is the Kamakura shogunate under the early fourteenth-century regency of Hōjō Takatoki. Takatoki's enthusiasm for cockfighting has sent the whole of Japan into a frenzy as every corner of the land is scoured for birds to send to Kamakura. In the nearby Kanazawa domain, a loyal peasant named Yoji is determined to obey his lord's orders and supply a suitable gamecock that will fulfill his duty. Traveling all the way to the far shore of Edo Bay, he somehow manages to find a worthy specimen, but back home his eleven-year-old son Yonosuke frees the bird from its cage and releases it straight into the jaws of the neighbor's dog. When Yoji discovers this, he storms off in search of Yonosuke only to find the boy's lifeless body floating in a nearby well.

After a sleepless, grief-filled night, Yoji and his wife are startled by a fluttering of wings outside their gate the next morning. Miraculously, the bird has come back to life and darts about more vigorously than ever, kicking and clawing the dog to death when it attacks a second time. Yoji rushes off to present this rare treasure to the governor, who immediately sends it onward to Kamakura. Takatoki is pleased beyond measure, and Yoji is rewarded with a large sum of silver. The following night, Yonosuke appears to his parents in their dreams. He explains that after falling into the well he found himself in the underworld, where he was received by Enma, the king of hell. Impressed by the boy's filial pleas and his father's loyalty to his feudal lord, Enma cast the boy's spirit into the dead gamecock to allow him to honor his father. His mission achieved, Yonosuke's spirit has been replanted in his mother's womb. Yoji's wife later bears a son who resembles Yonosuke in every way, and the family prospers in the years that follow.

Chūryō's foregrounding of the virtues of loyalty and filial piety represents an important departure from "The Cricket," whose primary focus is on the hardships inflicted by oppressive rule, corruption, and the abuse of power. Set during the reign of the Xuande emperor (r. 1425–35), Pu's tale depicts a cascade of abuses that trickle down from the top as a consequence of a fervor for cricket-fighting at court. Officials at every level seek desperately to please their superiors with worthy crickets, which they obtain at great cost to those beneath them who are tasked with finding them. Even as Chūryō asserts a new theme in the second half of the tale, the first half retains his source's focus on unvirtuous rule, beginning with a learned exposition that details Takatoki's obsession with cockfighting and the ill it bodes for the state through reference to numerous precedents from Chinese and Japanese antiquity:

> We find in ancient texts that King Xuan of the Zhou took pleasure in cockfighting and had Ji Xingzi raise birds for him, while Emperor Xuanzong of the Tang, upon ascending to the throne, requisitioned a thousand gamecocks from throughout Chang'an.[14] In our land, too, it seems that from ancient times cockfights were held for entertainment at the imperial court on the occasion of the festival on the third day of the third month.[15]

14. The *Zhuangzi*, "Mastering Life" ("Da sheng"), tells the story of Ji Xingzi 紀渻子 (which Chūryō mistakenly renders as Ji Juanzi 紀涓子) readying gamecocks for King Xuan. Xuanzong's passion for cockfighting is observed in the *Xin Tang shu*, books 34 and 81, among other sources. The demand for fit specimens is said to have driven the price sky-high, creating a bubble that bankrupted families in the process.

15. In China, cockfights were held during the Cold Food Festival (*hanshi*) in early spring. On this continental model, fights were held at the Heian court as part of the

Yet surpassing all others in his devotion to the sport was the Sagami lay monk Takatoki. Once he saw a pack of dogs attacking each other in the courtyard, and, finding it exciting, from then on he took pleasure only in dogfighting. Some time later he discovered the joys of cockfighting, too, and came to adore the sport down to the very marrow of his bones. Orders were sent out to governors and administrators in the provinces, who sought gamecocks through the levy of taxes and tribute and by issuing requests to wealthy and high-ranking families. In this way they raised ten birds here, twenty there, and sent every last one off to Kamakura.

This being no passing fancy on Takatoki's part, the number of gold-beaked, iron-spurred cocks at his command reached four or five thousand.[16] As there was little space available at his residence, a well-situated plot of land was set aside elsewhere and given the name Cock-Fighting Field.[17] Bouts were held there twelve times a month.

"Ah, what an exciting spectacle!" declared those little given to introspection. "It is no different from fighting in actual battle." They looked on with delight.

Those of a more thoughtful persuasion furrowed their brows. Among them was Nakanori, Deputy Commissioner of the Ministry of Punishments, a Confucian scholar of the Southern Fujiwara. Hearing of these events, he spoke as follows:

"Long ago in China, during the rule of the Zhou, Ji Pingzi and Earl Zhao of the Hou pitted their gamecocks against each other in a fight. The Ji spread mustard powder on the wings of their bird, so that it would get into the eyes of that of the Hou. The Hou fitted their bird with metal spurs, scheming to win the fight in that way. Through this a lasting enmity was born. Thus we find written in the *Huainanzi*: 'That from which disaster

---

festivities of the third day of the third month; the custom was later adopted among the warrior elite and spread to commoners in the early modern period.

16. Chūryō's language echoes the account of Emperor Xuanzong's cockfighting tournaments in the Tang story "The Old Man of the Eastern Wall" ("Dongcheng laofu zhuan"), in *Taiping guangji*, vol. 485. A translation appears in Robert Joe Cutter, *The Brush and the Spur: Chinese Culture and the Cockfight* (Hong Kong: Chinese University Press, 1989), 97–103.

17. The name refers to an area outside the east gate of Tsurugaoka Hachiman Shrine said to have been the site for dogfights and cockfights held by Takatoki, although he was not the first to designate the location for such use. Miura, *Kamakura no chimei yurai jiten*, 141.

was born began with the foot of a cock; when it reached its greatest, it went so far as to destroy the state.'[18]

"Moreover, because Emperor Xuanzong of the Tang enjoyed cockfighting, the scholars of the day thought: 'Cocks signify the year of the cock, in which the emperor was born. Fighting symbolizes armed men and portends military action.' So it is written in *The Treatise on the Five Phases*.[19]

"When we carefully consider the examples of the past, we see that they have foretold the fall of the ruling house and the destruction of the state. The present obsession with the pastime is a sign that we are perched on the brink of disaster."[20]

Where Pu has been shown to have lifted many details about crickets and the occasional choice phrase from a late Ming guide to Beijing titled *A Brief Account of the Sights of the Capital* (*Dijing jingwu lüe*), which he edited into an abridged version of his own, Chūryō scours a wider range of texts for this exposition on the history of cockfighting and its often portentous significance.[21] Most notably, he draws liberally and at times verbatim from the *Taiheiki*, the text that established the image of Takatoki as an archetype of the unvirtuous tyrant—a debauched and mentally unstable ruler with a weakness for pleasures of the flesh, including drink. In one well-known episode, a serving girl peers through a crack in the door and sees Takatoki asleep, surrounded by a multitude of demonic drinking companions. When the lamps are lit, all that remains is a mess of bird and animal tracks. A Confucian scholar named Nakanori declares this to portend the fall of the state. Takatoki subsequently descends into greater depths of hedonism. After witnessing a pack of dogs tear at each other in his courtyard, he acquires an enthusiasm for dogfighting that

18. Versions of the story of the Ji and the Hou are told in sources including the *Shiji*, book 33, and the *Huainanzi*, book 18. A translation of the latter may be found in John S. Major et al., trans., *The Huainanzi: A Guide to the Theory and Practice of Government in Early Han China* (New York: Columbia University Press, 2010), 740, where the characters 郈氏介其鷄 are interpreted to mean "the Hou armored their gamecock"; however, another interpretation of this line is "the Hou put mustard-seed on their gamecock," in line with the *Shiji* version. Ji Pingzi is not to be confused with Ji Xingzi.

19. These lines are from book 34 of the *Xin Tang shu*, known as *The Treatise on the Five Phases* (*Wuxing zhi*), 10b–11a. Xuanzong was born in 685, the year of the cock.

20. *Kogarashi zōshi*, in *MCS*, 196–97.

21. Barr, "Pu Songling and *Liaozhai Zhiyi*," 278–79.

"penetrated to the very marrow of his bones." Dogs are requisitioned through taxes and requests to prominent families, and governors and administrators across Japan raise ten dogs here, twenty there, sending the pampered animals off to Kamakura in litters. Soon they reach four or five thousand in number, and twelve days of every month are specified for fights. Some share in Takatoki's delight, while others of more thoughtful persuasion despair over the grotesque spectacle.[22]

Following the introduction, Chūryō's narrative turns to the disastrous effects of Takatoki's actions on the nearby Kanazawa domain. The domain's governor, Jōen, is determined to restore his honor after all of the birds he has submitted to Takatoki are killed in combat by those given by one of his rivals. Redoubling his efforts, he orders his retainer Agata Tannai to levy one bird from each household before the next competition. Failure to obey is to be severely punished. However, the countryside has already been thoroughly scoured for birds, and the few worthy ones that remain are being snatched up and sold for astronomical sums. The peasants of the domain resolve the matter by handing over inferior specimens at Tannai's office and ensuring his forbearance with bribes that he is more than happy to accept. The sole exception is Yoji. Revering Jōen as a living god, he wants more than anything to honor his demands. But he is faced with an impossible situation. In the end, he decides it is preferable to show up empty-handed rather than disrespect his lord by bribing Tannai. His strict sense of virtue earns him a violent beating. Only when his wife rushes in and slips several silver pieces into Tannai's sleeve do the blows stop. She drags Yoji home to tend to his wounds and desperately urges him to pay the bribe the next time.

When the day of the competition arrives and Jōen's birds are all defeated once more, Tannai's scheme is discovered. In a fit of rage, Jōen has him executed. Jōen, however, is more distraught by having been deceived than with the hardships imposed on his people. Indeed, he issues another decree for birds and warns that any attempts at bribery or supplying inferior specimens will be severely punished. It is at this point that Yoji sets out on his ultimately successful mission to fulfill his duty as subject, and the tale shifts from one of corruption and misrule to one of filial piety.

22. Helen Craig McCullough, trans., *The Taiheiki: A Chronicle of Medieval Japan* (New York: Columbia University Press, 1959), 131–33.

Previous commentators have discerned a measure of political criticism in *Tales from the Withering Wind*. Tokuda Takeshi sees the present tale as a broadly conceived critique of the abuse of power, one that surpasses "The Cricket" in intensity but does not specifically target the Tokugawa regime.[23] Ishigami Satoshi advances more ambitious readings of several tales, detecting attacks on contemporary targets throughout Chūryō's collection. These readings can be oddly specific. The opening lines of the first tale, for example, with their evocative description of Kamakura's fall into disrepair centuries after its golden age, are read as a coded lament for the fading cultural efflorescence of 1780s Edo.[24] However, there is little to support such a reading. Premodern and early modern Japanese literature is filled with passages infused with the language of impermanence (*mujō*), and there is no evidence that Chūryō sought to encode a hidden message in his rather conventional contribution to this corpus.

Ishigami sees in several tales a condemnation not only of the Tokugawa regime but of the very feudal system on which its power rested. These include the tale of Takatoki and his unvirtuous underlings.[25] Again, however, no specific details are offered that might push such a reading beyond mere speculation. It is difficult to read the depiction of unvirtuous rule in and of itself as an act of political resistance, and the fact that multiple tales are viewed through the same lens—including those depicting Yoritomo and Imagawa Yoshimoto—points to a dogged determination to find hidden meaning no matter the evidence. In fact, as cautionary depictions of the abuse of power, the tales in question are more readily seen as an extension of the collection's didactic tendencies. Taking this one step further, much as chapter 5 positioned the depiction of past warfare as an act of deference to contemporary authority, reminders of the misdeeds of the rulers of the past can be seen as a further manifestation of the *kidan*'s submission to Tokugawa power, painting the present in a positive light through implicit comparison with the past. In the absence of specific clues to suggest satirical intent, Tokugawa authorities

23. Tokuda, "*Kogarashi zōshi* to *Ryōsai shii*," 350–52.

24. Ishigami Satoshi, "*Kogarashi zōshi* ron: Morishima Chūryō no taisei hihan," *Okadai kokubun ronkō* 27 (1999): 13.

25. Ishigami, "*Kogarashi zōshi* ron," 15.

likely would have been sympathetic to a work that reminded readers of the merits of benevolent rule.

Still, supposing there were satirical intent encoded in the text, what form would it be likely to take? Early modern readers were trained to apprehend more than one meaning at once, looking beneath the surface of texts through the device of *mitate.* In this regard Ishigami is not off the mark in reading medieval Kamakura as present-day Edo, as this was among the most common substitutions, familiar from *Chūshingura* and many other works. However, more is required than this. Not every account of Kamakura is a veiled reference to Edo. Narrower practices that might guide our attention include the conventional use of certain historical figures as stand-ins for contemporary rulers and other officials, sometimes aided by the use of facial likenesses that associated them with popular actors of the day. Readers were also accustomed not only to Bunyanesque names like those of Bakin's numerical moneylending family, or Enjirō, the protagonist of Kyōden's *Playboy Roasted à la Edo* (whose name itself can be read to mean, more or less, "playboy"), or Yan Shang (lit. "Salt Trade"), the salt-merchant father in Nanpo's *Japan for This Guy!*, but also to names that evoked real-life personages, as in a 1780 satirical narrative detailing the harebrained schemes of one Haraga Bannai (representing Chūryō's mentor Hiraga Gennai) or an 1803 *kibyōshi* that featured a cunning Dutchman named Sunperupei (a comic garbling of the surname of the Swedish naturalist and Japanologist Carl Peter Thunberg).[26]

Approaching Chūryō's tale with such practices in mind draws out specific clues that lie hidden in plain sight, unnoted by previous commenters. Most intriguingly, alert readers would have observed a slight but perplexing naming discrepancy. Where the *Taiheiki* refers to Kanezawa Sadaaki, Takatoki's adviser and successor as regent, as "the lay monk Kanazawa no Taifu Sōken," in Chūryō's tale this has been changed to "the lay monk Kanazawa no Taifu Jōen." To account for this, it is necessary to read the story through the lens of one of the most frequently deployed historical substitutions: the use of Yoritomo and his successors, as

26. The satire of Gennai, titled (*Kūrai sensei*) *Honzō mōmoku*, is included in Mizuno Minoru et al., eds., *Sharebon taisei* (Chūō kōronsha, 1978–88), 10:169–79. On Sunperupei and Thunberg, see Screech, *Lens within the Heart*, 36.

well as the Hōjō regents, as stand-ins for the Tokugawa shoguns. Hōjō Tokimasa fills in for Tokugawa Ieyasu in puppet plays including *Three Generations in Kamakura* (*Kamakura sandaiki*, premiered 1781) and *A Mirror of Wise Women in Japan* (*Nippon kenjo kagami*, premiered 1794), while for later shoguns writers often turned to Yoritomo, as in several *kibyōshi* in which he stands in for Ieharu.[27] Takatoki was another proxy, representing the "dog shogun" Tsunayoshi in Chikamatsu's *The Sagami Lay Monk and the Thousand Dogs* as well as in a rehashing of the play in comic-book form published during Chūryō's lifetime.[28]

If we read Takatoki as a proxy for the shogun in Chūryō's tale, then Tannai and Jōen, as Takatoki's agents and the effective wielders of power, can be seen to represent Tanuma Okitsugu, who served as senior councilor through 1786, and Matsudaira Sadanobu, who succeeded him between 1787 and 1793. Tannai echoes Tanuma both in name and in deed, as he carries out Takatoki's agenda heartlessly and with flagrant corruption. Jōen, who relieves Tannai, evokes Sadanobu for similar reasons: he is equally ruthless but clamps down on corruption. (This tension is seen in the fact that while Yoji is delighted by Jōen's straightforwardness, his fellow peasants resent his crackdown on bribery.) Lest we remain unconvinced of this subtext to the tale, we have as evidence Chūryō's change of "Sōken" to "Jōen"—the only alteration he makes to the names and titles he borrows from the *Taiheiki*. The first character of Jōen's name, *jō* 定, is the "Sada" of Sadanobu.

However tantalizing, one solitary act of resistance does not necessitate a reevaluation of the *kidan*'s broader deference to authority. On the contrary, it is the exception that underscores the rule that, by and large, the Japanese strange tale positions the conflict and unvirtuous rulers of the

27. In a 1788 *kibyōshi* by Koikawa Harumachi, Yoritomo orders Yoshitsune on a mission of subjugation to the northern frontier, where they establish a kingdom whose policies can be seen to satirize those of the bakufu under Ieharu. In Kinkō and Kyōden's *A Mirror of History in Black and White*, the work that resulted in punishment for both men, the stand-in for Ieharu is an imaginary tenth-generation Kamakura shogun. For the most extensive discussion of the former piece, see Uda Toshihiko, "Kibyōshi ni okeru Roshia sono ta," *Edo bungaku* 32 (June 2005): 136–46.

28. A discussion of the comic-book rewriting, titled *Musume katakiuchi jōdai-some* (1775), appears in Tanahashi Masahiro, *Kibyōshi sōran*, in *Nihon shoshigaku taikei* 48 (Seishōdō shoten, 1986–2004), 1:40–43.

past as foils to the peace, prosperity, and moral rightness of the present. Even in this momentary departure from the rule, the genre's essential conservatism reasserts itself as the narrative marches toward its denouement, with its celebration of loyalty and filial piety. Such camouflaging of the satirical subtext is to be expected in an age when more transparent acts of political resistance invited draconian punishment, and in the hands of a man who would, just a few months after the tale appeared in print, take up employment under one of the targets of his satire. Chūryō's caution is such that he is unlikely to have risked incurring the regime's ire; one recalls Swift's oft-cited metaphor of satire as "a sort of glass wherein beholders do generally discover everybody's face but their own."[29]

Yet the reflection is there, however faint. Through the veneer of performed submission, we can glimpse subversive intent that complicates received narratives of resistance as an act that simmered upward from the lower classes. Chūryō was far from an ordinary townsman or a disaffected, low-ranking samurai, especially at the time he wrote this tale. Had he turned out the piece a decade or two earlier, we might dismiss it as a youthful indiscretion—perhaps not so dissimilar to the (unpublished) comic sketch of a daimyō attributed to Sadanobu himself.[30] But Chūryō's career was near its zenith in the early 1790s, as he navigated in and around the very highest reaches of the bakufu regime. This was an act of resistance from *within*, one that points to hidden stresses and fault lines in the edifice of power. Other writers may have feared similarly deviating from the script, but we may surmise that beneath the placid surface they too harbored a complicated mixture of conflicting sentiments and impulses, even, at times, questioning the moral legitimacy of the regime itself.

29. From the beginning of the author's preface to *The Battle of the Books* (1697). In Angus Ross and David Woolley, eds., *Jonathan Swift: The Major Works* (Oxford: Oxford University Press, 2003), 1.

30. While Mori Senzō, the first to describe the contents of Sadanobu's unpublished manuscript, speculated that he had written it at the age of fourteen or fifteen, Haruko Iwasaki has offered compelling evidence that it was in fact completed about a decade later. See Iwasaki, "Portrait of a Daimyō," 8.

Character List

"Aiqing zhuan" 愛卿傳
Akutagawa Ryūnosuke 芥川龍之介
"Amakusa nada ni haku-su" 泊天草灘
Arakida Reijo 荒木田麗女
Asai Ryōi 浅井了意
"Asaji ga yado" 浅茅が宿
Asano Baidō 浅野梅堂
"Ashininai no okina no hanashi" 蘆擔翁話

Bai jia xing 百家姓
Bai Juyi 白居易
"Bai qiulian" 白秋練
Baien nikki 梅園日記
Baijuken Sukeemon 梅寿軒助右衛門
baishi (J. haishi) 稗史
Bai-shi wenji 白氏文集
Bankoku shinwa 萬國新話
Banqiao zaji 板橋雜記
Baopuzi 抱樸子
Baoweng Laoren 抱甕老人
Bencao gangmu 本草綱目
Bi Yi'an 畢怡庵
biji (J. hikki) 筆記
biji xiaoshuo (J. hikki shōsetsu) 筆記小説
"Boxing nü" 博興女
Bun'eidō Hōgusai 文栄堂反古斎
bunbu nidō 文武二道
Bunbu nidō mangoku dōshi 文武二道万石通
bunjin 文人
Bunrui hakusai shomoku tsūran 分類舶載書目通覧
"Buppōsō" 仏法僧
Byōshōroku 病牀録

Caomuzi 草木子
"Chang hen ge" 長恨歌
"Chang'e" 嫦娥
Chanmen baoxun 禅門寶訓
Chayu kehua 茶餘客話
Chen Mengrong 陳孟榮
Chen Yaowen 陳耀文
Cheng weishi lun 成唯識論
Chibei outan 池北偶談
Chidōkan 致道館
Chikamatsu Monzaemon 近松門左衛門
Chiwen lu 咫聞錄
Chōkō ian 聽訟彙案
Chŏndŭng sinhwa kuhae (J. *Sentō shinwa kukai*) 剪燈新話句解
Chosakudō haisho mokuroku 著作堂俳書目録
chuanqi 傳奇
Chuogeng lu 輟耕錄
Chūsei nidenki 中世二傳奇

(*Kanadehon*) *Chūshingura* (仮名手本)
忠臣蔵
"Cui Meng" 崔猛
"Cuzhi" 促織

"Da sheng" 達生
Dahui Zonggao 大慧宗杲
Daishin manshō 代紳漫鈔
Daisō 大惣
Dan Minglun 但明倫
"Da'nan" 大男
dangibon 談義本
Danqian zonglu 丹鉛總錄
"Daoshi" 道士
Dazai Osamu 太宰治
Dazai Shundai 太宰春台
Detai 得泰
detchōsō 粘葉装
Dijing jingwu lüe 帝京景物略
Doi Gōga 土井聱牙
"Dongcheng laofu zhuan" 東城老父傳
Dongpo quanji 東坡全集
Dōyū Koji 道祐居士
dōza 銅座
Du Fu 杜甫
"Dugu sheng guitu nao meng" 獨孤生
歸途鬧夢
"Dugu Xiashu" 獨孤遐叔
Dunbi suiwen lu 盾鼻隨聞錄

Edo meisho zue 江戸名所圖會
Edo-umare uwaki no kabayaki 江戸生艶
気樺焼
Ehon sangaikyō 画本纂怪興
Erke Pai'an jingqi 二刻拍案驚奇
Ershi lu 耳食錄

"Fan Juqing jishu sisheng jiao" 范巨卿雞
黍死生交
Feng Menglong 馮夢龍
Feng Zhenluan 馮鎮巒
"Fengxian" 鳳仙
"Fengyang shiren" 鳳陽士人
Fūgetsu Shōzaemon 風月庄左衛門
Fujiwara Sukeyo 藤原佐世
fukkoku 覆刻
Furukawa Koshōken 古川古松軒
Fushimiya Zenroku 伏見屋善六
Futian ji 甫田集

Geien nisshō 秇苑日渉
Gekka seidan 月下清談
Gekkōtei Bokusen 月光亭墨僊
Geng qi you ci li 更豈有此理
Genji monogatari 源氏物語
Genji zōho goshojaku mokuroku 元治増補
御書籍目録
Gōga-ō hissu shomoku 聱牙翁必須書目
gōkan 合巻
"Gongsun Jiuniang" 公孫九娘
Gozan-ban 五山版
guai (J. kai) 怪
Guang xieshi 廣諧史
Guang xinwen 廣新聞
Guangqun fangpu 廣羣芳譜
Gufu yuting zalu 古夫于亭雜錄
"Gui ku" 鬼哭
Gujin shuohai 古今説海
Gujin tushu jicheng 古今圖書集成
Gujin xiaoshuo 古今小說
Gujin yan 古今諺
Guwang tingzhi 姑妄聽之
Guwen Xiaojing 古文孝經
Guwen Xiaojing Kong-shi zhuan 古文孝經
孔氏傳

Hakurai shomoku 舶來書目
Hakusai shomoku 舶載書目
Hakusai shomoku tsūran 舶載書目通覧
Han Shan 寒山
(*Kokon kidan*) *Hanabusa sōshi* 古今奇談英
草紙
Hanareya kenmonroku 離屋見聞録
Hanareya sensei bunshō 離屋先生文抄
Hanareya zōsho mokuroku 離屋蔵書目録
Hanjo 班女
hanshibon 半紙本
Hattori Nankaku 服部南郭
Hattori Shukushin 服部叔信
Hayashi Jussai 林述斎

Hayashi Razan 林羅山
Hedong ji 河東記
Heike monogatari 平家物語
"Hengniang" 恆娘
Hirade Jun'eki 平出順益
Hiraga Gennai 平賀源内
Hirose Kyokusō 広瀬旭荘
(*Kan'on kidan*) *Hitofutagusa* 寒温奇談一二草
Hitokotogusa 鄙都言種
(*Kokon kidan*) *Hitsujigusa* 古今奇談莠句冊
Hogo no uragaki 反古のうらがき
Hōhiron 放屁論
Hokusō sadan 北窓瑣談
Hon'ami Kōetsu 本阿弥光悦
Honchō Gu Sho shinshi 本朝虞初新誌
Hongloumeng 紅樓夢
(*Kūrai sensei*) *Honzō mōmoku* 空來先生翻艸盲目
Hōseidō Kisanji 朋誠堂喜三二
Hosono Yōsai 細野要斎
Hotta Masaatsu 堀田正敦
"Hu meng" 狐夢
Hu Yinglin 胡應麟
"Hua ma" 畫馬
"Hua pi" 畫皮
Huachanshi suibi 畫禪室隨筆
Huainanzi 淮南子
Huaixi zashi 槐西雜志
Huangchao jingshi wenbian 皇朝經世文編
Huangdi neijing 黃帝内經
Huangdi neijing Suwen zhuzheng fawei (J. *Kōtei naikyō Somon chūshō hatsubi*) 黄帝内經素問註證發微
Huanghua jiwen 皇華紀聞
Huaniao chunqiu 花鳥春秋
hyakki yagyō 百鬼夜行
hyakumantō darani 百万塔陀羅尼
hyōryūki 漂流記

Ichiwa ichigen 一話一言
Ihara Saikaku 井原西鶴
Ikari Teikyo 猪狩貞居
Im Ki 林芑
imayō 今様
Inaka shibai 田舎芝居
Inō mononoke roku 稲生物怪録
Ise monogatari 伊勢物語
Ishibe Kinkō 石部琴好
Ishii Shōsuke 石井庄助
Ishikawa Masamochi 石川雅望
Isshiki Tokimune 一色時棟
Isson sōsho (Ch. *Yicun congshu*) 佚存叢書
Itami Chin'en 伊丹椿園
Itō Jinsai 伊藤仁斎

"Jasei no in" 蛇性の淫
Ji Yun 紀昀
Jian du suibi 檢蠹隨筆
jianben 監本
Jiandeng conghua 剪燈叢話
Jiandeng xinhua 剪燈新話
Jiandeng yuhua 剪燈餘話
Jianwen lu 見聞錄
Jieziyuan huapu 芥子園畫譜
jigoku meguri 地獄めぐり
Jin Ping Mei 金瓶梅
Jin shishuo 今世説
Jinghua shuiyue 鏡花水月
Jinghua yuan 鏡花緣
Jingshi tongyan 警世通言
Jingu qiguan 今古奇觀
Jinshi congcan 近事叢殘
Jippensha Ikku 十返舎一九
jitsuroku 実録
Jiu Tang shu 舊唐書
"Jiuyou" 酒友
Jiyuan ji suoji 寄園寄所寄
jōruri 浄瑠璃
Jūtei goshojaku mokuroku 重訂御書籍目録
Juyi lu 居易錄

kabusebori 覆せ彫り (also 被せ彫り)
Kadōkun 家道訓
Kaibara Ekiken 貝原益軒
kaidan 怪談
Kaidan zensho 怪談全書
Kaigai ibun 海外異聞
Kaihō nissatsu 懐寶日札
kaihōgyō 回峰行

kaii shōsetsu 怪異小説
Kaii zenseki yawa 怪異前席夜話
kaimami 垣間見
Kairoku 海録
kakikudashi 書き下し
Kakinegusa 垣根草
Kamakura sandaiki 鎌倉三代記
Kamiya Kizaemon 神谷喜左衛門
kanazōshi 仮名草子
kanbun 漢文
Kaneuchi Kakuzō 金内格三
Kangxi zidian 康熙字典
Kankei satetsu (or *Kankei sōtetsu*) 寒檠璅綴
Kankyō manpitsu 感興漫筆
Kanō Motonobu 狩野元信
kanpan 官版
Kansan yoroku 閑散餘録
kanshibun 漢詩文
Kantei Denshō 関亭傳笑
kanzen chōaku 勧善懲悪
Kaopan yushi 考槃餘事
Karaito sōshi 唐糸草子
Kara nishiki 唐錦
"Kashiwagi" 柏木
Kasshi yawa 甲子夜話
Kasuga-ban 春日版
Katō Enao 加藤枝直
Katsukawa Shunzan 勝川春山
Katsuragawa Hoshū 桂川甫周
Katsushika Hokusai 葛飾北斎
"Kawa hitoe" 皮一重
Kawachiya Kihē 河内屋喜兵衛
Keiho yūtetsu 瓊浦又綴
Keiho zattetsu 瓊浦雑綴
Keisai Eisen 渓斎英泉
kenchō 見帳
"Kibitsu no kama" 吉備津の釜
kibyōshi 黄表紙
kidan 奇談
Kikuchi Sankei 菊池三渓
"Kikuka no chigiri" 菊花の約
Kimura Mokurō 木村黙老
Kinoshita Jun'an 木下順庵
Kinshūdan 錦繍段
Kita Seiro 北静廬
Kitagawa Utamaro 喜多川歌麿
Kitamura Intei 喜多村筠庭
Kitamura Kigin 北村季吟
Kitao Masayoshi 北尾政美
Kitao Shigemasa 北尾重政
Kitsune no kawagoromo 狐の裘
kiyogaki 清書
Kiyū shōran 嬉遊笑覧
Kizanroku sōkō 帰山録草稿
Kōda Rohan 幸田露伴
Kodera Gyokuchō 小寺玉晁
Koga Tōan 古賀侗庵
Koganei Kimiko 小金井喜美子
(*Hakushō kidan*) *Kogarashi zōshi* 拍掌奇談凩草紙
Kogetsushō 湖月抄
Koikawa Harumachi 恋川春町
Koitsu wa Nippon 此奴和日本
kokatsuji-ban 古活字版
Kokinshū 古今集
kōkishin 好奇心
Kokon chomonjū 古今著聞集
kokubungaku 国文学
Kokubyaku mizukagami 黒白水鏡
Kokuei shū (also *Kurokage shū*) 黒影集
Komiyama Fūken 小宮山楓軒
Kōmō zatsuwa 紅毛雑話
Konohana zōshi 梅冊紙
(*Katakiuchi*) *Kōsei kidan* 復讐曠世奇談
"Kosei kirei enshō o uttauru hanashi" 狐精鬼霊寃情を訴ふる話
Kotobuki shioya no konrei 寿塩商婚礼
Kottōkō 骨董羹
"Kubi ga ochita hanashi" 首が落ちた話
kundoku 訓読
Kunikida Doppo 國木田独歩
kunqu 昆曲
Kuranari Ryūsho 倉成龍渚
Kutsuki Masatsuna 朽木昌綱
Kyan taiheiki mukō hachimaki 侠太平記向鉢巻
Kyokutei Bakin 曲亭馬琴
Kyokutei denki hanakanzashi 曲亭傳奇花釵児
Kyokutei zōsho mokuroku 曲亭蔵書目録

"Kyūganbō ga senjutsu fumin o taburakasu koto" 久含坊が仙術富民を誑かす話
Kyūkeisōdō zuihitsu 九桂草堂随筆

"Laoshan daoshi" 勞山道士
"Le Zhong" 樂仲
"Leigong bei dai" 雷公被紿
Li Changqi 李昌祺
Li Chaowei 李朝威
Li Yu 李漁
"Lianhua gongzhu" 蓮花公主
"Lianxiang" 蓮香
Liaozhai zhiyi 聊齋誌異
Lienü zhuan 列女傳
Liezi 列子
"Lin shi" 林氏
Ling Mengchu 凌濛初
Liu Yi zhuan 柳毅傳
Liuhe neiwai suoyan 六合内外瑣言
Liutao 六韜
Liuya waibian 柳崖外編
Liuyanzhai biji 六研齋筆記
Liuyu yanyi 六諭衍義
"Longfei xianggong" 龍飛相公
Lu Mingzhai 陸明齋
Lu Xun 魯迅
Lü Zhan'en 呂湛恩
Luanyang xiaoxia lu 灤陽消夏錄
Lunyu jijie 論語集解
Lunyu yishu 論語義疏
Luo Guanzhong 羅貫中

"Maiyoulang duzhan huakui" 賣油郎獨占花魁
"Manju ga shīkō haha no kingoku o manukareshimuru koto" 満珠が至孝母の禁獄を遁れしむる話
Man'yōshū 萬葉集
Maruya Genbē 丸屋源兵衛
Matsudaira Sadanobu 松平定信
Matsuo Bashō 松尾芭蕉
Matsura Seizan 松浦静山
Meirindō 明倫堂
Mengqiu 蒙求
Mimeyori sōshi 美目与里艸紙
Minagawa Kien 皆川淇園
Minamikawa Kinkei 南川金渓
Ming shi gao 明史稿
Mingshan cang 名山藏
Mingshishuo xinyu 明世説新語
misemono 見世物
mitate 見立て
Miura Baien 三浦梅園
(*Konko kitan*) *Miyamagusa* 今古奇譚深山草
Mochi suolu 墨池瑣錄
Momijiyama Bunko 紅葉山文庫
Momokusa 百草
monogatari 物語
Mori Ōgai 森鴎外
Mōri Takasue 毛利高標
Morishima Chūryō 森島中良
"Motomezuka zokusetsu no idō tsuka no kami no rei mondō no koto" 求冢俗説の異同冢の神靈問答の話
Motoori Norinaga 本居宣長
Motoori Ōhira 本居大平
Mozu no kusaguki 百舌の草茎
"Muchū no kai sannin kizu o etaru koto" 夢中の怪三人疵を得たる話
"Mudan deng ji" 牡丹燈記
mujō 無常
Mukai Genchū 向井元仲
Murase Kōtei 村瀬栲亭
Musume katakiuchi jōdai-some 娘敵討上代染

Nagasaki kaisho 長崎会所
Nagasaki meishō zue 長崎名勝圖繪
Nagata Chōbē 永田調兵衛
Nakagawa Tadateru 中川忠英
Nan no tame ka wa 難廼為可話
Nansō Satomi hakkenden 南総里見八犬傳
Narushima Ryūhoku 成島柳北
negumichō 直組帳
Nemoto Bui 根本武夷
Nenashigusa 根南志具佐
Nihon-koku genzaisho mokuroku 日本國見在書目録

ninjōbon 人情本
Nippon kenjo kagami 日本賢女鑑
Nise Murasaki Inaka Genji 偐紫田舎源氏
Niyūdō 二酉洞
Noda Tekiho 野田笛浦

Ogyū Hokkei 荻生北渓
Ogyū Sorai 荻生徂徠
Oka Hakku 岡白駒
Okada Shinsen 岡田新川
Okajima Kanzan 岡島冠山
Oku no hosomichi 奥の細道
Ōmugaeshi bunbu no futamichi 鸚鵡返文武二道
"Ono no Takamura" 小野篁
Ōnoya Sōhachi 大野屋惣八
ōraimono 往来物
Oshibana おし花
Oshiedori ahō no kōmyō 押絵鳥癡漢高名
oshikirichō 押切帳
Ōta Nanpo 大田南畝
Otogibōko 伽婢子
otogizōshi 御伽草子
Ōtomo no Yakamochi 大伴家持
Ōtsuki Gentaku 大槻玄澤
Ozaki Kōyō 尾崎紅葉
Ozaki Masayoshi 尾崎雅嘉

Pai'an jingqi 拍案驚奇
Paimen lu 排悶錄
Peiwen yunfu 佩文韻府
Pengfu bian 捧腹編
Pinhua baojian 品花寶鑑
Pinzi jian 品字箋
"Pipa xing" 琵琶行
Pu Songling (Liuxian) 蒲松齡 (留仙)
qi (J. ki) 奇

"Qian xiucai cuozhan fenghuang chou" 錢秀才錯占鳳凰儔
Qianbainian yan 千百年眼
qianjie 遷界
Qianque leishu 潛確類書
Qianzi wen 千字文
"Qin xia" 禽俠
Qinding sijing 欽定四經
"Qingfeng" 青鳳
Qingketing 青柯亭
Qingshi 情史
"Qisongyuan nong jia cheng zhen" 七松園弄假成真
"Qiu Daniang" 仇大娘
Qiudeng conghua 秋鐙叢話
Qiuping xinyu 秋坪新語
Qixiu leigao 七修類稿
Qu You 瞿佑
Quan Tang shi 全唐詩
Qunshu zhiyao 群書治要
Qunsui lu 群碎錄

Rai San'yō 賴山陽
Rai Shunsui 賴春水
rakusatsuchō 落札帳
"Rashōmon" 羅生門
Reishū yoshu 蛎洲餘珠
Rizhi lu 日知錄
Ruan Yuan 阮元
"Ruiyun" 瑞雲
Rulin waishi 儒林外史
Rushi wowen 如是我聞
Ryūkyū banashi 琉球談
Ryūtei Senka 笠亭仙果
Ryūtei Tanehiko 柳亭種彦

Saeda Shigeru 小枝繁
Saga-bon 嵯峨本
Sagami nyūdō senbiki no inu 相模入道千疋犬
sairai shomoku 齎来書目
Saiyū zakki 西遊雜記
Saiyūki 西遊記
Sakai Tadahiro 酒井忠寛
sakoku 鎖国
San'yō Genkitsu 三要元佶
Sanguo yanyi 三國演義
Sanguozhi 三國志
Sanguozhi pinghua 三國志平話
Sanlüe 三略

Santō Kyōden 山東京傳
Sanyan 三言
Sanyan erpai 三言二拍
Sarashime 晒女
Sawa Tansai 佐羽淡斎
Sawada Issai 澤田一斎
Segawa Kikunojō 瀬川菊之丞
Seita Tansō 清田儋叟
Sekijichō 惜字帖
"Sennin" 仙人
setsuwa 説話
Shanhai yūki 上海游記
"Shanhu" 珊瑚
sharebon 洒落本
"Shi yan" 詩讖
Shibata Tenma 柴田天馬
Shichikei Mōshi kōbun hoi 七經孟子考文補遺
Shifa yuanliu 詩法源流
(*Kokon kidan*) *Shigeshige yawa* 古今奇談繁野話
shihan 私版
Shiji 史記
Shikitei Sanba 式亭三馬
Shina kidan shū 支那奇談集
Shina yūki 支那遊記
Shincho hyakushu 新著百種
Shinra Manzō 森羅萬象
Shinrashi 森羅子
Shinrotei 振鷺亭
Shinto Tōhon-ichi hikaechō 新渡唐本市控帳
Shinzō shojaku mokuroku 新增書籍目録
Shinzoku kibun 清俗紀聞
shirabyōshi 白拍子
"Shiramine" 白峯
Shisanjing zhushu 十三經注疏
Shishuo xinyu bu 世說新語補
Shitomi Kangetsu 蔀関月
Shoen ōkagami 諸艶大鑑
Shōhaku sairai shomoku 商舶載來書目
Shōheikō (Shōheizaka gakumonjo) 昌平黌 (昌平坂學問所)
shojaku motochō 書籍元帳
Shokusanjin zōsho mokuroku 蜀山人蔵書目録
Shomotsu aratameyaku 書物改役
Shōsetsu jii 小説字彙
Shōsetsu kigen 小説奇言
Shōsetsu seigen 小説精言
Shōsetsu suigen 小説粋言
Shōzu shii 椒圖志異
"Shu chi" 書痴
"Shu xi" 鼠戲
"Shuchū" 酒虫
Shugyōroku 修行録
Shuidong riji 水東日記
Shuihu houzhuan 水滸後傳
Shuihu zhuan 水滸傳
Shuofu 說郛
Shūsuien Shujin 秋水園主人
Shuyiji 述異記
sibu 四部
Siku quanshu 四庫全書
Siku quanshu tiyao 四庫全書提要
Siku quanshu zongmu tiyao 四庫全書總目提要
Siku weishou shumu tiyao 四庫未收書目提要
Sima Guang 司馬光
Sima Qian 司馬遷
Sōkan Sanjin 草官散人
Soushen ji 搜神記
Suminokura Soan 角倉素庵
Sun Zhu 孫洙
surimono 摺物
Suwen 素問
Suzuki Akira 鈴木朖
Suzuki Hakutō 鈴木白藤
Suzuki Tōya 鈴木桃野

Tachibana Nankei 橘南谿
Taiheiki 太平記
taiisho 大意書
Taiping guangji 太平廣記
Taiping qinghua 太平清話
Taiping yulan 太平御覽
tairai shomoku 帯来書目

"Taiyuan yu" 太原獄
Takebe Ayatari 建部綾足
(*Tōka no geboku*) *Tama no eda* 燈下戲墨玉之枝
Tama sudare 多満寸太礼
Tamakatsuma 玉勝間
Tamenaga Shunsui 為永春水
Tanaka Joan 田中恕庵
Tanaka Kōtarō 田中貢太郎
Tanki manroku 耽奇漫録
Tankikai 耽奇会
tanpen yomihon 短編読本
Tanuma Okitsugu 田沼意次
Tao Yuanming 陶淵明
Tao Zongyi 陶宗儀
Tawara Jinzaemon 田原仁左衛門
Ten'in Ryūtaku 天隠龍澤
Terasaki Reishū 寺崎蛎洲
Tianzhong ji 天中記
Tingyu jitan 聽雨紀談
(*Koto shinto*) *Tōhon ruisho kō* 古渡新渡唐本類書考
Tōhon'ya Seibē 唐本屋清兵衛
Tōjin yashiki 唐人屋敷
Tōkaidō Yotsuya kaidan 東海道四谷怪談
Tōkaidōchū hizakurige 東海道中膝栗毛
Tokō jii 徒杠字彙
Tokutai-sen hitsugo 得泰舩筆語
Tong ya 通雅
Tongzhitang jingjie 通志堂經解
Tosa Tsunetaka 土佐経隆
Tōyō Dekameron 唐様でかめろん
Tōyūki 東遊記
Tsubouchi Shōyō 坪内逍遥
Tsuga Teishō 都賀庭鐘
Tsuma gasane omoi no rangiku 棲重思乱菊
tsunogaki 角書き
Tsurezuregusa 徒然草
Tsuruya Nanboku 鶴屋南北
Tsusaka Tōyō 津阪東陽
Tsutaya Jūzaburō 蔦屋重三郎
tsūzoku 通俗
Tsūzoku Haimonroku 通俗排悶録
Tsūzoku Kokon kikan 通俗古今奇観
Tsūzoku Seisei kōgen 通俗醒世恒言
Tsūzoku sekijō kien 通俗赤縄奇縁
Tu Long 屠隆

Uchiike Nagatoshi 内池永年
Ueda Akinari 上田秋成
(*Kinko kidan*) *Ugetsu monogatari* 近古奇談雨月物語
Ukiyoburo 浮世風呂
ukiyoe 浮世絵
ukiyozōshi 浮世草子
"Unkon unjō o katatte hisashiki o chikau hanashi" 雲魂雲情を語つて久しきを誓ふ話
Unpukan Tenpo 雲府観天歩
Utagawa Toyohiro 歌川豊広

Vita Sexualis ヰタ・セクスアリス

wahon 和本
waka 和歌
Wakan sansai zue 和漢三才圖會
Wakoku Sangen 和刻三言
wakokubon 和刻本
wakokubon kanseki 和刻本漢籍
Wakuraba monogatari 邂逅物語
Wang Jian 王椷
Wang Peng 汪鵬
Wang Yangming 王陽明
Wang Yangming quanji 王陽明全集
Wang Zhuo 王晫
Wasōbyōe (also *Wasōbē*) 和荘兵衛
Wen Zhengming 文徵明
Wenhai pisha 文海披沙
Wenqi leilin 問奇類林
Wenxuan 文選
wenyan xiaoshuo 文言小説
Wubian tongjian 五編通鑑
wujing qishu 武經七書
Wumen huafang lu 呉門畫舫錄
Wumen huafang xulu 呉門畫舫續錄
Wuxing zhi 五行志
Wuzazu 五雜組

"Xia nü" 俠女
Xiangzhu Liaozhai zhiyi tuyong 詳註聊齋誌異圖詠
Xiangzu biji 香祖筆記
Xiaojing Zheng zhu 孝經鄭注
xiaoshuo (J. shōsetsu) 小說
Xichao leshi 熙朝樂事
Xie Zhaozhe 謝肇淛
Xieduo 諧鐸
Xieji bianfang shu 協紀辨方書
Xihu jiahua 西湖佳話
Xihu shiyi 西湖拾遺
Xihu zhiyu 西湖志餘
Xin qixie 新齊諧
Xin Tang shu 新唐書
Xingshi hengyan 醒世恆言
Xiqing sanji 西清散記
Xiying oulu 息影偶錄
Xiyou ji 西游記
Xuanzhong ji 玄中記
Xu shuofu 續説郛
Xude lu 畜德錄
Xue Yusi 薛漁思

Yamada Saburobē 山田三郎兵衛
Yamanoi Konron 山井崑崙
Yamato honzō 大和本草
Yamazaki Yoshishige 山崎美成
"Yang Dahong" 楊大洪
Yang Zhou 楊舟
Yanpu zaji 簷曝雜記
"Yanzhi" 臙脂
"Ye gou" 野狗
Yetan suilu 夜譚隨錄
Yi jing 易經
"Yi quan" 義犬
Yijiong baibian 翼駉稗編
Yilin fashan 藝林伐山
yishi shi 異史氏
Yiwen leiju 藝文類聚
Yoda Gakkai 依田學海
yōkai 妖怪
"Yokawa no kohijiri akuryō o gōbuku suru koto" 横河の小聖悪霊を降伏する話
yomihon 読本
Yomiuri shinbun 讀賣新聞
Yongzhuang xiaopin 涌幢小品
Youming lu 幽明錄
Youxianku 遊仙窟
Yu Chu xinzhi 虞初新志
Yu Hongjian 俞鴻漸
"Yu Jiang" 於江
Yu Liangfu 俞良甫
Yu saotou 玉搔頭
"Yu zhongcheng" 于中丞
Yuan Mei 袁枚
Yuanjian leihan 淵鑑類函
"Yuanyu" 冤獄
Yuchu xinzhi 虞初新志
Yue Fei 岳飛
Yuewei caotang biji 閱微草堂筆記
Yūkokushi 遊谷子
Yun Ch'un-nyŏn 尹春年
Yunjing 韻鏡
"Yūrei sho o bumo ni tsukawasu" 幽霊書を父母につかはす
Yushi mingyan 喻世明言
Yutang conghua 玉堂叢話
Yūzōkan 有造館

zenki yomihon 前期読本
Zhang Chao 張潮
"Zhang Cheng" 張誠
Zhanguo ce 戰國策
zhanhai 展海
"Zhao dajiangjun ci pilian guai" 趙大將軍刺皮臉怪
Zhao Mengfu 趙孟頫
Zhao Qigao 趙起杲
Zhao Yi 趙翼
Zhaoshibei 照世盃
Zheng shuofu 正説郛
Zhenguan zhengyao 貞觀政要
Zhengzi tong 正字通
"Zheyu" 折獄
Zhian zaji 芝庵雜記
Zhibuzuzhai congshu 知不足齋叢書
"Zhicheng" 織成

zhiguai 志怪
Zhinang 智囊
Zhiwen lu 咫聞錄
Zhu Liuzhu 朱劉諸
Zhuzi shiji 朱子實紀
Zhu'an Shigui 竹庵士珪
Zhuangzi 莊子
"Zhucheng moujia" 諸城某甲
Zhuge Liang 諸葛亮
Zhuoyuan 酌元
Zhuyu 麈餘
Zi bu yu 子不語
Zizhi tongjian 資治通鑑
Zōeki shojaku mokuroku 增益書籍目録
zuihitsu 随筆
Zuo zhuan 左傳

Bibliography

The place of publication for Japanese works is Tokyo unless otherwise noted.

Aeba Kōson 饗庭篁村, ed. *Chūshingura hinikuron, Chūshingura henchikiron, Inaka shibai Chūshingura* 忠臣蔵皮肉論・忠臣蔵偏痴気論・田舎芝居忠臣蔵. In *Shūchin meicho bunko* 袖珍名著文庫 48. Fuzanbō, 1912.

Akutagawa Ryūnosuke 芥川龍之介. *Akutagawa Ryūnosuke zenshū* 芥川龍之介全集. 12 vols. Iwanami shoten, 1977–78.

———. "Travels in China" (*Shina yūki*). Translated by Joshua A. Fogel and Kiyoko Morita. *Chinese Studies in History* 30, no. 4 (Summer 1997): 10–55.

Altenburger, Roland. *The Sword or the Needle: The Female Knight-Errant (Xia) in Traditional Chinese Narrative*. New York: Peter Lang, 2009.

Aoki Masaru 青木正児, ed. *Tsūzoku Kokon kikan, fu Gekka seidan* 通俗古今奇観・附月下清談. Iwanami shoten, 1932.

Asakura Haruhiko 朝倉治彦, ed. *Matsudaira Sadanobu zōsho mokuroku* 松平定信蔵書目録. Yumani shobō, 2005.

Asō Isoji 麻生磯次. *Edo bungaku to Shina bungaku: kinsei bungaku no Shina-teki genkyo to yomihon no kenkyū* 江戸文学と支那文学：近世文学の支那的原拠と読本の研究. Sanseidō, 1946.

Barr, Allan H. "The Later Classical Tale." In Victor H. Mair, ed., *Columbia History of Chinese Literature*, 675–96. New York: Columbia University Press, 2001.

———. "Pu Songling and *Liaozhai Zhiyi*: A Study of Textual Transmission, Biographical Background, and Literary Antecedents." PhD diss., University of Oxford, 1983.

Benjamin, Walter. *Illuminations*. Translated by Harry Zohn. New York: Harcourt, Brace & World, 1968.

Bentley, John R. *Tamakatsuma: A Window into the Scholarship of Motoori Norinaga*. Ithaca, NY: Cornell East Asia Program, 2013.

Berry, Mary Elizabeth. *Japan in Print: Information and Nation in the Early Modern Period*. Berkeley: University of California Press, 2006.

Biji xiaoshuo daguan 筆記小説大觀. Taibei: Xinxing shuju, 1960.

Biji xiaoshuo daguan xubian 筆記小説大觀續編. Taibei: Xinxing shuju, 1962.

Blair, Ann M. *Too Much to Know: Managing Scholarly Information before the Modern Age*. New Haven, CT: Yale University Press, 2010.

Boneh, Shahar, Arnon Boneh, and R. J. Caron. "Estimating the Prediction Function and the Number of Unseen Species in Sampling with Replacement." *Journal of the American Statistical Association* 93, no. 441 (1998): 372–79.

Burdick, Anne, Johanna Drucker, Peter Lunenfeld, Todd Presner, and Jeffrey Schnapp. *Digital Humanities*. Cambridge, MA: MIT Press, 2012.

Campany, Robert Ford. *Strange Writing: Anomaly Accounts in Early Medieval China*. Albany: State University of New York Press, 1996.

Chambers, Anthony H., trans. *Tales of Moonlight and Rain*. New York: Columbia University Press, 2007.

Chan, Leo Tak-hung. *The Discourse on Foxes and Ghosts: Ji Yun and Eighteenth-Century Literati Storytelling*. Honolulu: University of Hawai'i Press, 1998.

Chance, L. H., and J. N. Davis. "The Handwritten and the Printed: Issues of Format and Medium in Japanese Premodern Books." *Manuscript Studies* 1, no. 1 (2016): 90–114.

Chen Beinkuen 陳炳崑. "Edo bungaku to *Ryōsai shii*" 江戸文学と『聊斎志異』. *Shokō* 曙光 12 (2001): 50–63.

Chen Naiqian 陳乃乾, ed. *Guyi xiaoshuo congkan* 古佚小説叢刊. Haining: Shenchutang, 1929.

Clements, Rebekah. *A Cultural History of Translation in Early Modern Japan*. Cambridge: Cambridge University Press, 2015.

Cranston, Edwin A. *Grasses of Remembrance*. 2 vols. In *A Waka Anthology*, vol. 2. Stanford, CA: Stanford University Press, 2006.

Cuthbert, Michael Scott. "Tipping the Iceberg: Missing Italian Polyphony from the Age of Schism." *Musica Disciplina* 54 (2009): 39–74.

Cutter, Robert Joe. *The Brush and the Spur: Chinese Culture and the Cockfight*. Hong Kong: Chinese University Press, 1989.

DeWoskin, Kenneth, and J. I. Crump, trans. *In Search of the Supernatural*. Stanford, CA: Stanford University Press, 1996.

Ditter, Alexei Kamran, Jessey Choo, and Sarah M. Allen, eds. *Tales from Tang Dynasty China: Selections from the Taiping Guangji*. Cambridge, MA: Hackett Publishing, 2017.

Doi Gōga 土井贅牙. *Gōga-ō hissu shomoku* 贅牙翁必須書目. *Shinagaku* 支那学 2, no. 10 (1922): 70–75.

Efron, Bradley, and Ronald Thisted. "Estimating the Number of Unseen Species: How Many Words Did Shakespeare Know?" *Biometrika* 63, no. 3 (December 1976): 435–47.

Ekiken-kai 益軒会, ed. *Ekiken zenshū* 益軒全集. 8 vols. Ekiken zenshū kankōbu, 1910–11.

Emmerich, Michael. *The Tale of Genji: Translation, Canonization, and World Literature*. New York: Columbia University Press, 2013.

Fisher, R. A., A. Steven Corbet, and C. B. Williams. "The Relation between the Number of Species and the Number of Individuals in a Random Sample of an Animal Population." *Journal of Animal Ecology* 12, no. 1 (May 1943): 42–58.

Fleming, William D. "Strange Tales from Edo: *Liaozhai zhiyi* in Early Modern Japan." *Sino-Japanese Studies* 20 (2013).

Fogel, Joshua. "Texts, Contexts, and Intellectual Contacts." In Fogel, ed., *Crossing the Yellow Sea: Sino-Japanese Cultural Contacts, 1600–1950*, 5–9. Norwalk, CT: EastBridge, 2007.

Foster, Michael Dylan. *Pandemonium and Parade: Japanese Monsters and the Culture of Yōkai*. Berkeley: University of California Press, 2009.

Fraleigh, Matthew. *Plucking Chrysanthemums: Narushima Ryūhoku and Sinitic Literary Traditions in Modern Japan*. Cambridge, MA: Harvard University Asia Center, 2016.

Fuji Akio 冨士昭雄, Inoue Toshiyuki 井上敏幸, and Satake Akihiro 佐竹昭広, eds. *Kōshoku nidai otoko, Saikaku shokoku banashi, Honchō nijū fukō* 好色二代男・西鶴諸国ばなし・本朝二十不孝. In *SNKBT* 76. Iwanami shoten, 1991.

Fujii Otoo 藤井乙男. *Edo bungaku sōsetsu* 江戸文学叢説. Iwanami shoten, 1931.

Fujita Yūken 藤田祐賢. "Kunikida Doppo to Chūgoku kaii bungaku" 国木田独歩と中国怪異文学. *Geppō* 月報 accompanying *Kunikida Doppo zenshū* 国木田独歩全集 4 (June 1966): 322–23.

———. "*Ryōsai shii* no ichisokumen: toku ni Nihon bungaku to no kanren ni oite" 「聊斎志異」の一側面：特に日本文学との関連において. In *Keiō gijuku sōritsu hyakunen kinen ronbunshū* 慶應義塾創立百年記念論文集, 59–79. Keiō gijuku daigaku hōgakubu, 1958.

Giles, Herbert, trans. *Strange Stories from a Chinese Studio*. 2 vols. London: Thomas de la Rue, 1880.

Gotō Tanji 後藤丹治. *Senki monogatari no kenkyū* 戦記物語の研究. Tsukuba shoten, 1936.

Green, Jonathan, and Frank McIntyre. "Lost Incunable Editions: Closing in on an Estimate." In Flavia Bruni and Andrew Pettegree, eds., *Lost Books: Reconstructing the Print World of Pre-Industrial Europe*, 55–72. Boston: Brill, 2016.

Greenblatt, Stephen. *Marvelous Possessions: The Wonder of the New World*. Chicago: University of Chicago Press, 1991.

Haga Tōru 芳賀徹. *Hiraga Gennai* 平賀源内. Asahi shinbunsha, 1981.

Hamada Giichirō 浜田義一郎. *Ōta Nanpo* 大田南畝. In *Jinbutsu sōsho* 人物叢書 102. Yoshikawa kōbunkan, 1963.

———, ed. *Ōta Nanpo zenshū* 大田南畝全集. 21 vols. Iwanami shoten, 1985–90.

Hamada Keisuke 浜田啓介, ed. *Shinchō Nihon koten shūsei bekkan: Nansō Satomi hakkenden* 新潮日本古典集成別巻：南総里見八犬伝, vol. 2. Shinchōsha, 2003.

Hammond, Charles E. "Factual Framing in *Liao zhai zhi yi*." *Acta Orientalia Academiae Scientiarum Hungaricae* 59, no. 2 (2006): 205–30.

Hanan, Patrick. *The Chinese Vernacular Story*. Cambridge, MA: Harvard University Press, 1981.

———. "The Nature of Ling Meng-ch'u's Fiction." In Andrew Plaks, ed., *Chinese Narrative: Critical and Theoretical Essays*, 85–114. Princeton, NJ: Princeton University Press, 1977.

Handel, Zev. Review of Peter F. Kornicki, *Languages, Scripts, and Chinese Texts in East Asia* (Oxford University Press, 2018). H-Asia, H-Net Reviews. August 2019.

Hashiguchi Kōnosuke 橋口侯之介. "Edo no furuhon'ya" 江戸の古本屋. *Nihon kosho tsūshin* 日本古書通信 942 (January 2008): 30–31.

Hattori Hitoshi 服部仁, ed. *Bakin kenkyū shiryō shūsei* 馬琴研究資料集成. 5 vols. Kuresu shuppan, 2007.

Hayami, Akira. *Japan's Industrious Revolution: Economic and Social Transformations in the Early Modern Period*. New York: Springer, 2015.

Hearn, Lafcadio. *Kwaidan: Stories and Studies of Strange Things*. Boston: Houghton Mifflin, 1904.

Hedberg, William C. "Akutagawa Ryūnosuke's Uncanny Travels in Republican-Era China." *Japan Forum* 29, no. 2 (2016): 236–56.

———. "The Chinese Afterlives of Coxinga and the Forty-Seven Rōnin of Akō: Japanese Puppet Theatre and Cultural Encounter in Edo-Period Nagasaki." *Sino-Japanese Studies* 20 (2013): 34–65.

———. *The Japanese Discovery of Chinese Fiction: The Water Margin and the Making of a National Canon*. New York: Columbia University Press, 2019.

———. "Reclaiming the Margins: Seita Tansō's *Suikoden hihyōkai* and the Poetics of Cross-Cultural Influence." *International Journal of Asian Studies* 12, no. 2 (2015): 193–215.

Hegel, Robert E. *Reading Illustrated Fiction in Late Imperial China*. Stanford, CA: Stanford University Press, 1998.

Hess, Laura E. "Qing Reactions to the Reimportation of Confucian Canonical Works from Tokugawa Japan." In Joshua A. Fogel, ed., *Sagacious Monks and Bloodthirsty Warriors: Chinese Views of Japan in the Ming-Qing Period*, 126–57. Norwalk, CT: EastBridge, 2002.

Higashi, Masao, ed. *Kaiki: Uncanny Tales from Japan, Volume 1: Tales of Old Edo*. Fukuoka: Kurodahan Press, 2009.

Hirano, Katsuya. *The Politics of Dialogic Imagination: Power and Popular Culture in Early Modern Japan*. Chicago: University of Chicago Press, 2014.

Hou Zhongyi 侯忠義 and Liu Shilin 劉世林. *Zhongguo wenyan xiaoshuo shigao* 中國文言小説史稿. Beijing: Beijing daxue chubanshe, 1993.

Hui, Luo. "The Ghost of *Liaozhai*: Pu Songling's Ghostlore and Its History of Reception." PhD diss., University of Toronto, 2009.

Huntington, Rania. *Alien Kind: Foxes and Late Imperial Chinese Narrative*. Cambridge, MA: Harvard University Asia Center, 2003.

Hutcheon, Linda. *A Theory of Adaptation*. 2nd ed. New York: Routledge, 2013.

Idema, Wilt, and Lloyd Haft. *A Guide to Chinese Literature*. Ann Arbor: Center for Chinese Studies, University of Michigan, 1997.

Iikura Yōichi 飯倉洋一. "'Kidan' no ba" 「奇談」の場, *Gobun* 語文 78 (May 2002): 22–32.

———. "Kinsei bungaku no ichiryōiki to shite no 'kidan'" 近世文学の一領域としての「奇談」. *Nihon bungaku* 日本文学 61, no. 10 (October 2012): 24–35.

———, ed. *Zenki yomihon kaidan shū* 前期読本怪談集. In Kigoshi Osamu 木越治, ed., *Edo kaidan bungei meisakusen* 江戸怪談文芸名作選 2. Kokusho kankōkai, 2017.

Ikeda Yasaburō 池田弥三郎 et al., eds. *Nihon meisho fūzoku zue* 日本名所風俗図会 15. Kadokawa shoten, 1983.

Ikezawa Ichirō 池澤一郎 et al., eds. *Kanbun shōsetsu shū* 漢文小説集. In *SNKBT Meiji hen* 3. Iwanami shoten, 2005.

Imaizumi Mine 今泉みね. *Nagori no yume: ran'i Katsuragawa-ke ni umarete* 名ごりの夢：蘭医桂川家に生れて. In *Tōyō bunko* 東洋文庫 9. Heibonsha, 1963.

Inoue Keiji 井上啓治. "*Kaii zenseki yawa* ron, fu honkoku: zenki yomihon, zenki kokkeibon kenkyū (5)" 『怪異前席夜話』論・附翻刻：前期読本・前期滑稽本研究(五). *Shūjitsu ronsō: Jinbun hen* 就実論叢：人文篇 19 (February 1990): 21–52.

———. "*Morokoshi no Yoshino* joron, fu honkoku: zenki gesaku kenkyū (2)" 『唐土の吉野』序論・附翻刻：前期戯作研究(二). *Shūjitsu ronsō* 就実論叢 16 (February 1987): 85–134.

Isaka Kiyonobu 井坂清信. "Kokuritsu kokkai toshokan shozō no wakokubon kanseki gaikan" 国立国会図書館所蔵の和刻本漢籍概観. *Sankō shoshi kenkyū* 参考書誌研究 43 (September 1993): 1–17.

Ishigami Satoshi 石上敏. "Honkoku (*Tōka no geboku*) *Tama no eda*" 翻刻『灯下戯墨玉之枝』. *Yomihon kenkyū* 読本研究 8, no. 2 (September 1994): 112–45.

———. "*Kogarashi zōshi* ron: Morishima Chūryō no taisei hihan" 『凩草紙』論：森島中良の体制批判. *Okadai kokubun ronkō* 岡大国文論稿 (March 1999): 10–20.

———. *Manzōtei Morishima Chūryō no bunji* 万象亭森島中良の文事. Kanrin shobō, 1995.

———, ed. *MCS*. In Takada Mamoru 高田衛 and Hara Michio 原道生, eds., *Sōsho Edo bunko* 叢書江戸文庫 32. Kokusho kankōkai, 1994.

Ishikawa Masamochi 石川雅望. *Tsūzoku Haimonroku* 通俗排悶録. Edo, Ōsaka, and Kyōto: Kadomaruya Jinsuke et al., 1828–29.

Ishikawa Ryō 石川了. "Shodai Ryūtei Senka nenpu kō: sono ichi" 初代笠亭仙果年譜稿：その一. *Ōtsuma joshi daigaku bungakubu kiyō* 大妻女子大学文学部紀要 11 (March 1979): 25–37.

Ishizaki Matazō 石崎又造. *Kinsei Nihon ni okeru Shina zokugo bungakushi* 近世日本における支那俗語文学史. Kōbundō, 1940.

Isobe Akira 磯部彰. "*Saiyūki* to *Tsūzoku Saiyūki*" 『西遊記』と『通俗西遊記』. In Wakan hikaku bungakukai 和漢比較文学会, ed., *Wakan hikaku bungaku sōsho* 和漢比較文学叢書 7: *Kinsei bungaku to kanbungaku* 近世文学と漢文学, 87–148. Kyūko shoin, 1988.

Isobe Yūko 磯部祐子 and Moriga Kazue 森賀一惠. *Toyama bungaku no reimei* 富山文学の黎明. 2 vols. Toyama: Katsura shobō, 2017.

Iwao Seiichi 岩生成一. "Kinsei Nis-Shi bōeki ni kansuru sūryōteki kōsatsu" 近世日支貿易に関する数量的考察. *Shigaku zasshi* 史学雑誌 62, no. 11 (November 1953): 1–40.

Iwasaki, Haruko. "Portrait of a Daimyō: Comical Fiction by Matsudaira Sadanobu." *Monumenta Nipponica* 38, no. 1 (Spring 1983): 1–19.

Jiu Tang shu 舊唐書. Beijing: Zhonghua shuju, 1975.

Jōo, Fumiko. "'The Peony Lantern' and Fantastic Tales in Late Imperial China and Tokugawa Japan: Local History, Religion, and Gender." PhD diss., University of Chicago, 2011.

Jūtei goshojaku mokuroku 重訂御書籍目録 (1836). Collection of the National Archives of Japan.

Kaempfer, Engelbert. *The History of Japan, Together with a Description of the Kingdom of Siam, 1690–92*. Translated by J. G. Scheuchzer. New York: Macmillan, 1906.

Kaibara Ekiken 貝原益軒. *Yamato honzō* 大和本草. Kyōto: Ono Zensuke, 1709.

Kaidan meisaku shū 怪談名作集. In *Nihon meicho zenshū: Edo bungei no bu* 日本名著全集：江戸文芸之部 10. Nihon meicho zenshū kankōkai, 1927.

Kanda Masayuki 神田正行. "*Suikoden* no shohon to Bakin" 『水滸伝』の諸本と馬琴. In Suwa Haruo 諏訪春雄 and Takada Mamoru 高田衛, eds., *Fukkō-suru Hakkenden* 復興する八犬伝, 249–86. Bensei shuppan, 2008.

Kaneuchi Kakuzō 金内格三. *Tokō jii* 徒杠字彙. Edo: Suwaraya Mohē et al., 1860.

Kawaguchi Matsutarō 川口松太郎. *Ugetsu monogatari* 雨月物語. Tōgensha, 1954.

Kawase Kazuma 川瀬一馬. "Baijuken no isho kaihan ni tsuite" 梅寿軒の医書開版について. *Shoshigaku* 書誌学 9 (1967): 1–10.

———. *Gozan-ban no kenkyū* 五山版の研究. Nihon koshosekishō kyōkai, 1970.

———. *Kokatsuji-ban no kenkyū* 古活字版之研究. 3 vols. Rev. ed. Nihon koshosekishō kyōkai, 1967.

Keene, Donald. *World within Walls: Japanese Literature of the Pre-Modern Era, 1600–1867*. New York: Holt, Rinehart & Winston, 1976.

Kern, Adam L. *Manga from the Floating World: Comicbook Culture and the Kibyōshi of Edo Japan*. Cambridge, MA: Harvard University Asia Center, 2006.

———. "The Writer at His Desk: The Professionalization of Authorship in Eighteenth-Century Japan." In Wilt L. Idema, ed., *Books in Numbers*, 267–307. Cambridge, MA: Harvard-Yenching Library, 2007.

Kigoshi Osamu 木越治, ed. *Edo kaidan bungei meisakusen* 江戸怪談文芸名作選. 5 vols. Kokusho kankōkai, 2016–19.

———, ed. *Ukiyozōshi kaidan shū* 浮世草子怪談集. In Takada Mamoru 高田衛 and Hara Michio 原道生, eds., *Sōsho Edo bunko* 叢書江戸文庫 34. Kokusho kankōkai, 1994.

Kimura Yaeko 木村八重子, Uda Toshihiko 宇田敏彦, and Koike Masatane 小池正胤, eds. *Kusazōshi shū* 草双紙集. In *SNKBT* 83. Iwanami shoten, 1997.

Kinoshita Kazuo 木下一雄. "Kyōikushi to rinri: Edo jidai shoki rinri ni shuzai shite" 教育史と論理：江戸時代初期論理に取材して. *Kyōikugaku kenkyū* 教育学研究 21, no. 6 (January 1955): 2–18.

Kishino Toshihiko 岸野俊彦. *Owari-han shakai no bunka, jōhō, gakumon* 尾張藩社会の文化・情報・学問. Ōsaka: Seibundō shuppan, 2002.

Koakimoto Dan 小秋元段. "Saga-bon *Shiki* no shoshiteki kōsatsu" 嵯峨本『史記』の書誌的考察. *Hōsei daigaku bungakubu kiyō* 法政大学文学部紀要 49 (2003): 109–41.

Koike Masatane 小池正胤, Uda Toshihiko 宇田敏彦, Nakayama Yūshō 中山右尚, and Tanahashi Masahiro 棚橋正博, eds. *Edo no gesaku [parodī] ehon* 江戸の戯作絵本. 4 vols. *Zokkan* 続巻. 2 vols. Shakai shisōsha, 1980–85.

Kokumin tosho kabushiki kaisha 国民図書株式会社, ed. *Nihon zuihitsu zenshū* 日本随筆全集, vol. 1. Kokumin tosho, 1927.

Kokuritsu kokkai toshokan toshobu 国立国会図書館図書部, ed. *Kokuritsu kokkai toshokan shozō kokatsujiban zuroku* 国立国会図書館所蔵古活字版図録. Kokuritsu kokkai toshokan, 1989.

Kornicki, Peter F. *The Book in Japan: A Cultural History from the Beginnings to the Nineteenth Century*. Honolulu: University of Hawai'i Press, 2001.

———. "The *Hyakumantō Darani* and the Origins of Printing in Eighth-Century Japan." *International Journal of Asian Studies* 9, no. 1 (2012): 43–70.

———. *Languages, Scripts, and Chinese Texts in East Asia*. Oxford: Oxford University Press, 2018.

———. "Manuscript, Not Print: Scribal Culture in the Edo Period." *Journal of Japanese Studies* 32, no. 1 (2006): 23–52.

———. "*Nishiki no Ura*: An Instance of Censorship and the Structure of a *Sharebon*." *Monumenta Nipponica* 32, no. 2 (Summer 1977): 153–88.

Krusenstern, Adam Johann von. *Voyage Round the World in the Years 1803, 1804, 1805, & 1806 [. . .]*. Translated by Richard Belgrave Hoppner. London: John Murray, 1813.

Kunikida Doppo zenshū hensan iinkai 国木田独歩全集編纂委員会, ed. *Teihon Kunikida Doppo zenshū* 定本国木田独歩全集. 2nd ed. 11 vols. Gakushū kenkyūsha, 1978.

Li, Wai-yee. "Early Qing to 1723." In Kang-i Sun Chang and Stephen Owen, eds., *Cambridge History of Chinese Literature Volume 2: From 1375*, 152–244. Cambridge: Cambridge University Press, 2010.

Love, Harold. *Scribal Publication in Seventeenth-Century England*. Oxford: Clarendon Press, 1993.

Lu Xun 魯迅. *Zhongguo xiaoshuo shilüe* 中國小說史略. Shanghai: Shanghai guji chubanshe, 1998.

Lurie, David. *Realms of Literacy: Early Japan and the History of Writing*. Cambridge, MA: Harvard University Asia Center, 2011.

Mair, Victor. "Buddhism and the Rise of the Written Vernacular in East Asia: The Making of National Languages." *Journal of Asian Studies* 53, no. 3 (1994): 707–51.

Major, John S., et al., trans. *The Huainanzi: A Guide to the Theory and Practice of Government in Early Han China*. New York: Columbia University Press, 2010.

Makiyama Masayuki 槙山雅之. "'Setsuwa-kei kidan' no isō josetsu: Shinrotei *Kan'on kidan hitofutagusa* no hōhō" 《説話系奇談》の位相 序説：振鷺亭『寒温奇談一二草』の方法. *Kokusai bunka kenkyūka ronshū* 国際文化研究科論集 (Tōhoku daigaku) 5 (December 1997): 23–29.

Markus, Andrew. "The Daisō Lending Library of Nagoya, 1767–1899." *Gest Library Journal* 3, no. 3 (Winter 1989–90): 5–34.

Maruya Genbē 丸屋源兵衞. *Zōeki shojaku mokuroku* 増益書籍目録. Kyōto: Maruya Genbē, 1709.

Maruyama, Masao. *Studies in the Intellectual History of Tokugawa Japan*. Princeton, NJ: Princeton University Press, 1974.

Masuda Wataru 増田渉, ed. *Gen Kōran* [*Ruan Jianglan*] *shussetan: Shina shōsetsu, hoka nihen* 阮江蘭出世譚：支那小説、他二編. In *Kindai bungei senshū* 近代文芸選集 5. Kenbunsha, 1926.

Masuda Wataru et al., trans. *Ryōsai shii* [*Liaozhai zhiyi*] 聊斎志異. In *Chūgoku koten bungaku zenshū* 中国古典文学全集 21. Heibonsha, 1958.

Matsuda Osamu 松田修, Watanabe Morikuni 渡辺守邦, and Hanada Fujio 花田富二夫, eds. *Otogi bōko* 伽婢子. In *SNKBT* 75. Iwanami shoten, 2001.

Matsudaira Sadamitsu 松平定光, ed. *Uge no hitokoto, Shugyōroku* 宇下人言・修行録. Iwanami shoten, 1942.

Matsura Seizan 松浦静山. *Kasshi yawa* 甲子夜話, vol. 1. In Nakamura Yukihiko 中村幸彦 and Nakano Mitsutoshi 中野三敏, eds., *Tōyō bunko* 東洋文庫 306. Heibonsha, 1977.

McCullough, Helen Craig, trans. *The Taiheiki: A Chronicle of Medieval Japan*. New York: Columbia University Press, 1959.

McDermott, Joseph. "The Ascendance of the Imprint in China." In Cynthia J. Brokaw and Kai-wing Chow, eds., *Printing and Book Culture in Late Imperial China*, 55–104. Berkeley: University of California Press, 2005.

McGee, Dylan. "Hirade Jun'eki no *Daisui manshō* kara ukagaeru bassui shōroku to Daisō-bon no kashidashi" 平出順益の『代睡漫抄』から窺える抜粋抄録と大惣本の貸出. *Gengo bunka ronshū* 言語文化論集 37, no. 1 (October 2015): 35–42.

Minford, John, trans. *Strange Tales from a Chinese Studio*. New York: Penguin Books, 2006.

Mitamura Engyo 三田村鳶魚, ed. *Mikan zuihitsu hyakushu* 未刊随筆百種, vol. 12. Chūō kōronsha, 1978.

Miura Katsuo 三浦勝男, ed. *Kamakura no chimei yurai jiten* 鎌倉の地名由来辞典. Tōkyōdō shuppan, 2005.

Miyamoto Tsuneichi 宮本常一, Haraguchi Torao 原口虎雄, and Higa Shunchō 比嘉春潮, eds. *Nihon shomin seikatsu shiryō shūsei* 日本庶民生活史料集成. 31 vols. San'ichi shobō, 1968–84.

Mizuno Kiyoshi 水野清. "Suzuki Akira no shakushobo" 鈴木朖の借書簿. *Bunbaku* 文莫 4 (1979): 47–125.

Mizuno Minoru 水野稔 et al., eds. *Sharebon taisei* 洒落本大成. 30 vols. Chūō kōronsha, 1978–88.

Mizuta Norihisa 水田紀久, Rai Tsutomu 頼惟勤, and Naoi Fumiko 直井文子, eds. *Kan Chazan, Rai San'yō shishū* 菅茶山頼山陽詩集. In *SNKBT* 66. Iwanami shoten, 1996.

Mizutani Futō 水谷不倒. *Mizutani Futō chosakushū* 水谷不倒著作集. 8 vols. Chūō kōronsha, 1973–77.

Monbushō 文部省, ed. *Nihon kyōikushi shiryō* 日本教育史資料, vol. 7. Monbu daijin kanbō hōkokuka, 1892.

Mori Junzaburō 森潤三郎. *Momijiyama bunko to shomotsu bugyō* 紅葉山文庫と書物奉行. Shōwa shobō, 1933.

Mori Senzō 森銑三, ed. *Zuihitsu hyakkaen* 随筆百花苑, vol. 3. Chūō kōronsha, 1980.

Mori Senzō and Kitagawa Hirokuni 北川博邦, eds. *ZNZT*. 12 vols. Yoshikawa kōbunkan, 1979–81.

Morishima Chūryō 森島中良. *Daishin manshō* 代紳漫鈔. Unpaginated manuscript, collection of National Diet Library.

———. (*Hakushō kidan*) *Kogarashi zōshi* 拍掌奇談凩草紙. Edo and Ōsaka: Kazusaya Rihē et al., 1792.

———. *Sekijichō* 惜字帖. Unpaginated album, collection of Waseda University Library.

Mueller, Pam A., and Daniel M. Oppenheimer. "The Pen Is Mightier Than the Keyboard: Advantages of Longhand over Laptop Note Taking." *Psychological Science* 25, no. 6 (June 2014): 1159–68.

Mukai Nobuo 向井信夫. "Kansei nendai ni okeru Bakin chosaku no ni san ni tsuite" 寛政年代に於ける馬琴著作の二三について. *Biburia* ビブリア 61 (October 1975): 20–26.

Nabeshima Naotomo 鍋島直共. "Shokusanjin no Nagasaki taizai: sakuhin *Mozu no kusaguki* sono ta ni miru" 蜀山人の長崎滞在：作品「百舌の草茎」その他にみる. *Nagasaki daigaku kyōyōbu kiyō: jinbun kagaku* 長崎大学教養部紀要：人文科学 7 (1967): 1–6.

Nagasaki bugyōsho 長崎奉行所. *Shojaku motochō* 書籍元帳, 1842–54. 6 fascicles. Handwritten manuscript, dated 1946. Collection of Waseda University Library.

Nagasawa Kikuya 長澤規矩也, ed. *Tōwa jisho ruishū* 唐話辞書類集. 20 vols. Kyūko shoin, 1959–76.

———, ed. *Wakokubon kanseki bunrui mokuroku* 和刻本漢籍分類目録. Rev. ed. Kyūko shoin, 2006.

———. *Wakokubon kanseki zuihitsu shū* 和刻本漢籍随筆集, vol. 2. Kyūko shoin, 1972.

Nagasawa Kikuya sensei kiju kinenkai 長澤規矩也先生喜寿記念会, ed. *Nagasawa Kikuya chosakushū* 長澤規矩也著作集. 11 vols. Kyūko shoin, 1982–87.

Nagoya-shi Hōsa bunko 名古屋市蓬左文庫, ed. *Nagoya-shi Hōsa bunko kanseki bunrui mokuroku* 名古屋市蓬左文庫漢籍分類目録. Nagoya: Nagoya-shi kyōiku iinkai, 1975.

Nagoya-shi kyōiku iinkai 名古屋市教育委員会, ed. *Nagoya sōsho* 名古屋叢書, vol. 19: *Zuihitsu hen 2* 随筆編(二). Nagoya: Nagoya-shi kyōiku iinkai, 1960.

———, ed. *Nagoya sōsho* 名古屋叢書, vol. 20: *Zuihitsu hen 3* 随筆編(三). Nagoya: Nagoya-shi kyōiku iinkai, 1961.

Nakajima Takashi 中島隆. "Hanpon jidai no 'shahon' to wa nani ka" 板本時代の「写本」とは何か. *Kokubungaku: Kaishaku to kyōzai no kenkyū* 国文学：解釈と教材の研究 42, no. 11 (1997): 49–53.

Nakamura Yukihiko 中村幸彦. *Chūgoku bunka sōsho* 中国文化叢書 9: *Nihon kangaku* 日本漢学. Taishūkan, 1968.

———, ed. *Fūrai Sanjin shū* 風来山人集. In *NKBT* 55. Iwanami shoten, 1961.

———. *Kinsei bungei shichōron* 近世文芸思潮論. In *Nakamura Yukihiko chojutsu shū* 中村幸彦著述集 1. Chūō kōronsha, 1982.

———. *Kinsei sakka kenkyū* 近世作家研究. San'ichi shobō, 1961.

———. *Kinsei shōsetsu shi* 近世小説史. In *Nakamura Yukihiko chojutsu shū* 中村幸彦著述集 4. Chūō kōronsha, 1987.

———. *Kinseiteki hyōgen* 近世的表現. In *Nakamura Yukihiko chojutsu shū* 中村幸彦著述集 2. Chūō kōronsha, 1982.

———, ed. *Ueda Akinari shū* 上田秋成集. In *NKBT* 56. Iwanami shoten, 1959.

Nakamura Yukihiko, Takada Mamoru 高田衛, and Nakamura Hiroyasu 中村博保, eds. *Hanabusa sōshi, Nishiyama monogatari, Ugetsu monogatari, Harusame monogatari* 英草紙・西山物語・雨月物語・春雨物語. In *SNKBZ* 78. Shōgakkan, 1995.

Nakano Mitsutoshi 中野三敏. *Gesaku kenkyū* 戯作研究. Chūō kōronsha, 1981.

Nguyen, Nam. "Writing as Response and as Translation: *Jiandeng xinhua* and the Evolution of the *Chuanqi* Genre in East Asia, Particularly in Vietnam." PhD diss., Harvard University, 2005.

"*Nihon meicho zenshū* (dai-ikki shuppan): *Edo bungei no bu* (zen nijūrokkan oyobi tsuika hen nikan) shomoku yotei ichiran" 日本名著全集 (第一期出版) : 江戸文芸之部 (全廿六巻及追加篇二巻) 書目予定一覧. Supplement to *Nihon meicho zenshū: Edo bungei no bu* 日本名著全集 : 江戸文芸之部, vol. 26: *Senryū zappai shū* 川柳雑俳集. Nihon meicho zenshū kankōkai, 1927.

Nihon meicho zenshū: Edo bungei no bu 日本名著全集 : 江戸文芸之部. 28 vols. Nihon meicho zenshū kankōkai, 1925–29.

Nihon zuihitsu taisei henshūbu 日本随筆大成編集部, ed. *NZT*. 3 series, 71 vols. Yoshikawa kōbunkan, 1973–78.

Ning Jiayu 寧稼雨. *Zhongguo wenyan xiaoshuo zongmu tiyao* 中國文言小說總目提要. Jinan: Qilu shushe, 1996.

Nishimura Masamori 西村正守 and Sano Chikara 佐野力. *Tōkyō shojakukan ni okeru kyūhan zōsho no shūshū* 東京書籍館における旧藩蔵書の収集. In *Toshokan kenkyū shirīzu* 図書館研究シリーズ 15. Kokuritsu kokkai toshokan, 1973.

Nishino Haruo 西野春雄, ed. *Yōkyoku hyakuban* 謡曲百番. In *SNKBT* 57. Iwanami shoten, 1998.

Noda Tekiho 野田笛浦 and Zhu Liuzhu 朱劉諸. *Tokutai-sen hitsugo* 得泰船筆語. 2 vols. Ki-han: Hyōyōkan, ca. 1826.

Ōba Osamu 大庭脩. *Books and Boats: Sino-Japanese Relations in the Seventeenth and Eighteenth Centuries*. Translated by Joshua A. Fogel. Portland, ME: Merwin Asia, 2012.

———. "Chinese Travelers to Nagasaki." In Joshua A. Fogel, ed., *Sagacious Monks and Bloodthirsty Warriors: Chinese Views of Japan in the Ming-Qing Period*, 111–25. Norwalk, CT: EastBridge, 2002.

———. *Edo jidai ni okeru Chūgoku bunka juyō no kenkyū* 江戸時代における中国文化受容の研究. Kyōto: Dōhōsha, 1984.

———. *Edo jidai ni okeru Tōsen mochiwatarisho no kenkyū* 江戸時代における唐船持渡書の研究. Suita-shi: Kansai daigaku shuppanbu, 1967.

———. *Edo jidai no Nit-Chū hiwa* 江戸時代の日中秘話. Tōhō shoten, 1980.

———. "Genroku gannen no Tōhon mokuroku" 元禄元年の唐本目録. *Shisen* 史泉 35–36 (December 1967): 151–67.

———, ed. *Hakusai shomoku* 舶載書目. 2 vols. Suita-shi: Kansai daigaku shuppanbu, 1972.

———. *Kanseki yunyū no bunkashi: Shōtoku taishi kara Yoshimune e* 漢籍輸入の文化史 : 聖徳太子から吉宗へ. Kenbun shuppan, 1997.

———. "Naikaku bunko no *Kōrai shoseki mokuroku* (honkoku)" 内閣文庫の購来書籍目録〔翻刻〕. *Kansai daigaku tōzai gakujutsu kenkyūjo kiyō* 関西大学東西学術研究所紀要 1 (March 1968): 33–84.

———. "Seidō bunko no *Fueki fukenshi mokuroku*" 聖堂文庫の賦役府県志目録. *Kansai daigaku tōzai gakujutsu kenkyūjo kiyō* 関西大学東西学術研究所紀要 3 (March 1970): 91–97.

Ōba Osamu and Wang Yong 王勇. *Tenseki* 典籍. In *Nit-Chū bunka kōryūshi sōsho* 日中文化交流史叢書 9. Taishūkan shoten, 1996.

Odagiri Hiroko 小田桐弘子. "Hon'yaku bungaku no keifu: Kimiko yaku 'Kawa hitoe'" 翻訳文学の系譜 : きみ子訳「皮一重」. *Fukuoka jogakuin tanki daigaku kiyō* 福岡女学院短期大学紀要 24 (February 1988): 1–19.

Ōga Junji 大賀順治, ed. *Shina kidan shū: dai ippen, dai nihen, sanjūkyūnen gogatsu [dai sanpen]* 支那奇談集：第一編、第二編、卅九年五月[第三編]. Kinji gahōsha, 1906.

Ogata Tsutomu 尾形仂, ed. *Shōsetsu sangen* 小説三言. Yumani shobō, 1976.

Ogawa Takehiko 小川武彦 and Kanai Yasushi 金井康, eds. *Tokugawa bakufu zōshomoku* 徳川幕府蔵書目. 10 vols. In *Shoshi shomoku shirīzu* 書誌書目シリーズ 16. Yumani shobō, 1985.

Okada Kesao 岡田袈裟男. "Morishima Chūryō bannen tansaku: arui wa ichibunjin no gengo uchū" 森島中良晩年探索：あるいは一文人の言語宇宙. *Nihon bungaku* 日本文学 32, no. 1 (January 1983): 62–73.

———. "Morishima Chūryō no mita kaihi no bunka: *Kōmō zatsuwa*, *Bankoku shinwa* o chūshin ni" 森島中良の見た海彼の文化：『紅毛雑話』『万国新話』を中心に. *Kokubungaku kenkyū* 国文学研究 151 (March 2007): 59–71.

Okada Minoru 岡田稔 and Ichihashi Taku 市橋鐸. *Suzuki Akira: hyakusanjūnenki kinen* 鈴木朖：百三十年忌記念. Nagoya: Suzuki Akira kenshōkai, 1967.

Ono Takeo 小野武雄. *Edo bukka jiten* 江戸物価事典. Tenbōsha, 1979.

Ōtaka Yōji 大高洋司. "Edo yomihon no tenkai: Kansei, Kyōwa nenkan" 江戸読本の展開：寛政・享和年間. In Yokoyama Kuniharu 横山邦治, ed., *Yomihon no sekai: Edo to Kamigata* 読本の世界：江戸と上方, 9–34. Sekai shisōsha, 1985.

Ōtaka Yōji and Kondō Mizuki 近藤瑞木, eds. *Shoki Edo yomihon kaidan shū* 初期江戸読本怪談集. Vol. 1 of Takada Mamoru 高田衛, ed., *Edo kaii kisō bungei taikei* 江戸怪異綺想文芸大系, 5 vols. Kokusho kankōkai, 2000–2003.

Ōtsuki Nyoden 大槻如電, ed. *Shinsen yōgaku nenpyō* 新選洋学年表. Ōtsuki Shigeo, 1927.

Park, Si Nae. *The Korean Vernacular Story Telling Tales of Contemporary Chosŏn in Sinographic Writing*. New York: Columbia University Press, 2020.

Pastreich, Emanuel. *The Observable Mundane: Vernacular Chinese and the Emergence of a Literary Discourse on Popular Narrative in Edo Japan*. Seoul: Seoul National University Press, 2011.

Plutschow, Herbert. *A Reader in Edo Period Travel*. Folkestone, Kent: Global Oriental, 2006.

Reider, Noriko T. "The Appeal of *Kaidan* Tales of the Strange." *Asian Folklore Studies* 59, no. 2 (2000): 265–83.

———. "The Emergence of *Kaidan-shū*: The Collection of Tales of the Strange and Mysterious in the Edo Period." *Asian Folklore Studies* 60, no. 1 (2001): 79–99.

Roberts, Luke S. "Shipwrecks and Flotsam: The Foreign World in Edo-Period Tosa." *Monumenta Nipponica* 70, no. 1 (2015): 83–122.

Ross, Angus, and David Woolley, eds. *Jonathan Swift: The Major Works*. Oxford: Oxford University Press, 2003.

Ryūtei Senka 笠亭仙果. *Hanareya sensei bunshō* 離屋先生文抄. Manuscript, collection of National Diet Library.

———. *Mimeyori sōshi* 美目与里艸紙. Edo: Yamamotoya Heikichi, 1847.

———. *Oshibana* おし花. Manuscript, collection of National Diet Library.

Saigusa Hiroto 三枝博音, ed. *Miura Baien shū* 三浦梅園集. Iwanami bunko, 1953.

Saishō Hazuki 最相葉月. *Hoshi Shin'ichi: sen'ichiwa o tsukutta hito* 星新一：一〇〇一話をつくった人. Shinchōsha, 2007.

Saitō Gesshin 斎藤月岑, Saitō Yukio 斎藤幸雄, Saitō Yukitaka 斎藤幸孝, and Hasegawa Settan 長谷川雪旦. *Edo meisho zue* 江戸名所図会. Edo: Suwaraya Mohē, 1834–36.

Sakaki, Atsuko. *Obsessions with the Sino-Japanese Polarity in Japanese Literature*. Honolulu: University of Hawai'i Press, 2005.

Sasagawa Taneo 笹川種郎. *Kinsei bungeishi* 近世文芸志. Meiji shoin, 1931.

Satō Satoru 佐藤悟. "Honkoku *Izumi no Chikahira monogatari*" 翻刻『泉親衡物語』. *Jissen kokubungaku* 実践国文学 42 (September 1992): 91–169.

Screech, Timon. *The Lens within the Heart: The Western Scientific Gaze and Popular Imagery in Later Edo Japan*. 2nd ed. Honolulu: University of Hawai'i Press, 2002.

Seida Keiko 清田啓子. "Honkoku Kyokutei Bakin no kibyōshi (3)" 翻刻 曲亭馬琴の黄表紙 (三). *Komazawa tanki daigaku kenkyū kiyō* 駒沢短期大学研究紀要 5 (March 1977): 19–95.

Seki Senshū 尺仙秀, trans. *Tōyō Dekameron* 唐様でかめろん. Mikasa shobō, 1933.

Shen Jin [Chum Shum] 沈津. "Ming dai fangke tushu zhi liutong yu jiage" 明代坊刻圖書之流通與價格. *Guojia tushuguan guankan* 國家圖書館館刊 1 (June 1996): 101–18.

Shibata Mitsuhiko 柴田光彦 and Kanda Masayuki 神田正行, eds. *Bakin shokan shūsei* 馬琴書翰集成. 7 vols. Yagi shoten, 2002–2004.

Shibata Tenma 柴田天満, trans. *Ryōsai shii* [*Liaozhai zhiyi*] 聊斎志異, vol. 9. Sōgensha, 1952.

Shimada Isao 島田勇雄, Takeshima Atsuo 竹島淳夫, and Higuchi Motomi 樋口元巳, eds. *Wakan sansai zue* 和漢三才図会. 18 vols. In *Tōyō bunko* 東洋文庫 447, 451, 456, 458, 462, 466, 471, 476, 481, 487, 494, 498, 505, 510, 516, 521, 527, and 532. Heibonsha, 1985–91.

Shimada, Ryuto. *The Intra-Asian Trade in Japanese Copper by the Dutch East India Company during the Eighteenth Century*. Boston: Brill, 2006.

Shimazaki, Satoko. *Edo Kabuki in Transition: From the Worlds of the Samurai to the Vengeful Female Ghost*. New York: Columbia University Press, 2016.

Shinbo Hiroshi 新保博. *Kinsei no bukka to keizai hatten: zen-kōgyōka shakai e no sūryōteki sekkin* 近世の物価と経済発展：前工業化社会への数量的接近. Tōyō keizai shinpōsha, 1978.

Shinrotei 振鷺亭. (*Katakiuchi*) *Kōsei kidan* 復讐曠世奇談. Ōsaka, Nagoya, Edo, and Kyōto: Akitaya Taemon et al., 1818.

Shively, Donald H. "Bakufu versus Kabuki." *Harvard Journal of Asiatic Studies* 18, no. 3/4 (December 1955): 326–56.

———. "Chikamatsu's Satire on the Dog Shogun." *Harvard Journal of Asiatic Studies* 18, no. 1/2 (June 1955): 159–80.

Sibau, Maria Franca. *Reading for the Moral: Exemplarity and the Confucian Moral Imagination in Seventeenth-Century Chinese Short Fiction*. Albany: State University of New York Press, 2018.

Shokusanjin zōsho mokuroku [*Nanpo bunko zōshomoku*] 蜀山人蔵書目録 [南畝文庫蔵書目]. In Shoshi kenkyūkai 書誌研究会, ed., *Shoshi shomoku shirīzu* 書誌書目シリーズ 13. Yumani shobō, 1984.

Smits, Gregory. *Visions of Ryukyu: Identity and Ideology in Early-Modern Thought and Politics*. Honolulu: University of Hawai'i Press, 1999.

Sonoda Yutaka 園田豊. "*Kogarashi zōshi* to *Ugetsu monogatari*" 『凩草紙』と『雨月物語』. *Sōsho Edo bunko geppō* 叢書江戸文庫月報 32 (accompanying *MCS*) (July 1994): 5–8.

———. "Manzōtei to Kyōden no zekkō ni tsuite: Bakin kyokuhitsu setsu e no ichi shiron" 万象亭と京伝の絶交について：馬琴曲筆説への一試論. *Edo jidai bungakushi* 江戸時代文学誌 4 (November 1985): 23–37.

Steininger, Brian. *Chinese Literary Forms in Heian Japan: Poetics and Practice.* Cambridge, MA: Harvard University Asia Center, 2017.

Sugimoto Yoshinobu 杉本好伸, ed. *Inō mononokeroku emaki shūsei* 稲生物怪録絵巻集成. Kokusho kankōkai, 2004.

Suwa Haruo 諏訪春雄, ed. *Tōkaidō Yotsuya kaidan* 東海道四谷怪談. In *Kabuki on sutēji* 歌舞伎オン・ステージ 18. Hakusuisha, 1999.

Suzuka Sanshichi 鈴鹿三七. *Chokuhan shūei* 勅版集影. Rinsen shoten, (1930) 1986.

Suzuki Jun 鈴木淳. *Waka ga kakareru toki* 和歌が書かれるとき. Vol. 2 of Asada Tōru 浅田徹 et al., eds., *Waka o hiraku* 和歌をひらく. Iwanami shoten, 2005.

Suzuki Jūzō 鈴木重三. *Ehon to ukiyoe* 絵本と浮世絵. Bijutsu shuppansha, 1979.

———. "Gōkan-mono no daizai tenki to Tanehiko" 合巻物の題材転機と種彦. *Kokugo to kokubungaku* 国語と国文学 38, no. 4 (April 1961): 57–71.

Suzuki Jūzō and Tokuda Takeshi 徳田武, eds. *Wakae no hato, Sangoku ichiya monogatari* 稚枝鳩・三国一夜物語. In *Bakin chūhen yomihon shūsei* 馬琴中編読本集成 2. Kyūko shoin, 1995.

Tagawa Kuniko 田川邦子, ed. *Edo sakusha jōruri shū* 江戸作者浄瑠璃集. In Takada Mamoru 高田衛 and Hara Michio 原道生, eds., *Sōsho Edo bunko* 叢書江戸文庫 15. Kokusho kankōkai, 1989.

Takada Mamoru 高田衛, ed. *Edo kaii kisō bungei taikei* 江戸怪異綺想文芸大系. 5 vols. Kokusho kankōkai, 2000–2003.

———. *Takizawa Bakin: momotose nochi no chiin o matsu* 滝沢馬琴：百年以後の知音を俟つ. Kyōto: Mineruva shobō, 2006.

Takahashi Akinori 高橋章則. "'Hanpon' no 'shahon' o tsukuru no wa naze ka: Tōhoku no kokugakusha Uchiike Nagatoshi o rei ni" 「板本」の「写本」を作るのはなぜか：東北の国学者内池永年を例に. *Nao de la China* 6 ナオ・デ・ラ・チーナ (2004): 23–28.

Takahashi Noriko 高橋則子. *Kusazōshi to engeki: yakusha nigaoe sōshiki o chūshin ni* 草双紙と演劇：役者似顔絵創始期を中心に. Kyūko shoin, 2004.

Takahashi Satoshi 高橋智. "Shōnai-han Chidōkan kyūzō kanseki ni tsuite" 荘内藩致道館旧蔵漢籍について. *Shidō bunko ronshū* 斯道文庫論集 49 (2014): 49–95.

———. *Umi o watatte kita kanseki: Edo no shoshigaku nyūmon* 海を渡ってきた漢籍：江戸の書誌学入門. Nichigai asoshiētsu, 2016.

Takamaki Minoru 高牧実. *Bakin ikka no Edo-gurashi* 馬琴一家の江戸暮らし. Chūō kōron shinsha, 2003.

Takayanagi Shinzō 高柳真三 and Ishii Ryōsuke 石井良助, eds. *Ofuregaki shūsei* 御觸書集成, vol. 5: *Ofuregaki Tenpō shūsei* (*ge*) 御触書天保集成(下). Iwanami shoten, 1941.

Tanahashi Masahiro 棚橋正博. *Edo gesaku sōshi* 江戸戯作草紙. Shōgakukan, 2000.

———. *Kibyōshi no kenkyū* 黄表紙の研究. Wakakusa shobō, 1997.

———. *Kibyōshi sōran* 黄表紙総覧. 5 vols. In *Nihon shoshigaku taikei* 日本書誌学大系 48. Seishōdō shoten, 1986–2004.

———. "Shinrotei nenpu kō" 振鷺亭年譜稿. *Yomihon kenkyū* 読本研究 10, no. 2 (1996): 1–60.

Tanaka Kōtarō 田中貢太郎, trans. *Ren'ai kigo* 恋愛鬼語. Ten'yūsha, 1921.

———. *Ryōsai shii* [*Liaozhai zhiyi*] 聊斎志異. In *Shina bungaku taikan* 支那文学大観 12. Shina bungaku taikan kankōkai, 1926.

Tanki manroku 耽奇漫録. Manuscript, collection of National Diet Library.

Thunberg, Carl Peter. *Travels in Europe, Africa, and Asia, Performed between the Years 1770 and 1779*. 3rd ed. London: F. and C. Rivington, 1796.

Tian, Xiaofei. *Tao Yuanming and Manuscript Culture: The Record of a Dusty Table*. Seattle: University of Washington Press, 2005.

Toby, Ronald. *Engaging the Other: "Japan" and Its Alter-Egos, 1550–1850*. Leiden: Brill, 2019.

———. "Reopening the Question of *Sakoku*: Diplomacy in the Legitimation of the Tokugawa Bakufu." *Journal of Japanese Studies* 3, no. 2 (Summer 1977): 323–63.

———. *State and Diplomacy in Early Modern Japan: Asia in the Development of the Tokugawa Bakufu*. Princeton, NJ: Princeton University Press, 1984.

Tokuda Takeshi 徳田武. *Edo kangaku no sekai* 江戸漢学の世界. Perikansha, 1990.

———. *Kinsei kindai shōsetsu to Chūgoku hakuwa bungaku* 近世近代小説と中国白話文学. Kyūko shoin, 2004.

———. "*Min Shin gundan* to *Gu Sho shinshi* 'Gonin den'" 『明清軍談』と『虞初新志』「五人伝」. *Kokubungaku: Kaishaku to kyōzai no kenkyū* 国文学：解釈と教材の研究 50, no. 6 (2005): 24–32.

———. *Nihon kinsei shōsetsu to Chūgoku shōsetsu* 日本近世小説と中国小説. In *Nihon shoshigaku taikei* 日本書誌学大系 51. Musashimurayama-shi: Seishōdō shoten, 1987.

———, ed. *Shōseihai, fu Chūsei nidenki* 照世盃・付中世二伝奇. Yumani shobō, 1976.

Tokuda Takeshi and Yokoyama Kuniharu 横山邦治, eds. *Shigeshige yawa, Kyokutei denki hanakanzashi, Saibara kidan, Toribeyama shirabeno itomichi* 繁野話・曲亭伝奇花釵児・催馬楽奇談・鳥辺山調綫. In *SNKBT* 80. Iwanami shoten, 1992.

Treat, John Whittier. "Japan Is Interesting: Modern Japanese Literary Studies Today." *Japan Forum* 30, no. 3 (2018): 1–20.

Tsusaka Tōyō 津阪東陽. *Chōkō ian* 聴訟彙案. Tsu: Yūzōkan, 1831.

Tsutsumi Kunihiko 堤邦彦 and Sugimoto Yoshinobu 杉本好伸, eds. *Kinsei minkan ibun kaidan shūsei* 近世民間異聞怪談集成 (2003). Vol. 5 of Takada Mamoru 高田衛, ed., *Edo kaii kisō bungei taikei* 江戸怪異綺想文芸大系, 5 vols. Kokusho kankōkai, 2000–2003.

Uda Toshihiko 宇田敏彦. "Kibyōshi ni okeru Roshia sono ta" 黄表紙におけるロシアその他. *Edo bungaku* 江戸文学 32 (June 2005): 136–46.

Uehara Rorō 上原路郎. *Soba jiten* 蕎麦辞典. Tōkyōdō shuppan, 1972.

Utano Hiroshi 歌野博. "Edo jidai no hon no nedan kō" 江戸時代の本の値段考. *Nihon kosho tsūshin* 日本古書通信 772 (November 1993): 11–14.

Wada Hiromichi 和田博通, ed. *Shokusanjin kibyōshi shū* 蜀山人黄表紙集. Koten bunko, 1984.

Wakayama Zenzaburō 若山善三郎, ed. *Hirade-shi zōsho mokuroku* 平出氏蔵書目録. Nagoya: Bunkōdō shoten, 1939.

Walley, Glynne. "'I Would Rather Be a Faithful Dog than an Unrighteous Man': Virtue and Vice in Kyokutei Bakin's *Nansō Satomi hakkenden*." PhD diss., Harvard University, 2009.

Walthall, Anne. "Edo Riots." In James L. McClain, John W. Merriman, and Ugawa Kaoru, eds., *Edo and Paris: Urban Life and the State in the Early Modern Era*, 407–28. Ithaca, NY: Cornell University Press, 1994.

Wang, Aihe. *Cosmology and Political Culture in Early China*. Cambridge: Cambridge University Press, 2000.

Washburn, Dennis. *Translating Mount Fuji*. New York: Columbia University Press, 2007.

Widmer, Ellen. "Tragedy or Travesty? Perspectives on Langxian's 'The Siege of Yangzhou.'" In Eva Hung, ed., *Paradoxes of Traditional Chinese Literature*, 167–98. Hong Kong: Chinese University Press, 1994.

Wile, Douglas. *Art of the Bedchamber: The Chinese Sexual Yoga Classics, Including Women's Solo Meditation Texts*. Albany: State University of New York Press, 1992.

Winkel, Margarita. "Entertainment and Education: An Antiquarian Society in Edo, 1824–25." In Anna Beerens and Mark Teeuwen, eds., *Uncharted Waters: Intellectual Life in the Edo Period*, 13–34. Leiden: Brill, 2012.

Wu, Laura Hua. "From *Xiaoshuo* to Fiction: Hu Yinglin's Genre Study of *Xiaoshuo*." *Harvard Journal of Asiatic Studies* 55, no. 2 (December 1995): 339–71.

Xiangzhu Liaozhai zhiyi tuyong 詳註聊齋志異圖詠. Shanghai: Tongwen shuju, 1886.

Xiao Hanzhen 蕭涵珍. "Li Yu yu Jianghu wenyi: Ryūtei Senka de *Seidan Tokiwa no iroka* ji *Mimeyori sōshi*" 李漁與江戸文藝：論笠亭仙果的《清談常磐色香》及《美目与利草紙》. *Minsu quyi* 民俗曲藝 189 (September 2015): 119–55.

Yajima Genryō 矢島玄亮. *Nihon-koku genzaisho mokuroku: shūshō to kenkyū* 日本国見在書目録：集証と研究. Kyūko shoin, 1984.

Yamada Hiromitsu 山田博光. "*Ryōsai shii* to Nihon kindai bungaku" 聊斎志異と日本近代文学. In Tezukayama gakuin daigaku sōritsu nijūgo shūnen kinen ronshū henshū iinkai 帝塚山学院大学創立25周年記念論集編集委員会, ed., *Sekai to Nihon* 世界と日本, 35–55. Ōsakasayama-shi: Tezukayama gakuin daigaku, 1992.

Yamaguchi Takeshi 山口剛. "Yomihon no hassei: Teishō to Akinari to no kankei" 読本発生：庭鐘と秋成との関係 (1926). Reprinted in Konoe Noriko 近衛典子, ed., *Akinari kenkyū shiryō shūsei* 秋成研究資料集成 11. Kuresu shuppan, 2003.

Yamamoto Noritsuna 山本紀綱. *Nagasaki Tōjin yashiki* 長崎唐人屋敷. Kenkōsha, 1983.

Yamanaka Hiroyuki 山中浩之. "Shinshutsu Ozaki Masayoshi hen *Hakurai shomoku* genpon ni tsuite" 新出尾崎雅嘉編『舶来書目』原本について. *Higashi Ajia bunka kōshō kenkyū* 東アジア文化交渉研究 8 (March 2015): 1–21.

Yamanaka Kōichi 山中光一. "Kokubungaku kenkyū shiryōkan zō maikuro shiryō mokuroku dēta kara suikei sareru kinsei no shuppan no henka" 国文学研究資料館蔵マイクロ資料目録データから推計される近世の出版の変化. *Kokubungaku kenkyū shiryōkan kiyō* 国文学研究資料館紀要 12 (March 1986): 119–51.

Yamawaki Teijirō 山脇悌二郎. *Nagasaki no Tōjin bōeki* 長崎の唐人貿易. In Nihon rekishi gakkai 日本歴史学会, ed., *Nihon rekishi sōsho* 日本歴史叢書 6. Yoshikawa kōbunkan, 1964.

Yamazaki Fumoto 山崎麓, ed. *Nihon shōsetsu shomoku nenpyō* 日本小説書目年表. Revised by Shoshi kenkyūkai 書誌研究会. In *Shoshi shomoku shirīzu* 書誌書目シリーズ 6. Yumani shobō, 1977. Rev. ed. of *Nihon shōsetsu nenpyō* 日本小説年表 (1929).

Yamazaki Yoshishige 山崎美成. *Kairoku* 海録. Kokusho kankōkai, 1915.

Yang Shuang 楊爽. "Yoda Gakkai to *Ryōsai shii*: 'Ono no Takamura' to 'Lianhua gongzhu' to no hikaku kenkyū o chūshin ni" 依田学海と『聊斎志異』:「小野篁」と「蓮花公主」との比較研究を中心に. *Nihon kanbungaku kenkyū* 日本漢文学研究 12 (2017): 119–51.

Yang, Shuhui, and Yunqin Yang, trans. *Stories Old and New*. Seattle: University of Washington Press, 2000.

Yayoshi Mitsunaga 彌吉光長. *Mikan shiryō ni yoru Nihon shuppan bunka* 未刊史料による日本出版文化. 8 vols. Yumani shobō, 1988–93.

———. *Yayoshi Mitsunaga chosakushū* 彌吉光長著作集. 6 vols. Nichigai asoshiētsu, 1980–83.

Yicun congshu 佚存叢書. Hushang: Huang shi muhuozi yinben qianyin 黃氏木活字印本鉛印, 1882.

Yokoyama Kuniharu 横山邦治. *Yomihon no kenkyū: Edo to Kamigata to* 読本の研究:江戸と上方と. Kazama shobō, 1974.

———, ed. *Yomihon no sekai: Edo to Kamigata* 読本の世界:江戸と上方. Sekai shisōsha, 1985.

Yuan Xingpei 袁行霈 and Hou Zhongyi 侯忠義, eds. *Zhongguo wenyan xiaoshuo shumu* 中國文言小説書目. Beijing: Beijing daxue chubanshe, 1981.

Zeitlin, Judith T. *Historian of the Strange: Pu Songling and the Chinese Classical Tale*. Stanford, CA: Stanford University Press, 1993.

Zenkoku kanseki dētabēsu 全國漢籍データベース (Japan-Wide Database of Chinese Texts). http://kanji.zinbun.kyoto-u.ac.jp/kanseki.

Zhang Youhe 張友鶴, ed. *LZ*. 3 vols. Beijing: Zhonghua shuju, 1962.

Zhu Yixuan 朱一玄, ed. *Liaozhai zhiyi ziliao huibian* 聊齋志異資料彙編. Zhengzhou: Zhongzhou guji chubanshe, 1986.

Zolbrod, Leon M., trans. *Ugetsu Monogatari: Tales of Moonlight and Rain*. Vancouver: University of British Columbia Press, 1974.

Zwicker, Jonathan. *Practices of the Sentimental Imagination: Melodrama, the Novel, and the Social Imaginary in Nineteenth-Century Japan*. Cambridge, MA: Harvard University Asia Center, 2006.

Index

Page numbers in *italics* refer to figures and tables.

Harvard East Asian Monographs
(most recent titles)

417. Joshua Hill, *Voting as a Rite: A History of Elections in Modern China*
418. Kirsten L. Ziomek, *Lost Histories: Recovering the Lives of Japan's Colonial Peoples*
419. Claudine Ang, *Poetic Transformations: Eighteenth-Century Cultural Projects on the Mekong Plains*
420. Evan N. Dawley, *Becoming Taiwanese: Ethnogenesis in a Colonial City, 1880s–1950s*
421. James McMullen, *The Worship of Confucius in Japan*
422. Nobuko Toyosawa, *Imaginative Mapping: Landscape and Japanese Identity in the Tokugawa and Meiji Eras*
423. Pierre Fuller, *Famine Relief in Warlord China*
424. Diane Wei Lewis, *Powers of the Real: Cinema, Gender, and Emotion in Interwar Japan*
425. Maram Epstein, *Orthodox Passions: Narrating Filial Love during the High Qing*
426. Margaret Wan, *Regional Literature and the Transmission of Culture: Chinese Drum Ballads, 1800–1937*
427. Takeshi Watanabe, *Flowering Tales: Women Exorcising History in Heian Japan*
428. Jürgen P. Melzer, *Wings for the Rising Sun: A Transnational History of Japanese Aviation*
429. Edith Sarra, *Unreal Houses: Character, Gender, and Genealogy in the* Tale of Genji
430. Yi Gu, *Chinese Ways of Seeing and Open-Air Painting*
431. Robert Cliver, *Red Silk: Class, Gender, and Revolution in China's Yangzi Delta Silk Industry*
432. Kenneth J. Ruoff, *Japan's Imperial House in the Postwar Era, 1945–2019*
433. Erin L. Brightwell, *Reflecting the Past: Place, Language, and Principle in Japan's Medieval Mirror Genre*
434. Janet Borland, *Earthquake Children: Building Resilience from the Ruins of Tokyo*
435. Susan Blakely Klein, *Dancing the Dharma: Religious and Political Allegory in Japanese Noh Theater*
436. Yukyung Yeo, *Varieties of State Regulation: How China Regulates Its Socialist Market Economy*
437. Robert Goree, *Printing Landmarks: Popular Geography and* Meisho zue *in Late Tokugawa Japan*
438. Lawrence C. Reardon, *A Third Way: The Origins of China's Current Economic Development Strategy*
439. Eyck Freymann, *One Belt One Road: Chinese Power Meets the World*

440. Yung Chul Park, Joon Kyung Kim, and Hail Park, *Financial Liberalization and Economic Development in Korea, 1980–2020*
441. Steven B. Miles, *Opportunity in Crisis: Cantonese Migrants and the State in Late Qing China*
442. Grace Huang, *Chiang Kai-shek's Politics of Shame: Leadership, Legacy, and National Identity*
443. Adam Lyons, *Karma and Punishment: Prison Chaplaincy in Japan*
444. Craig A. Smith, *Chinese Asianism, 1894–1945*
445. Sachiko Kawai, *Uncertain Powers: Sen'yōmon and Landownership by Royal Women in Early Medieval Japan*
446. Juliane Noth, *Transmedial Landscapes and Modern Chinese Painting*
447. Susan Westhafer Furukawa, *The Afterlife of Toyotomi Hideyoshi: Historical Fiction and Popular Culture in Japan*
448. Nongji Zhang, *Legal Scholars and Scholarship in the People's Republic of China: The First Generation (1949–1992)*
449. Han Sang Kim, *Cine-Mobility: Twentieth-Century Transformations in Korea's Film and Transportation*
450. Brian Hurley, *Confluence and Conflict: Reading Transwar Japanese Literature and Thought*
451. Simon Avenell, *Asia and Postwar Japan: Deimperialization, Civic Activism, and National Identity*
452. Maura Dykstra, *Empire of Routine: The Administrative Revolution of the Eighteenth-Century Qing State*
453. Marnie S. Anderson, *In Close Association: Local Activist Networks in the Making of Japanese Modernity, 1868–1920*
454. John D. Wong, *Hong Kong Takes Flight: Commercial Aviation and the Making of a Global Hub, 1930s–1998*
455. Martin K. Whyte and Mary C. Brinton, compilers, *Remembering Ezra Vogel*
456. Lawrence Zhang, *Power for a Price: The Purchase of Appointments in Qing China*
457. J. Megan Greene, *Building a Nation at War: Transnational Knowledge Networks and the Development of China during and after World War II*
458. Miya Qiong Xie, *Territorializing Manchuria: The Transnational Frontier and Literatures of East Asia*
459. Dal Yong Jin, *Understanding Korean Webtoon Culture: Transmedia Storytelling, Digital Platforms, and Genres*
460. Takahiro Yamamoto, *Demarcating Japan: Imperialism, Islanders, and Mobility, 1855–1884*
461. Elad Alyagon, *Inked: Tattooed Soldiers and the Song Empire's Penal-Military Complex*
462. Borje Ljunggren and Dwight H. Perkins, eds., *Vietnam: Navigating a Rapidly Changing Economy, Society, and Political Order*
463. En Li, *Betting on the Civil Service Examinations: The Lottery in Late Qing China*
464. Matthieu Felt, *Meanings of Antiquity: Myth Interpretation in Premodern Japan*
465. William D. Fleming, *Strange Tales from Edo: Rewriting Chinese Fiction in Early Modern Japan*